Lecture Notes in Computer Science 15451

Founding Editors

Gerhard Goos
Juris Hartmanis

Editorial Board Members

Elisa Bertino, *Purdue University, West Lafayette, IN, USA*
Wen Gao, *Peking University, Beijing, China*
Bernhard Steffen ⓘ, *TU Dortmund University, Dortmund, Germany*
Moti Yung ⓘ, *Columbia University, New York, NY, USA*

The series Lecture Notes in Computer Science (LNCS), including its subseries Lecture Notes in Artificial Intelligence (LNAI) and Lecture Notes in Bioinformatics (LNBI), has established itself as a medium for the publication of new developments in computer science and information technology research, teaching, and education.

LNCS enjoys close cooperation with the computer science R & D community, the series counts many renowned academics among its volume editors and paper authors, and collaborates with prestigious societies. Its mission is to serve this international community by providing an invaluable service, mainly focused on the publication of conference and workshop proceedings and postproceedings. LNCS commenced publication in 1973.

Ritse M. Mann · Tianyu Zhang · Tao Tan ·
Luyi Han · Danial Truhn · Shuo Li · Yuan Gao ·
Shannon Doyle · Robert Martí Marly ·
Jakob Nikolas Kather · Katja Pinker-Domenig ·
Shandong Wu · Geert Litjens
Editors

Artificial Intelligence and Imaging for Diagnostic and Treatment Challenges in Breast Care

First Deep Breast Workshop, Deep-Breath 2024
Held in Conjunction with MICCAI 2024
Marrakesh, Morocco, October 10, 2024
Proceedings

Editors
Ritse M. Mann
Radboudumc
Nijmegen, The Netherlands

Tao Tan
Macao Polytechnic University
Macao, China

Danial Truhn
University Hospital Aachen
Aachen, Germany

Yuan Gao
Netherlands Cancer Institute
Amsterdam, The Netherlands

Robert Martí Marly
University of Girona
Girona, Spain

Katja Pinker-Domenig
Irving Medical Center
Columbia University
New York, NY, USA

Geert Litjens
Radboudumc
Nijmegen, The Netherlands

Tianyu Zhang
Radboudumc
Nijmegen, The Netherlands

Luyi Han
Radboudumc
Nijmegen, The Netherlands

Shuo Li
Case Western Reserve University
Cleveland, OH, USA

Shannon Doyle
Netherlands Cancer Institute
Amsterdam, The Netherlands

Jakob Nikolas Kather
Dresden University of Technology
Dresden, Germany

Shandong Wu
University of Pittsburgh
Pittsburgh, PA, USA

ISSN 0302-9743   ISSN 1611-3349 (electronic)
Lecture Notes in Computer Science
ISBN 978-3-031-77788-2   ISBN 978-3-031-77789-9 (eBook)
https://doi.org/10.1007/978-3-031-77789-9

© The Editor(s) (if applicable) and The Author(s), under exclusive license to Springer Nature Switzerland AG 2025

This work is subject to copyright. All rights are solely and exclusively licensed by the Publisher, whether the whole or part of the material is concerned, specifically the rights of translation, reprinting, reuse of illustrations, recitation, broadcasting, reproduction on microfilms or in any other physical way, and transmission or information storage and retrieval, electronic adaptation, computer software, or by similar or dissimilar methodology now known or hereafter developed.
The use of general descriptive names, registered names, trademarks, service marks, etc. in this publication does not imply, even in the absence of a specific statement, that such names are exempt from the relevant protective laws and regulations and therefore free for general use.
The publisher, the authors and the editors are safe to assume that the advice and information in this book are believed to be true and accurate at the date of publication. Neither the publisher nor the authors or the editors give a warranty, expressed or implied, with respect to the material contained herein or for any errors or omissions that may have been made. The publisher remains neutral with regard to jurisdictional claims in published maps and institutional affiliations.

This Springer imprint is published by the registered company Springer Nature Switzerland AG
The registered company address is: Gewerbestrasse 11, 6330 Cham, Switzerland

If disposing of this product, please recycle the paper.

Preface

The 1st Workshop on AI and Imaging for Diagnostic and Treatment Challenges in Breast Care (Deep-Breath 2024) was held in Marrakesh, Morocco, on October 10, 2024. The Deep-Breath workshop provides an international platform for presentation of - and discussion on - studies related to AI in breast imaging. Deep-Breath aims to promote the development of this research area by sharing insights in academic research and clinical practice between clinicians and AI experts, and by exploring together the opportunities and potential challenges of AI applications in breast health. The Deep-Breath workshop provides, therefore, a unique forum to discuss the possibilities in this challenging field, aiming to create value that eventually truly leads to benefit for physicians and patients.

The Deep-Breath 2024 MICCAI workshop was held as a half-day event and received 51 submissions, including both full papers and abstracts - a strong outcome given the number of competing workshops. All submissions were peer-reviewed by at least two experts, and ultimately, 23 full papers were accepted for presentation at the workshop and inclusion in these proceedings. Together, they provide an excellent overview of the state of the art in contemporary AI for breast imaging, covering many different imaging modalities and clinical questions.

We would like to take this opportunity to express our sincere gratitude to MICCAI for providing an excellent platform for our workshop. Special thanks to ScreenPoint Medical, ODELIA, SAFE-MRI, and BIG for their sponsorship and valuable support. Additionally, we would like to thank our dedicated committee members, chairs, and all the authors who contributed to the success of Deep-Breath 2024.

October 2024

Ritse M. Mann
Tianyu Zhang
Tao Tan
Luyi Han
Daniel Truhn
Shuo Li
Yuan Gao
Shannon Doyle
Robert Martí Marly
Jakob Nikolas Kather
Katja Pinker-Domenig
Shandong Wu
Geert Litjens

Organization

General Chairs

Tianyu Zhang   Radboudumc, the Netherlands
Tao Tan   Macao Polytechnic University, China
Ritse M. Mann   Radboudumc, the Netherlands

Organizing Committee

Tianyu Zhang   Radboudumc, the Netherlands
Tao Tan   Macao Polytechnic University, China
Daniel Truhn   University Hospital RWTH Aachen, Germany
Shuo Li   Case Western Reserve University, USA
Yuan Gao   Maastricht University, the Netherlands
Shannon Doyle   Netherlands Cancer Institute, the Netherlands
Robert Martí Marly   University of Girona, Spain
Jakob Nikolas Kather   Dresden University of Technology, Germany
Katja Pinker-Domenig   Columbia University Irving Medical Center, USA
Shandong Wu   University of Pittsburgh, USA
Geert Litjens   Radboudumc, the Netherlands
Ritse M. Mann (in-chief)   Radboudumc, the Netherlands

Chairs

Jarek van Dijk   Radboudumc, the Netherlands
Yuan Gao   Maastricht University, the Netherlands
Luyi Han Aleksandra   Radboudumc, the Netherlands
Osowska-Kurczab   Warsaw University of Technology, Poland
Nika Rasoolzadeh   Radboudumc, the Netherlands
Oliver Lester Saldanha   EKFZ for Digital Health, Germany
Xin Wang   Netherlands Cancer Institute, the Netherlands
Tianyu Zhang   Radboudumc, the Netherlands

Keynote Speakers

Jaap Kroes — ScreenPoint Medical, the Netherlands
Geert Litjens — Radboudumc, the Netherlands
Ritse M. Mann — Radboudumc, the Netherlands
Jonas Teuwen — Netherlands Cancer Institute, the Netherlands
Daniel Truhn — University Hospital RWTH Aachen, Germany

Technical Committee

Jarek van Dijk — Radboudumc, the Netherlands
Luyi Han — Radboudumc, the Netherlands
Menghan Hu — East China Normal University, China
Xiaohong Liu — Shanghai Jiao Tong University, China
Xinglong Liang — Radboudumc, the Netherlands
Cheng Lu — Guangdong Provincial People's Hospital, Guangdong Academy of Medical Sciences, China
Chunyao Lu — Radboudumc, the Netherlands
Ehsan Kozegar — University of Guilan, Iran
Raneim Nabil Hossni Mohamed — Radboudumc, the Netherlands
Nika Rasoolzadeh — Radboudumc, the Netherlands
Oliver Lester Saldanha — EKFZ for Digital Health, Germany
Xin Wang — Netherlands Cancer Institute, the Netherlands

Clinical Committee

Anna D'Angelo — Fondazione Policlinico Universitario A. Gemelli IRCCS, Italy
Ritse M. Mann — Radboudumc, the Netherlands
Antonio Portaluri — University of Messina, Italy
Carla Sitges — Hospital Clinic de Barcelona, Spain
Marialena Tsarouchi — Radboudumc, the Netherlands

Additional Reviewers

Haoran Dou
Yunzhi Huang
Hao Yang

Contents

Evaluation of Bagging Ensembles on Multimodal Data for Breast Cancer
Diagnosis 1
   Abdulganiyu Jimoh, Fatima-Zahrae Nakach, Ali Idri, and Ikram Chairi

HF-Fed: Hierarchical Based Customized Federated Learning Framework
for X-Ray Imaging 13
   Tajamul Ashraf and Tisha Madame

DuEU-Net: Dual Encoder UNet with Modality-Agnostic Training
for PET-CT Multi-modal Organ and Lesion Segmentation 23
   Jinhong Song, Xiao Yang, Xinglong Liang, Jiaju Huang, Junqiang Ma,
   Yue Sun, Wuman Luo, SengPeng Mok, Ying Wang, and Tao Tan

One for All: UNET Training on Single-Sequence Masks for Multi-sequence
Breast MRI Segmentation 32
   Jarek M. van Dijk, Luyi Han, Luuk Balkenende, Nika Rasoolzadeh,
   Karine R. Morche, Tianyu Zhang, and Ritse M. Mann

Multimodal Breast MRI Language-Image Pretraining (MLIP):
An Exploration of a Breast MRI Foundation Model 42
   Nika Rasoolzadeh, Tianyu Zhang, Yuan Gao, Jarek M. van Dijk,
   Qiuhui Yang, Tao Tan, and Ritse M. Mann

Enhancing the Utility of Privacy-Preserving Cancer Classification Using
Synthetic Data 54
   Richard Osuala, Daniel M. Lang, Anneliese Riess, Georgios Kaissis,
   Zuzanna Szafranowska, Grzegorz Skorupko, Oliver Diaz,
   Julia A. Schnabel, and Karim Lekadir

Efficient Generation of Synthetic Breast CT Slices By Combining
Generative and Super-Resolution Models 65
   Zhikai Yang, Mehdi Astaraki, Örjan Smedby, and Rodrigo Moreno

Exploring Patient Data Requirements in Training Effective AI Models
for MRI-Based Breast Cancer Classification 75
   Solha Kang, Wesley De Neve, Francois Rameau, and Utku Ozbulak

Virtual Dynamic Contrast Enhanced Breast MRI Using 2D U-Net
Architectures 85
    Hannes Schreiter, Jessica Eberle, Lorenz A. Kapsner,
    Dominique Hadler, Sabine Ohlmeyer, Ramona Erber,
    Julius Emons, Frederik B. Laun, Michael Uder, Evelyn Wenkel,
    Sebastian Bickelhaupt, and Andrzej Liebert

Optimizing BI-RADS 4 Lesion Assessment Using Lightweight
Convolutional Neural Network with CBAM in Contrast Enhanced
Mammography 96
    Oladosu Oladimeji, Hamail Ayaz, Ian McLoughlin,
    and Saritha Unnikrishnan

Mammographic Breast Positioning Assessment via Deep Learning 107
    Toygar Tanyel, Nurper Denizoglu, Mustafa Ege Seker, Deniz Alis,
    Esma Cerekci, Ercan Karaarslan, Erkin Aribal, and Ilkay Oksuz

Endpoint Detection in Breast Images for Automatic Classification
of Breast Cancer Aesthetic Results 117
    Nuno Freitas, Carlos Veloso, Carlos Mavioso, Maria J. Cardoso,
    Hélder P. Oliveira, and Jaime S. Cardoso

Thick Slices for Optimal Digital Breast Tomosynthesis Classification
With Deep-Learning 127
    Paul Terrassin, Mickael Tardy, Hassan Alhajj, Nathan Lauzeral,
    and Nicolas Normand

Predicting Aesthetic Outcomes in Breast Cancer Surgery: A Multimodal
Retrieval Approach 137
    Mohammad Hossein Zolfagharnasab, Nuno Freitas, Tiago Gonçalves,
    Eduard Bonci, Carlos Mavioso, Maria J. Cardoso, Hélder P. Oliveira,
    and Jaime S. Cardoso

Vision Mamba for Classification of Breast Ultrasound Images 148
    Ali Nasiri-Sarvi, Mahdi S. Hosseini, and Hassan Rivaz

Breast Cancer Molecular Subtyping from H&E Whole Slide Images Using
Foundation Models and Transformers 159
    Lauren Jimenez-Martin, Carlos Hernández-Pérez, and Veronica Vilaplana

Graph Neural Networks for Modelling Breast Biomechanical Compression 169
    Hadeel Awwad, Eloy García, and Robert Martí

A Generative Adversarial Approach to Remove Moiré Artifacts
in Dark-Field and Phase-Contrast X-Ray Images 181
   Eloy García, Diego García-Pinto, Victor Sánchez-Lara,
   Ricardo Montoya delÁngel, and Robert Martí

MRI Breast Tissue Segmentation Using nnU-Net for Biomechanical
Modeling 191
   Melika Pooyan, Hadeel Awwad, Eloy García, and Robert Martí

Fat-Suppressed Breast MRI Synthesis for Domain Adaptation in Tumour
Segmentation 202
   Lidia Garrucho, Eve Delegue, Richard Osuala, Dimitri Kessler,
   Kaisar Kushibar, Oliver Díaz, Karim Lekadir, and Laura Igual

Guiding Breast Conservative Surgery by Augmented Reality
from Preoperative MRI: Initial System Design and Retrospective Trials 212
   Rasoul Sharifian, Sabrina Madad-Zadeh, Nicolas Bourdel, Alexia Giro,
   Wissam Marraoui, Christophe Pomel, and Adrien Bartoli

ELK: Enhanced Learning Through Cross-Modal Knowledge
Transfer for Lesion Detection in Limited-Sample Contrast-Enhanced
Mammography Datasets 221
   Ricardo Montoya-del-Angel, Marawan Elbatel,
   Jorge Patricio Castillo-Lopez, Yolanda Villaseñor-Navarro,
   Maria-Ester Brandan, and Robert Marti

Safe Breast Cancer Diagnosis Resilient to Mammographic Adversarial
Samples 232
   Degan Hao, Dooman Arefan, Margarita L. Zuley, Wendie A. Berg,
   and Shandong Wu

Author Index 245

Evaluation of Bagging Ensembles on Multimodal Data for Breast Cancer Diagnosis

Abdulganiyu Jimoh[1]($\boxtimes$), Fatima-Zahrae Nakach[2], Ali Idri[3], and Ikram Chairi[1,2,3]

[1] School of Collective Intelligence, UM6P, Rabat 11103, Morocco
{abdulganyu.jimoh,ikram.chairi}@um6p.ma
[2] Faculty of Medical Sciences, UM6P, Ben Guerir 43150, Morocco
fatimazahra.nakach@um6p.ma
[3] College of Computing, UM6P, Ben Guerir 43150, Morocco
ali.idri@um6p.ma

Abstract. In this paper, we evaluate bagging ensembles for breast cancer diagnosis using a multimodal dataset "PathoEMR" which combines pathology images and electronic medical records. We implement the bagging ensemble method to two deep learning models (Densenet201 and VGG16) for pathological images and seven machine learning classifiers for electronic medical records. The best bagging ensemble for electronic medical records achieved an accuracy mean value of 92.31%, a precision of 95.56%, a recall of 90.66%, an F1-score of 92.99%, and a specificity of 95.87%. While the best bagging ensemble for the classification of pathological images achieved an accuracy mean value of 85.59%, a precision of 86.87%, a recall of 90.45%, and an f1-score of 88.60%. We compare the bagging ensembles with different number of base learners between them and with the single models based on the Scott-Knott statistical method and the Borda count voting method. All our bagging ensemble models outperform the single models for breast cancer classification. Moreover, we found that the best bagging ensembles outperform the state-of-the-art models applied to the same dataset, which achieved an accuracy of 83.60% with VGG16 applied to pathological images and 78.50% with the auto-encoder applied to electronic medical records.

Keywords: Machine Learning · Deep Learning · Ensemble Learning · Image Processing · Pathology Image · Medical Records · Breast Cancer

1 Introduction

With an expected 2.3 million new cancer cases (1 in 4 new cases) and 685,000 cancer deaths (1 in 6 deaths) in 2020, breast cancer (BC) is the most common disease diagnosed in women globally and the leading cause of cancer mortality in women [6]. Population expansion and ageing alone would increase breast cancer to 3 million new cases and 1 million deaths by 2040 [7]. According to the report from the International Agency for Research on Cancer (IARC) in 2020, which analyzed data from the Global Cancer Observatory, breast cancer continues to hold the highest incidence rate in Morocco [8]. Among women, it constitutes approximately 38.9% of all newly diagnosed cancer cases reported in the previous year. Breast cancer is the foremost cancer, accounting for 19.8% of all cancer cases in the country. These figures highlight the need for efforts in breast cancer research, awareness, and healthcare interventions to address this prevalent health concern in the country [12]. Goodfellow et al. [14] stated that machine learning (ML) techniques have increasingly replaced aspects of human involvement (as cited in [15]). Deep learning (DL) allow computers to learn from experience and comprehend the world in concepts of hierarchy's [14]. Since any complex model technical error or bias may have an impact on people's health, privacy, and ultimately their entire lives [2], it is important to have a variety of medical modalities, such as pathological images and electronic medical records (EMR), for training ML and DL models to detect cancers. Artificial Intelligence (AI) will be used more and more in the healthcare industry because of the complexity and growth of data in the sector [1]. Care providers and life sciences institutions currently use a variety of AI technologies [1], an automated disease detection system lowers the risk of death while assisting medical professionals in early disease detection and diagnosis and providing a dependable, efficient, and speedy response [13]. DL techniques have been widely used in numerous healthcare applications, including mortality prediction, patient subtyping, and diagnostic prediction, with the rapid increase and accumulation of EMR data [5].

With the rapid growth and accumulation of electronic medical records (EMR) data, deep learning methods have been widely applied in many healthcare tasks, such as mortality prediction, patients subtyping, and diagnosis prediction.

A potential area for raising base classifier performance is ensemble learning which aims to improve predicted accuracy by combining various models. The use of ensemble learning improved the diagnostic accuracy of breast tumors, making it easier to identify the tumor's stage and whether it was benign or malignant [9]. Nakach et al. [3] introduced a novel bagged ensemble approach for binary classification of histopathological images from the BreakHis dataset using convolutional neural networks (CNNs) and transfer learning strategies. In their method, a CNN is trained independently on different bootstrapped samples (bags) of the training data, and the predictions are aggregated using majority voting to obtain the final classification result of the deep bagging ensemble. Building on this approach, the current paper aims to apply a similar bagging ensemble technique to a multimodal dataset, "PathoEMR," which contains both histopathological images and EMR. We evaluate the performance of the bagging ensemble on this integrated dataset to assess its effectiveness in improving breast cancer diagnosis through the combined use of pathology images and EMR data.

2 Materials and Methods

2.1 Data Acquisition

We used the PathoEMR dataset already curated by [4] through a cooperative collaboration with Peking University International Hospital in Beijing, China. This dataset, created for the classification of both benign and malignant breast cancer patients, consists of pathological images and a wide range of features taken from clinical EMR. We utilized the EMR of 185 patients, as shown in Table 1, and later preprocessed them using one-hot encoding to obtain 31 features. These features serve as organized descriptors of the patients' medical conditions and show a clear relationship regarding diagnosis. The original EMR contains 29 features, including age, gender, disease course type, prior history of tumors, adhesion to pectoral muscles, orange peel appearance, prophase treatment details, breast deformity, neoadjuvant chemotherapy status, presence of the dimple sign, redness and swelling of the skin, skin ulcers, tumor presence, axillary lymphadenectasis, changes in the nipple, nipple discharge, lymph node swelling, tumor position, tenderness, surface smoothness, tumor morphology, activity level, presence of capsules, skin adhesion, and diagnosis. The pathology whole slide images (WSI) for each patient consists of 3,764 high-resolution pathological images, each with 2048 × 1536 pixel dimensions. Each one of these pathological images was obtained with the same medical equipment, at 100X or 200X magnification level. Each image has been clearly labeled as benign or malignant by medical experts depending on the predominant cancer type shown in the image to aid in the classification task. Histolab python library was used to extract tiles from the WSI as a grids where we capture every accessible tile, as opposed to choosing a tile at random. The Grid Tiler extractor as function in Histolab carefully extracts tiles from the greatest identified tissue area in the WSI by adhering to a grid layout. In our particular situation, we want to extract 512-pixel square tiles at level 0 from the pathology slide. The amount of tissue found in the images has no bearing on how tiles should be extracted. These tiles are preset by default to not overlap, therefore the "pixeloverlap" function in Histolab, which determines how many pixels overlap between adjacent tiles, is set to 0.

Table 1. The overall description of the PathoEMR datasets

Description	Value
Number of medical records	185 (82 benign, 103 malignant)
Number of pathological images	3764 (1332 benign, 2432 malignant)
Size of pathological images	2048×1536 pixels
Color model of pathological images	R(ed)G(reen)B(lue)
Memory space of pathological images	3–20 MB
Number of features extracted from each case	29
Number of pre-processed features from each case	31

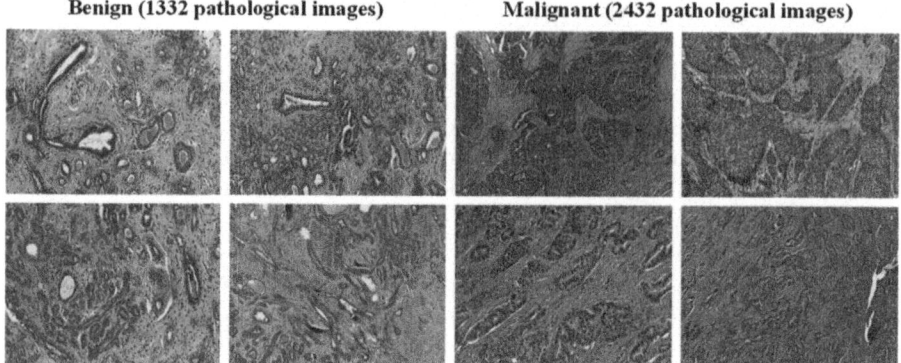

Fig. 1. The Pathological Whole Slide Images Dataset.

2.2 Methodology

Feature Selection Method. Regarding the number of features in the EMR data, we conducted feature selection to focus on the most relevant features and enhance the interpretability of our insights. By using techniques such as Chi2, Mutual Information Gain (MIG), and SHapley Additive exPlanations (SHAP), we were able to identify and prioritize the features that contribute most significantly to the classification task. This approach not only streamlined our analysis but also provided clearer insights into the factors most pertinent to breast cancer diagnosis, thereby improving both the precision and interpretability of our model's predictions. SelectKBest was used to find the most informative features from the training data based on Chi2 and MIG, the chosen ML classifier was then trained on the given features and assessed on the validation set. The evaluation functions are first defined in our code implementation, along with the model name, the input data (X and y), the scoring function, the number of features that have been chosen (k), and other hyperparameters like the sizes of the hidden layers, the number of iterations, and the random state. Similarly, we evaluated the effectiveness of various ML while also determining the significance of features using the SHAP library that selects top 10 picked features based on their mean absolute SHAP values.

ML Classifiers. Seven machine learning classifiers were utilized for processing EMR data: Multi-Layer Perceptron (MLP), XGBoost (XGB), Random Forest (RF), Extremely Randomized Trees (EBM), Support Vector Machine (SVM), Decision Tree (DT), and K-Nearest Neighbors (KNN). Each classifier was optimized and fine-tuned with specific parameters tailored to the characteristics of the PathoEMR dataset. For instance, SVM was configured with a radial basis function kernel and tuned for regularization parameter C and gamma, while XGBoost parameters included learning rate, maximum depth, and number of estimators. A thorough approach for carrying out cross-validation using a variety

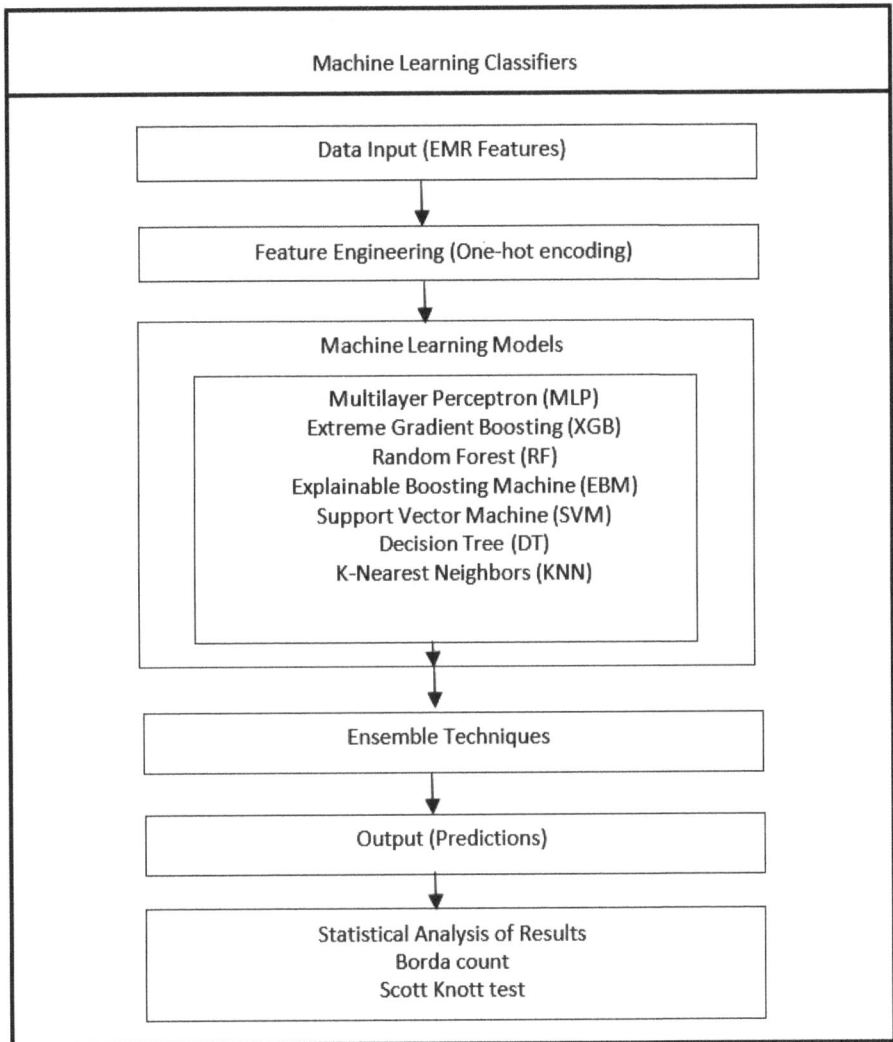

Fig. 2. Flowchart of the application of the bagging method based ML classifiers for the EMR modality of the PathoEMR dataset.

of machine learning classifiers is implemented in the coding function. The Python program makes use of well-known techniques from the scikit-learn library, such as the ExplainableBoostingClassifier (EBM) from the interpret module and the KNeighborsClassifier, DecisionTreeClassifier, RandomForestClassifier, and XGBClassifier. The performance of these classifiers will be extensively assessed and compared across a range of assessment criteria, including accuracy, precision, recall, F1-score, and specificity. The followings shows the mathematical representation of the seven ML models we used in this research paper:

Multi-Layer Perceptron (MLP):

$$\mathbf{h}^{(l)} = \phi(\mathbf{W}^{(l)}\mathbf{h}^{(l-1)} + \mathbf{b}^{(l)})$$

XGBoost (XGB):

$$\hat{y}_i = \sum_{k=1}^{K} f_k(\mathbf{x}_i)$$

Random Forest (RF):

$$\hat{y} = \frac{1}{T}\sum_{t=1}^{T} h_t(\mathbf{x})$$

Explainable Boosting Machine (EBM):

$$\hat{y}_i = \mathbf{f}(\mathbf{x}_i) = \beta_0 + \sum_{j=1}^{p} f_j(x_{ij})$$

$$\mathbf{f}(\mathbf{x}_i) = \beta_0 + \sum_{j=1}^{p} [f_j(x_{ij}) + \text{boosting residuals}]$$

Support Vector Machine (SVM):

$$f(\mathbf{x}) = \mathbf{w} \cdot \mathbf{x} + b$$

Decision Tree (DT):

$$\hat{y} = h(\mathbf{x})$$

K-Nearest Neighbors (KNN):

$$\hat{y} = \frac{1}{k} \sum_{i \in \mathcal{N}_k(\mathbf{x})} y_i$$

DL Methods. For the classificatiob of pathological images, we employed two CNNs: Densenet201 and VGG16. Densenet201 was used to process images at 100X magnification, while VGG16 was applied to images at 200X magnification. These models were chosen for their proven effectiveness in image classification tasks related to medical diagnostics. Each layers in DenseNet block receives

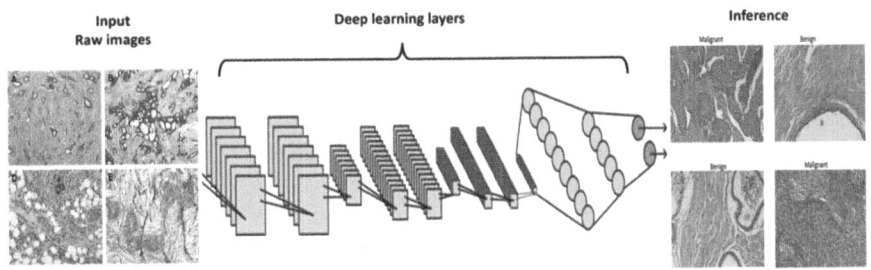

Fig. 3. Deep Learning Model for Pathological Images Dataset.

inputs from all connected preceding layers. The output of the model l^{th} layer x_l can be mathematically described as:

$$x_l = H_l([x_0, x_1, x_2, \ldots, x_{l-1}]) \qquad (1)$$

The mathematical description of forward pass through the VGG16 network architecture can be expressed as follows:

$$\mathbf{y} = \mathbf{W}_3 \cdot \text{ReLU}(\mathbf{W}_2 \cdot \text{ReLU}(\mathbf{W}_1 \cdot \text{ConvLayers}(\mathbf{x}) + \mathbf{b}_1) + \mathbf{b}_2) + \mathbf{b}_3 \qquad (2)$$

Ensemble Method. In ensemble learning, the method known as bagging (i.e., bootstrapping or aggregating) consists of creating several subsets of the dataset (bags), and train each model (also know as base learner) on a single bag, the final prediction is made by aggregating the predictions of the different base learners, and has the mathematical representation described as:

$$\hat{y}_i = \frac{1}{B} \sum_{b=1}^{B} h_b(\mathbf{x}_i)$$

To enhance classification performance, we employed bagging ensembles with varying numbers of base learners for both pathological imaging and EMR modalities. Specifically: 1. For Densenet, four bagging ensembles were implemented with different numbers of base learners: 3, 5, 7, and 9. 2. For VGG16, four bagging ensembles were implemented with different numbers of base learners: 3, 5, 7, and 9. 3. For ML classifiers, five bagging ensembles were implemented with different numbers of base learners: 3, 7, 10, 15 and 20.

These ensembles were compared with each of their base learners as well as the single models to investigate the effectiveness of the bagging method for the classification of multimodal data.

Model Evaluation. Our evaluation set up a StratifiedKFold cross-validation approach with five folds, ensuring data stratification and shuffling for thorough model assessment. Accuracy, precision, recall, F1-score, and specificity performance metrics are computed for each fold as part of the assessment process. We compare the models based on the Scott-Knott test and the Borda count voting method.

For the bagging ensembles, the model uses a controlled randomization approach to divide the training data into smaller subsets, or "bags," with each bag making up 60% of the whole training dataset. It is essential for introducing diversity into the various models that the training data are purposefully varied. DL models that are based on the Densenet201 and VGG16 architecture are then painstakingly created during code execution for each bag. Then, in order to hasten the convergence process, these models are placed through accelerated training on Tensor Processing Units (TPUs), a high-performance computing resource and notably, checkpoints are meticulously kept up to track these models' performance during training.

3 Results and Discussion

Tables 1–2 report the performance of ML classifiers on EMR modality from the PathoEMR dataset as singles and ensembles. The evaluation performance of ML classifiers for EMR modality with and without feature selection revealed that the top models are MLP, XGBoost, RF, and EBM with Chi2 achieving an accuracy of 92.31%, 92.57%, and 91.14% respectively. MIG was the best feature section method for SVM with an accuracy of 91.95%, while DT and KNN performed better without feature selection. For the ensembles, we observed a shift in the ranking of models. Although the performance of the bagging ensembles applied to the top single models did not improve, the bagging ensemble based on SVM and DT showed a significant performance increase. This ensemble outperformed those based on MLP, XGB, and EBM.

When evaluating the DL models for pathology images we found that VGG16 achieves an accuracy of 82.92% outperforming Densenet with 0.16%. However, this order changed when applying bagging method, it was found that the top-performing ensembles are based on Denesenet with 7 base learner, VGG16 with 7 base learner, and VGG16 with 9 base learner achieving an accuracy of 85.59%, 84.99% and 84.99% respectively. Moreover, these ensembles consistently outperform all their individual base learner, in terms of classification accuracy, precision, recall, and f1-score, as shown in Tables 4–5. Furthermore, our best-ranked models for EMR and digital pathological imaging achieved an accuracy of 92.31%, 85.59% respectively, outperforming the state-of-the-art (Yan et al., 2021) accuracy results that achieved 78.50% using an autoencoder for EMR and 83.60% using VGG16 for digital pathological imaging.

In comparing the performance across modalities, it is evident that the choice of model and feature selection technique plays a significant role in achieving high classification accuracy. For the EMR modality, traditional ML classifiers with optimized feature selection methods like Chi2 and MIG demonstrate strong performance, with Chi2-enhanced models notably leading in accuracy. The shift in ensemble performance, where bagging SVM and DT outperformed other ensembles, highlights the potential benefits of combining different models, particularly when feature selection is appropriately managed.

Conversely, in the pathology images modality, the DL models exhibit a different performance trend. While VGG16 initially shows better accuracy than DenseNet, applying the bagging method enhances the performance of DenseNet-based ensembles more significantly. This suggests that for DL models, the benefit of ensemble methods may be more pronounced, possibly due to the increased diversity and complementary strengths of the base learners in handling complex image features. The consistency of ensemble models in outperforming individual models across various metrics (accuracy, precision, recall, and F1-score) reinforces the robustness of ensemble approaches in DL tasks.

Overall, these results underscore the nuanced interplay between model selection, feature extraction, and ensemble techniques. While traditional ML models with advanced feature selection methods are highly effective for EMR classification, DL models with ensemble methods offer superior performance for pathology image classification. This comparative analysis suggests that ensemble learning can be a powerful strategy in both contexts, but its impact may vary depending on the specific modality and model type (Table 3).

Table 2. Performance evaluation of ML classifiers on EMR modality from the PathoEMR dataset.

Model	Feature Selection	Accuracy	Precision	Recall	F1 Score	Specificity	Borda Score
MLP	Chi2	92.31%	95.56%	90.66%	92.99%	95.87%	21
XGB	Chi2	92.57%	96.57%	89.77%	92.65%	96.05%	21
RF	Chi2	91.14%	96.57%	87.99%	91.88%	96.55%	15
EBM	Chi2	91.14%	93.99%	90.76%	92.96%	92.90%	15
SVM	MIG	90.95%	96.31%	86.89%	91.89%	96.56%	13
DT	Without	90.95%	94.98%	88.59%	91.86%	92.46%	7
KNN	Without	89.99%	93.52%	86.99%	89.60%	92.76%	2

Table 3. Performance evaluation of bagging method based ML classifiers on the EMR modality.

Model	Ensemble of	Accuracy	Precision	Recall	F1 Score	Specificity	Borda Score
SVM	10	91.35%	95.78%	88.42%	91.89%	95.14%	21
DT	15	90.81%	94.19%	89.33%	91.16%	92.50%	17
EMB	3	90.81%	92.16%	91.28%	91.16%	90.22%	13
MLP	20	90.27%	92.93%	89.38%	91.04%	91.47%	11
XGB	7	90.27%	91.48%	91.28%	91.31%	88.82%	9
XGB	7	90.27%	91.48%	91.28%	91.31%	88.82%	9
KNN	10	89.18%	92.86%	87.47%	89.99%	91.54%	6

Table 4. Performance evaluation of single and bagging ensemble based DL models for pathological image classification.

Model	Type	Accuracy	Precision	Recall	F1 Score	Borda Score
Densenet	Ensemble of 7	85.59%	86.87%	90.45%	88.60%	15
VGG16	Ensemble of 7	84.99%	83.99%	91.30%	86.06%	14
VGG16	Ensemble of 9	84.99%	82.75%	91.29%	86.06%	12
Densenet	Ensemble of 9	84.99%	85.99%	90.86%	88.79%	11
Densenet	Ensemble of 5	84.98%	85.99%	90.84%	88.79%	7
VGG16	Ensemble of 5	81.68%	81.85%	91.79%	86.88%	7
VGG16	Single	82.92%	80.34%	97.88%	84.78%	4
Densenet	Ensemble of 3	82.64%	85.45%	90.88%	87.87%	3
Densenet	Single	82.76%	85.28%	90.31%	87.82%	3
V_Ens	Ensemble of 3	82.18%	81.47%	90.86%	85.99%	3

Table 5. Performance evaluation of the best base learners (DL models trained on 60% of training dataset) according to the ensemble they construct for classification of pathology images.

Base learner	Belonging to	Accuracy	Precision	Recall	F1 Score	Borda Score
Densenet	Ensemble of 5	81.78%	84.06%	90.8%3	87.31%	24
Densenet	Ensemble of 7	81.39%	83.94%	90.46%3	87.02%	20
Densenet	Ensemble of 3	80.70%	84.70%	88.07%3	86.29%	15
VGG16	Ensemble of 5	79.63%	82.80%	88.97%3	85.77%	12
VGG16	Ensemble of 9	78.09%	82.01%	87.53%3	84.64.77%	11
VGG16	Ensemble of 9	77.56%	80.76%	88.97%3	84.48%	6

4 Conclusion

Our research findings underscore the effectiveness of employing bagging ensembles with ML and DL models and position them as promising tools for BC classification using EMR and digital pathology imaging. The bagging ensembles consistently outperformed their base learners, single classifiers, and state-of-the-art models when applied to the "PathoEMR" dataset. Additionally, our results confirmed the effectiveness of feature selection techniques such as Chi2, MIG, and SHAP in enhancing classification precision and accuracy.

Comparing the two modalities, our findings highlighted the superior predictive capabilities of DL models in handling complex medical data, reaffirming the potential of these models in healthcare applications. For future work, we recommend exploring both late and early fusion techniques to combine EMR and pathology imaging data, aiming to further enhance breast cancer classification accuracy.

Acknowledgments. This work was conducted under the research project "Machine Learning based Breast Cancer Diagnosis and Treatment", 2023–2025. The authors would like to thank the Moroccan Ministry of Higher Education and Scientific Research, Digital Development Agency (ADD), National Center for Scientific and Technical Research (CNRST), and Mohammed VI Polytechnic University (UM6P) for their support.

References

1. Davenport, T., Kalakota, R.: The potential for artificial intelligence in healthcare. Futur. Healthc. J. **6**(2), 94 (2019)
2. Wenzel, M.A., Wiegand, T.: Towards international standards for the evaluation of artificial intelligence for health. In: 2019 ITU Kaleidoscope: ICT for Health: Networks, Standards and Innovation (ITU K), pp. 1–10. IEEE (2019). https://doi.org/10.23919/ITUK48006.2019.8996131
3. Nakach, F.Z., Idri, A.: A novel bagged ensemble approach for accurate histopathological breast cancer classification using transfer learning and convolutional neural networks. In: Rocha, A.P., Steels, L., van den Herik, J. (eds.) Agents and Artificial Intelligence. ICAART 2023. LNCS, vol. 14546. Springer, Cham (2024). https://doi.org/10.1007/978-3-031-55326-4_16
4. Yan, R., et al.: Richer fusion network for breast cancer classification based on multimodal data. BMC Med. Inform. Decis. Mak. **21**(1), 1–15 (2021)
5. Zhang, C., Gao, X., Ma, L., Wang, Y., Wang, J., Tang, W.: GRASP: generic framework for health status representation learning based on incorporating knowledge from similar patients. In: Proceedings of the AAAI Conference on Artificial Intelligence, vol. 35, no. 1, pp. 715–72, May 2021. https://doi.org/10.1609/aaai.v35i1.16152
6. Sedeta, E.T., Jobre, B., Avezbakiyev, B.: Breast cancer: global patterns of incidence, mortality, and trends (2023)
7. Arnold, M., et al.: Current and future burden of breast cancer: global statistics for 2020 and 2040. Breast **66**, 15–23 (2022)
8. Bray, F., Ferlay, J., Soerjomataram, I., Siegel, R.L., Torre, L.A., Jemal, A.: Global cancer statistics 2018: GLOBOCAN estimates of incidence and mortality worldwide for 36 cancers in 185 countries. CA Cancer J. Clin. **68**(6), 394–424 (2018)
9. Osman, A.H., Aljahdali, H.M.A.: An effective of ensemble boosting learning method for breast cancer virtual screening using neural network model. IEEE Access **8**, 39165–39174 (2020)
10. Esteva, A., et al.: Dermatologist-level classification of skin cancer with deep neural networks. Nature **542**(7639), 115–118 (2017)
11. He, B., et al.: TOOme: a novel computational framework to infer cancer tissue-of-origin by integrating both gene mutation and expression. Front. Bioeng. Biotechnol. **8**, 394 (2020)
12. WHO. Globocan. 2020. Morocco: Incidence, Mortality and Prevalence by cancer site. https://gco.iarc.who.int/media/globocan/factsheets/populations/504-morocco-fact-sheet.pdf. Accessed 25 July 2024
13. Mahesh, T.R., Vinoth Kumar, V., Vivek, V., Karthick Raghunath, K.M., Sindhu Madhuri, G.: Early predictive model for breast cancer classification using blended ensemble learning. Int. J. Syst. Assur. Eng. Manag. 1–10 (2022)

14. Goodfellow, I., Bengio, Y., Courville, A.: Deep Learning. MIT Press, Cambridge (2016)
15. Houssein, E.H., Emam, M.M., Ali, A.A., Suganthan, P.N.: Deep and machine learning techniques for medical imaging-based breast cancer: a comprehensive review. Expert Syst. Appl. **167**, 114161 (2021)

HF-Fed: Hierarchical Based Customized Federated Learning Framework for X-Ray Imaging

Tajamul Ashraf[✉][iD] and Tisha Madame[iD]

Indian Institute of Technology Delhi, New Delhi 110016, India
tajamul@sit.iitd.ac.in

Abstract. In clinical applications, X-Ray technology plays a crucial role in noninvasive examinations like mammography, providing essential anatomical information about patients. However, the inherent radiation risk associated with X-Ray procedures raises significant concerns. X-Ray reconstruction is crucial in medical imaging for creating detailed visual representations of internal structures, and facilitating diagnosis and treatment without invasive procedures. Recent advancements in deep learning (DL) have shown promise in X-Ray reconstruction. Nevertheless, conventional DL methods often necessitate the centralized aggregation of substantial large datasets for training, following specific scanning protocols. This requirement results in notable domain shifts and privacy issues. To address these challenges, we introduce the Hierarchical Framework-based Federated Learning method (HF-Fed) for customized X-Ray Imaging. HF-Fed addresses the challenges in X-Ray imaging optimization by decomposing the problem into two components: local data adaptation and holistic X-Ray Imaging. It employs a hospital-specific hierarchical framework and a shared common imaging network called Network of Networks (NoN) for these tasks. The emphasis of the NoN is on acquiring stable features from a variety of data distributions. A hierarchical hypernetwork extracts domain-specific hyperparameters, conditioning the NoN for customized X-Ray reconstruction. Experimental results demonstrate HF-Fed's competitive performance, offering a promising solution for enhancing X-Ray imaging without the need for data sharing. This study significantly contributes to the evolving body of literature on the potential advantages of federated learning in the healthcare sector. It offers valuable insights for policymakers and healthcare providers holistically. The source code and pre-trained HF-Fed model is available at this link.

1 Introduction

X-Ray imaging is vital for clinical diagnosis, providing noninvasive insights into patient anatomy, especially in breast mammography [9,26,27]. However, potential radiation risks related to genetic and cancer diseases have raised concerns [12]. Common strategies to mitigate these risks, like adjusting the X-Ray tube's current/voltage and reducing scanning views, often degrade imaging quality [31], negatively impacting image analysis and diagnoses. To address these challenges, researchers have explored deep learning (DL) for low-dose X-Ray (LD-Xray) reconstruction [13], with promising results. However, current methods depend on centralized training (CL) with large datasets from various hospitals, overlooking privacy concerns and domain shifts that cause low accuracy. Anonymizing data has proven insufficient in ensuring robust patient privacy [25, 28].

In light of privacy, legal, and ethical concerns, there is an increasing demand for a collaborative, privacy-preserving approach in multi-hospital training. Federated Learning (FL) is a paradigm designed to enhance data security and privacy by decentralizing the training process, keeping information on individual devices, and sharing only the updated model parameters [11, 18]. FL stands out as a decentralized solution explicitly crafted to safeguard data and its confidentiality [14]. Unlike CL methods, which involve the transfer of private patient data, FL methods exclusively exchange gradients, thereby minimizing privacy risks associated with data content. FL offers a privacy-conscious alternative for training models on X-Ray data from multiple sources, addressing the limitations of centralized approaches and fostering a more secure and ethically sound framework for medical imaging. A significant challenge in FL arises from the non-independence and non-identically distributed (Non-IID) nature of data, a particularly pronounced issue in X-Ray Imaging compared to other analysis tasks. The diverse hardware and scanning protocols across different scanners or hospitals exacerbate this challenge. Unfortunately, the holistic model in FL is limited to capturing general statistical patterns and lacks the specificity required for individual data sources, leading to inaccurate results. To address these problems, recent efforts focus on customized FL methods, aiming to train local models tailored to specific data distributions. Certain methods employ hypernetworks [30] to attain personalization by creating customized weights for the target network. Nevertheless, numerous currently available hypernetwork-based Federated Learning approaches often overlook the underlying physical processes and come with significant additional training expenses. In computer-aided diagnosis, the precision of imaging (upstream) tasks significantly impacts subsequent processes like segmentation and detection (downstream). This paper presents an in-depth FL framework for upstream tasks, focusing on post-processing and reconstruction. Our hierarchical customized FL framework (HF-Fed) for X-Ray Imaging addresses holistic optimization by personalizing feature adaptation and extracting invariant holistic imaging features. In X-Ray Imaging, maintaining structural similarity is crucial. Our HF-Fed framework trains a universally shared imaging network using varied client data to capture consistent holistic characteristics. Recognizing the impact of scanning protocols and geometry parameters, HF-Fed introduces a hierarchical hypernetwork that dynamically adjusts imaging features using embedded knowledge.

HF-Fed integrates a hospital-specific hierarchical framework and a Network of Networks (NoN). The hypernetwork adapts scanning parameters to customize features, enhancing invariant features of the imaging network. Utilizing FL, it facilitates comprehensive gradient exchange for robust model training. The hospital-specific hypernetwork ensures domain-specific personalization, while NoN learns universal features across diverse domains.

The contributions of this work are as follows:

1. Introduction of HF-Fed for customized X-Ray imaging using FL. This is the first attempt at applying Federated Learning for customized X-Ray imaging.
2. The proposed HF-Fed framework comprises two components: the hospital-specific hierarchical hypernetwork and the Network of Networks (NoN). The hypernetwork is designed for customization to address Non-IID challenges, while NoN captures invariant and stable features across diverse data distributions.
3. A flexible framework that can be easily extended to various X-Ray imaging tasks, including post-processing and reconstruction.

2 Related Work

X-Ray imaging technology has advanced significantly, enhancing diagnostic capabilities [22]. Reconstruction methods include sinogram filtration, iterative reconstruction (IR), and postprocessing. Sinogram filtration involves filtering raw or log-transformed data using adaptive techniques such as weighted least-squares with penalties [7]. IR methods improve objective functions by incorporating prior knowledge like total variation and non-local means filters [5], along with regularization terms. Postprocessing methods offer convenience but lack flexibility without raw data. Deep Learning (DL) has shown promise in low-dose computed tomography (LDCT) reconstruction with models like RED-CNN for denoising [4], GAN-based approaches for super resolution [33], and parameter-dependent frameworks (PDF) [32]. However, these centralized models raise privacy concerns and limit clinical applicability.

2.1 Customized Federated Learning

Federated Learning (FL) adopts a decentralized approach that emphasizes data privacy while allowing models to learn from diverse data sources [29]. The traditional FL method, FedAvg, introduced by McMahan et al. [24], builds a comprehensive model by averaging local models from various parties. FedProx [18] improves upon FedAvg by enforcing proximity between local and global models. Li et al. [16] introduced the model-contrastive (MOON) technique, which minimizes contrastive distances between local and global models. FL's privacy-preserving features have been applied in various medical tasks [14].

In the realm of medical imaging advancements, Guo et al. [10] introduced an intermediate latent feature alignment approach for MRI reconstruction, requiring knowledge of target domain data, which poses practical challenges. Dinh et al. [6] addressed non-iid challenges in multitask learning within federated learning (FL), aiming for a universally applicable model but facing significant hurdles. Zhang et al. [34] proposed a semi-asynchronous FL framework for short-term solar power forecasting, showing robust performance. Liang et al. [20] introduced LG-FedAvg, linking learning representation and FL, primarily for high-level tasks, potentially less seamless in low-level imaging assignments. Ditto [17], a comprehensive-regularized multitask learning framework, integrates local and holistic models effectively, showing promising outcomes.

Ma et al. [23] introduced an approach to assess layer significance across diverse clients for tailored model aggregation. Li et al. [19] presented FedBN, integrating local batch normalization (BN) to mitigate feature shift and achieve personalization in local hospital settings. Shamsian et al. [30] proposed pFedHN, using a hypernetwork for local model parameter generation, particularly effective in simple models. Ashraf et al. [1] explored network customization for transformer-based client-side models, limiting broad applicability. Chen et al. developed cyclic knowledge distillation for extracting semantic features from local models, focusing on classification tasks aligning semantic features across clients. Hanzely [11] incorporated regularization to minimize optimization gaps in federated models. Feng et al. [8] proposed an MRI denoising model with shared encoders, addressing non-iid challenges in X-Ray reconstruction due to protocol sensitivity. Here, we introduce a hierarchical X-Ray reconstruction framework adaptable for diverse imaging tasks.

3 Proposed Method

3.1 Problem Statement

In the context of X-Ray reconstruction, the general optimization problem can be expressed as follows:

$$\min_{a} \frac{1}{2}\|Xa - b\|_2^2 + Y(a) \tag{1}$$

In this context, $\|\cdot\|_2^2$ signifies the L2 norm, and X symbolizes the system matrix. The variables a and b denote the image for reconstruction and the measured data, respectively. The regularization term $Y(\cdot)$ integrates prior knowledge. In customized Federated Learning (FL), hospitals strive to attain customized models from local data, improving performance through collaborative FL methods, such as sharing specific layers. If there are K hospitals, the learning process can be expressed as:

$$\min_{\theta_1,\ldots,\theta_K} \sum_{k=1}^{K} W_k \mathbb{E}_{(a_l,b,a_n)\sim D_k} \|F_k(a_l, b, \theta_k) - a_n\|_2^2$$

In this formulation, F^k denotes the optimization model in the k-th hospital, W_k represents the weight of the k-th hospital in holistic optimization, and D_k signifies the dataset in the k-th hospital. The aim of customized Federated Learning is to discover optimal local models for different hospitals without sharing raw data.

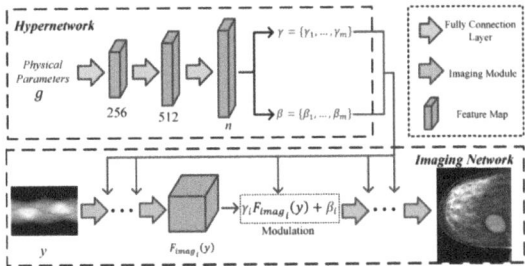

Fig. 1. The proposed HF-Fed architecture consists of a globally shared imaging network and a hospital-specific, hierarchically-driven hypernetwork.

3.2 HF-Fed Architecture

Given the substantial impact of scanning protocol and geometry parameters on the physical X-Ray reconstruction process, it is reasonable to leverage this knowledge for guiding the network in predicting normal X-Ray images. Motivated by this concept, we introduce the Hierarchical Framework-based Federated Learning (HF-Fed), which consists of a hospital-specific hypernetwork and a holistically shared imaging framework. The complete assimilation process of the current imaging framework, denoted as $L_{\text{imag}}(a, b, w)$, involves feeding inputs into the model L_{imag} with parameters w, without any constraint. While assuming a uniform distribution of inputs can reduce complexity, meeting this assumption in real scenarios is challenging, leading to the non-iid problem. To tackle this, the hospital-specific hypernetwork functions as a monitor, adjusting the process. As a result, the assimilation process of HF-Fed is redefined as $L_{\text{imag}}(a, b, w, \theta)$, where θ denotes the result from the hypernetwork $H(\cdot)$ constrained with ξ. In particular, the vector n, encompassing crucial scanning and geometry parameters, is input into $H(\cdot)$ to generate the sets of scaling factors γ and biases β. These sets are employed to adjust the features of F_{imag}, and this procedure is expressed as $\gamma, \beta = H(n, \xi)$. Some elements in n with large magnitudes, such as the numbers of views and detector bins, and the photon number of incident X-Ray, undergo normalization and logarithmization. The normalization is defined as

$$n_j = \frac{n_j - \min(n_j)}{\max(n_j) - \min(n_j)} \quad (2)$$

Figure 1 illustrates the architecture of our proposed HF-Fed. The structure of the hypernetwork is closely tied to the imaging network and is designed as a three-layer fully-connected network in this article. It generates scaling factors γ and biases β based on a 7-dimensional physical parameter vector n. The output sizes of the two subsequent linear layers are 256 and 512, respectively, with the final output dimensionality dependent on the imaging network's feature dimension, which is twice the imaging feature dimension.

To enhance parameter efficiency, RED-CNN adopts a strategy where the encoder and decoder layers share two groups of modulation factors. Similarly, in

LEARN, all IR blocks share the same modulation factors. The modulation function is represented as:
$$L^*_{\text{imag}}(b) = \gamma L_{\text{imag}}(b) + \beta.$$
This operation is applied to feature maps from various modules in the imaging network, resulting in the modification of equation (6):
$$L^*_{\text{imag}_i}(b) = \gamma_i L_{\text{imag}_i}(b) + \beta_i,$$
where $L_{\text{imag}_i}(b)$ and $L^*_{\text{imag}_i}(b)$ represent the feature map from the ith module and its modulated counterpart, respectively. γ_i and β_i signify the regularization factor and bias for the ith module.

As highlighted earlier, the imaging network in HF-Fed is adaptable for various tasks, with imaging units varying based on different imaging methods. For instance, convolution layers serve as imaging units for postprocessing methods like RED-CNN [5]. Conversely, for unrolled iteration methods such as LEARN [3], the imaging unit represents an unrolled iteration module.

3.3 Implementation of NoN (Network of Networks)

In this research, we propose HF-Fed, a hypernetwork-based federated learning framework designed to tackle the non-iid challenge in X-Ray image reconstruction. Similar to FedAvg and FedProx, HF-Fed involves local updates for both the hypernetwork and imaging network, with only the imaging network's updates aggregated on the server. Unlike FedBN, which normalizes data globally, HF-Fed adapts by performing local normalization due to varied X-Ray data distributions from different machines, challenging FedBN's assumptions [21]. To address this, we introduce a hypernetwork to modulate feature maps within the imaging network, enabling hierarchical-driven self-normalization.

Privacy and security challenges in inter-hospital collaboration are addressed by HF-Fed, ensuring that local data remains private. Each hospital refines its local model by minimizing the loss:
$$\ell_k = \frac{1}{2}\mathbb{E}_{(a_i,n,b)\sim D_k}\left[L_k(\delta_k, b, n) - a_i\right]^2$$
where $L_k(\cdot)$ represents the local network at the k-th hospital, parameterized by δ_k. Optimization of parameters w_k and ξ_k of L_{imag} and $H(\cdot)$ at the k-th hospital is conducted iteratively:
$$w_k^{w+1}, \xi_k^{w+1} = w_k^w, \xi_k^w - \lambda \nabla_{w_k^w, \xi_k^w} L^k$$
where λ denotes the learning rate. After training epochs, gradients from the imaging network are sent to the server for aggregation, while the hypernetwork remains locally for modulation.

Table 1. HF-Fed's SSIM scores for the post-processing task

# Models	SSIM Scores						
	w/o FL	Fedavg	FedProx	FedBN	Ditto	pFedHN	HF-Fed
Hospital #1	94.55 ± 0.15	92.21 ± 0.08	92.94 ± 0.13	93.68 ± 0.13	93.91 ± 0.17	95.25 ± 0.11	**96.87 ± 0.12**
Hospital #2	90.42 ± 4.22	94.28 ± 4.23	91.85 ± 1.50	91.23 ± 1.93	93.02 ± 0.88	90.20 ± 0.95	**94.64 ± 0.22**
Hospital #3	**94.86 ± 0.99**	94.01 ± 0.12	92.41 ± 0.16	95.70 ± 0.14	91.23 ± 0.32	91.72 ± 0.16	91.19 ± 0.18
Hospital #4	92.26 ± 0.61	93.57 ± 0.52	91.45 ± 0.87	92.13 ± 0.67	93.08 ± 0.72	**94.94 ± 0.91**	93.25 ± 0.77
Hospital #5	91.75 ± 0.22	94.46 ± 0.11	94.25 ± 0.69	91.13 ± 0.84	94.61 ± 0.45	95.05 ± 0.47	**96.63 ± 0.98**
Average	92.57 ± 1.65	93.11 ± 1.65	92.58 ± 1.65	92.70 ± 1.65	93.57 ± 1.65	93.03 ± 1.65	**95.12 ± 1.65**
STD	1.65	0.91	1.22	1.63	1.23	2.04	1.62

4 Experiments and Results

The "RSNA Screening Mammography Breast Cancer Detection" dataset [2] includes 54.7K X-Ray mammogram images from 1,000 patients, split into 4,000, 1,000, and 1,000 images for training, validation, and testing respectively. No overlap exists between these sets, with validation occurring every 200 rounds during training. The dataset is divided into five groups on average, resulting in diverse client-specific data distributions, posing a severe non-iid challenge. Evaluation uses the correlation coefficient (CC) to assess denoised image quality. Each hospital handles a single data type with strict transmission restrictions. Post-processing uses RED-CNN [5], and reconstruction employs LEARN [3] with a learning rate of 1×10^{-4}. RED-CNN undergoes 3 epochs over 1000 rounds, while LEARN uses 200 rounds. HF-Fed is compared with FedAvg [24], FedProx [18], FedBN [19], Ditto [17], pFedHN [30], and original models without federated learning (w/o FL). FedProx applies a penalty constant of 1×10^{-4}, and FedBN adds personalized BN layers post-convolution. Optimization uses Adam [15] with Mean Squared Error (MSE) loss. Experiments are conducted on NVIDIA GTX 3090 and A100 GPUs using PyTorch.

4.1 Experiments on the Large-Scale Training Set

In this section, we compare FL-based methods and original imaging models without FL, using a large-scale local dataset with RED-CNN as the backbone network. Hyperparameters remain consistent, except each hospital has 200 images in the training set. Table 1 demonstrates that FL-based methods significantly improve performance with larger datasets, mitigating the non-iid problem. HF-Fed consistently delivers high performance across different dataset sizes, enhancing imaging quality effectively. All methods benefit from larger training samples, with HF-Fed remaining competitive. Our hypernetwork uses X-Ray geometry parameters to modulate feature maps, balancing stability and imaging performance, proving effective in achieving consistent and competitive results.

4.2 Ablation Study

In this section, we conduct ablation studies to highlight the effectiveness of various components in HF-Fed. The experiments follow the settings outlined

Table 2. Results of Ablation Studies

Model	PSNR	SSIM
W/o FL "†"	36.58	0.9384
W/o FL "‡"	38.15	0.9348
FedAvg "†"	35.51	0.8726
FedAvg "‡"	36.85	0.9158
"HF-Fed ◇"	38.62	0.9644
"HF-Fed ★"	38.95	0.9667
"HF-Fed ○"	39.51	0.9691
HF-Fed	**39.95**	**0.9654**

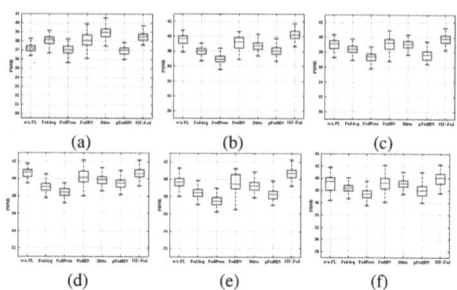

Fig. 2. Boxplots of PSNR scores for post-processing

in Sect. 3.2, with results summarized in Table 2. "†" and "‡" denote imaging networks without and with the hypernetwork, respectively, showing the significant role of the hypernetwork in improving imaging performance by addressing domain gap issues. Further, we evaluate our learning strategy by aggregating only the hypernetwork in rounds labeled "HF-Fed◇", addressing the challenge of heterogeneous scanning parameters. Additional experiments explore the modulation scope of the hypernetwork, where "HF-Fed★" and "HF-Fed○" scenarios focus on encoder and decoder modulation, respectively. Figure 2 shows the boxplots of PSNR based on w/o FL, FedAvg, FedProx, FedBN. Ditto, pFedHN, and HF-Fed for the postprocessing task. Results suggest similar performances across all modulation scenarios, indicating the effectiveness of modulating all layers for consistency and generality.

5 Conclusion

Current X-Ray imaging networks typically use centralized learning (CL), which overlooks privacy concerns and faces challenges with non-iid data due to varied scanning protocols and equipment. Introducing HF-Fed, a hierarchical-based hypernetwork for X-Ray imaging, addresses these issues by seamlessly integrating into diverse networks (CNN-based, IR-based, transformer-based). HF-Fed features hospital-specific hierarchical-driven hypernetworks and a shared Network of Networks (NoN), which adaptively extract stable imaging features across domains. Ablation experiments demonstrate that while FL-absent methods achieve customized X-Ray reconstruction, they suffer from detail loss with limited data. In contrast, FL-based HF-Fed maintains stability, recovering more details across hospitals and achieving superior reconstruction quality.

Disclosure of Interests. The authors have no competing interests to declare relevant to this article's content.

References

1. Ashraf, T., Bin Afzal Mir, F., Gillani, I.A.: Transfed: a way to epitomize focal modulation using transformer-based federated learning. In: Proceedings of the IEEE/CVF Winter Conference on Applications of Computer Vision, pp. 554–563 (2024)
2. Carr, C., et al.: RSNA screening mammography breast cancer detection (2022). https://kaggle.com/competitions/rsna-breast-cancer-detection
3. Chen, H., et al.: Learn: learned experts' assessment-based reconstruction network for sparse-data CT. IEEE Trans. Med. Imaging **37**(6), 1333–1347 (2018)
4. Chen, H., et al.: Low-dose CT with a residual encoder-decoder convolutional neural network. IEEE Trans. Med. Imaging **36**(12), 2524–2535 (2017)
5. Chen, Y., et al.: Bayesian statistical reconstruction for low-dose x-ray computed tomography using an adaptive-weighting nonlocal prior. Comput. Med. Imaging Graph. **33**(7), 495–500 (2009)
6. Dinh, C.T., Vu, T.T., Tran, N.H., Dao, M.N., Zhang, H.: A new look and convergence rate of federated multitask learning with laplacian regularization. IEEE Trans. Neural Netw. Learn. Syst. (2022)
7. Donoho, D.L.: Compressed sensing. IEEE Trans. Inf. Theory **52**(4), 1289–1306 (2006)
8. Feng, C.M., Yan, Y., Wang, S., Xu, Y., Shao, L., Fu, H.: Specificity-preserving federated learning for MR image reconstruction. IEEE Trans. Med. Imaging (2022)
9. Geras, K.J., Mann, R.M., Moy, L.: Artificial intelligence for mammography and digital breast tomosynthesis: current concepts and future perspectives. Radiology **293**(2), 246–259 (2019)
10. Guo, P., Wang, P., Zhou, J., Jiang, S., Patel, V.M.: Multi-institutional collaborations for improving deep learning-based magnetic resonance image reconstruction using federated learning. In: Proceedings of the IEEE/CVF Conference on Computer Vision and Pattern Recognition, pp. 2423–2432 (2021)
11. Hanzely, F., Richtárik, P.: Federated learning of a mixture of global and local models. arXiv preprint arXiv:2002.05516 (2020)
12. Hasegawa, B.H.: The physics of medical x-ray imaging (1990)
13. Ikuta, M., Zhang, J.: A deep convolutional gated recurrent unit for CT image reconstruction. IEEE Trans. Neural Netw. Learn. Syst. (2022)
14. Kaissis, G.A., Makowski, M.R., Rückert, D., Braren, R.F.: Secure, privacy-preserving and federated machine learning in medical imaging. Nat. Mach. Intell. **2**(6), 305–311 (2020)
15. Kingma, D.P., Ba, J.: Adam: a method for stochastic optimization. arXiv preprint arXiv:1412.6980 (2014)
16. Li, Q., He, B., Song, D.: Model-contrastive federated learning. In: Proceedings of the IEEE/CVF Conference on Computer Vision and Pattern Recognition, pp. 10713–10722 (2021)
17. Li, T., Hu, S., Beirami, A., Smith, V.: Ditto: fair and robust federated learning through personalization. In: International Conference on Machine Learning, pp. 6357–6368. PMLR (2021)

18. Li, T., Sahu, A.K., Zaheer, M., Sanjabi, M., Talwalkar, A., Smith, V.: Federated optimization in heterogeneous networks. In: Proceedings of Machine Learning and Systems, vol. 2, pp. 429–450 (2020)
19. Li, X., Jiang, M., Zhang, X., Kamp, M., Dou, Q.: FedBN: Federated learning on non-IID features via local batch normalization. arXiv preprint arXiv:2102.07623 (2021)
20. Liang, P.P., et al.: Think locally, act globally: federated learning with local and global representations. arXiv preprint arXiv:2001.01523 (2020)
21. Lim, B., Son, S., Kim, H., Nah, S., Mu Lee, K.: Enhanced deep residual networks for single image super-resolution. In: Proceedings of the IEEE Conference on Computer Vision and Pattern Recognition Workshops, pp. 136–144 (2017)
22. Lu, Z., et al.: M 3 NAS: multi-scale and multi-level memory-efficient neural architecture search for low-dose CT denoising. IEEE Trans. Med. Imaging **42**(3), 850–863 (2022)
23. Ma, X., Zhang, J., Guo, S., Xu, W.: Layer-wised model aggregation for personalized federated learning. In: Proceedings of the IEEE/CVF Conference on Computer Vision and Pattern Recognition, pp. 10092–10101 (2022)
24. McMahan, B., Moore, E., Ramage, D., Hampson, S., Arcas, B.A.: Communication-efficient learning of deep networks from decentralized data. In: Artificial Intelligence and Statistics, pp. 1273–1282. PMLR (2017)
25. Narayanan, A., Shmatikov, V.: Robust de-anonymization of large sparse datasets. In: 2008 IEEE Symposium on Security and Privacy (SP 2008), pp. 111–125. IEEE (2008)
26. Rodríguez-Ruiz, A., et al.: Detection of breast cancer with mammography: effect of an artificial intelligence support system. Radiology **290**(2), 305–314 (2019)
27. Rodriguez-Ruiz, A., et al.: Stand-alone artificial intelligence for breast cancer detection in mammography: comparison with 101 radiologists. JNCI: J. Natl. Cancer Inst. **111**(9), 916–922 (2019). https://doi.org/10.1093/jnci/djy222
28. Schwarz, C.G., et al.: Identification of anonymous MRI research participants with face-recognition software. N. Engl. J. Med. **381**(17), 1684–1686 (2019)
29. Shah, S.M., Lau, V.K.: Model compression for communication efficient federated learning. IEEE Trans. Neural Netw. Learn. Syst. (2021)
30. Shamsian, A., Navon, A., Fetaya, E., Chechik, G.: Personalized federated learning using hypernetworks. In: International Conference on Machine Learning, pp. 9489–9502. PMLR (2021)
31. Slovis, T.L.: The alara concept in pediatric CT: myth or reality? Radiology **223**(1), 5–6 (2002)
32. Xia, W., et al.: CT reconstruction with pdf: parameter-dependent framework for data from multiple geometries and dose levels. IEEE Trans. Med. Imaging **40**(11), 3065–3076 (2021)
33. You, C., et al.: Ct super-resolution GAN constrained by the identical, residual, and cycle learning ensemble (GAN-circle). IEEE Trans. Med. Imaging **39**(1), 188–203 (2019)
34. Zhang, W., et al.: Semi-asynchronous personalized federated learning for short-term photovoltaic power forecasting. Digit. Commun. Netw. **9**(5), 1221–1229 (2023)

DuEU-Net: Dual Encoder UNet with Modality-Agnostic Training for PET-CT Multi-modal Organ and Lesion Segmentation

Jinhong Song[1], Xiao Yang[2], Xinglong Liang[3], Jiaju Huang[1], Junqiang Ma[1], Yue Sun[1], Wuman Luo[1], SengPeng Mok[4], Ying Wang[2(✉)], and Tao Tan[1(✉)]

[1] Faculty of Applied Science, Macao Polytechnic University, Macao 999078, China
taotanjs@gmail.com
[2] Department of Nuclear Medicine, The Fifth Affiliated Hospital, Sun Yat-sen University, Zhuhai, China
wangy9@mail.sysu.edu.cn
[3] Department of Radiology and Nuclear Medicine, Radboud University Medical Centre, Nijmegen, The Netherlands
[4] Faculty of Science and Technology, University of Macau, Macau, China

Abstract. Multimodal PET-CT segmentation plays a crucial role in medical image analysis, offering vital localization and quantification of tumors and organs. However, automatic segmentation of multimodal medical images remains a significant challenging. In this study, we developed a deep learning-based segmentation model for PET-CT that can simultaneously segment organs and tumor. For the PET and CT, we design dual encoders separately to comprehensively capture the features of both modalities, and then the multimodal features are input to a shared decoder. Additionally, to address the challenge of limited PET-CT data, we developed a model capable of generating PET images from CT scans. This approach allows us to include CT-only datasets in the training process, thereby enhancing the model's generalization and performance. Experimental evaluations on publicly available datasets demonstrate the superiority of our method over benchmark approaches. In addition, we also test the generalization ability of our model on an internal breast cancer dataset. Our code is available at https://github.com/MD7sjh/DuEU-Net.

Keywords: PET-CT · Segmentation · Organ · Tumor

1 Introduction

With advancements in medical science and technology, medical imaging has become indispensable in modern diagnostics. Among these technologies, nuclear

---

J. Song X. Yang—Contributed equally to this work.

medicine imaging, particularly positron emission tomography (PET) and computed tomography (CT), has made a significant impact on clinical practice due to its unique capabilities. PET-CT integrates the strengths of both modalities, offering enhanced biological tissue information and comprehensive physiological and anatomical insights [1]. PET imaging reveals metabolic activity at a molecular level, complemented by CT's detailed anatomical structure. This combined modality has found extensive applications in cancer diagnosis, treatment planning, and therapeutic response assessment, providing a more nuanced understanding of disease states. Despite its benefits, automatic segmentation of PET-CT remains a challenging endeavor [2].

In recent years, deep learning has achieved significant advancements in medical image processing, particularly in the domains of tumor detection and organ segmentation. The most representative model among them is U-Net [3]. U-Net employs a full convolutional network that facilitates pixel-level predictions while preserving original image dimensions. There are many representative models based on U-Net. Özgün Çiçek et al. introduced 3D U-Net, which extends U-Net's capabilities to 3D data, enhancing its applicability in volumetric medical imaging [4]. X. Li et al. proposed a hybrid dense join U-Net, integrating 2D Dense-UNet for efficient in-slice feature extraction and a 3D counterpart for hierarchical aggregation of volume contexts, effectively leveraging comprehensive information features [5]. To address the challenge of integrating local and global context information, Konstantinos Kamnitsas et al. employed a dual-path architecture capable of processing input images across multiple scales simultaneously [6]. H. Xia et al. proposed a multi-scale context attention network to mitigate detail loss during coding by exploring valuable information across diverse scales and contexts [7]. Xian Lin et al. introduced ConvFormer, a CNN-style transformer designed to enhance attention convergence and improve segmentation performance [8]. Isensee.F et al. developed nnU-Net, focusing on simplifying network design to enhance adaptability and universality across various medical imaging tasks [9]. Recognizing the potential of larger models in medical image segmentation. Zhou et al. introduced nnFormer, incorporating interleaved convolution and self-attention operations along with novel local and global volume-based self-attention mechanisms to advance volume representation learning [10]. Recently, Huang, Ziyan et al. developed STU-Net based on nnU-Net principles, harnessing enhanced performance capabilities and leveraging nnU-Net's strengths in data preprocessing [11]. These innovations highlight the significant strides made in leveraging deep learning to improve medical image analysis, particularly in enhancing accuracy, robustness, and efficiency in clinical applications.

However, UNet exhibits limitations such as its inability to handle multimodal images effectively. Moreover, its direct one-to-one skip connections hinder the fusion of multi-level features. To address these shortcomings, we propose a method for PET-CT multimodal nuclear medicine image segmentation. Our approach aims to leverage the complementary strengths of PET and CT modalities to enhance segmentation accuracy and preserve details. The primary contributions of our method are outlined as follows:

- We designed a novel network which contains two parallel encoding branches for different modalities. Each encoder is constructed with multiple residual blocks designed to extract mode-specific features comprehensively, facilitating the integration of information across different modalities.
- We developed a model to generate PET images from CT scans, enabling the inclusion of CT-only datasets in training. This approach addresses the challenge of insufficient PET-CT data and enhances the model's generalization ability.
- We compared our method with the current state-of-the-art segmentation model, nnU-Net. Experimental evaluations on publicly available datasets demonstrate the superiority of our method.

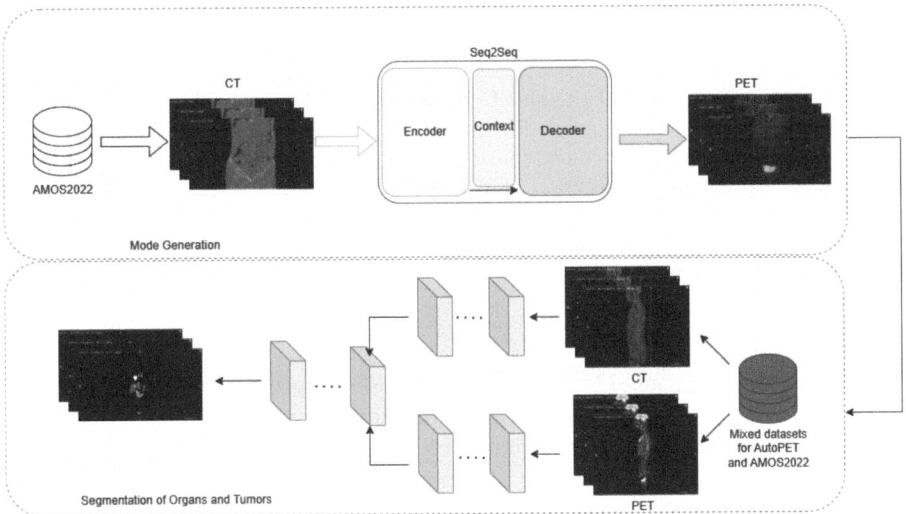

Fig. 1. A brief overview of the overall approach. The pseudo-PET images for the CT-only dataset were generated using the generation model. Then, both the pseudo-PET-CT and PET-CT datasets were input into the segmentation model for organ and tumor segmentation.

2 Method

Our method consists of two main parts: PET images generation and organ-tumor segmentation. First, we trained a generative model using the AutoPET [12] dataset to generate corresponding PET images from CT scans. This generative model employs the Seq2Seq architecture, a state-of-the-art approach for medical image generation [13]. We then extended the CT-only dataset into a pseudo-PET-CT dataset using our generative model. This augmented dataset was combined with the PET-CT dataset and fed into the segmentation model. Our framework was shown on Fig. 1.

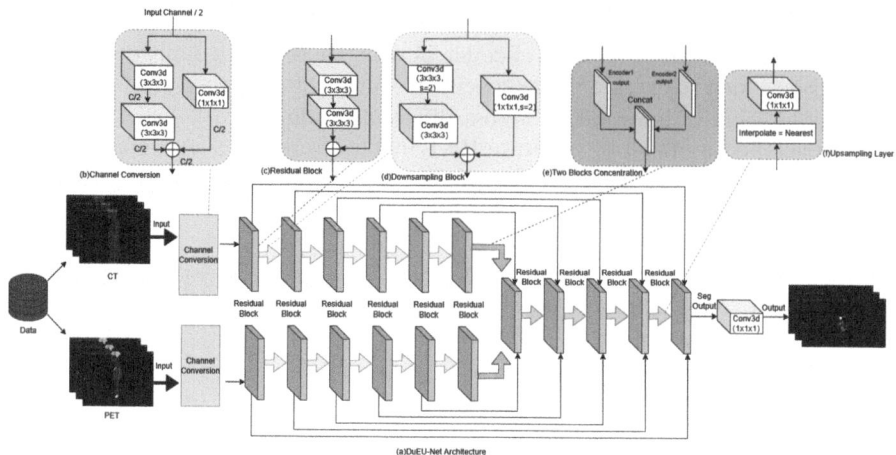

Fig. 2. (a) Overall overview of the DuEU-Net architecture: Two encoders dealing with two different modes, yellow arrows for downsampling, green arrows for upsampling, and pink arrows showing the concatenation of the outputs from both encoders before upsampling. (b) Channel conversion of the input. (c) Residual blocks. (d) Downsampling block. (e) Concatenation of the output of the two encoders. (f) The layer used to perform the nearest neighbor upsampling operation (Color figure online)

2.1 DuEU-Net Architecture

As we know, the traditional U-Net is generally used to process single-modal data, and it only contains one encoder which has limitations for multimodal data. Therefore, for multimodal data such as PET-CT, we designed DuEU-Net, which utilizes two parallel encoder paths (Encoder 1 and Encoder 2). This design is mainly based on DC-Net [14]. This innovative architecture enables simultaneous feature extraction from two distinct input sources, such as medical images with different modalities or differently preprocessed versions of the same image. Each encoder comprises a sequence of residual blocks that progressively reduce spatial dimensions through downsampling (pooling operations) while enhancing feature dimensions to capture contextual information across various scales. Unlike conventional methods, DuEU-Net's decoder section handles progressive upsampling and integration of deep features extracted by the encoders to produce finely segmented high-resolution outputs. Importantly, at each upsampling stage, the outputs of Encoder 1 and Encoder 2 are merged. This approach not only incorporates multi-scale features but also integrates information from two distinct encoding paths, thereby enhancing the model's ability to comprehend complex image structures and improving segmentation accuracy. Moreover, DuEU-Net employs nearest neighbor upsampling operations to gradually increase the size of feature maps. This simple approach involves directly copying the value of the nearest low-resolution pixel to the new location, avoiding complex computations and ensuring efficient implementation. The detailed design diagram of the network structure is shown in Fig. 2.

Table 1. The table uses Mean Validation DSC as the evaluation metric. The methods without "*" use the AutoPET dataset without organ labels and AMOS2022. The methods with "*" are AutoPET datasets with organ labels and AMOS2022. DuEU-NET* (weight=5.0) means to assign a weight to the Tumor label during the execution of the loss function, and the value of this weight is 5.0. The specific explanation is given in implementation details.

Class Tag	nnU-Net	DuEU-Net	nnU-Net*	DuEU-Net*	DuEU-Net* (Weight = 5.0)
Spleen	0.9548	**0.9619**	0.9560	0.9589	0.9561
Right Kidney	0.9593	**0.9599**	0.9525	0.9536	0.9533
Left Kidney	0.9403	0.9436	0.9551	**0.9556**	0.9551
Gallbladder	0.8079	0.7973	0.8432	0.8463	**0.8503**
Esophagus	0.8144	0.8307	0.8634	0.8694	**0.8695**
Liver	0.9647	0.9659	0.9710	0.9720	**0.9724**
Stomach	0.8834	0.8857	0.9260	**0.9332**	0.9262
Aorta	0.9480	0.9473	0.9528	**0.9548**	0.9547
Inferior Vena Cava	0.8846	0.8893	0.9155	0.9172	**0.9180**
Pancreas	0.8494	0.8564	0.8914	0.8925	**0.8956**
Right Adrenal Gland	0.7573	0.7978	0.8138	0.8146	**0.8159**
Left Adrenal Gland	0.7635	0.7648	0.8127	0.8173	**0.8197**
Duodenum	0.8038	0.8009	0.8423	**0.8529**	0.8491
Bladder	0.8768	0.8840	0.8636	0.8850	**0.8867**
Prostate/Uterus	0.8285	0.8442			
Tumor	0.7207	**0.7270**	0.6160	0.6638	0.6855
Mean	0.8598	0.8641	0.8783	0.8858	**0.8872**

3 Experiments

3.1 Dataset and Evaluation Metrics

We conducted experiments on two public datasets: AutoPET [12] which contains 501 whole-body FDG-PET/CT examinations with identified lesions and AMOS2022 [16] which contains 500 examinations. Given the differences between the two datasets, we performed specific preprocessing steps as follows: For AutoPET, since it only contains tumor labels, we use TotalSegmentator [15] to generate organ labels for this dataset. For AMOS2022, it only contains CT scans and organ labels, so we generate pseudo-PET for it through our trained generative model. Finally, the two datasets were merged into one large dataset with 15 organs and tumor labels. Subsequently, 560 subjects were allocated for training, 140 for validation, and 101 for testing purposes. The details are shown in Table 2. The evaluation metric used was the Dice similarity coefficient (DSC), where higher scores indicate better segmentation performance. For data preprocessing, we use the same data preprocessing method as nnU-Net, and need to make the information of dataset naming and resolution comply with nnU-Net specifications [9].

$$DSC = \frac{2 \times |A \cap B|}{|A| + |B|} \qquad (1)$$

Table 2. This table describes the labels, quantity, and modality of our dataset. The 15 organs are Spleen, Right Kidney, Left Kidney, Gallbladder, Esophagus, Liver, Stomach, Aorta, Inferior Vena Cava, Pancreas, Right Adrenal Gland, Left Adrenal Gland, Duodenum, Bladder, Prostate/Uterus.

Diagnosis	Quantity	Modality
Melanoma	188	PET/CT
Lymphoma	145	PET/CT
Lung Cancer	168	PET/CT
15 organs	500	Pseudo-PET/CT

3.2 Qualitative Comparison and Visualization

The results on two datasets were shown in Table 1. The method name without "*" is the result that directly combines AutoPET without organ labels and AMOS2022 into a dataset, and the method name with "*" is the result of a large dataset containing 15 organs and tumor labels. We can see that our method outperforms the benchmark method for two datasets, especially in organ segmentation. Additionally, we conducted tests on an internal breast cancer PET/CT dataset, achieving a Dice coefficient of 0.32. This demonstrates that our model can find the tumor location and retain generalization capability on unseen data, providing a basis for the future development of a universal tumor segmentation model. We also show some segmentation results in Fig. 3. Note that the red rectangle shows the difference in the segmentation of the specific labels in more detail. In a sense, our approach is closer to GroundTruth in more detail than the benchmark. In addition, we also show examples of generating Pseudo-PET images from CT images. Specifically, we show the CT and PET of the AutoPET, and the Pseudo-PET refers to the PET image generated only based on the CT image using the generative model. Figure 4 presents a comparison between the image data generated by our method and real images.

3.3 Implementation Details

These models were implemented using PyTorch and trained on a NVIDIA GeForce RTX 4090D graphics processors. The basic training configuration utilized the nnU-Net data preprocessing framework, with manual adjustments made for a patch size of $128 \times 128 \times 128$, an initial learning rate set to 1e-3, and training conducted over 1000 epochs. The entire training and validation process required

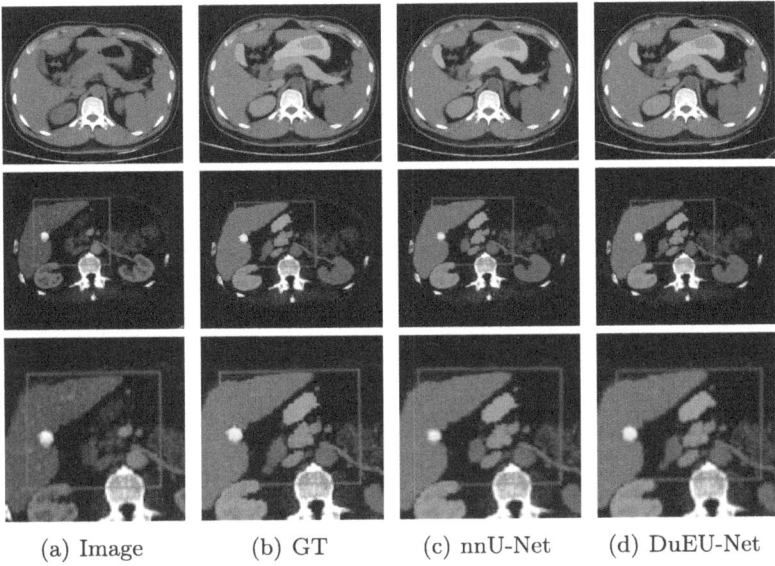

(a) Image (b) GT (c) nnU-Net (d) DuEU-Net

Fig. 3. The first row is the different CT scans from AMOS2022 dataset, and the two rows below are the same PET-CT datas from the AutoPET dataset. (Color figure online)

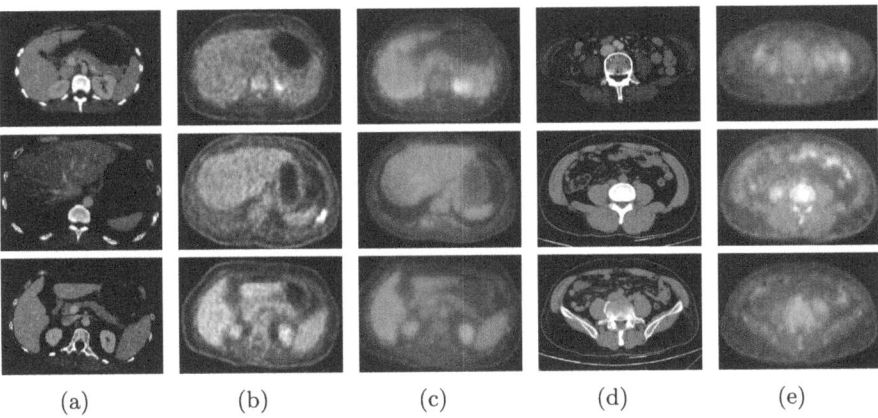

(a) (b) (c) (d) (e)

Fig. 4. The images generated using the generation model is shown here compared to the original datas.(a) CT (AutoPET); (b) PET (AutoPET); (c) Pseudo-PET (AutoPET); (d) CT (AMOS2022); (e) Pseudo-PET (AMOS2022)

approximately 26 h. It is worth noting that in order to maintain the lesion segmentation effect to the maximum extent, we adjusted the weight of the loss function related to the lesion in the training and set it to 5.0.

$$L(y, \hat{y}) = -\sum_{i=1}^{N} \begin{cases} 5.0 \cdot [y_i \log(\hat{y}_i)] & \text{if } i = N \\ 1.0 \cdot [y_i \log(\hat{y}_i)] & \text{if } i \neq N \end{cases} \qquad (2)$$

4 Conclusions

This study presents a PET-CT multimodal nuclear medicine image segmentation method designed for simultaneous organ and lesion segmentation, supported by extensive experimentation. Our experiments demonstrate that the CT-to-PET generative model we trained effectively compensates for the lack of PET-CT data, thereby expanding the training set. Results demonstrate superior performance compared to existing methods. Future research will focus on expanding our approach to include segmentation across additional modal combinations.

Acknowledgment. This work is supported by the Macao Polytechnic University [RP/FCA-15/2022]; the Science and Technology Development Fund of Macao (0105/2022/A); the Science and Technology Development Fund of Macao (0021/2022/AGJ).

References

1. Xu, H., Li, Y., Zhao, W., Quellec, G., Lu, L., Hatt, M.: Joint nnU-net and radiomics approaches for segmentation and prognosis of head and neck cancers with PET/CT images. In: Andrearczyk, V., Oreiller, V., Hatt, M., Depeursinge, A. (eds.) HECK-TOR 2022. LNCS, vol. 13626, pp. 154–165. Springer, Cham (2023). https://doi.org/10.1007/978-3-031-27420-6_16
2. Asgari Taghanaki, S., Abhishek, K., Cohen, J.P., Cohen-Adad, J., Hamarneh, G.: Deep semantic segmentation of natural and medical images: a review. Artif. Intell. Rev. **54**(1), 137–178 (2020). https://doi.org/10.1007/s10462-020-09854-1
3. Ronneberger, O., et al.: U-net: convolutional networks for biomedical image segmentation. arXiv abs/1505.04597 (2015)
4. Çiçek, Ö., Abdulkadir, A., Lienkamp, S.S., Brox, T., Ronneberger, O.: 3D u-net: learning dense volumetric segmentation from sparse annotation. In: Ourselin, S., Joskowicz, L., Sabuncu, M.R., Unal, G., Wells, W. (eds.) MICCAI 2016. LNCS, vol. 9901, pp. 424–432. Springer, Cham (2016). https://doi.org/10.1007/978-3-319-46723-8_49
5. Li, X., Chen, H., Qi, X., Dou, Q., Fu, C.-W., Heng, P.-A.: H-DenseUNet: hybrid densely connected unet for liver and tumor segmentation from CT volumes. IEEE Trans. Med. Imaging **37**(12), 2663–2674 (2018). https://doi.org/10.1109/TMI.2018.2845918
6. Kamnitsas, K., et al.: Efficient multi-scale 3D CNN with fully connected CRF for accurate brain lesion segmentation. Med. Image Anal. **36**, 61–78 (2017). https://doi.org/10.1016/j.media.2016.10.004. ISSN 1361-8415
7. Xia, H., Ma, M., Li, H., Song, S.: MC-net: multi-scale context-attention network for medical CT image segmentation. Appl. Intell. **52**(2), 1508–1519 (2021). https://doi.org/10.1007/s10489-021-02506-z

8. Lin, X., et al.: ConvFormer: plug-and-play CNN-style transformers for improving medical image segmentation. In: International Conference on Medical Image Computing and Computer-Assisted Intervention (2023)
9. Isensee, F., Jaeger, P.F., Kohl, S.A.A., et al.: nnU-Net: a self-configuring method for deep learning-based biomedical image segmentation. Nat. Methods **18**, 203–211 (2021). https://doi.org/10.1038/s41592-020-01008-z
10. Zhou, H.-Y., et al.: nnFormer: volumetric medical image segmentation via a 3D transformer. IEEE Trans. Image Process. **32**, 4036–4045 (2023). https://doi.org/10.1109/TIP.2023.3293771
11. Huang, Z., et al.: STU-net: scalable and transferable medical image segmentation models empowered by large-scale supervised pre-training. arXiv abs/2304.06716 (2023)
12. Gatidis, S., Kuestner, T.: A whole-body FDG-PET/CT dataset with manually annotated tumor lesions (FDG-PET-CT-Lesions) [Dataset]. Cancer Imaging Arch. (2022). https://doi.org/10.7937/gkr0-xv29
13. Han, L., et al.: An explainable deep framework: towards task-specific fusion for multi-to-one MRI synthesis. In: Greenspan, H., et al. (eds.) MICCAI 2023. LNCS, vol. 14229, pp. 45–55. Springer, Cham (2023). https://doi.org/10.1007/978-3-031-43999-5_5
14. Lou, A., et al.: DC-UNet: rethinking the U-Net architecture with dual channel efficient CNN for medical image segmentation. Med. Imaging (2020)
15. Wasserthal, J., et al.: TotalSegmentator: robust segmentation of 104 anatomic structures in CT images. Radiol. Artif. Intell. **5**(5), e230024 (2022)
16. Ji, Y., et al.: AMOS: a large-scale abdominal multi-organ benchmark for versatile medical image segmentation. arXiv abs/2206.08023 (2022)

One for All: UNET Training on Single-Sequence Masks for Multi-sequence Breast MRI Segmentation

Jarek M. van Dijk[1,2], Luyi Han[1,2], Luuk Balkenende[1,2], Nika Rasoolzadeh[1,2], Karine R. Morche[1], Tianyu Zhang[1,2(✉)], and Ritse M. Mann[1,2(✉)]

[1] Department of Radiology and Nuclear Medicine, Radboud University Medical Centre, Geert Grooteplein 10, 6525 GA Nijmegen, The Netherlands
{Tianyu.Zhang,Ritse.Mann}@radboudumc.nl

[2] Department of Radiology, The Netherlands Cancer Institute, Plesmanlaan 121, 1066 CX Amsterdam, The Netherlands

Abstract. The segmentation of fibroglandular (FGT) and breast tissue in MRI remains an important step for computer assisted radiology and for risk assessment of breast cancer. Currently, all automatic segmentation methods are trained exclusively on T1-based images and segmentations, and there is no existing literature on segmenting non-T1 sequences. To address this research gap, we trained an nnUNet to perform multi-sequence segmentation using solely T1-based masks. Evaluation based on Dice Similarity Scores and visual inspection reveals distinct segmentations per sequence with reasonable overall performance. Our findings indicate that the architecture is able to overcome partially incorrect labels and make use of general breast-specific masks. However, despite the reasonable results, the segmentations missed some potential FGT sites and is likely to improve from sequence-specific masks. Furthermore, the prediction quality is relatively poor for non-dense breasts. Future studies should include reader studies or sequence-specific segmentations as well as a comparative study with and without such sequence-specific segmentations.

Keywords: MRI · Segmentation · Breast cancer · Deep Learning

1 Introduction

Breast cancer was the most commonly diagnosed cancer and the leading cause of cancer-related death among women in 2023 [1,2]. A key factor in advancing clinical outcome lies in risk assessment and earlier detection of lesions [3,4]. Facilitating earlier detection, Magnetic Resonance Imaging (MRI) has become a highly sensitive imaging method, particularly in contrast-enhanced formats [5]. Additionally it offers wide sequence variety to support clinical decision-making and lesion evaluation [6,7].

Yet, the interpretation of MRI remains a labor-intensive task in clinical settings. Therefore, algorithms are continually developed to assist clinicians in analyzing MRI scans and performing related tasks, such as using the ratio of breast tissue to fibroglandular tissue (FGT) in risk evaluation [8–10], as well as lesion evaluation and detection. For such algorithms, the segmentation of breast and FGT can be an important step [11]. Thus, automatic segmentation algorithms have been developed for breast MRI over time. However, all methods have have focused on the segmentation of T1 sequences, which are most often used for evaluating FGT volume, and no work has been done on breast and FGT segmentation in other MRI sequences. Although segmenting these sequences may be redundant for estimating FGT volume, especially considering the low resolution in Diffusion Weighted Image (DWI), identifying the general areas where the breast and FGT are located could still be valuable for downstream tasks such as lesion detection and malignancy evaluation.

Therefore the aim of this study is twofold: firstly, to develop and train a neural network capable of segmenting breast tissue and FGT across multiple MRI sequences. Secondly, we aim to investigate the feasibility of using solely T1-based segmentations in training models for non-T1 sequences. We hypothesize that a neural network trained on T1-based segmentations can generalize to other sequences despite inherent differences between them, and will be able to focus on sequence-specific features relevant for segmentation. Moreover, we expect the network to find sequence-specific indications of breast and FGT for the purpose of segmentation.

Building on the approach by Samperna et al. [12], who used a single segmentation mask across different phases of Dixon sequences, we propose a similar strategy for multi-sequence MRI images of the same breast. However, compared to their work, we anticipate that a single mask will be less effective across all MRI sequences due to the greater variability among them. More concretely, this could result in false positive (FP) segmentations of irrelevant areas and false negative (FN) segmentations of relevant ones. Although recent research shows a neural network's ability to overcome FN segmentations in prostate histology slides [13], similar results have not yet been demonstrated for MRI breast images. Furthermore, there is no evidence of the network's ability to effectively disregard FP segmentations in breast MRI.

2 Material and Methods

In this study, we trained an nnUNet [14] to predict segmentations on Dynamic Contrast Enhanced (DCE), subtraction of in-wash DCE phase (Sinwash), subtraction of out-wash DCE phase (Soutwash), T2, as well as DWI acquisitions and corresponding apparent diffusion coefficient (ADC) maps. The ground truth (GT) segmentation is made from the first DCE timepoint (DCE1). Additionally, we checked whether including multiple sequences affects the quality of DCE1 segmentations by training a second nnUNet with only DCE1 images.

2.1 Data

A dataset of 89 patients from the Netherlands Cancer Institute (NKI), including multi-sequence measurements and DCE1-based segmentations was used. Each patient scan includes multiple T1-fatsat DCE images, T2, DWI (b_0, b_{150}, b_{800}, and b_{1500}), ADC, Sinwash, and Soutwash images. The number of DCE phases per patient ranged from two to six, with three phases being most common. Some patients had breast lesions, but the segmentation of lesions was omitted from this study and included in the FGT segmentation. The population for this dataset consisted of woman between the age of 30 and 61 ($\mu = 51$). Scans were made with the Phillips Ingenia and Achieva dStream. T1 repetition times varied between 3.24–3.67 ms ($\mu = 3.56$), echo times between 1.68–1.85 ms ($\mu = 1.71$) and flip angles were either 10° or 12°.

2.2 Datasets

The datasets for the nnUNet were created by selecting patients for training and testing using an 85-15 train split, resulting in 75 patients for training and 14 patients for testing. This approach ensured consistent test samples between subsets of the network and prevented data leakage from different sequences of a single patient between the train and test sets. For the multi-sequence dataset (DS2), all sequences of a patient were included, and for the T1-only dataset (DS1) only the DCE images were selected. The resulting T1-only dataset contained 260 images for training/validation and 48 for testing, whereas the multi-sequence dataset had 837 images for training/validation and 158 for testing. As apparent in Table 1, some discrepancy exists between the relative number of images between the train and test sets, as some patients were missing T2 or Soutwash images and the number of DCE phases was not always the same.

Table 1. Amount of images for each sequence in the train- and test data per dataset

Dataset		DCE	T2	DWI	ADC	Sinwash	Soutwash	total
DS1	Train	260	0	0	0	0	0	260 (84%)
	Test	48	0	0	0	0	0	48 (16 %)
DS2	Train	260	55	300	75	75	72	837 (84%)
	Test	48	12	56	14	14	14	158 (16%)

2.3 Architecture and Training

Before training, all sequences were resampled to a ($1 \times 1 \times 1$ mm) spacing for consistent spacing and thickness. To correct size artifacts where segmentations were larger along the longitudinal axis or both the longitudinal and frontal axes, cropping was applied to the lateral or both lateral and superior slices of the segmentations. Deletions of a single superior slice were most common although some multi-slice deletions occurred. Preprocessing and training was performed using the nnUNet's 3D high-resolution architecture with default settings. A 5-fold split, stratified on patient level, was used for validation during training. Training continued for 1000 epochs per split. For inference an ensemble of the five folds was used. Each image was treated as an unique training sample, rather than stacking the inputs.

2.4 Evaluation Metrics

To evaluate the quality of DCE1 predicted segmentations, the dice similarity coefficient (DSC; Eq. 1) is computed separately for FGT and breast as a binary segmentation task, with the background not being considered a segmentation. Differences in performance between DS1-trained and DS2-trained networks were evaluated by a paired t-test, for which the assumption of normality was validated with the Shapiro-Wilk test [15]. All statistical tests were performed using SciPy v1.11.4 in Python.

$$\text{DSC(A,B)} = \frac{2|A \cap B|}{|A| + |B|} \quad (1)$$

where:

$|A \cap B|$ = the area in which A and B have the same segmentation
$|A|$ = the total area of segmentation A
$|B|$ = the total area of segmentation B

To evaluate whether segmentation predictions differ between sequences, we calculated the similarity of the sequence-specific segmentation predictions per patient. Formally, for each patient p of total patients N, we compared the predicted segmentations of sequence A with those sequence B (Eq. 2). For each pair of sequences A and B, where the number of images per sequence $(n_A; n_B)$ may vary, DSC between all sequence pairs was determined as:

$$\text{DSC}_{AB} = \frac{1}{N} \sum_{p=1}^{N} \left\{ \text{DSC}(A_i^p, B_j^p) \mid i = 1, 2, \ldots, n_A, \, j = 1, 2, \ldots, n_B \right\} \quad (2)$$

where:

$|A_i^p|$ = represent a segmentation i from sequence A for patient p
$|B_j^p|$ = represent a segmentation j from sequence B for patient p

Additionally, we determined the average DSC between sequence-based predictions and its corresponding DCE1-based GT to evaluate how well the general breast and FGT area are segmented.

3 Results

3.1 T1-Performance

For DS1, the DSC between the ground truth and predicted segmentation of DCE1 was 0.93 ($\sigma = 0.04$) for breast tissue and 0.86 ($\sigma = 0.13$) for FGT. For DS2, these values were 0.92 ($\sigma = 0.03$) and 0.85 ($\sigma = 0.13$), respectively. Despite these small differences, the performance difference was significant for breast ($p = 0.023$) and FGT ($p = 0.046$), and the t-test's normality assumption was not rejected ($p = 0.692$ for breast; $p = 0.354$ for FGT).

3.2 Sequence Similarities

Table 2 compares the DSC scored between sequences, with the comparisons for DCE's various timepoints and DWI's various b-values being averaged. Overall, the breast segmentations are more similar between sequences than FGT segmentations. The sequences DCE, T2, Sinwash, and Soutwash consistently showed higher DSC values with each other than with ADC or DWI. Similarly, these sequences generally have higher similarity to the ground truth, with DCE being most similar, followed by T2, Sinwash, and Soutwash.

Table 2. Average DSC and standard deviation between sequences and with the DCE1-based ground truth

		T1-GT	DCE	T2	DWI	ADC	Sinwash	Soutwash
DCE	breast	0.91 ± 0.04	NAN	0.95 ± 0.03	0.90 ± 0.06	0.90 ± 0.06	0.94 ± 0.03	0.94 ± 0.03
	FGT	0.83 ± 0.12	NAN	0.84 ± 0.12	0.70 ± 0.15	0.69 ± 0.16	0.78 ± 0.11	0.80 ± 0.09
T2	breast	0.90 ± 0.04	0.95 ± 0.03	NAN	0.91 ± 0.06	0.90 ± 0.07	0.94 ± 0.03	0.94 ± 0.02
	FGT	0.76 ± 0.14	0.84 ± 0.12	NAN	0.69 ± 0.16	0.68 ± 0.17	0.75 ± 0.13	0.79 ± 0.13
DWI	breast	0.87 ± 0.06	0.90 ± 0.06	0.91 ± 0.06	NAN	0.95 ± 0.02	0.91 ± 0.06	0.91 ± 0.05
	FGT	0.66 ± 0.15	0.70 ± 0.15	0.69 ± 0.16	NAN	0.84 ± 0.11	0.72 ± 0.15	0.72 ± 0.15
ADC	breast	0.87 ± 0.06	0.90 ± 0.06	0.90 ± 0.07	0.95 ± 0.02	NAN	0.91 ± 0.06	0.90 ± 0.06
	FGT	0.65 ± 0.16	0.69 ± 0.16	0.68 ± 0.17	0.84 ± 0.11	NAN	0.71 ± 0.16	0.71 ± 0.16
Sinwash	breast	0.89 ± 0.03	0.94 ± 0.03	0.94 ± 0.03	0.91 ± 0.06	0.91 ± 0.06	NAN	0.95 ± 0.03
	FGT	0.72 ± 0.13	0.78 ± 0.11	0.75 ± 0.13	0.72 ± 0.15	0.71 ± 0.16	NAN	0.81 ± 0.09
Soutwash	breast	0.89 ± 0.04	0.94 ± 0.03	0.94 ± 0.02	0.91 ± 0.05	0.90 ± 0.06	0.95 ± 0.03	NAN
	FGT	0.72 ± 0.12	0.80 ± 0.09	0.79 ± 0.13	0.72 ± 0.15	0.71 ± 0.16	0.81 ± 0.09	NAN

3.3 DWI Specific

Table 3 presents the average DSC between various DWI sequences for breast tissue and FGT. As was the case for the inter-sequence comparison, the breast-segmentations are more similar than the FGT-segmentations. Overall, the DWI sequences show higher similarity among themselves than with other non-DWI sequences. The lowest within-DWI similarity was 0.94 for breast tissue and 0.80 for FGT tissue, which was only surpassed by the DWI-ADC similarity of 0.95 for breast tissue and 0.84 for FGT tissue.

Furthermore, the average similarity of the b-values with the T1-based GT are very similar, with b_{150} performing best, b_{1500} performing worst and b_0 performing equal to b_{800}. For inter-DWI similarity, b_0 and b_{150} become more similar to other b-values as these b-values increases. Conversely, the reverse is seen for b_{1500} as the inter-DWI similarity increases with the b-value. On the other hand, b_{800} shows no consistent trend and has highest similarity with b_{150}, followed by b_0, and is least similar to b_{1500}.

Table 3. Average DSC between DWIs and GT

		T1-GT	b_0	b_{150}	b_{800}	b_{1500}
b_0	breast	0.87 ± 0.06	NAN	0.98 ± 0.01	0.96 ± 0.02	0.94 ± 0.04
	FGT	0.66 ± 0.15	NAN	0.92 ± 0.06	0.86 ± 0.09	0.80 ± 0.10
b_{150}	breast	0.87 ± 0.06	0.98 ± 0.01	NAN	0.96 ± 0.02	0.94 ± 0.04
	FGT	0.67 ± 0.15	0.92 ± 0.06	NAN	0.88 ± 0.08	0.81 ± 0.09
b_{800}	breast	0.87 ± 0.06	0.96 ± 0.02	0.96 ± 0.02	NAN	0.95 ± 0.03
	fgt	0.66 ± 0.15	0.86 ± 0.09	0.88 ± 0.08	NAN	0.85 ± 0.09
b_{1500}	breast	0.87 ± 0.05	0.94 ± 0.04	0.94 ± 0.04	0.95 ± 0.03	NAN
	fgt	0.64 ± 0.15	0.80 ± 0.10	0.81 ± 0.09	0.85 ± 0.09	NAN

3.4 Visual Results

For visual evaluation, a test-case with scattered or FGT was segmented (Fig. 1). Notably, the FGT DSC with the GT is below average for all sequences except DCE1. Additionally, the breast predictions are fairly consistent while the FGT predictions show greater variability. Overall, the segmentation of DCE1 and T2 are most refined, whereas the Sinwash and Soutwash are more globular. Conversely, ADC and all DWI sequences lack fine-grained details in FGT segmentation.

In the DCE1 image, several spots annotated in the ground truth are missing in the predicted output, particularly in the right breast (left in the image). Interestingly, a segmentation is added for a bright spot in the anterior-right (top-right in image) of the left breast that was not annotated in the GT, indicating either an oversight in the ground truth or FP of the network. For the T2 segmentation, many darkened fibers are segmented, especially where they are also found in the DCE1-GT. However, a darkened area in the left breast –likely an artifact– shows less segmentation, which explains some of the decreased DSC score for this case. In the ADC images, segmentations are predicted in brightened areas, somewhat corresponding to FGT in the GT and other images. Sinwash and Soutwash cover similar areas as the other images, but there is no clearly discernible pattern. In the DWI images, increasing b-value generally reduces total segmented FGT. In the right breast, the brighter area is consistently annotated across images, but the segmentation volume at the anterior side of right breast reduces. Overall, most images show segmentations in the same general area, but differ in total covered area, segmented sites and overall coarseness of segmentation.

Notably, the similarity of FGT-segmentations was higher for images with heterogeneous dense breast tissue, as is illustrated by Fig. 3. This is also reflected by the above-average DSC. Similarly, the segmentations of DWI, ADC, Sinwash and Soutwash and ADC are less refined than the T2 and DCE1 cases. For images with of few and scattered FGT, as is the case in Fig. 3, the inter-sequence similarity of FGT segmentation is lower. The most likely cause is the loss of small FGT detections in the sequences other than DCE1 and T2, as such strands are less present in the images.

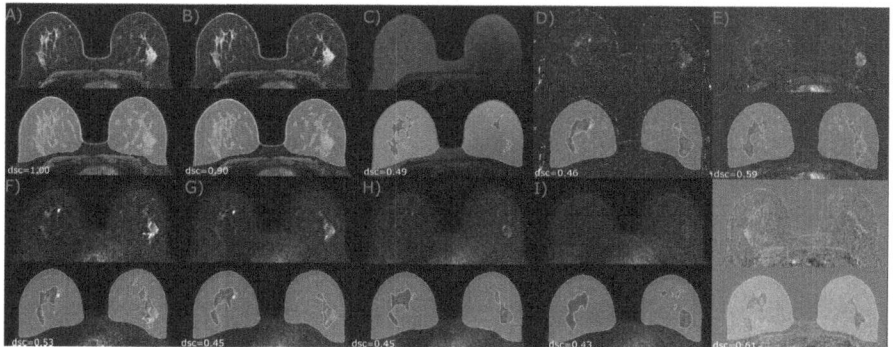

Fig. 1. Segmentation results of multiple sequences for one of the test patients, with the left side of the image corresponding to the right breast. A) and B) respectively display the ground truth and predicted segmentations for DCE1. C) shows the predicted segmentation for T2, D) for ADC, and E) for Sinwash. F) to I) depict predicted segmentations for DWI sequences: b_0, b_{150}, b_{800}, and b_{1500} respectively. J) shows the predicted segmentation for Soutwash. DSC scores of FGT with the ground truth are added in the bottom-left corner.

4 Discussion

The goal of this research was to train a network for sequence-specific segmentations using the mask of only one sequence. The results (Table 2; Fig. 1; Table 3) indicate that the network indeed differs in its segmentations per sequence. Additionally, visually similar sequences, such as DCE and T2 or inter-DWI pairs, produce more similar segmentations compared to dissimilar sequences like DCE and DWI. Moreover, the general overlap in segmented areas between sequences and the ground-truth indicates that the network is able to capture features indicating breast and FGT in each sequence. This is further supported by the visual differences in segmented areas, such as bright FGT strands in DCE and darker strands in T2.

A possible explanation for the network's specificity to each sequence, despite the training segmentations containing both correct and incorrect labels, may be

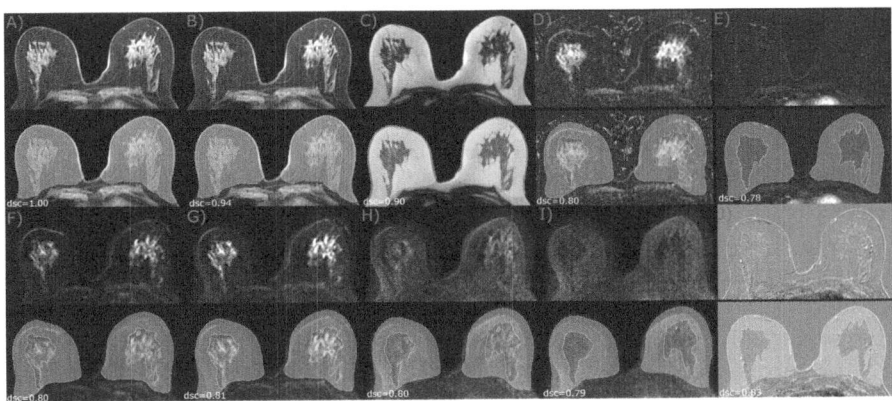

Fig. 2. Segmentation results of multiple sequences for a test patient with heterogeneous dense breast, with the left side of the image corresponding to the right breast. A) and B) respectively display the ground truth and predicted segmentations for DCE1. C) shows the predicted segmentation for T2, D) for ADC, and E) for Sinwash. F) to I) depict predicted segmentations for DWI sequences: b_0, b_{150}, b_{800}, and b_{1500} respectively. J) shows the predicted segmentation for Soutwash. DSC scores of FGT with the ground truth are added in the bottom-left corner.

Fig. 3. Segmentation results of a test case with scattered and few FGT strands, with the left side of the image corresponding to the right breast. A) and B) respectively display the ground truth and predicted segmentations for DCE1. C) shows the predicted segmentation for T2, D) for ADC, and E) for Sinwash. F) to I) depict predicted segmentations for DWI sequences: b_0, b_{150}, b_{800}, and b_{1500} respectively. J) shows the predicted segmentation for Soutwash. DSC scores of FGT with the ground truth are added in the bottom-left corner.

lack of patterns in the incorrect labels. Generally, a network learns by identifying patterns in the data that are salient for correct classification. If the FP and FN segmentations lack consistent discernible features, the network cannot extract meaningful patterns from these errors and only the true-positive segmentations of the GT will guide most of the learning.

Compared to the average DSC (Table 2) and the heterogeneous dense case in the supplementary (Fig. 2), the performance for the case in Fig. 1 was relatively poor; another less dense case (Fig. 3) even worse. A possible explanation may be that small amounts of scattered FGT makes accurate detection more challenging due to lack of signal. The proxy-mask may also be less accurate for these cases as each strand is smaller and has less segmented area overall. Additionally, this lower overall segmentation volume might make the DSC more sensitive to errors, as the ratio of incorrectly segmented to total volume increases [16]. Thus, although segmentations of dense breasts show better overall performance, assessing errors for finer details can be more complex compared to scattered breasts, where such inaccuracies are more noticeable.

Comparing the networks, the addition of new sequences resulted in a slight but statistically significant performance decrease in the DCE1 segmentations, as the DS2-network's performance on this sequence was marginally worse than that of the DS1-network. However, to conclusively attribute this effect to the addition of sequence, rather than chance from re-training, some repetition studies are needed. If the reduced performance is indeed caused by the inclusion of additional sequences, it could be worthwhile to investigate whether sequence-specific networks would improve performance over the currently used all-sequence network.

Overall, there is room for improvement. More varied data could be used as the network is unable to overcome the artifact presented in the T2 segmentation (Fig. 1). Accurately evaluating FGT segmentation is also challenging due to reliance on the DCE1 proxy mask, and sequences like DWI are expected to be less effective at capturing FGT, particularly at higher b-values. Additionally, a more precise assessment of segmentation quality could be achieved by using sequence-specific ground truths or conducting reader studies, possibly combined with a comparative study of results with and without such masks.

Thus, the network's utility is currently limited to tasks where general segmentation is sufficient, such as cropping breasts, applying attention mechanisms, or measuring relative breast density. The use of proxy masks becomes especially relevant due to the lack of publicly available non-T1 segmented data for training. For tasks requiring highly accurate segmentations, particularly for low-density breasts, it is likely better to provide sequence-specific segmentations.

5 Conclusion

In this work, we trained a UNET to segment DCE, T2, DWI, ADC, wash-in subtraction, and wash-out subtraction sequences using only DCE masks for breast and FGT. The network successfully segmented sequence-specific features and produced varying segmentation results across different sequences. Our study demonstrates that reasonable segmentations across multiple sequences are feasible without individual masks for each sequence, though with some loss in quality.

Disclosure of Interests. Authors have no conflict of interest to declare.

References

1. Bray, F., Laversanne, M., Sung, H., et al.: Global cancer statistics 2022: GLOBOCAN estimates of incidence and mortality worldwide for 36 cancers in 185 countries. CA Cancer J. Clin. **74**(3), 229–263 (2024)
2. Zhang, T., Tan, T., Samperna, R., et al.: Radiomics and artificial intelligence in breast imaging: a survey. Artif. Intell. Rev. **56**(Suppl 1), 857–892 (2023)
3. Etzioni, R., et al.: The case for early detection. Nat. Rev. Cancer **3**, 243–252 (2003)
4. Dibden, A., Offman, J., Duffy, S.W., Gabe, R.: Worldwide review and meta-analysis of cohort studies measuring the effect of mammography screening programmes on incidence-based breast cancer mortality. Cancers **12**(4), 976 (2020)
5. Mann, R., Kuhl, C., Moy, L.: Contrast-enhanced MRI for breast cancer screening. J. Magn. Reson. Imaging **50**, 377–390 (2019)
6. Mann, R.M., Cho, N., Moy, L.: Breast MRI: state of the art. Radiology **292**(3), 520–536 (2019)
7. Baltzer, P., Mann, R.M., Iima, M., et al.: Diffusion-weighted imaging of the breast—a consensus and mission statement from the EUSOBI International Breast Diffusion-Weighted Imaging working group. Eur. Radiol. **30**, 1436–1450 (2020)
8. Kerlikowske, K., et al.: Combining quantitative and qualitative breast density measures to assess breast cancer risk. Breast Cancer Res. **19**(1) (2017)
9. Wang, Y., Deasy, J.: SU-E-I-70: semi-automatic, user-driven breast, chest wall and FGT segmentations based on hough transform, morphology tools and histogram technology. Med. Phys. **39**(6Part5), 3641–3641 (2012)
10. Vachon, C.M., van Gils, C.H., Sellers, T.A., et al.: Mammographic density, breast cancer risk and risk prediction. Breast Cancer Res. **9**, 217 (2007)
11. Wu, S., Weinstein, S.P., Conant, E.F., Schnall, M.D., Kontos, D.: Automated chest wall line detection for whole-breast segmentation in sagittal breast MR images. Med. Phys. **40**(4) (2013)
12. Samperna, R., Moriakov, N., Karssemeijer, N., Teuwen, J., Mann, R.M.: Exploiting the Dixon method for a robust breast and Fibro-Glandular tissue segmentation in breast MRI. Diagnostics **12**(7), 1690 (2022)
13. Anklin, V., et al.: Learning whole-slide segmentation from inexact and incomplete labels using tissue graphs. In: de Bruijne, M., et al. (eds.) MICCAI 2021. LNCS, vol. 12902, pp. 636–646. Springer, Cham (2021). https://doi.org/10.1007/978-3-030-87196-3_59
14. Isensee, F., Jaeger, P.F., Kohl, S.A., Petersen, J., Maier-Hein, K.H.: nnU-Net: a self-configuring method for deep learning-based biomedical image segmentation. Nat. Methods **18**(2), 203–211 (2021)
15. Shapiro, S.S., Wilk, M.B.: An analysis of variance test for normality (complete samples). Biometrika **52**(3–4), 591–611 (1965)
16. Reinke, A., et al.: Common limitations of performance metrics in biomedical image analysis. OpenReview (2021)

Multimodal Breast MRI Language-Image Pretraining (MLIP): An Exploration of a Breast MRI Foundation Model

Nika Rasoolzadeh[1,2], Tianyu Zhang[1,2,3(✉)], Yuan Gao[1,2,3], Jarek M. van Dijk[1,2], Qiuhui Yang[4], Tao Tan[1,2,4], and Ritse M. Mann[1,2]

[1] Department of Radiology and Nuclear Medicine, Radboud University Medical Center, 6525 GA Nijmegen, The Netherlands
Tianyu.Zhang@radboudumc.nl
[2] Department of Radiology, Netherlands Cancer Institute (NKI), Plesmanlaan 121, 1066 CX Amsterdam, The Netherlands
[3] GROW School for Oncology and Developmental Biology, Maastricht University Medical Centre, 6202 AZ Maastricht, The Netherlands
[4] Faculty of Applied Sciences, Macao Polytechnic University, Macao 999078, China

Abstract. Breast magnetic resonance imaging (MRI) is widely recognized for its high sensitivity in detecting breast cancer. However, interpreting breast MRI scans remains a complex, time-consuming, and resource-intensive task, even for experienced radiologists. To address these challenges, artificial intelligence-based methods are increasingly being employed. In this study, we developed a multimodal breast MRI language-image pre-training (MLIP) approach as an initial exploration of a breast MRI foundation model to aid in the interpretation of scans. Two types of inferences were used to evaluate MLIP's performance. First, MLIP could retrieve corresponding MRI cases from a dataset based on a query, achieving an area under the receiver operating characteristic curve of 0.717 for suspicious and malignant cases, 0.640 for dense breasts, and 0.601 for low background parenchymal enhancement (BPE). Second, MLIP demonstrated the ability to predict the level of disease suspicion for a given MRI case. The results suggest that MLIP has the potential to serve as a foundation model for breast MRI interpretation. Future work will focus on expanding its capabilities through various downstream tasks and integrating additional models to enhance overall performance.

Keywords: Breast Imaging · MRI · NLP · Contrastive Learning · Foundation model

1 Introduction

Breast cancer has consistently been one of the leading causes of death among women for many years. Recent statistics show that, rather than decreasing, the numbers remain high [3]. In fact, the global incidence has steadily increased across all age groups in recent years, with some variations by region and age [8]. One of the reasons contributing to this number is suboptimal screening practices. Screening has been a contentious topic in the breast cancer world mainly due to the promotion of scientifically false concepts about the risk-benefit ratio of screening. Fortunately, the number of studies highlighting the importance of screening and proposing updated guidelines has been increasing.

The use of mammography in breast cancer screening has been shown to reduce the breast cancer mortality rates by at least 20–25% [13] and can reduce the rate of advanced breast cancers by 25% [2]. Therefore, it is reasonable that mammography remains to be the most common method of screening. However, mammography is not without its limitations. Besides the painful procedure, its sensitivity is affected by density masking, where the dense breast tissue obscures the tumors. Therefore, supplemental screenings with ultrasound and magnetic resonance imaging (MRI) are essential for women with high risk and women with extremely dense breasts. The first group is recommended to have annual breast MRI with a potential yearly or biennial mammography starting at the age of 35–40. And the later, is recommended to have breast MRI at least every 4 years from age of 50 to 70 [12].

As the most sensitive detection method, breast MRI can improve breast cancer surgery, provide earlier stage detection and low interval cancer rates across diverse populations [11]. Limited availability, a relatively high cost, and exam duration limit widespread implementation of MRI in screening programs. Abbreviated protocols offer a potential solution for lengthy examinations. Another vital concern that needs to be addressed, is the false positives and false negative occurrences. Confusion arising from artifacts and difficulty distinguishing between normal enhancing structures and tumors can lead to false positives, whereas false negatives occur due to background-enhancing breast tissue, missed or misinterpretation of enhancements as benign. A retrospective review of previous MRI studies shows a potential reader error in 47% of cases, primarily due to misinterpretation rather than missed detection or improper management of the cancers [14].

Artificial intelligence (AI) based approaches are becoming more widely implemented to address these challenges [21]. Apart from cancer detection in mammography, primarily covered in the literature [1,6], AI can enhance several areas within breast imaging, such as risk assessment, breast density evaluation, therapy assessment are only a few examples among many. Previous studies have demonstrated that a commercial AI model can reduce the radiologist reading workload by 33.5% [7]. Additionally, the clinical safety of AI-supported mammography screening with the aforementioned model was confirmed in a trial, where it demonstrated comparable cancer detection rates to standard double reading while significantly reducing the screen-reading workload [10].

Unfortunately, similar conclusions cannot be made for AI-supported breast MRI screening, as it has not been extensively studied due to challenges associated with breast MRI, including a lack of standardized data, limited availability of publicly annotated datasets, high costs, and accessibility issues of MRI machines, and the complexity of MRI images. Nevertheless, interest and research in breast MRI AI are steadily increasing. A recent study demonstrated that an AI-based score can effectively select patients for supplemental MRI after a negative mammogram, helping to detect many missed cancers and making the cost per cancer detected comparable to that of mammography screening [16].

To address the current research gap in AI for breast MRI, we propose to explore the potential of a foundation model utilizing a CLIP-based (Contrastive Language-Image Pretraining) approach as a preliminary step. In 2021, OpenAI introduced CLIP, aimed at integrating visual and textual information. Since then, medical imaging researchers have developed various models to address challenges such as small datasets [17], 3D medical image analysis [18], a model for brain fMRI [9], a Pathology Language and Image Pre-Training (PLIP) [4], and segmentation [5,19]. However, to our knowledge, there has yet to be a CLIP-based model specifically designed for breast MRI [23].

In this study, we seek to address the challenges associated with the lack of structured data and data annotations in breast MRI by implementing two key strategies. First, we will enable data retrieval based on specific text queries, allowing users to access relevant data more efficiently. Second, we will enable downstream tasks for annotation generation. In the first part, we focus on MRI retrieval for cases categorized by likely benign vs. suspicious or likely malignant, dense vs. fatty tissue, and low vs. high BPE cases, based on the Breast Imaging Reporting and Data System (BI-RADS) classification, breast density, and BPE-related text queries, respectively.

2 Materials and Methods

In this section, we first present the dataset used for training, validation, and testing. Next, we review the CLIP framework for 2D images, introduce our Breast MRI Language Pretraining (MLIP) model, and describe its application for image retrieval and a zero-shot downstream task, BI-RADS prediction.

2.1 Data Collection

The training dataset was curated from dynamic contrast-enhanced (DCE) and subtraction MRI images, along with their corresponding radiological reports, provided by the Netherlands Cancer Institute between January 2010 and December 2021, encompassing a total of 15,005 cases. It should be noted that multiple exams and reports may exist for individual patients. In total, it included 2672 cases of BI-RADS 1, 4423 cases of BI-RADS 2, 1057 of BI-RADS 3, 865 of BI-RADS 4, 279 of BI-RADS 5, and 2602 cases of BI-RADS 6. Subsequently, we process the validation and test sets to remove the cases with no BI-RADS information for a better evaluation of the model performance for two inference steps. The unprocessed validation and test sets include 3013 and 738 cases, respectively. BI-RADS 0 indicates incomplete information, often requiring additional imaging for a conclusive assessment, while BI-RADS 6 represents confirmed malignant breast tumors. Therefore, cases classified as BI-RADS 0 and 6 were excluded from the study. The resulted validation set consists of 1704 image-report pairs, including 589 cases of BI-RADS 1, 904 cases of BI-RADS 2, 162 cases of BI-RADS 3, 114 cases of BI-RADS 4, 19 cases of BI-RADS 5. The processed test has a size of 380 with 135 cases of BI-RADS 1, 190 cases of BI-RADS 2, 37 cases of BI-RADS 3, 29 cases of BI-RADS 4, and 4 cases of BI-RADS 5. The test sets used for the density and BPE inference consist of 100 and 155 image-report pairs, respectively. These sets were specifically chosen to ensure the availability of ground truth for distinguishing between dense and fatty tissue, as well as low and high BPE.

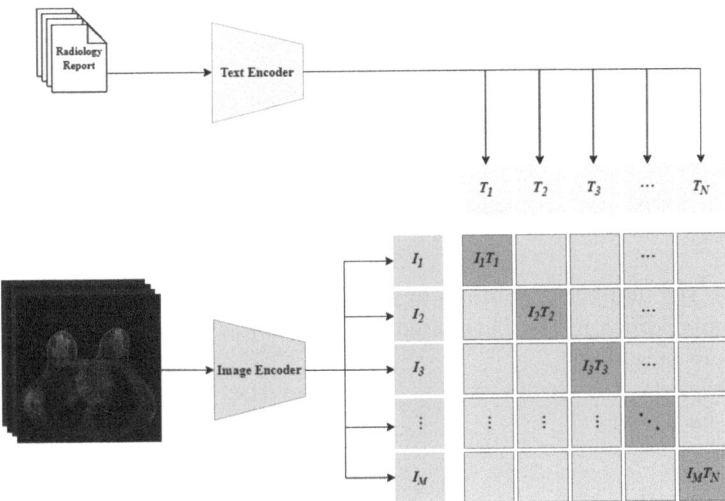

Fig. 1. Contrastive learning approach for breast MRI images and radiology report pairs.

2.2 Contrastive Learning

Contrastive Learning is a deep learning method where the model learns about similar and dissimilar data by contrasting positive pairs (similar samples) against negative pairs (dissimilar samples). When the data consists of both image and text, embeddings for each modality are projected into a common representation space, often referred to as the projection space [15]. The goal is to learn a representation of data such that similar instances are close together in the representation space, while dissimilar instances are far apart. This is achieved through a loss function that emphasizes the similarity between positive pairs and the dissimilarity between negative pairs based on the embeddings.

The same approach is applied, with the primary difference from CLIP being the 3D nature of MRI images. Unlike 2D images, the model processes volumetric data, having spatial information across three dimensions, which adds complexity to the embedding and the contrastive learning process. For a batch of image-text pairs (I_i, T_i), where each image I_i is paired with the corresponding text T_i, the contrastive loss is calculated in two parts: (1) Image-to-Text loss: maximizes the similarity between an image and its correct text. (2) Text-to-Image loss: maximizes the similarity between a text and its correct image. The final loss is the average of both losses. Cosine similarity between the embeddings is used as the similarity measure:

$$s(z_i, z_t) = \frac{z_i \cdot z_t}{\|z_i\| \|z_t\|} \tag{1}$$

where z_i is the image embedding of image I_i, z_t is the text embedding of text T_t.

For each image I_i, the image-to-text loss uses a softmax over the cosine similarities to convert them into probabilities, and cross-entropy loss is used to maximize the probability of the correct text for each image:

$$\mathcal{L}_{\text{image-to-text}} = -\frac{1}{N} \sum_{i=1}^{N} \log \frac{\exp(s(\mathbf{z}_i, \mathbf{z}_i)/\tau)}{\sum_{j=1}^{N} \exp(s(\mathbf{z}_i, \mathbf{z}_j)/\tau)} \tag{2}$$

where N is the number of samples in the batch, and the denominator sums over all text embeddings in the batch, making the contrastive comparison. τ is the temperature parameter.

Similarly, the text-to-image loss maximizes the probability of the correct image for each text:

$$\mathcal{L}_{\text{text-to-image}} = -\frac{1}{N} \sum_{i=1}^{N} \log \frac{\exp(s(\mathbf{z}_i, \mathbf{z}_i)/\tau)}{\sum_{j=1}^{N} \exp(s(\mathbf{z}_j, \mathbf{z}_i)/\tau)} \tag{3}$$

where the denominator sums over all image embeddings in the batch. The overall MLIP loss is the average of the image-to-text and text-to-image losses:

$$\mathcal{L}_{\text{MLIP}} = \frac{1}{2} \left(\mathcal{L}_{\text{image-to-text}} + \mathcal{L}_{\text{text-to-image}} \right) \tag{4}$$

2.3 Experiment Settings

The MRI images have a size of 352 × 352 × 176 with a voxel spacing of (1, 1, 1). As shown in Fig. 1, the input of MLIP includes DCE MRI (pre-contrast and subtraction of pre-contrast and post-contrast) and the corresponding radiology report. The image encoder is based on a 3D ResNet50 architecture, while the text encoder utilizes the RadioLOGIC language model [22]. All parameters in the model were trainable during the training process. The image encoder outputs an image feature vector of 2048 dimensions, and the text encoder produces a text feature vector of 768 dimensions. Both feature vectors were passed through separate projection heads (one for images and one for text) to ensure they reside in the same embedding space of 256 dimensions. The initial temperature parameter τ was set to 0.07 in Eqs. 2 and 3. The initial learning rate for image encoder was 4e-6, while the initial learning rate for the text encoder was 1e-6. The projection heads had an initial learning rate of 1e-3. The batch size was set to 4, and the model was trained for 20 epoches. AdamW optimizer was applied to update the model parameters. The MLIP model was trained on NVIDIA RTX A6000 graphics processing unit (GPU), 48 Gigabytes of GPU memory.

2.4 Inference

The trained model is subsequently utilized for two types of inference: (1) image retrieval based on a query and (2) BI-RADS prediction as a downstream task. During the first inference, MRI images are ranked based on their cosine similarity scores, calculated between the image and query embeddings. Three query categories are used separately: (1) "BI-RADS X" with X being 1, 2, 3, 4, or 5; (2) a selection of Dutch expressions used for reporting dense breast tissue for categories C and D; and (3) a selection of Dutch expressions used for reporting low BPE. The length of each query is adjusted to be similar to the average reports length in the dataset. The retrieved images are then ordered from most to least similar, with the top-ranked images having the highest agreement to the query. In the second inference, we use zero-shot learning to enable the model to predict BI-RADS classification of the MRI images in the test set. Although zero-shot learning has gained considerable attention in the field of 2D classification, there has been relatively little exploration of its application in the 3D domain [20]. In this study, we predicted BI-RADS classifications using a pretrained model and a separately fine-tuned version of the same model. We evaluated the results by analyzing Sankey plots to visually compare ground truth and predicted values.

2.5 Statistical Analysis

Statistical analysis was performed by Python 3.9. Area under the receiver operating characteristic curve (AUC), sensitivity, specificity were used as figures of merit to evaluate the performance of the model. The operating point of AI model was generated based on the maximum Youden index. 95% confidence intervals were generated with bootstrap method with 1000 replications. Agreement between human reader and AI model for BI-RADS categories was assessed using the Gwet agreement coefficient (AC1 value).

3 Results and Discussion

This section focuses on the results derived from the two inference procedures conducted. The first one consists of image retrieval based on a text query. We performed queries for BI-RADS 4 and BI-RADS 5 as a reference point to distinguish between benign and malignant cases, density categories C, D, and low

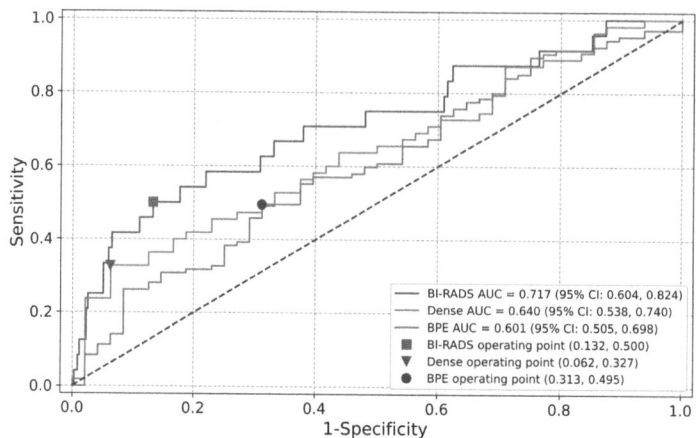

Fig. 2. Performance of the proposed MLIP model for image retrieval based on BI-RADS, Dense and BPE queries, evaluated using a similarity-based ROC curve.

BPE. For the second inference, a downstream task, zero-shot BI-RADS classification, is performed using this model for BI-RADS score prediction.

The evaluation for BI-RADS 4/5, dense breast, and low BPE is conducted using long queries on the test set. The ROC curves in Fig. 2 shows the performance of the proposed MLIP model in image retrieval based on BI-RADS, Dense and BPE queries using similarity-based evaluation. The results show that the pre-trained MLIP can be used to retrieve the required images from the database, with an AUC of 0.717 (95% CI: 0.604, 0.824) for BI-RADS 4/5 abnormal MRI images retrieval, and the BI-RADS operating point selected based on the maximum Youden index (similarity threshold = 0.433) corresponds to a sensitivity of 0.500 and a specificity of 0.868. Figure 3(a) shows some examples of retrieved images with BI-RADS 4/5. The AUC for dense breast MRI images retrieval is 0.640 (95% CI: 0.538, 0.740), and the Dense operating point selected based on the maximum Youden index (similarity threshold = 0.435) corresponds to a sensitivity of 0.327 and a specificity of 0.938. Figure 3(b) shows some examples of retrieved images with dense breast. The AUC for Low BPE MRI images retrieval is 0.601 (95% CI: 0.505, 0.698), and the BPE operating point selected based on the maximum Youden index (similarity threshold = 0.354) corresponds to a sensitivity of 0.518 and a specificity of 0.667. Figure 3(c) shows some examples of retrieved images with low BPE. The prediction results of BI-RADS scores based on MRI images are shown in Fig. 4. Figure 4(a) shows the zero-shot results, where the Gwet's AC1 of the human readers and the AI model was initially 0.18 (95% CI, 0.10, 0.26), indicating a relatively low level of agreement. A notable proportion of BI-RADS 1/2 cases were classified into higher BI-RADS categories, such as BI-RADS 3 or BI-RADS 4/5. However, as shown in Fig. 4(b), after fine-tuning, the agreement improved, with Gwet's AC1 of 0.23 (95% CI, 0.15, 0.30). This result incorporates the zero-shot outcomes and

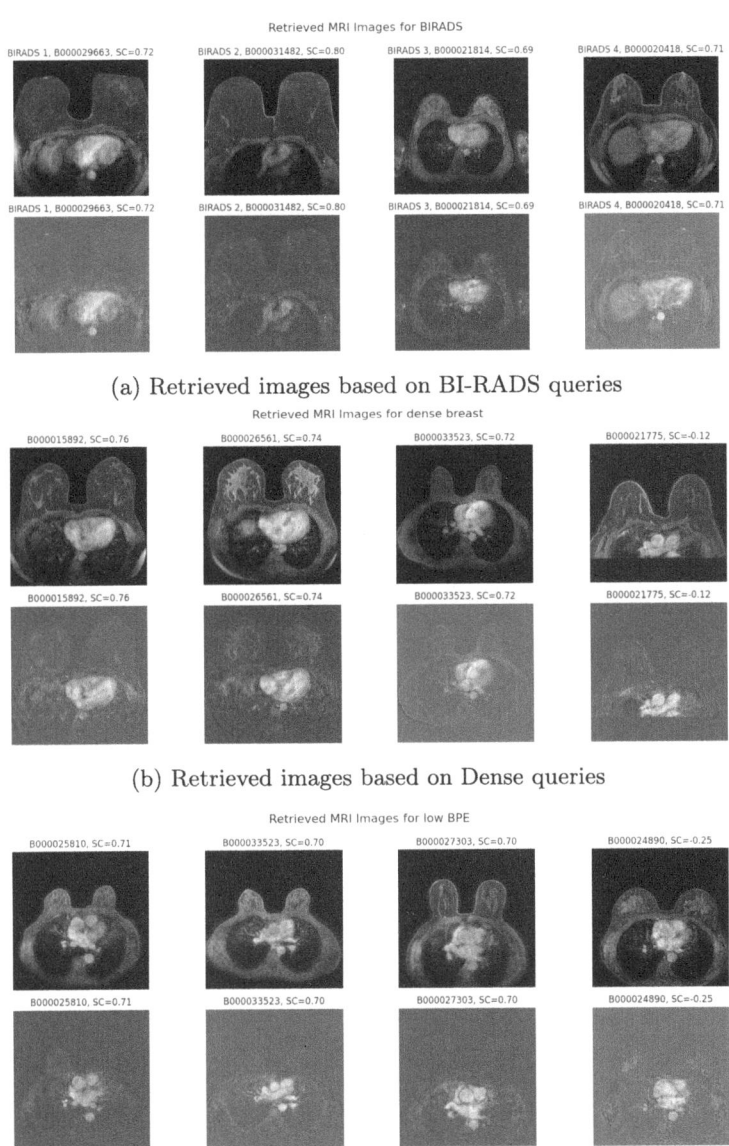

Fig. 3. Some examples of retrieved images with BI-RADS 4/5, dense breast and low BPE; DCE images in the first row and subtracted images in the second row. (a) Each column corresponds to the retrieved MRI image for the queried BI-RADS class with the highest similarity score (b) The first three columns correspond to the retrieved images with highest similarity scores, showing breasts with C category density and the last column dispalying an example from the bottom of the list corresponding to a fatty tissue. (c) The first three columns show the retrieved images with highest alignment to low BPE query and the last column displays an example from the bottom of the list. SC, similarity score.

reflects a moderate enhancement in alignment between the AI model and human reader's assessments, suggesting that the fine-tuning process led to more consistent classifications. Figure 4(c) and (d) shows the results in more detail.

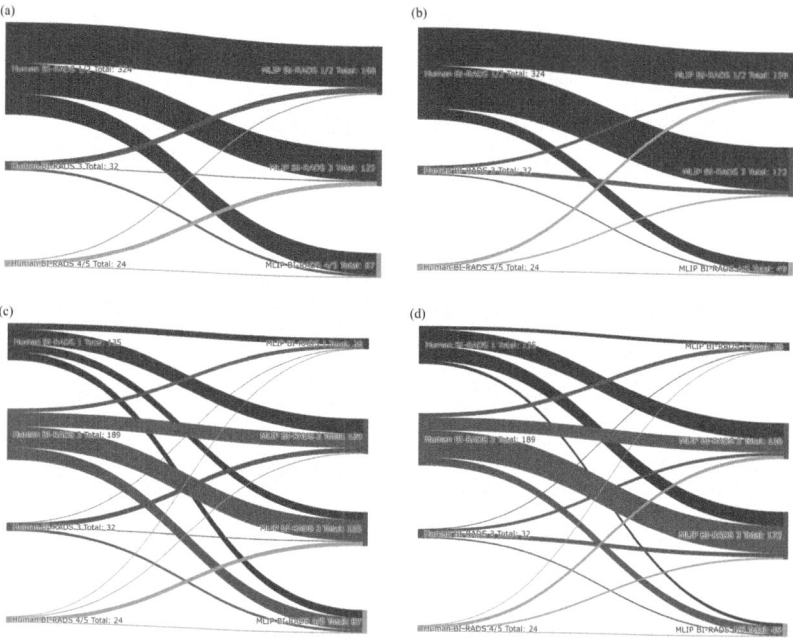

Fig. 4. Sankey plots showing changes in Breast Imaging Reporting and Data System (BI-RADS) clinical management categories between human reader and AI model. (b) and (d) correspond to the fine-tuned model result. Human-AI agreement was assessed between the original radiologists who wrote the breast imaging reports and the outputs from AI model.

The model demonstrates a significantly improved ability to differentiate between positive and negative cases for BI-RADS-based queries in inference one, compared to density and BPE queries. This improvement may be attributed to the substantial presence of BI-RADS information in the radiology reports of the training set. In contrast, these reports often lack evaluations of density and BPE, containing information that is not directly descriptive of MRI images, such as details about biopsies and pathological responses. The absence of consistent parameters, such as density categories A, B, C, and D, as well as low vs. high BPE information, along with the variability in the language used to describe density and BPE, may introduce additional complexity. Furthermore, the noise present in the reports of the image-text pairs may also limit the model's performance.

To name a few of the other limitations, first, the use of full MRI images, which include the torso and other anatomical structures, increases the complexity of embeddings and the contrastive learning process. Second, the sample sizes for BI-RADS 4 and BI-RADS 5 categories were relatively small because the dataset used was based on screening. Third, this is a feasibility exploratory study that obtained cases from a single center, and subsequent studies will collect more cases from multiple centers to externally verify the performance of the model. Finally, the downstream tasks of the model currently only focus on BI-RADS classification. Future work will expand more downstream tasks and continue to explore the potential of MLIP.

Overall, the model still holds substantial potential for further improvement. Future work could focus on enhancing the model to achieve better outcomes using a more complex embedding encoding and an improved projection process. Additionally, integrating well-established models, such as segmentation models, to direct the MLIP's attention specifically to the breast region-while eliminating redundant information from the MRI, such as thoracic structures-could further optimize the model's performance.

4 Conclusion

In conclusion, this study explored the potential of utilizing a contrastive language-image pretraining approach for 3D breast MRI images, resulting in the development of a pretrained model tested across two inference scenarios. The model effectively learned the relationship between full radiology reports and their corresponding MRI images, enabling it to retrieve the most relevant MRI images based on an input query. The promising results suggest that this model can be further enhanced to perform more advanced diagnostic tasks and support structured radiology report generation, holding significant potential to serve as a robust foundation model for breast MRI analysis. By integrating this model with the developed models, future work will focus on improving overall diagnostic performance.

Disclosure of Interests. Authors have no conflict of interest to declare.

References

1. Dembrower, K., Crippa, A., Colón, E., Eklund, M., Strand, F.: Artificial intelligence for breast cancer detection in screening mammography in Sweden: a prospective, population-based, paired-reader, non-inferiority study. Lancet Digit. Health **5**(10), e703–e711 (2023). https://doi.org/10.1016/S2589-7500(23)00153-X
2. Duffy, S.W., et al.: Mammography screening reduces rates of advanced and fatal breast cancers: results in 549,091 women. Cancer **126**(13), 2971–2979 (2020). https://doi.org/10.1002/cncr.32859
3. Ferlay, J., et al.: Global cancer observatory: cancer today. International Agency for Research on Cancer, Lyon, France (2024). https://gco.iarc.who.int/today. Accessed 28 June 2024

4. Huang, Z., Bianchi, F., Yuksekgonul, M., Montine, T.J., Zou, J.: A visual–language foundation model for pathology image analysis using medical Twitter. Nat. Med. **29**(9), 2307–2316 (2023). https://doi.org/10.1038/s41591-023-02504-3
5. Koleilat, T., Asgariandehkordi, H., Rivaz, H., Xiao, Y.: Medclip-SAM: bridging text and image towards universal medical image segmentation (2024). https://arxiv.org/abs/2403.20253
6. Kooi, T., et al.: Large scale deep learning for computer aided detection of mammographic lesions. Med. Image Anal. **35**, 303–312 (2017). https://doi.org/10.1016/j.media.2016.07.007. https://www.sciencedirect.com/science/article/pii/S1361841516301244
7. Lauritzen, A.D., et al.: Early indicators of the impact of using AI in mammography screening for breast cancer. Radiology **311**(3), e232479 (2024). https://doi.org/10.1148/radiol.232479, pMID: 38832880
8. Lima, S.M., Kehm, R.D., Terry, M.B.: Global breast cancer incidence and mortality trends by region, age-groups, and fertility patterns. EClinicalMedicine **38**, 100985 (2021). https://doi.org/10.1016/j.eclinm.2021.100985
9. Liu, Y., Ma, Y., Zhou, W., Zhu, G., Zheng, N.: Brainclip: bridging brain and visual-linguistic representation via clip for generic natural visual stimulus decoding (2023). https://arxiv.org/abs/2302.12971
10. Lång, K., et al.: Artificial intelligence-supported screen reading versus standard double reading in the mammography screening with artificial intelligence trial (MASAI): a clinical safety analysis of a randomised, controlled, non-inferiority, single-blinded, screening accuracy study. Lancet Oncol. **24**(8), 936–944 (2023). https://doi.org/10.1016/S1470-2045(23)00298-X
11. Mann, R.M., Cho, N., Moy, L.: Breast MRI: state of the art. Radiology **292**(3), 520–536 (2019). https://doi.org/10.1148/radiol.2019182947, pMID: 31361209
12. Marcon, M., Fuchsjäger, M.H., Clauser, P., Mann, R.M.: ESR Essentials: screening for breast cancer - general recommendations by EUSOBI. Eur. Radiol. (2024). https://doi.org/10.1007/s00330-024-10740-5
13. Marmot, M.G., Altman, D.G., Cameron, D.A., Dewar, J.A., Thompson, S.G., Wilcox, M.: The benefits and harms of breast cancer screening: an independent review. Br. J. Cancer **108**(11), 2205–2240 (2013). https://doi.org/10.1038/bjc.2013.177
14. Pages, E.B., Millet, I., Hoa, D., Doyon, F.C., Taourel, P.: Undiagnosed breast cancer at MR imaging: analysis of causes. Radiology **264**(1), 40–50 (2012). https://doi.org/10.1148/radiol.12111917
15. Radford, A., et al.: Learning transferable visual models from natural language supervision (2021). https://arxiv.org/abs/2103.00020
16. Salim, M., et al.: AI-based selection of individuals for supplemental MRI in population-based breast cancer screening: the randomized ScreenTrustMRI trial. Nat. Med. **30**(9), 2623–2630 (2024). https://doi.org/10.1038/s41591-024-03093-5
17. Wolf, D., et al.: Self-supervised pre-training with contrastive and masked autoencoder methods for dealing with small datasets in deep learning for medical imaging. Sci. Rep. **13**(1), 20260 (2023). https://doi.org/10.1038/s41598-023-46433-0
18. Wu, L., Zhuang, J., Chen, H.: VOCO: a simple-yet-effective volume contrastive learning framework for 3D medical image analysis (2024). https://arxiv.org/abs/2402.17300
19. Wu, Y., Zeng, D., Wang, Z., Shi, Y., Hu, J.: Distributed contrastive learning for medical image segmentation. Med. Image Anal. **81**, 102564 (2022). https://doi.org/10.1016/j.media.2022.102564. https://www.sciencedirect.com/science/article/pii/S1361841522002079

20. Zhang, R., et al.: Pointclip: point cloud understanding by clip (2021). https://arxiv.org/abs/2112.02413
21. Zhang, T., et al.: Radiomics and artificial intelligence in breast imaging: a survey. Artif. Intell. Rev. **56**(Suppl 1), 857–892 (2023)
22. Zhang, T., et al.: Radiologic, a healthcare model for processing electronic health records and decision-making in breast disease. Cell Rep. Med. **4**(8) (2023)
23. Zhao, Z., et al.: Clip in medical imaging: a comprehensive survey (2024). https://arxiv.org/abs/2312.07353

Enhancing the Utility of Privacy-Preserving Cancer Classification Using Synthetic Data

Richard Osuala[1,2,3(✉)], Daniel M. Lang[2,3], Anneliese Riess[2,3], Georgios Kaissis[2,3,4], Zuzanna Szafranowska[1], Grzegorz Skorupko[1], Oliver Diaz[1,5], Julia A. Schnabel[2,3,6], and Karim Lekadir[1,7]

[1] Departament de Matemàtiques i Informàtica, Universitat de Barcelona, Barcelona, Spain
richard.osuala@ub.edu
[2] Helmholtz Center Munich, Munich, Germany
[3] Technical University of Munich, Munich, Germany
[4] Imperial College London, London, UK
[5] Computer Vision Center, Bellaterra, Spain
[6] Kings College London, London, UK
[7] Institució Catalana de Recerca i Estudis Avançats (ICREA), Barcelona, Spain

Abstract. Deep learning holds immense promise for aiding radiologists in breast cancer detection. However, achieving optimal model performance is hampered by limitations in availability and sharing of data commonly associated to patient privacy concerns. Such concerns are further exacerbated, as traditional deep learning models can inadvertently leak sensitive training information. This work addresses these challenges exploring and quantifying the utility of privacy-preserving deep learning techniques, concretely, (i) differentially private stochastic gradient descent (DP-SGD) and (ii) fully synthetic training data generated by our proposed malignancy-conditioned generative adversarial network. We assess these methods via downstream malignancy classification of mammography masses using a transformer model. Our experimental results depict that synthetic data augmentation can improve privacy-utility tradeoffs in differentially private model training. Further, model pretraining on synthetic data achieves remarkable performance, which can be further increased with DP-SGD fine-tuning across all privacy guarantees. With this first in-depth exploration of privacy-preserving deep learning in breast imaging, we address current and emerging clinical privacy requirements and pave the way towards the adoption of private high-utility deep diagnostic models. Our reproducible codebase is publicly available at https://github.com/RichardObi/mammo_dp.

Keywords: Differential Privacy · Generative Models · Breast Imaging

1 Introduction

Breast cancer accounts for staggering estimates of 684.000 deaths and 2,26 million new cases worldwide per year [11]. Part of this burden could be reduced

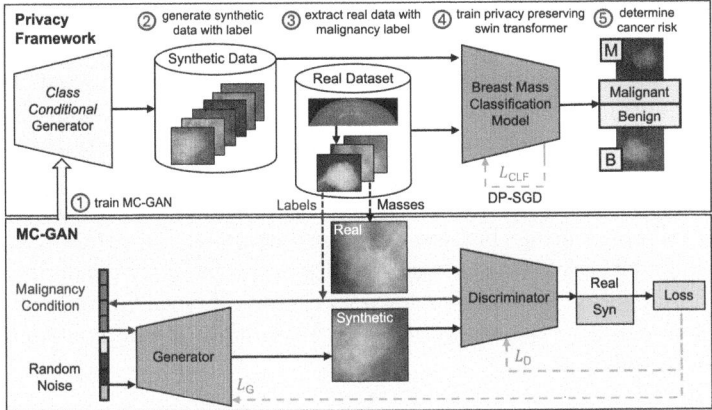

Fig. 1. Overview of our privacy-preserving deep learning pipeline and malignancy-conditioned generative adversarial network (MCGAN).

through earlier detection and timely treatment. Screening mammography is a cornerstone for early detection and further associated with a reduction in breast cancer mortality [21]. Recent literature emphasizes the potential of deep learning-based computer-aided diagnosis (CAD) [15,22,24,30], e.g., demonstrating that a symbiosis of deep learning models with radiologist assessment yields the highest breast cancer detection performances [21]. However, training deep learning models on patient data poses a risk of leakage of sensitive person-specific information during and after training [24], as models have the capacity to memorise sufficient information to allow for high-fidelity image reconstruction [3,13]. To avoid such leakage of private patient information, data needs to be protected during model training, in particular when the objective is to develop models to be used in clinical practice or shared among entities. Furthermore, international data protection regulations grant patients the right to request the removal of their information from data holders. For instance, point (b) of article 17(1) of the EU General Data Protection Regulation (GDPR) [9] stipulates that data subjects have a "right to be forgotten". Given, for instance, the proven possibility of reconstructing training data given a model's weights [3,13], these rights can extend to the removal of patient-specific information from already trained deep learning models [29]. However, it is known to be difficult to "reliably" and "provably" remove patient information—present in only one or few specific training data points—from already trained model weights [29]. A generic and verifiable alternative is given by the removal of a patient's data point from the training data and retraining of the respective model with the reminder of the dataset. This procedure is not only likely to have negative impacts on the performance of algorithms, but also emerges as a deterrence and risk for hospitals to adopt deep learning models, due to extensive economic, organisational, and environmental costs caused by retraining. Anticipating patient consent withdrawals, costly retraining can be avoided by demonstrating that deep learning model weights do not include personally identifiable information (PII) about any specific patient. To this end, a powerful technique to ensure privacy during model training is given by Differentially Private Stochastic Gradient Descent (DP-SGD) [1], which quantifiably reduces the effect each single training sample can have on the resulting model weights. Furthermore, privacy-preservation can also be achieved by diagnostic models exclusively trained on synthetic data, which is not (unambiguously) attributable to any specific patient but rather contains anonymous samples representing the essence of the dataset [12,24]. The caveat of both DP-SGD and synthetic data strategies is, however, that they generally lead to a reduction in model performance, known as the privacy-utility trade-off. Investigating this trade-off in the realm of breast imaging, our core contributions are summarised as follows:

- We design and validate a transformer model, achieving promising performance as a backbone for privacy-preserving breast mass malignancy classification.
- We propose and validate a conditional generative adversarial network capable of differentiating between benign and malignant breast mass generation.
- We empirically quantify privacy-utility-tradeoffs in mass malignancy classification, assessing various differential privacy guarantees, and further combine and compare them with training on synthetic data.

2 Methods and Materials

Datasets and Preprocessing

We use the open-access Curated Breast Imaging Subset of Digital Database for Screening Mammography (CBIS-DDSM) dataset [16], which consists of 891 scanned film mammography cases with segmented masses with biopsy-proven malignancy status. After extracting mass images from craniocaudal view (CC) and mediolateral oblique (MLO) views, we follow the predefined per-patient train-test split [16], allocating 1296 mass images for training and 402 (245 benign, 157 malignant) mass images to testing. We further divided this training set randomly per-patient into a training (1104 mass images, 525 malignant) and a validation set (192 mass images, 102 malignant). As external test set, we further adopt the publicly available BCDR cohort [19], which comprises 1010 patients, totalling 1493 lesions (639 masses) with contours and biopsy information from both digital mammograms (BCDR-DM) and film mammograms (BCDR-FM). Our final BCDR test set contains 1106 mass images extracted from CC and MLO views, 486 of which are malignant and 620 benign. To obtain mass patches from the mammograms, the lesion contour information is used to define bounding boxes, which enclose the mass. We then create a square patch around each bounding box with a minimum length and width of 128 pixels. Next, we increase the patch size by adding a margin of 60 pixels in each direction, before extracting the resulting patch, and resizing it to a pixel dimensions of 128×128 using inter-area interpolation. For classification, the mass patches are further resized to 224×224px maintaining image ratios, and stacked to 3 channels. Models were trained on either a single 8 GB NVIDIA RTX 2080 Super or 48 GB RTX A6000 GPU using PyTorch and opacus [31] for DP-SGD.

Cancer Classification Transformer Model

Given its reported high performance on classifying the presence of a lesion in mammography patches [30] and its shifted window mechanism, allowing to effectively attend to shapes of varying sizes, we adopt a swin transformer (Swin-T) [17] as cancer classification model, to distinguish between benign and malignant masses. We inititalize ImageNet-pretrained [6] network weights and, after following the Swin-T hyperparameter setup [17] (stride, window size), we adjust the last fully-connected layer of the swin transformer reinitializing it with two output nodes each one outputting the logits for one of our respective classes (i.e., malignant or benign). We only set the parameters of the adjusted fully-connected layer as trainable and apply a learning rate of 1e–5. A weight decay of 1e–8 is used following the fine-tuning experiment described in [17]. Furthermore, an adamw optimizer [20], label smoothing of 0.1, and a batch size of 128 are used. During training, random horizontal and vertical flips are applied as data augmentation and a cross entropy loss is backpropagated. Training for 300 epochs using a cross entropy loss function, the model from the epoch with the lowest area under the precision-recall curve (AUPRC) on the validation set is selected for testing.

Malignancy-Conditioned Generative Adversarial Network

Going beyond unconditional mass synthesis in the literature [2,30], we propose a malignancy conditioned generative adversarial network (MCGAN) to control the generation of either benign or malignant synthetic breast masses. In general, GANs consist of a generator (G) and a discriminator (D) network, which engage in a two-player zero-sum game, where G generates synthetic samples that D strives to distinguish from real ones [12]. We design G and D as deep convolutional neural networks [27] and, as shown in Fig. 1, integrate class-conditional information [23]. To this end, we extract the histopathology report's biopsy information for each mass from the metadata, and convert it into a discrete malignancy label. Then, we transform this label into a multi-dimensional embedding vector to either represent the (a) malignant or (b) benign class, before passing it through a fully-connected layer yielding a representation with the corresponding dimensionality to concatenate it to the generator input (100 dim noise vector) and to the discriminator input (128 × 128 input image). As D learns to associate class labels with patterns in the input images, it has to learn whether or not a given class corresponds to a given synthetic sample. Furthermore, as the discriminator loss is backpropagated into the generator, G is forced to synthesize samples corresponding to the provided class condition. This results in G learning a conditional distribution based on the value function

$$\min_G \max_D V(D,G) = \min_G \max_D [\mathbb{E}_{x \sim p_{\text{data}}}[\log D(x|y)] + \mathbb{E}_{z \sim p_z}[\log(1 - D(G(z|y)))]].$$

Optimizing the discriminator via binary cross-entropy [12], we define its loss in a class-conditional setup as

$$L_{D_{\text{MCGAN}}} = -\mathbb{E}_{x \sim p_{\text{data}}}[\log D(x|y)] + \mathbb{E}_{z \sim p_z}[\log(1 - D(G(z|y)))].$$

We train our MCGAN on the CBIS-DDSM training data, applying random horizontal (p = 0.5) and vertical (p = 0.5) flipping as well as random cropping with resizing, where the resize scale ranges from 0.9 to 1.1 and aspect ratio from 0.95 to 1.1. We further include one-sided label smoothing [27] in a range of [0.7, 1.2]. Following [2], we employ a discriminator convolutional kernel size of 6 and a generator kernel size of 4. We observe that this reduces checkerboard artefacts as D's field-of-view now requires G to create realistic transitions between the kernel-sized patches in the image. MCGAN is trained for 10k epochs with a batch size of 16. Based on the best quality-diversity tradeoff, we select the model from epoch 1.4k after qualitative visual assessment of generated samples.

Patient Privacy Preservation Framework

Privacy protection is an ethical norm and legal obligation, e.g. granting patients the right of their (retrospective) removal from databases [9]. Since (biomedical) deep learning models are vulnerable to information leakage, e.g. sensitive patient attributes [3,13,29], they can be affected by such (and future) regulations. However, privacy-preserving techniques can be integrated into deep learning frameworks and, to some extent, avoid compromising confidential data. For instance, (i) model training with DP-SGD [1] or (ii) training exclusively on synthetic data.

From a legal perspective, models trained on only synthetic data remain unaffected by patient consent withdrawal if "relatedness" between the data and the data subject cannot be established, or if "personal data has been rendered synthetic in such a manner that the data subject is no longer identifiable" [18] e.g., according to article 4(1) and recital 26 of the GDPR [9]. It is to be noted that in the "acceptable-risk" legal interpretation, a data subject's re-identification risk is reduced to an "acceptable" level rather than fully eradicated [18]. Hence, this interpretation enables approaches such as synthetic data and/or Differential Privacy (DP) model training to be used as legally compliant privacy preservation methods despite not guaranteeing a "zero-risk" of patient re-identification.

DP is a mathematical framework that allows practitioners to provide (worst-case scenario) theoretical privacy guarantees for an individual sharing their data to train a deep learning model. Consider two databases (e.g., containing image-label pairs), we call them adjacent if they differ in a single data point, i.e., one image is present in one database but not in the other. Then, a randomised mechanism $\mathcal{M}: \mathcal{D} \to \mathcal{R}$ with domain $\mathcal{D}$ and range $\mathcal{R}$ is said to satisfy (ε, δ)-differential privacy, if for any two adjacent databases $d, d' \in \mathcal{D}$ and for any subset of outputs $S \subseteq \mathcal{R}$, $\Pr[\mathcal{M}(d) \in S] \leq e^{\varepsilon} \Pr[\mathcal{M}(d') \in S] + \delta$ holds. ε and δ bound a single data point's influence on a model's output (e.g. the models' weights or predictions). Thus, the smaller the value of these parameters, the higher the model's privacy and the harder it is for an attacker to retrieve information about any training data point. DP-SGD [1] is the DP variant of the well-known SGD algorithm, and facilitates the training of a model under DP conditions. In particular, a model trained under (ε, δ)-DP is robust to post-processing, meaning only using its output for further computations also satisfies (ε, δ)-DP. Moreover, the choice of these parameters is application-dependent and normative [5] and varies strongly across real-world deployments [7]. In the case of mammography, multiple lesions of the same patient are available in the datasets, i.e. one from the CC view and one from the MLO view. Therefore, to preserve the privacy of one patient it is necessary to protect all their data points (i.e. all images). In such a case, DP group privacy is used to estimate a patient's DP privacy guarantee. However, for simplicity, in our subsequent experiments, we provide image-level privacy guarantees rather than per patient.

3 Experiments and Results

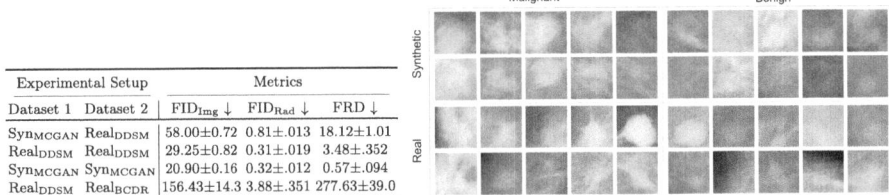

Fig. 2. Qualitative and quantitative synthesis results: Images are randomly selected malignant and benign real (CBIS-DDSM [16]) and MCGAN-generated masses. ImageNet [6] and RadImageNet [22,26] based FID [14] and FRD [25] scores are reported as mean ± standard deviation based on 3 subsets randomly sampled per patient ($N_{real} \approx 360$, $N_{syn} \approx 3240$). Row 4 indicates an BCDR-based[19] upper bound for comparison with synthetic data metrics in row 1.

Synthetic Data Evaluation. Qualitatively assessing the synthetic images in Fig. 2, it is not readily possible to distinguish synthetic from real masses in terms of image fidelity or diversity. We note the absence of clear visual indicators to distinguish between malignant and benign images for both real and synthetic images. This is in line with the difficulty of determining the malignancy of a mammographic lesion shown by high clinical error rates and inter-observer variability [8]. However, results for training our malignancy classification model on only synthetic data (see *Syn* and *SynPre* in Table 1) show that the synthetic data captures the conditional distribution effectively generating either malignant or benign masses. Both, vanilla ImageNet-based Fréchet Inception Distance (FID) [6,14] and radiology domain-specific RadImageNet-based FID [22,26], concur that the synthetic data ($FID_{Img} = 58 \pm .72$) is substantially closer to the real CBIS-DDSM [16] distribution compared to BCDR [19] ($FID_{Img} = 156.43 \pm 1.43$). This is even more pronounced when comparing the

Table 1. Results for within-domain (CBIS-DDSM [16]) and out-of-domain (BCDR [19]) breast cancer malignancy classification masses extracted from mammograms. *Syn* indicates 3k synthetic images being part of the fine-tuning training data, while *Syn-Pre* represents pretraining all trainable model params with those 3k synthetic images (without DP guarantee), before fine-tuning the last two layers on real data with DP guarantee (*RealFT*). AUROC and AUPRC are reported as mean ± std based on 3 random seed runs. Best results in bold.

Experimental Setup			CBIS-DDSM [16]		BCDR [19]	
Model	ε	δ	AUROC ↑	AUPRC ↑	AUROC ↑	AUPRC ↑
SwinT$_{\text{Real}}$	∞	∞	0.778±.001	0.85±.001	0.695±.002	0.726±.003
SwinT$_{\text{Syn}}$	∞	∞	0.597±.011	0.696±.011	0.566±.064	0.602±.048
SwinT$_{\text{SynPre}}$	∞	∞	0.639±.016	0.733±.001	0.622±.032	0.660±.017
SwinT$_{\text{Real}}$	1	$1e^{-4}$	0.525±.043	0.640±.030	0.487±.020	0.549±.020
SwinT$_{\text{Real+Syn}}$	1	$1e^{-4}$	**0.553±.040**	**0.665±.025**	**0.521±.023**	**0.573±.024**
SwinT$_{\text{SynPre+RealFT}}$	∞—1	∞—$1e^{-4}$	0.661±.018	0.741±.007	0.637±.026	0.67±.0013
SwinT$_{\text{Real}}$	6	$1e^{-4}$	0.572±.031	0.679±.019	0.532±.031	0.579±.029
SwinT$_{\text{Real+Syn}}$	6	$1e^{-4}$	**0.617±.013**	**0.708±.015**	**0.609±.027**	**0.647±.024**
SwinT$_{\text{SynPre+RealFT}}$	∞—6	∞—$1e^{-4}$	0.677±.014	0.752±.009	0.647±.022	0.679±.009
SwinT$_{\text{Real}}$	12	$1e^{-4}$	0.596±.023	0.702±.013	0.559±.033	0.600±.030
SwinT$_{\text{Real+Syn}}$	12	$1e^{-4}$	**0.624±.010**	**0.704±.012**	**0.625±.020**	**0.663±.012**
SwinT$_{\text{SynPre+RealFT}}$	∞—12	∞—$1e^{-4}$	0.688±.012	0.758±.011	0.654±.019	0.685±.007
SwinT$_{\text{Real}}$	20	$1e^{-4}$	0.611±.018	**0.715±.012**	0.581±.028	0.618±.026
SwinT$_{\text{Real+Syn}}$	20	$1e^{-4}$	**0.630±.003**	0.699±.008	**0.641±.018**	**0.685±.012**
SwinT$_{\text{SynPre+RealFT}}$	∞—20	∞—$1e^{-4}$	0.697±.012	0.763±.012	0.659±.017	0.689±.006
SwinT$_{\text{Real}}$	60	$1e^{-4}$	0.622±.014	**0.721±.110**	0.605±.019	0.640±.017
SwinT$_{\text{Real+Syn}}$	60	$1e^{-4}$	**0.629±.002**	0.694±.005	**0.650±.013**	**0.696±.007**
SwinT$_{\text{SynPre+RealFT}}$	∞—60	∞—$1e^{-4}$	0.712±.013	0.776±.013	0.671±.014	0.697±.004

variation of extracted radiomics features for CBIS-DDSM to synthetic (FRD = 18.12) and BCDR (FRD = 277.63) images using the Fréchet Radiomics Distance (FRD) [25]. While this indicates desirable synthetic data fidelity, we also observe good diversity. The latter is shown by comparing subsets of the same datasets with each other, where the variation within the synthetic data (e.g., FID$_{\text{Rad}}$ = 0.32±.12) closely resembles the variation within the real CBIS-DDSM dataset (e.g., FID$_{\text{Rad}}$ = 0.31±.19). Notwithstanding less variation in radiomics imaging biomarkers within the synthetic data (FRD$_{\text{Syn}}$ = 0.57 vs. FRD$_{\text{Real}}$ = 3.48), this overall points to a valid coverage of the distribution and an absence of mode collapse.

Mass Malignancy Classification. As shown in Table 1, we conduct experiments with and without formal privacy guarantees. For scenarios where a formal privacy guarantee is not strictly required and, thus, synthetic data suffices as privacy mechanism, we compare the results of training SwinT on synthetic data (*Syn*) and on real data (*Real*) with DP-SGD. *Kaissis et al.* [15] defined

$\varepsilon = 6$ as suitable privacy budget for their medical imaging dataset. Compared to DP-SGD with $\varepsilon = 6$, synthetic data achieves better AUPRCs for within-domain tests on CBIS-DDSM (SwinT$_{\text{Syn}}$ = 0.696 vs SwinT$_{\text{Real}(\varepsilon=6)}$ = 0.679) and is on par for out-of-domain (ood) tests on BCDR (SwinT$_{\text{Syn}}$ = 0.602 vs SwinT$_{\text{Real}(\varepsilon=6)}$ = 0.600). However, training all SwinT layers using synthetic data (*SynPre*), achieves substantially better performance only approximated by DP results for $\varepsilon = 60$ for within-domain (SwinT$_{\text{SynPre}}$ = 0.733 vs SwinT$_{\text{Real}(\varepsilon=60)}$ = 0.721) and ood (SwinT$_{\text{SynPre}}$ = 0.66 vs SwinT$_{\text{Real}(\varepsilon=60)}$ = 0.64) tests. Further fine-tuning SwinT$_{\text{SynPre}}$ on real data using DP-SGD results in additional improvement across all privacy parameters for within-domain and ood testing. For instance, training SwinT$_{\text{SynPre+RealFT}}$ with $\varepsilon = 1$ results in an AUPRC of 0.74 and 0.67 for CBIS-DDSM and BCDR, respectively. To assess scenarios where a formal guarantee is required, we further compare DP-SGD training of SwinT on real data (*Real*) with DP-SGD training on a mix of real and synthetic data (*Real+Syn*). To this end, our experiments show that such synthetic data augmentation can improve the privacy-utility tradeoff. This is exemplified by SwinT$_{\text{Real+Syn}(\varepsilon=6)}$ accomplishing an AUPRC of 0.708 within-domain and 0.647 ood, while SwinT$_{\text{Real}(\varepsilon=6)}$ achieved 0.679 and 0.579, respectively. We further observe the trend that stricter privacy budgets (i.e., smaller ε) can be associated with more added performance of synthetic data as additional classification model training data.

4 Discussion and Conclusion

We introduce a privacy preservation framework based on differential privacy (DP) and synthetic data and apply it to the diagnostic task of classifying the malignancy of breast masses extracted from screening mammograms. We further propose, train, and evaluate a malignancy-conditioned generative adversarial network to generate a dataset of benign and malignant synthetic breast masses. Next, we train a swin transformer model on mass malignancy classification and assess, compare and combine training under DP and training on synthetic data. This analysis revealed that when training with DP, synthetic data augmentation can notably improve classification performance for within-domain and out-of-domain test cases. Apart from that, we show, across privacy mechanisms and across domains, that the performance of models pretrained on synthetic data can be further improved by DP fine-tuning on real data.

This finding is particularly important considering that synthetic data, if not directly attributable to any specific patient, can become a valid, legally compliant alternative to strict DP guarantees in clinical practice. Consequently, it is to be further investigated where and when deterministic mechanisms without formal DP guarantees can suffice to shield against different privacy attacks [4]. In particular, we motivate future work to analyse the extent to which the inherent properties of synthetic data generation algorithms can provide empirical protection against attacks. In this regard, a comparison of generation algorithms such as GANs [12] and denoising probabilistic diffusion models (DDPMs)

[28] can provide insights towards further improving conditional mass synthesis, while also enabling to quantify and compare the extent and effect of training data memorization in these models. A methodological alternative to our approach is to assess privacy-utility tradeoffs when training the generative model itself using DP-SGD [10,24], resulting in formal privacy guarantees of the generated synthetic datasets. Thus, a further avenue to explore then lies within the question whether randomness inherent in randomised data synthesis algorithms (e.g., based on the noise in DDPMs or GANs) can be used to amplify the privacy of the DP versions of such synthesis algorithms, thereby potentially further enhancing privacy-utility tradeoffs. To this end, our study constitutes a crucial first step leading towards the clinical adoption of diagnostic deep learning models, enabling practical privacy-utility tradeoffs all while anticipating respective legal obligations and clinical requirements.

Acknowledgments. research and innovation programme under grant agreement No 952103 (EuCanImage) and No 101057699 (RadioVal). It was further partially supported by the project FUTURE-ES (PID2021-126724OB-I00) from the Ministry of Science and Innovation of Spain. RO acknowledges a research stay grant from the Helmholtz Information and Data Science Academy (HIDA). GK received support from the German Federal Ministry of Education and Research and the Bavarian State Ministry for Science and the Arts under the Munich Centre for Machine Learning (MCML), from the German Ministry of Education and Research and the Medical Informatics Initiative as part of the PrivateAIM Project, from the Bavarian Collaborative Research Project PRIPREKI of the Free State of Bavaria Funding Programme "Artificial Intelligence – Data Science", and from the German Academic Exchange Service (DAAD) under the Kondrad Zuse School of Excellence for Reliable AI (RelAI).

Disclosure of Interests. The authors have no competing interests to declare that are relevant to the content of this article.

References

1. Abadi, M., et al.: Deep learning with differential privacy. In: Proceedings of the 2016 ACM SIGSAC Conference on Computer and Communications Security, pp. 308–318 (2016)
2. Alyafi, B., Diaz, O., Marti, R.: DCGANs for realistic breast mass augmentation in x-ray mammography. In: Medical Imaging 2020: Computer-Aided Diagnosis, vol. 11314, p. 1131420. International Society for Optics and Photonics (2020)
3. Balle, B., Cherubin, G., Hayes, J.: Reconstructing training data with informed adversaries. In: 2022 IEEE Symposium on Security and Privacy (SP), pp. 1138–1156. IEEE (2022)
4. Cohen, A., Nissim, K.: Towards formalizing the gdpr's notion of singling out. Proc. Natl. Acad. Sci. **117**(15), 8344–8352 (2020)
5. De, S., Berrada, L., Hayes, J., Smith, S.L., Balle, B.: Unlocking high-accuracy differentially private image classification through scale. arXiv preprint arXiv:2204.13650 (2022)
6. Deng, J., Dong, W., Socher, R., Li, L.J., Li, K., Fei-Fei, L.: ImageNet: a large-scale hierarchical image database. In: 2009 IEEE Conference on Computer Vision and Pattern Recognition, pp. 248–255. IEEE (2009)

7. Dwork, C., Kohli, N., Mulligan, D.: Differential privacy in practice: expose your epsilons! J. Priv. Confidentiality **9**(2) (2019)
8. Ekpo, E.U., Alakhras, M., Brennan, P.: Errors in mammography cannot be solved through technology alone. Asian Pacific J. Can. Preven. APJCP **19**(2), 291 (2018)
9. European Parliament and Council of European Union: General Data Protection Regulation (GDPR), Regulation (EU) 2016/679 of The European Parliament and of the Council. https://eur-lex.europa.eu/legal-content/EN/TXT/HTML/?uri=CELEX:32016R0679/ (2018)
10. Ghalebikesabi, S., et al.: Differentially private diffusion models generate useful synthetic images. arXiv preprint arXiv:2302.13861 (2023)
11. Global Cancer Observatory: The global cancer observatory (gco) is an interactive web-based platform presenting global cancer statistics to inform cancer control and research. https://gco.iarc.fr/ (2023), Accessed 17 Jan 2023
12. Goodfellow, I., et al.: Generative adversarial nets. In: Advances in Neural Information Processing Systems, pp. 2672–2680 (2014)
13. Haim, N., Vardi, G., Yehudai, G., Shamir, O., Irani, M.: Reconstructing training data from trained neural networks. arXiv preprint arXiv:2206.07758 (2022)
14. Heusel, M., Ramsauer, H., Unterthiner, T., Nessler, B., Hochreiter, S.: GANs trained by a two time-scale update rule converge to a local nash equilibrium. arXiv preprint arXiv:1706.08500 (2017)
15. Kaissis, G., et al.: End-to-end privacy preserving deep learning on multi-institutional medical imaging. Nat. Mach. Intell. **3**(6), 473–484 (2021)
16. Lee, R.S., Gimenez, F., Hoogi, A., Miyake, K.K., Gorovoy, M., Rubin, D.L.: A curated mammography data set for use in computer-aided detection and diagnosis research. Sci. Data **4**(1), 1–9 (2017)
17. Liu, Z., et al.: Swin transformer: Hierarchical vision transformer using shifted windows. In: Proceedings of the IEEE/CVF International Conference on Computer Vision, pp. 10012–10022 (2021)
18. López, C.A.F.: On the legal nature of synthetic data. In: NeurIPS 2022 Workshop on Synthetic Data for Empowering ML Research (2022)
19. Lopez, M.G., et al.: BCDR: a breast cancer digital repository. In: 15th International Conference on Experimental Mechanics, vol. 1215 (2012)
20. Loshchilov, I., Hutter, F.: Decoupled weight decay regularization. In: International Conference on Learning Representations (2019)
21. McKinney, S.M., et al.: International evaluation of an AI system for breast cancer screening. Nature **577**(7788), 89–94 (2020)
22. Mei, X., et al.: RadImageNet: an open radiologic deep learning research dataset for effective transfer learning. Radiol. Artif. Intell. e210315 (2022)
23. Mirza, M., Osindero, S.: Conditional generative adversarial nets. arXiv preprint arXiv:1411.1784 (2014)
24. Osuala, R., Kushibar, K., Garrucho, L., Linardos, A., Szafranowska, Z., Klein, S., Glocker, B., Diaz, O., Lekadir, K.: Data synthesis and adversarial networks: a review and meta-analysis in cancer imaging. Med. Image Anal. **84**, 102704 (2023)
25. Osuala, R., et al.: Towards learning contrast kinetics with multi-condition latent diffusion models. arXiv preprint arXiv:2403.13890 (2024)
26. Osuala, R., Skorupko, G., Lazrak, N., Garrucho, L., García, E., Joshi, S., Jouide, S., Rutherford, M., Prior, F., Kushibar, K., et al.: medigan: a python library of pretrained generative models for medical image synthesis. J. Med. Imaging **10**(6), 061403 (2023)

27. Radford, A., Metz, L., Chintala, S.: Unsupervised representation learning with deep convolutional generative adversarial networks. arXiv preprint arXiv:1511.06434 (2015)
28. Sohl-Dickstein, J., Weiss, E., Maheswaranathan, N., Ganguli, S.: Deep unsupervised learning using nonequilibrium thermodynamics. In: International Conference on Machine Learning, pp. 2256–2265. PMLR (2015)
29. Su, R., Liu, X., Tsaftaris, S.A.: Why patient data cannot be easily forgotten? In: Medical Image Computing and Computer Assisted Intervention–MICCAI 2022: 25th International Conference, Singapore, 18–22 September 2022, Proceedings, Part VIII, pp. 632–641. Springer (2022)
30. Szafranowska, Z., Osuala, R., Breier, B., Kushibar, K., Lekadir, K., Diaz, O.: Sharing generative models instead of private data: a simulation study on mammography patch classification. In: 16th International Workshop on Breast Imaging (IWBI2022), vol. 12286, pp. 169–177. SPIE (2022)
31. Yousefpour, A., et al.: Opacus: user-friendly differential privacy library in pytorch. arXiv preprint arXiv:2109.12298 (2021)

Efficient Generation of Synthetic Breast CT Slices By Combining Generative and Super-Resolution Models

Zhikai Yang[✉], Mehdi Astaraki, Örjan Smedby, and Rodrigo Moreno

Department of Biomedical Engineering and Health Systems,
KTH Royal Institute of Technology, Stockholm, Sweden
zhikai@kth.se

Abstract. High-quality synthetic medical images can enlarge training datasets in different deep learning-based applications. Recently, diffusion-based methods for image synthesis have outperformed GAN-based methods, even for medical images. Unfortunately, using diffusion models is costly in terms of training time and computational resources. We propose a two-stage method that combines diffusion models and GANs to tackle this problem. First, we use diffusion models or GANs to generate low-resolution images. Then, we use a GAN-based super-resolution model to interpolate high-resolution images from these low-resolution images. Experimental results on synthetic breast CT slices show that the proposed framework is more efficient and performs better than state-of-the-art methods that generate the images in a single step. The proposed methods will be available at https://github.com/xiaoerlaigeid/Image-Frequency-Score.git.

Keywords: Medical Image Generation · Generative Adversarial Network · Diffusion Model · Super-Resolution · Frequency Information

1 Introduction

Deep generative models, such as generative adversarial networks (GANs), have shown great potential in synthesizing realistic-looking images [5,24,25]. Recently, diffusion-based models have shown even better performance in several image generation tasks [7,14]. However, a problem with diffusion-based methods is that they require more computational resources and longer inference time than GAN-based methods. Several approaches have been proposed to reduce sampling times to accelerate inference time [15,18].

In medical imaging, the scarcity of public data, partly related to ethical and legal concerns, makes it urgent to devise methods to synthesize high-fidelity and anatomically meaningful medical images in a reasonable computational time. Fu et al. [3] propose using a registration-based method to generate new medical image dataset while maintaining the anatomical structure. However, this method can only generate images from the original dataset. The degree of realism is based on image quality and anatomical structure. Kelkar et al. [10] proposed using image statistics metrics to evaluate the anatomical aspects of synthetic images. The results of the proposed metric show that the GAN-based methods could learn the basic first- and second-order statistics with high perceptual quality, but they still need to learn other relevant statistics.

Frequency information plays a vital role in the quality of the generated images. In this context, several studies have been conducted to improve the quality of generated images in the frequency domain [8,17,20]. According to [19], generative models tend to optimize low-frequencies first before optimizing high-frequencies, which they call the frequency principle (F-principle). This principle has been confirmed in further studies [11,12]. To improve the performance for high-frequencies, for example, Liu et al. [13] proposed a guidance branch to increase the focus of generative networks to high-frequency information.

In this study, we propose a framework to synthesize high-quality breast computed tomography (CT) slices that leverage the use of both low- and high-frequency information. The method incorporates two stages. In the first stage, we use a generative model to generate low-resolution (LR) images, which could focus more on anatomical structures encoded in low-frequency components (LFC). In the second stage, a super-resolution (SR) network restores parts of the high-frequency component (HFC) unavailable in LR images. The advantage of this framework is two-fold. First, generating low-resolution images and super-resolution is more efficient than using a single network, allowing for using otherwise unaffordable models in most applications, especially diffusion models. Second, we expect to obtain better quality than using a single network. According to the F-principle, the generative network will learn quicker and better low frequencies in low-resolution images. The loss of accuracy in high frequencies is then tackled by using super-resolution. Thus, our main contributions are as follows.

- Propose a two-stage method to generate realistic-looking breast CT slices efficiently. To the best of our knowledge, such an approach has not been explored for the generation of breast images so far.
- Propose image measurements to quantify the quality of synthesized images in the frequency domain. These measurements are general and can be employed in other generative tasks.

2 Methodology

Low-frequency information encodes coarse details or global variations in an image, while high-frequency information encodes fine details and local variations. In our case, low frequencies encode information about large-scale structures, such as the shape of the breast or other anatomical structures. LR images contain fewer spatial details than HR images of the same scene. This reduction in resolution leads to a loss of HFC, such as sharp edges, fine textures, or small details. However, LR images still retain the low-frequency information, representing the image's general shape, structure, and overall variations. This LFC is typically

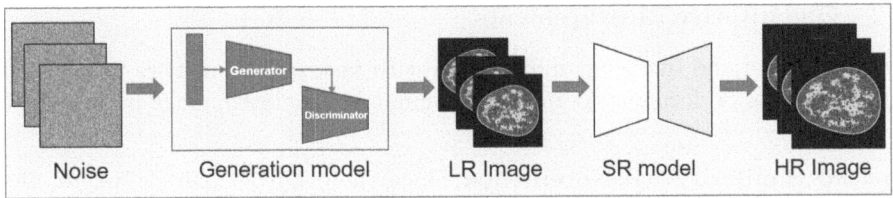

Fig. 1. The framework of the proposed two-stage breast image generation framework. In the first stage, the generation model generates low-resolution (LR) images. Then, these LR images are used as the input of a super-resolution (SR) model input to generate high-resolution (HR) images.

related to the global content or coarse features of the scene. The ratio between LFC and HFC in LR images is higher than in HR images. Thus, according to the F-principle, generative models will tend to yield better results on LR images since they contain a higher ratio between LFC and HFC. We argue that the loss in performance on the HFC due to LR can be partially compensated by using super-resolution methods.

2.1 Overall Framework

We propose a two-stage image generation framework (Fig. 1). In the first stage, we use generative methods to generate LR images. Our hypothesis is that these generative models will be more efficient in capturing the LFC of the image since LR images contain a higher ratio between LFC and HFC compared to HR ones. In the second stage, we use a GAN-based super-resolution method to upsample the images to HR images. Thus, the missing HFC that are not available in LR images are restored/learned during this stage. In the experiments, we compared the performance of three state-of-the-art generative methods for the generation of LR images:

Denoising Diffusion GAN (DDG): This is a generative model that combines elements from denoising diffusion models and generative adversarial networks [18].

Denoising Diffusion Implicit Model (DDIM): The DDIM is a widely used diffusion-based method, which has a U-Net architecture with three residual blocks and self-attention modules [7].

StyleGAN2: Unlike classical GAN, this is a progressive, growing technique where the generator and discriminator networks gradually grow during training. StyleGAN2 has demonstrated its ability to generate highly realistic and visually appealing images [9].

In the second stage, we use the **Enhanced Super-Resolution GAN (ESR-GAN),ch7wang2018esrgan** method to upsample the first stage generated breast images with more detailed fine structure to recover more HFC. It is a stable and widely used GAN-based super-resolution method.

2.2 Quantitative Measurements

We use spatial and frequency information with task-specific metrics to measure the generation performance of different commonly generated image performance metrics.

Spatial Similarity Measurements: Since there are no paired images, the Structural Similarity Index Measure (SSIM) and Peak Signal Noise Ratio (PSNR) cannot used as metrics. For the spatial distribution measurement, the Fréchet Inception Distance (FID) [6] is commonly used, which use deep learning extrated features. It is computed as:

$$FID = \|\mu_r - \mu_g\|_2^2 + \text{Tr}(\Sigma_r + \Sigma_g - 2(\Sigma_r \Sigma_g)^{\frac{1}{2}}), \quad (1)$$

where μ_r and μ_g are the means of the feature representations of authentic and generated images, respectively, in which feature representation is a 1-dimension vector extracted with a pre-trained convolutional neural network; Tr means trace operation; Σ_r and Σ_g are the covariance matrices of the feature representations of authentic and generated images, respectively; and $\|\cdot\|_2$ denotes the Euclidean distance.

Although the FID can be seen as a perceptual metric, it is also essential to quantify anatomical structure. Kelkar et al. [10] proposed using the Kolmogorov-Smirnov (KS) statistic to measure the similarity of real breast image spatial features distribution and generated breast image spatial features distribution, which is computed as:

$$S_s = KS(F_{Rs}, F_{Gs}), \quad (2)$$

where S_s is the KS statistics score computed on the spatial feature vectors F_{Rs} and F_{Gs} for the real and generated images, respectively. More specifically, these spatial features are extracted from the generated image set G and the real image set R. The spatial feature vector is defined as:

$$f_s = [size, fat, glandular, ratio\_fg, mean, var, skew, kur, bal] \quad (3)$$

which are breast image anatomical structure features by the size of the breast area, $size$, fat area, fat, glandular area, $glandular$, the ratio of fat and glandular, $ratio\_fg$, and the mean, variance, skewness and kurtosis of image pixel intensity, $mean\ var$, $skew$, kur, and balance $bal = \frac{i_{70} - mean}{mean - i_{30}}$, in which i_{70} and i_{30} denoted the 70% and 30% intensity values from the image. This feature vector f_s is computed per image, where $f_s \in F_s$.

Frequency Similarity Measurements: To better analyze the generation method in the frequency domain, we propose a criterion to compute the similarity distribution between two image sets in the LFC and HFC. The metric S_{ksf} is inspired by the method proposed in [10], which also uses KS statistics score, but with frequency feature vector set F_{Rf} and F_{Gf} instead:

$$S_f = KS(F_{Rf}, F_{Gf}). \quad (4)$$

Table 1. Performance of different generative models on 1,000 synthetic images. The best-performing methods are marked in bold.

Methods	FID ↓	S_s ↓	mean S_L ↓	mean S_H ↓	W-S_L ↓	W-S_H ↓
Real Images	3.25	0.005	0.012	0.267	–	–
DDIM-256	9.9	0.055	**0.037**	0.367	**0.005**	0.071
DDG-256	11.2	0.053	**0.037**	0.366	**0.005**	0.066
StyleGAN2-256	**9.8**	**0.019**	0.064	**0.324**	0.016	**0.057**
StyleGAN2-512	28.6	0.023	0.411	0.372	0.063	0.081

For this, the spatial domain images i_s are transformed into the frequency domain images i_f using the Fourier transform. Then, the frequency domain images are centered-cropped with a given image crop ratio r to decouple LFC l_r and HFC h_r, where $i_f = h_r \cup l_r$. We then apply the logarithm to these images to prevent the low-frequency information from becoming dominant. We estimate the reduced dimension feature vectors f_{Rf}, f_{Gf} using principal component analysis (PCA) to extract primary information. Finally, Eq. 4 is applied independently to the high- and low-frequency vector components to estimate KS scores between real and generated images. We referred to these estimations as S_L and S_H, respectively.

3 Experimental Results

We conducted experiments to evaluate the image quality of the synthetic images in both quantitative and qualitative terms. In the proposed method, we combined DDG, DDIM, and StyleGAN2 at resolution 256 × 256 with ESR-GAN to obtain 2D images of size 512 × 512. For comparison, we also implemented StyleGAN2 at 512 × 512.

Model Training: For the two-stage generation method, first, the generation models are trained to generate images of 256 × 256, and the super-resolution method is trained to go from 256 × 256 to 512 × 512. Due to hardware limitations, the diffusion-based method cannot be trained directly in high resolution. Training and inference were conducted on an NVIDIA A100 GPU with 80 GB memory.

Dataset: All models were trained on the AAPM2023 DGM-Image Challenge dataset [2,4]. It consists of 100,000 images with size 512 × 512, which is a typical resolution in breast CT, generated in a virtual imaging clinical trial for regulatory evaluation (VICTRE) of breast phantom creation software [1]. These images emulate coronal slices of anthropomorphic breast phantoms. They contain fibroglandular structures interspersed with fatty tissue and ligament networks.

3.1 Quantitative Evaluation

Generation Performance: Table 1 shows the score in the FID, S_s, mean, and Wasserstein (W) metric of S_L and S_H for the LFC and HFC at different crop

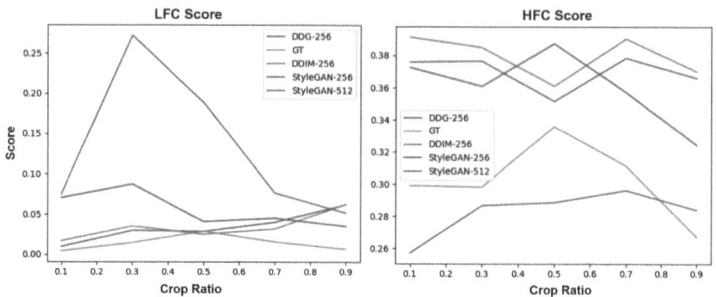

Fig. 2. LFC and HFC scores S_L and S_H with different crop ratios.

ratios from 0.1–0.9 in steps of 0.2. We use the Wasserstein distance at different crop rate scores to compare them with the statistics of real images. We used 1,000 real and synthetic images were used to compute the metric. As shown, all models that use super-resolution outperform StyleGAN2-512, the only one that does not use it.

We note that the StyleGAN2-512 performs worse than the two-stage StyleGAN2-256. The StyleGAN2 has a better spatial score than diffusion models, achieving 0.019, although the DDIM method has similar results in the FID score. Regarding the S_L, the diffusion-based techniques are better than the GAN-based methods: DDIM-256 and DDG-256 both achieve 0.037 in the mean S_L. Regarding the mean S_H, the two-stage method has similar scores, both diffusion-based and the GAN-based method, and they are superior to StyleGAN2-512. The results show the importance of evaluating the image quality of image generation methods with different measurements.

Figure 2 illustrates the LFC and HFC scores S_L and S_H at different crop ratios. As shown, these scores fluctuate with varying crop ratios. Notice that the methods using two stages get closer trends to the ones of the real data (Real Image in the figure). Also, the diffusion-based methods have lower scores compared to the GAN-based method in terms of S_L. In addition, two-stage methods score better in the low-frequency domain than the single-stage generation method, which follows the F-principle assumption. In addition, although the DDIM-256 has a similar FID score compared to StyleGAN2-256, they differ in the other metrics. Compared to real images, we still have room for improvement.

Computation Performance: Table 2 illustrates the model parameters, training times per epoch, and inference times for every 100 generated images. The diffusion model has more model parameters, and it also takes more time for training and inference. We cannot train diffusion model with 512 image size. In addition to that, the GAN-based model has a smaller model parameter to achieve the same level of performance.

Table 2. Comparison with different model parameters, training and inference time

Method	Nr. Params	Training [min/epoch]	Inference [s/100 images]
DDIM-256	113M	105	1255.0
DDG-256	68M	60	13.4
StyleGAN2-256	59M	8	**2.3**
StyleGAN2-512	59M	12	3.6

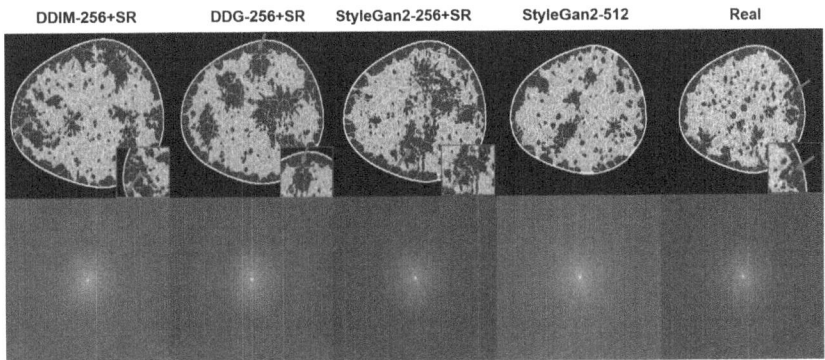

Fig. 3. Generated images from different spatial (top) and frequency domain methods. The red arrows indicate calcifications. The highlighted image with red boxes indicating the calcification. (Color figure online)

3.2 Qualitative Evaluation

Figure 3 shows the generated images with different methods in spatial and frequency domains, including the real images. In the spatial domain visualization results, StyleGAN2-512 has similar anatomy structures. However, it lacks calcification areas (bright spots indicated with red arrows in the figure), which can be found in images generated with the other methods. This issue results in a lack of diversity in the images generated by StyleGAN2-512. In the frequency domain visualization, we notice the ratio between LFC and HFC is lower for StyleGAN2-512 than for both real and other two-stage generation methods, as it has less contrast. To some extent, the calcification area is more related to high-frequency information, which can align with these image's appearance in the spatial domain.

Spatial similarity metric. Figure 4 illustrates the 2D spatial feature f_s distribution after PCA for DDG-256, DDIM-256, StyleGAN2-256, and StyleGAN2-512. The red and green points represent PCA features of generation synthetic and dataset real images, respectively. As shown, StyleGAN2-256 has the best overlap with the distribution of real images. On the other hand, StyleGAN2-512 yields the worst overlap. Note that it is not desirable to have a perfect over-

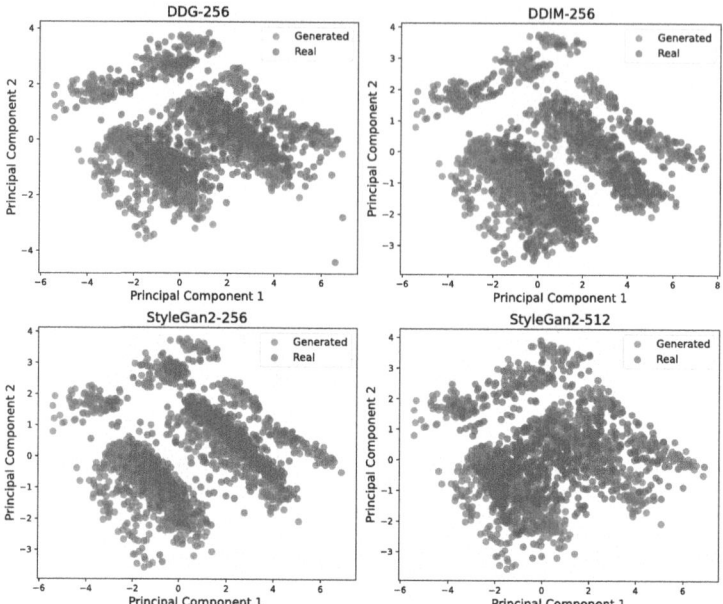

Fig. 4. Visualization of the spatial features distribution in real images and generated images by generation model.

lap with the dataset's real images since we also want to add variability in the generated images.

4 Discussion and Conclusion

We proposed a two-stage image generation framework to generate synthetic breast CT slices that exploit the F-principle. The framework avoids large GPU memory requirements usually needed for generating high-resolution images with diffusion models and improves image quality compared with one-stage generation methods. Our method vastly reduces the computational cost consumption without significantly decreasing performance. Moreover, we proposed S_L and S_H scores to compare real and generated images in the frequency domain that can complement the standard FID score and KS spatial metrics.

From the results from Table 1, it is difficult to decide whether diffusion-based or GANs are better for the first task, which aligned with the AAPM2023 DGM-Image Challenge report [2]. We argue that such a decision is application-dependent. For example, segmentation tasks might benefit from methods with better S_L scores, while detecting small structures (e.g., calcifications) can be easier with higher S_H scores. The FID score alone is insufficient to assess image quality. From the F-principle, deep learning models update the knowledge during training from low-frequency to high-frequency information. Thus, it is natural to measure low and high-frequency information as we propose in this paper.

High and low-frequency information correspond to different spatial information of the image. For example, in this breast CT dataset, the HFC is more related to calcification spot areas, and the LFC is more related to the whole image anatomy structure.

An advantage of virtual clinical trials' software-generated images is that the image distribution is more stable than natural images. For example, each tissue type has an intensity within a specific range. This feature is helpful in better quantifying the quality of the generative method. Clearly, the next step will be to validate the proposed pipeline on real breast imaging datasets. But the proposed method still has limitations, we did not compared the proposed method in the class gudied generation problem. In future work, we plan to implement class-guided generation and train a deep learning model on the generated dataset for various downstream breast diagnosis task based on our previous work [21–23], further validating our proposed method.

Acknowledgement. This work was supported by grants from Marie Skłodowska-Curie Doctoral Networks Actions (HORIZON-MSCA-2021-DN-01-01; 101073222), Cancerfonden (22-2389 Pj) and HKUST-KTH Global Knowledge Network Awards. The computations were enabled by the Berzelius resource provided by the Knut and Alice Wallenberg Foundation at the National Academic Infrastructure for Supercomputing in Sweden.

Disclosure of Interests. The authors have no competing interests to declare.

References

1. Badano, A., et al.: Evaluation of digital breast tomosynthesis as replacement of full-field digital mammography using an in silico imaging trial. JAMA Netw. Open **1**(7), e185474–e185474 (2018)
2. Deshpande, R., et al.: Report on the AAPM grand challenge on deep generative modeling for learning medical image statistics. ArXiv (2024)
3. Fu, J., Tzortzakakis, A., Barroso, J., Westman, E., Ferreira, D., Moreno, R.: Fast three-dimensional image generation for healthy brain aging using diffeomorphic registration. Hum. Brain Mapp. **44**(4), 1289–1308 (2023). https://doi.org/10.1002/hbm.26165
4. Gotsis, D., et al.: Data for the 2023 AAPM grand challenge on deep generative modeling for learning medical image statistics (2023). https://doi.org/10.13012/B2IDB-2773204_V1
5. Han, L., et al.: Synthesis-based imaging-differentiation representation learning for multi-sequence 3D/4D MRI. Med. Image Anal. **92**, 103044 (2024)
6. Heusel, M., Ramsauer, H., Unterthiner, T., Nessler, B., Hochreiter, S.: GANs trained by a two time-scale update rule converge to a local Nash equilibrium. Adv. Neural. Inf. Process. Syst. **30** (2017)
7. Ho, J., Jain, A., Abbeel, P.: Denoising diffusion probabilistic models. Adv. Neural. Inf. Process. Syst. **33**, 6840–6851 (2020)
8. Hu, X., et al.: HDNet: high-resolution dual-domain learning for spectral compressive imaging. In: Proceedings of the IEEE/CVF Conference on Computer Vision and Pattern Recognition, pp. 17542–17551 (2022)

9. Karras, T., Laine, S., Aittala, M., Hellsten, J., Lehtinen, J., Aila, T.: Analyzing and improving the image quality of StyleGAN. In: Proceedings of the IEEE/CVF Conference on Computer Vision and Pattern Recognition, pp. 8110–8119 (2020)
10. Kelkar, V.A., et al.: Assessing the ability of generative adversarial networks to learn canonical medical image statistics. IEEE Trans. Med. Imaging (2023)
11. Khayatkhoei, M., Elgammal, A.: Spatial frequency bias in convolutional generative adversarial networks. In: Proceedings of the AAAI Conference on Artificial Intelligence, vol. 36, pp. 7152–7159 (2022)
12. Li, Z., Xia, P., Rui, X., Li, B.: Exploring the effect of high-frequency components in GANs training. ACM Trans. Multimed. Comput. Commun. Appl. **19**(5), 1–22 (2023)
13. Liu, F., Shao, M., Wang, F., Zhang, L.: High-fidelity GAN inversion by frequency domain guidance. Comput. Graph. (2023)
14. Múller-Franzes, G., et al.: Diffusion probabilistic models beat GANs on medical images. arXiv preprint arXiv:2212.07501 (2022)
15. Song, J., Meng, C., Ermon, S.: Denoising diffusion implicit models. arXiv preprint arXiv:2010.02502 (2020)
16. Wang, X., et al.: ESRGAN: enhanced super-resolution generative adversarial networks. In: Proceedings of the European Conference on Computer Vision (ECCV) Workshops, pp. 1–16 (2018)
17. Wu, Z., Liu, W., Li, J., Xu, C., Huang, D.: SFHN: spatial-frequency domain hybrid network for image super-resolution. IEEE Trans. Circ. Syst. Video Technol. (2023)
18. Xiao, Z., Kreis, K., Vahdat, A.: Tackling the generative learning trilemma with denoising diffusion GANs. arXiv preprint arXiv:2112.07804 (2021)
19. Xu, Z.-Q.J., Zhang, Y., Xiao, Y.: Training behavior of deep neural network in frequency domain. In: Gedeon, T., Wong, K.W., Lee, M. (eds.) ICONIP 2019. LNCS, vol. 11953, pp. 264–274. Springer, Cham (2019). https://doi.org/10.1007/978-3-030-36708-4_22
20. Yang, M., Wang, Z., Chi, Z., Feng, W.: WaveGAN: frequency-aware GAN for high-fidelity few-shot image generation. In: Avidan, S., Brostow, G., Cissé, M., Farinella, G.M., Hassner, T. (eds.) ECCV 2022. LNCS, vol. 13675, pp. 1–17. Springer, Cham (2022). https://doi.org/10.1007/978-3-031-19784-0_1
21. Yang, Z., Fan, T., Smedby, Ö., Moreno, R.: 3D breast ultrasound image classification using 2.5 D deep learning. In: 17th International Workshop on Breast Imaging (IWBI 2024), vol. 13174, pp. 443–449. SPIE (2024)
22. Yang, Z., Fan, T., Smedby, Ö., Moreno, R.: Lesion localization in digital breast tomosynthesis with deformable transformers by using 2.5 d information. In: Medical Imaging 2024: Computer-Aided Diagnosis, vol. 12927, pp. 85–90. SPIE (2024)
23. Yang, Z., Wu, W., Zhang, J., Zhao, Y., Gu, L.: Deep co-training active learning for mammographic images classification. In: 2020 Chinese Automation Congress (CAC), pp. 1059–1062. IEEE (2020)
24. Zhang, T., et al.: Synthesis of contrast-enhanced breast MRI using T1-and multi-b-value DWI-based hierarchical fusion network with attention mechanism. In: Greenspan, H., et al. (eds.) MICCAI 2023. LNCS, vol. 14226, pp. 79–88. Springer, Cham (2023). https://doi.org/10.1007/978-3-031-43990-2_8
25. Zhang, T., et al.: Important-net: integrated MRI multi-parametric increment fusion generator with attention network for synthesizing absent data. Inf. Fusion **108**, 102381 (2024)

Exploring Patient Data Requirements in Training Effective AI Models for MRI-Based Breast Cancer Classification

Solha Kang[1], Wesley De Neve[1,3], Francois Rameau[2], and Utku Ozbulak[1,3(✉)]

[1] Center for Biosystems and Biotech Data Science, Ghent University Global Campus, Incheon, Republic of Korea
utku.ozbulak@ghent.ac.kr
[2] The State University of New York Korea, Incheon, Republic of Korea
[3] Department of Electronics and Information Systems, Ghent University, Ghent, Belgium

Abstract. The past decade has witnessed a substantial increase in the number of startups and companies offering AI-based solutions for clinical decision support in medical institutions. However, the critical nature of medical decision-making raises several concerns about relying on external software. Key issues include potential variations in image modalities and the medical devices used to obtain these images, potential legal issues, and adversarial attacks. Fortunately, the open-source nature of machine learning research has made foundation models publicly available and straightforward to use for medical applications. This accessibility allows medical institutions to train their own AI-based models, thereby mitigating the aforementioned concerns. Given this context, an important question arises: how much data do medical institutions need to train effective AI models? In this study, we explore this question in relation to breast cancer detection, a particularly contested area due to the prevalence of this disease, which affects approximately 1 in every 8 women. Through large-scale experiments on various patient sizes in the training set, we show that medical institutions do not need a decade's worth of MRI images to train an AI model that performs competitively with the state-of-the-art, provided the model leverages foundation models. Furthermore, we observe that for patient counts greater than 50, the number of patients in the training set has a negligible impact on the performance of models and that simple ensembles further improve the results without additional complexity.

1 Introduction

Although AI-based models that utilize deep neural networks have demonstrated successful results in various medical imaging tasks, such as tumor detection [9], organ segmentation [14], and disease classification [10, 26], these models have not yet been widely adopted in clinical settings due to several factors that limit their

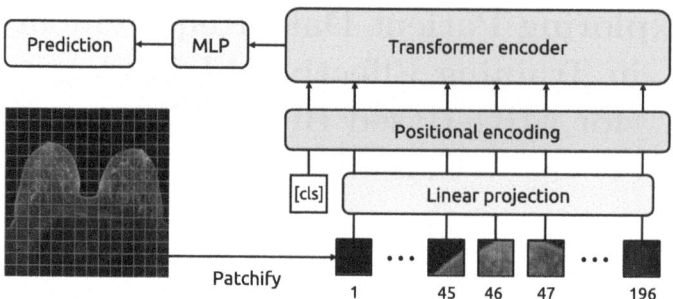

Fig. 1. Visualization of the ViT architecture and image patch tokenization.

usage [16]. First, the critical nature of medical decision-making demands exceptionally high accuracy and reliability, as errors can have severe consequences for patient health. Consequently, developing AI algorithms for medical applications requires not only a deep understanding of both computer science and medicine but also compliance with various regulations and standards, such as the Health Insurance Portability and Accountability Act (HIPAA) [1]. This complexity makes it challenging for private companies to develop and commercialize their products effectively.

Second, the lack of standardized and high-quality medical data complicates the training and validation of AI models. Variations in imaging modalities, the use of different medical devices, and inconsistencies in data annotation all contribute to this complexity [20]. For example, although breast cancer is one of the most researched types of cancer, the majority of studies investigating breast cancer via MRI or mammography imaging use private datasets, making comparisons across various methods nearly impossible [2] (Fig. 1).

Lastly, concerns about data privacy and security receive a lot of attention in the medical field. Various adversarial attacks, such as data poisoning attacks, which can taint training datasets, pose substantial risks [23,25]. The potential for such attacks introduces legal and ethical issues that further hinder the deployment of AI in healthcare settings.

All of the aforementioned factors contribute to the decision of medical institutions, such as university hospitals, to develop their own AI-based solutions, typically in collaboration with computer science departments [21,22]. Until recently, such efforts required tremendous amounts of data and expertise, as the models had to be specifically created for each task at hand. This posed considerable challenges in terms of resources and specialized knowledge, often limiting the ability of smaller institutions to develop effective AI solutions [15].

The emergence of foundation models [5], which are mostly based on the transformer architecture, has been a game changer for medical AI, including breast cancer detection [3]. These models, pre-trained on vast amounts of diverse data, provide a robust and versatile base upon which researchers can build their applications [6]. For a comprehensive overview on foundation models, we refer the interested readers to the work of [5]. By leveraging these foundation models in the form of transfer learning, medical institutes can substantially reduce the amount of data and time needed to develop accurate and reliable AI solutions. This not only democratizes access to advanced AI technologies but also enhances the feasibility of creating in-house solutions tailored to specific medical needs [4].

Given the ability of such pretrained models to discover relationships with potentially fewer images, we ask the following question: how many patients would a medical institute need to create a model comparable to the state-of-the-art if they utilize foundation models? Specifically, can a medical institute avoid the need to spend a decade collecting and annotating MRI data to train an effective breast cancer detection model? To answer this question, we employ the DUKE Breast Cancer Dataset [28], curated over 14 years, aimed at detecting malignant breast tumors in MRI data. Through large-scale experiments, we investigate and identify the diminishing returns of image quantities in the training set for breast cancer detection via MRI data, and we make the following contributions:

- We demonstrate that pretrained models can achieve state-of-the-art results in MRI-based breast cancer detection even with a limited number of images, showcasing their efficiency in data-scarce scenarios.
- We observe minimal performance differences among various pretraining methods, indicating that the choice of pretraining technique may have a negligible impact on the overall outcomes.
- We observe that the selection of patients in the training set has a negligible impact on the performance of models for patient counts as few as 50.
- We experimented with simple ensemble methods and demonstrated their effectiveness in improving overall performance without adding substantial complexity.

2 Methodology

In this section, we provide a description of the dataset used, outline the models utilized, and describe the proposed method in detail.

2.1 Models

To investigate the impact of data scarcity on model training, we employ the most commonly used transformer-based computer vision architecture, Vision Transformer-Base/16 (ViT-B/16) [8]. Vision transformers are known to be data-hungry and perform poorly compared to convolutional neural networks in data-scarce regimes. To overcome this limitation, numerous self-supervised learning (SSL) frameworks have been proposed in the past couple of years [6,12,13]. For a detailed overview of SSL frameworks, we refer interested readers to the following surveys [17,24]. Among these SSL frameworks, we employ two models pretrained using (1) DINO [6], a discriminative SSL framework, and (2) MAE [12], which

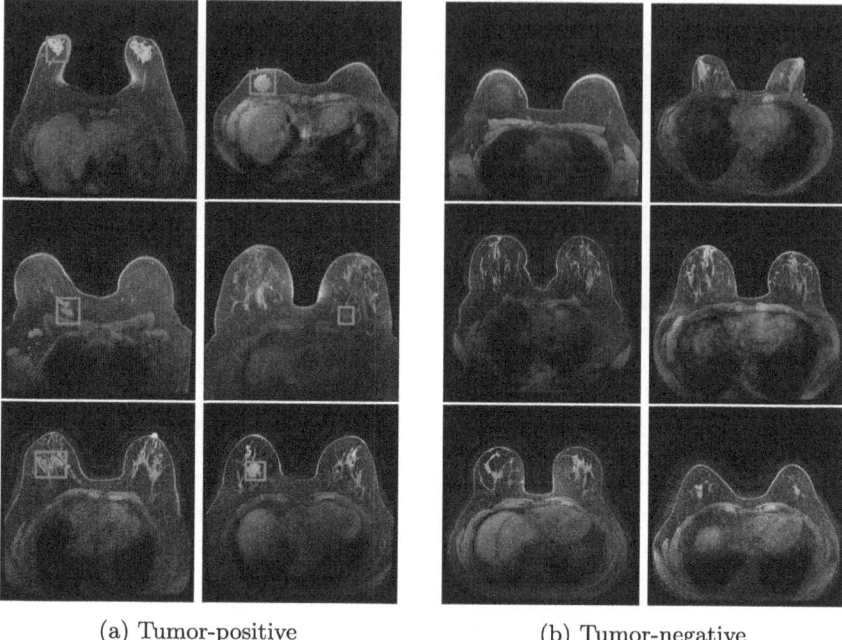

Fig. 2. An example set of images from the Duke breast MRI dataset: (a) Tumor-positive breast MRI images, overlaid with bounding boxes indicating tumor locations, and (b) Tumor-negative breast MRI images.

relies on a generative approach. Pretraining for these models is performed on the ImageNet dataset [27], a large-scale dataset containing natural images. In addition to these two models, we also experiment with two additional ViTs: one that is randomly initialized and another that is pretrained in a supervised fashion on the same (ImageNet) dataset. Models that are pretrained using the aforementioned methods on large datasets typically serve as foundation models. Note that fine-tuning a foundation model for a specific dataset falls under the category of transfer learning and has been studied extensively for the past decade [29].

As suggested by [8], we use ViTs for images of size 224×224 with image tokens/patches of size 16×16, resulting in a total of 196 tokens. We modify the final linear layer of the model to accommodate the two-class classification problem tackled in this work.

2.2 Dataset

The Duke Breast Cancer Dataset, sourced from 922 patients with invasive breast cancer treated at Duke Hospital over a span of 14 years, stands as one of the largest publicly available datasets of 3D MRI breast cancer images [28]. The primary task with this dataset is to determine the presence of breast tumors in the

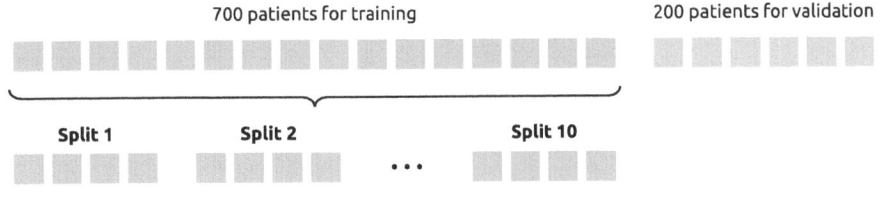

Fig. 3. Overview of the generation of training splits. A fixed validation set of 200 patients is randomly sampled from a total of 900 patients. From the remaining 700 patients, 10 training splits of $n \in \{1, 5, 10, 50, 100, 200, 400, 700\}$ patients are randomly sampled for each patient count.

MRI images based on 2D slices. For 3D to 2D conversion, we follow the procedure detailed in [18,19]. When the 3D images of this dataset are separated into 2D slices, this operation results in more than 100,000 2D images corresponding to approximately 130 images for each patient. Due to the large quantity of data, the majority of research efforts employing this dataset use only a subset of these images to showcase experimental results. Unlike those efforts, we use the entire DUKE dataset for a comprehensive analysis and incorporate a data-splitting methodology to investigate potential disparities in patient selection for the training set. Example images from the DUKE dataset are displayed in Fig. 2, highlighting regions with tumors in tumor-positive images, thereby showcasing the complexity of the tackled problem.

Patient-based data splitting for consistent evaluation – To ensure consistent evaluation, we first sample a fixed validation set consisting of images obtained from 200 patients. Then, to perform a thorough investigation that accounts for potential disparities in the selected patients in the training set, we employ stratified sampling to create multiple training subsets with varying numbers of patients. Specifically, we randomly sample images from 1, 5, 10, 50, 100, 200, 400, and 700 patients from the cohort of the remaining 722 patients and generate ten unique training splits per patient count. This results in a total of 80 unique training datasets (8 different patient counts × 10 unique splits). For each patient count, the ten training splits contain an equal number of positive and negative images. A visual description of the patient splitting technique we employ can be found in Fig. 3.

The aforementioned approach provides a comprehensive set of training datasets for model evaluation and enables us to assess potential discrepancies in model performance with respect to the selection of patients within the training set.

2.3 Training

We train our foundation models using a grid-search strategy, applying the SGD optimizer with learning rates of 0.1, 0.01, and 0.001, paired with weight decay

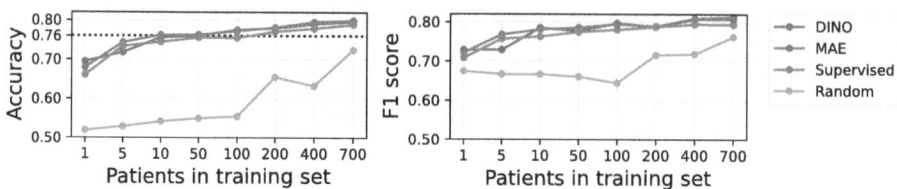

Fig. 4. (left) Validation accuracies of the best-performing ViT models trained with 1, 5, 10, 50, 100, 200, 400, 700 patients across all 10 training splits, and (right) corresponding F1-scores for the selected models.

settings of either 0 or 0.0001. Our training process employs the Cross-Entropy Loss function, with a batch size of 32. We adopt a cosine annealing learning rate scheduler in alignment with the research on downstream transferability of self-supervised models. We experiment with a momentum of 0 and 0.1. For augmentation, we exclusively use random resized crops of size 224 × 224 to maintain the fidelity of MRI images. Additionally, early stopping is implemented in all training runs, with a patience threshold set at 5 epochs. Based on the aforementioned grid-search approach, we select models with the highest validation performances on their respective data splits to demonstrate experimental results.

3 Experimental Results

As detailed in Sect. 2.1, we train four ViT-B/16 models where three of those models: three pretrained on the ImageNet dataset using DINO, MAE, and supervised training, and a fourth model with random initialization. We train those models with the grid-search approach detailed in Sect. 2.3 and present results in Fig. 4 and Fig. 5.

Specifically, Fig. 4 displays the effectiveness of the best-performing models on the validation set, measured by accuracy and F1-score, for each patient split. To quantify the influence of selecting different patients for training, we select best-performing models on their respective patient splits and represent the distribution of accuracies in Fig. 5. In figures comparing the accuracy, the dashed line represents the state-of-the-art results obtained from the work of [18]. Based on these results, we make the observations listed below.

Foundation Models do not Require Substantial MRI Training Data for State-of-the-Art Results. Unsurprisingly, we observe a steady improvement in model performance with an increased number of patients in the training set. Moreover, we find that in the best-case scenario, having a training set consisting of only 10 patients and using foundation models is enough to reach the accuracy obtained in the work of [18]. From patient counts of 50 to 700, a 14-fold increase in the patient count only leads to approximately a 4% increase in accuracy, suggesting that there is a point at which increasing the number of patients in the training set yields diminishing returns in performance enhancement.

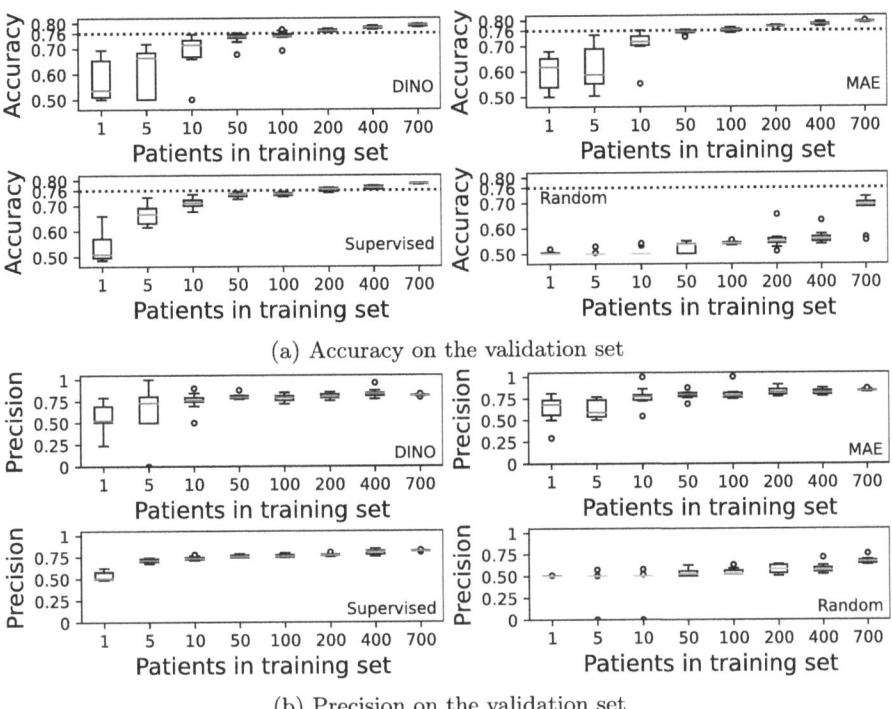

Fig. 5. Box plots illustrating the distribution of (a) accuracy as well as (b) precision on validation sets across ViT models trained with 1, 5, 10, 50, 100, 200, 400, and 700 patients. For each patient count in the training set, patients are randomly sampled from the training dataset to create 10 training splits.

The Pre-training Method used has Minimal Impact on Model Performance. As shown in Fig. 4 and Fig. 5, the models exhibit a similar increase in performance regardless of the training method. This suggests that the specific pre-training method used for the models might not significantly impact their performance. This finding highlights the robustness of the pre-trained models, indicating that once a certain amount of training data is reached, the choice of pre-training approach becomes less critical to the model's success.

Patient Selection for Training Data is not Critical. In Fig. 5, we illustrate the distribution of the highest validation accuracies as well as precision scores obtained for each training split. We observe that, especially for the three foundation models, the variability across different splits decreases with the increase in the number of patients used for training. Contrary to the findings of [7], for patient counts of 50 and onward, all training splits achieve similar performances, indicating that patients in the training set do not have a noticeable impact on model performance.

Table 1. For 10 splits containing only the data of 50 patients in the training set, the performance of three foundation models and a simple majority vote-based ensemble model of the three foundation models are provided. For each row, the highest accuracy value and F1-score are highlighted with <u>underlined text</u> and **bold text**, respectively.

Data Split	DINO Accuracy	F1	MAE Accuracy	F1	Supervised Accuracy	F1	Ensemble Accuracy	F1
1	0.760	0.776	0.759	0.789	0.749	0.775	<u>0.765</u>	**0.791**
2	0.743	0.763	0.720	0.763	0.729	0.750	<u>0.756</u>	**0.783**
3	0.757	0.778	0.763	0.779	0.744	0.765	<u>0.766</u>	**0.787**
4	0.755	0.788	0.761	0.789	0.752	0.772	<u>0.768</u>	**0.797**
5	0.740	0.766	<u>0.753</u>	0.775	0.725	0.758	0.749	**0.776**
6	0.763	0.774	0.770	**0.791**	0.746	0.754	<u>0.770</u>	0.785
7	0.751	0.760	0.751	0.769	0.733	0.767	<u>0.760</u>	**0.784**
8	0.756	0.770	0.766	**0.790**	0.741	0.759	<u>0.766</u>	0.785
9	0.735	0.756	0.759	0.769	0.713	0.708	<u>0.759</u>	**0.771**
10	0.750	0.763	0.763	**0.791**	0.755	0.766	<u>0.769</u>	0.789

Simple Ensembles Increase the Performance. Ensemble models in machine learning are generally known to have improved performance over the individual models that comprise the ensembles [11]. Utilizing the three best-performing pre-trained models for individual splits, we experimented with a simple ensemble using majority voting for the case of 50 patients in the training data, provided accuracy values and F1-scores in Table 1. As can be seen, for 9 out of 10 splits, the ensemble model achieves higher accuracy compared to the best-performing individual model, highlighting the potential for improved diagnostic accuracy in medical applications with minimal additional complexity.

4 Conclusions

In this research effort, we demonstrated that medical institutes that perform MRI-based breast cancer detection do not need a decade of data curation to train an effective AI model that performs comparably to the state-of-the-art. In particular, we showed that minimal training data, requiring as few as 50 patients, can match previous accuracy benchmarks, with ensemble methods further improving the results.

Our goal with this research effort is to encourage medical institutes to adopt AI-based diagnostic tools more rapidly by demonstrating the feasibility of achieving high accuracy with limited amounts of data. Indeed, approaches that take advantage of foundation models can substantially reduce the time and resources required for data collection, enabling faster implementation of advanced diagnostic technologies and improving patient outcomes. We hope that our findings will drive innovation in medical diagnostics and contribute to more widespread and equitable access to state-of-the-art healthcare solutions.

That being said, we would like to highlight that observations made in this work may be partial to the employed dataset. As such, we believe that a future work exploring a wider-range of datasets is necessary to solidify our findings.

Although we demonstrated the diminishing returns of image quantities on the models' performance, it is nevertheless more beneficial to employ all existing data to make marginal gains in model performance. As such, we believe future research efforts investigating the optimal amount of data, training time, and performance would greatly benefit the medical AI community.

References

1. Act, A.: Health insurance portability and accountability act of 1996. Public Law **104**, 191 (1996)
2. Adam, R., Dell'Aquila, K., Hodges, L., Maldjian, T., Duong, T.Q.: Deep learning applications to breast cancer detection by magnetic resonance imaging: a literature review. Breast Cancer Res. **25**(1), 87 (2023)
3. Awais, M., et al.: Foundational models defining a new era in vision: a survey and outlook. arXiv preprint arXiv:2307.13721 (2023)
4. Azad, B., et al.: Foundational models in medical imaging: a comprehensive survey and future vision. arXiv preprint arXiv:2310.18689 (2023)
5. Bommasani, R., et al.: On the opportunities and risks of foundation models. arXiv preprint arXiv:2108.07258 (2021)
6. Caron, M., Touvron, H., Misra, I., Jégou, H., Mairal, J., Bojanowski, P., Joulin, A.: Emerging properties in self-supervised vision transformers. In: Proceedings of the IEEE/CVF International Conference on Computer Vision, pp. 9650–9660 (2021)
7. Dakka, M., et al.: Automated detection of poor-quality data: case studies in healthcare. Sci. Rep. **11**(1), 18005 (2021)
8. Dosovitskiy, A., et al.: An image is worth 16×16 words: transformers for image recognition at scale. arXiv preprint arXiv:2010.11929 (2020)
9. Esteva, A., et al.: Dermatologist-level classification of skin cancer with deep neural networks. Nature **542**(7639), 115–118 (2017)
10. Gulshan, V., et al.: Development and validation of a deep learning algorithm for detection of diabetic retinopathy in retinal fundus photographs. jama **316**(22), 2402–2410 (2016)
11. Hansen, L.K., Salamon, P.: Neural network ensembles. IEEE Trans. Pattern Anal. Mach. Intell. **12**(10), 993–1001 (1990)
12. He, K., Chen, X., Xie, S., Li, Y., Dollár, P., Girshick, R.: Masked autoencoders are scalable vision learners. In: Proceedings of the IEEE/CVF Conference on Computer Vision and Pattern Recognition, pp. 16000–16009 (2022)
13. He, K., Fan, H., Wu, Y., Xie, S., Girshick, R.: Momentum contrast for unsupervised visual representation learning. In: Proceedings of the IEEE/CVF Conference on Computer Vision and Pattern Recognition, pp. 9729–9738 (2020)
14. Heller, N., et al.: The state of the art in kidney and kidney tumor segmentation in contrast-enhanced CT imaging: Results of the kits19 challenge. Med. Image Anal. **67**, 101821 (2021)
15. Iliashenko, O., Bikkulova, Z., Dubgorn, A.: Opportunities and challenges of artificial intelligence in healthcare. In: E3S Web of Conferences, vol. 110, p. 02028. EDP Sciences (2019)

16. Kelly, C.J., Karthikesalingam, A., Suleyman, M., Corrado, G., King, D.: Key challenges for delivering clinical impact with artificial intelligence. BMC Med. **17**, 1–9 (2019)
17. Khan, A., AlBarri, S., Manzoor, M.A.: Contrastive self-supervised learning: a survey on different architectures. In: 2022 2nd International Conference on Artificial Intelligence (ICAI), pp. 1–6. IEEE (2022)
18. Konz, N., Gu, H., Dong, H., Mazurowski, M.A.: The intrinsic manifolds of radiological images and their role in deep learning. In: International Conference on Medical Image Computing and Computer-Assisted Intervention, pp. 684–694. Springer (2022)
19. Konz, N., Mazurowski, M.A.: The effect of intrinsic dataset properties on generalization: Unraveling learning differences between natural and medical images. arXiv preprint arXiv:2401.08865 (2024)
20. Liu, X., Glocker, B., McCradden, M.M., Ghassemi, M., Denniston, A.K., Oakden-Rayner, L.: The medical algorithmic audit. Lancet Digit. Health **4**(5), e384–e397 (2022)
21. Maleki Varnosfaderani, S., Forouzanfar, M.: The role of AI in hospitals and clinics: transforming healthcare in the 21st century. Bioengineering **11**(4), 337 (2024)
22. Mekki, Y.M.: Physicians should build their own machine-learning models. Patterns **5**(3) (2024)
23. Mozaffari-Kermani, M., Sur-Kolay, S., Raghunathan, A., Jha, N.K.: Systematic poisoning attacks on and defenses for machine learning in healthcare. IEEE J. Biomed. Health Inform. **19**(6), 1893–1905 (2014)
24. Ozbulak, U., et al.: Know your self-supervised learning: a survey on image-based generative and discriminative training. arXiv preprint arXiv:2305.13689 (2023)
25. Ozbulak, U., Van Messem, A., De Neve, W.: Impact of adversarial examples on deep learning models for biomedical image segmentation. In: Shen, D., et al. (eds.) MICCAI 2019. LNCS, vol. 11765, pp. 300–308. Springer, Cham (2019). https://doi.org/10.1007/978-3-030-32245-8_34
26. Rajpurkar, P., et al.: Chexnet: radiologist-level pneumonia detection on chest x-rays with deep learning. arXiv preprint arXiv:1711.05225 (2017)
27. Russakovsky, O., et al.: ImageNet large scale visual recognition challenge. Int. J. Comput. Vision **115**(3), 211–252 (2015)
28. Saha, A., et al.: A machine learning approach to radiogenomics of breast cancer: a study of 922 subjects and 529 dce-mri features. Br. J. Cancer **119**(4), 508–516 (2018)
29. Tan, C., Sun, F., Kong, T., Zhang, W., Yang, C., Liu, C.: A survey on deep transfer learning. In: International Conference on Artificial Neural Networks, pp. 270–279. Springer (2018)

Virtual Dynamic Contrast Enhanced Breast MRI Using 2D U-Net Architectures

Hannes Schreiter[1(✉)], Jessica Eberle[1], Lorenz A. Kapsner[1,2], Dominique Hadler[1], Sabine Ohlmeyer[1], Ramona Erber[3], Julius Emons[4], Frederik B. Laun[1], Michael Uder[1], Evelyn Wenkel[1,5], Sebastian Bickelhaupt[1], and Andrzej Liebert[1]

[1] Institute of Radiology, University Hospital Erlangen, Friedrich-Alexander University Erlangen-Nürnberg, Erlangen, Germany
hannes.schreiter@uk-erlangen.de
[2] Medical Center for Information and Communication Technology, University Hospital Erlangen, Friedrich-Alexander University Erlangen-Nürnberg, Erlangen, Germany
[3] Institute of Pathology, University Hospital Erlangen, Friedrich-Alexander University Erlangen-Nürnberg, Erlangen, Germany
[4] Department of Gynecology and Obstetrics, University Hospital Erlangen, Erlangen, Germany
[5] Radiologie München GbR, München, Germany

Abstract. Breast Magnetic Resonance Imaging (MRI) examinations routinely include contrast-agent based dynamic contrast-enhanced (DCE) acquisitions. Expanding the accessibility and personalization of breast MRI might be supported amongst others by advancing non-contrast-enhanced MRI, such as virtual dynamic contrast-enhanced techniques (vDCE) utilizing neural networks. This IRB-approved retrospective study includes n = 540 breast MRI examinations acquired on a single 3T MRI scanner. Two 2D U-Net architectures were trained using non-contrast-enhanced MRI acquisitions including T1w, T2w and multi-b-value diffusion weighted imaging acquisitions as inputs and either a single (SCO-Net) or multiple (MCO-Net) time points of a DCE series as ground truth. The neural networks predicted a vDCE series corresponding to five consecutive DCE time points. Across all time points, no significant differences in structural similarity index (SSIM) could be found between the SCO-Net and MCO-Net, both achieving a mean SSIM of 0.86. For peak-signal-to-noise-ratio and normalized root-mean-square error, significantly better results could be observed for the MCO-Net reaching scores of 24.42dB and 0.087 respectively. Comparison of manual segmentations of findings on DCE and vDCE images reached a DICE score of 0.61 and an intersection over union (IoU) of 0.47 without significant differences between SCO-Net and MCO-Net. These findings suggest a technical feasibility of generating vDCE image series from unenhanced input acquisitions using neural networks. However, the analysis does not allow drawing any conclusion on the clinical assessment of lesion specific curve kinetics, which need to be assessed prior determining on the feasibility of deriving diagnostically meaningful enhancement characteristics in individual lesions.

Keywords: Contrast-enhanced MRI · Breast MRI · Deep Learning

1 Introduction

Dynamic contrast-enhanced (DCE) Magnetic Resonance Imaging (MRI), a core element of multiparametric breast MRI examinations, acquires several T1-weighted (T1w) images before and after gadolinium-based contrast agent (GBCA) administration. This acquisition commonly employs intervals of 60–90 s in between the acquisitions, enabling assessment of enhancement characteristics in tissue and suspicious lesions [1]. Despite its diagnostic accuracy, DCE MRI has certain drawbacks when considered for specific diagnostic applications, especially in the context of breast cancer screening in healthy persons: GBCA administration is associated to direct and indirect costs [2], multi-time point DCE breast examinations commonly occupy significant scanner time [3, 4] and despite a contextual comparatively high safety profile, GBCA administration have been reported to be associated with certain side effects like allergic reactions and the "symptoms associated to gadolinium exposure" (SAGE) complex [5]. Additionally, the use of GBCAs contributes to environmental gadolinium pollution with GBCA contamination affecting surface waters [6–8].

Due to these factors, there's a growing interest in breast MRI approaches reducing GBCA administration in the screening context, yet providing visual characteristics of contrast-enhanced acquisitions by generating artificial contrast-enhanced images from non-enhanced acquisitions. Such methods were previously shown in breast studies [9–12], albeit deriving only one of the multiple time points considered in DCE breast MRI.

However, technically such methods might allow as well for generating images reflecting different time points of dynamic acquisitions by training distinct networks for each time points acquired over several minutes. This assumption is supported by several studies using different post-contrast acquisition intervals as training data. For example, in Chung et al. 90-s intervals [9], in Muller-Franzes et al. 60-s intervals [11], and in Kim et al. both 60 and 90 s [10] were used. These variations thus fuel and support the hypothesis of a principal possibility to predict post-contrast images across a series of time points in an individual patient. Furthermore, Zhang et al. [13] showed that besides synthesizing multiple different MRI sequences a feasibility to synthesize DCE in breast MRI is given. However, resulting in unsatisfying outputs as stated by the authors [13].

Our study therefore investigates neural networks' ability to predict contrast enhancement for creating virtual dynamic contrast-enhanced (vDCE) breast MRI at various time points. It assesses two methods: using five separate networks for each time point (single-channel output - SCO-Net) and another using a single network with five time points as output channels (multi-channel output - MCO-Net), with the latter potentially benefiting by learning the dependencies of cross-time point latency information within a single training step. Both approaches were quantitatively assessed across the entire breast and in segmentations of findings, including delineation comparisons between second time point DCE and vDCE images, akin to Chung et al.'s work [9].

2 Materials and Methods

2.1 Dataset, Imaging Sequences and Data Preprocessing

This IRB approved retrospective study includes n = 540 clinically indicated breast MRI examinations of female patients (mean age: 52 ± 12 years) acquired between 2017 and June 2020 at University Hospital Erlangen, Germany. Acquisitions were conducted on a single 3 T MRI scanner (MAGNETOM Skyra Fit, Siemens Healthineers, Erlangen, Germany) with a dedicated 18-Channel breast coil (Siemens Healthineers, Erlangen, Germany). The dataset was randomly split on patient level into training, validation and an independent test set with n = 377, n = 81, and n = 82 examinations, respectively.

Each examination included pre-contrast T1w, T2-weighted (T2w), multi-b-value (b-values: 0, 750 and 1500 s/mm2) diffusion weighted imaging (DWI) and T1w subtraction series after administration of GBCA (T1w-sub) at five consecutive time points. The acquisition of T1w-sub began 20 s after GBCA injection with each scan lasting 60 s. Detailed acquisition parameters are provided in Supplement Table 1.

The DICOM files were transformed to NIfTI format using dcm2niix tool [14], followed by preprocessing using in-house Python (version 3.9.10) scripts utilizing SimpleITK framework (version 2.2.1) including resampling, intensity normalization, intensity clamping and rescaling.

All images' field of view (FoV) was resampled to match the FoV of DWI acquisitions as well as common spatial dimensions with an in-plane matrix of 448x280 and n = 96 slices. Z-score normalization was applied individually on T1w, T2w and different DWI acquisitions. To maintain the intensity uptake over time in T1w-sub normalization was applied to the entire series. Intensities were clamped at boundaries of -1 and 15, to minimize outlier impact. Finally, T1w, T2w and the DWI acquisitions were scaled to a [0, 1] domain, while T1w-sub volumes were scaled to a [−1,1] domain.

Binary breast volume masks were calculated from T1w data using an in-house developed algorithm based on mean thresholding of multiple maximum intensity projections (MIP) in slice (z-) direction. Each *slice* of T1w data was processed into individual MIPs of adjacent slices (n_{slices}) to account for varying anatomical shapes, as defined in Eq. (1). MIPs were then binarized using mean thresholding followed by binary dilation with a 5-pixel diameter disk-shaped kernel and a binary closing operation to ensure homogeneous masks. The resulting masks were stored in NIfTI format with the same spacing, direction and origin of the T1w data. This algorithm was also previously described in Liebert et al. [15]. Supplement Fig. 1 shows an exemplary binary mask.

$$n_{slices}(slice) = \begin{cases} [0, 6] & \text{if } slice \leq 3 \\ [slice - 3, slice + 3] & \text{if } 3 < slice < 9 \\ [slice - 3, slice + 3] & \text{if } 87 < slice < 93 \\ [90, 96] & \text{if } slice \geq 93 \\ [slice - 8, slice + 8] & \text{otherwise} \end{cases} \quad (1)$$

2.2 Neural Network Architecture and Training

Two 2D U-net architectures, were implemented, both consisting of three encoder and three decoder stages with a bottleneck layer in-between. Detailed information of the composition of each layer is presented in Fig. 1.

In SCO-Net, five individual networks were trained each predicting a single time point of the DCE series. MCO-Net utilized a five-channel output representing the whole DCE time series. The networks were trained using native T1w, T2w and the multi-b-value DWI series as inputs and T1w-sub series as targets. Inspired by Chen et al.[16] the loss function was a combination of structural similarity index metric (SSIM)[17] and L1-norm as shown in the Eq. (2) below.

$$L(y_i, y_{i'}) = (1 - SSIM(y_i, y_{i'})) + L1(y_i, y_{i'}) \qquad (2)$$

Training utilized all slices of the datasets with ADAM optimizer and a batch size of 30 random slices. A dedicated workstation (Linux Ubuntu 20.04, AMD Ryzen Threadripper PRO 3945WX 3.4 Ghz, 64 GB RAM) with one Nvidia Quadro RTX 6000 GPU-card with 24 GB RAM was used. The networks were trained for 35 epochs without early stopping. Experiments were implemented using PyTorch (version 1.13.1), PyTorch-Lightning (version 1.8.6) and MONAI (version 0.8.0) frameworks.

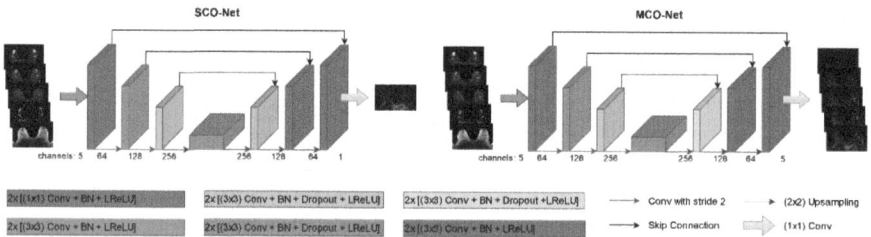

Fig. 1. Schematic overview of 2D-Unet Architectures. Left: Architecture for SCO-Net. Right: Architecture for MCO-Net. Both networks use 5 images as input channels. In SCO-Net, five individual networks were trained, each using a different time point of the DCE series as ground-truth. The MCO-Net uses each time point of the DCE series as a channel of the ground truth. Encoder stages consisted of two blocks of either a 1×1 or 3×3 convolution (Conv) layers followed by a batch normalization (BN) layer and a leaky rectified linear unit (LReLU) layer. Each decoder stage incorporates a concatenation with features of the encoder to represent the skip connections. The decoder stages on the 2nd and 1st level consisted of two 3×3 Conv layers followed by a BN layer and a LReLU layer. The deepest encoder and decoder stage and the bottleneck contain an additional dropout layer with a probability of 0.5. For encoder down-sampling, 2×2 Conv with a stride of 2 were used. Decoder up-sampling was performed using 2×2 transposed Conv with a stride of 2. After the final decoder stage, a 1×1 Conv was performed followed by a *tanh* operation in order to map the predictions to the expected output channels and [-1, 1] domain.

2.3 Performance Evaluation

The vDCE series were quantitatively evaluated on the holdout test set using the following metrics also used in previous literature: SSIM, peak signal-to-noise-ratio (PSNR), normalized root mean square error (NRMSE) and median symmetric accuracy (MEDSY-MAC) which addresses robust analysis of symmetric prediction errors [10, 12, 18, 19]. These metrics were calculated for both the whole image volume and separately for bounding boxes placed around segmented target findings as detailed below. Differences in mean values per time point and subject between the two network architecture approaches were evaluated using a two-way Repeated Measurements Anova, with the pingouin Python framework (version 0.5.3).

To assess the proposed techniques' effectiveness in depicting contrast uptake, segmentations were conducted on n = 48 subjects of the test set with findings that stood out against background tissue in the DCE acquisitions including 8 BI-RADS <= 2 cases (ranging from 5.0–31.4 mm) and 40 BI-RADS > 2 cases (ranging from 4.7–85.1 mm). Per patient, the largest appearing finding was volumetrically segmented in DCE and both vDCE methods at the second time point using 3D Slicer Software (version:4.11) [20] carried out by a medical student (>2 years' experience) under a single radiologist's (>10 years' experience) guidance. Segmentations were compared using following metrics: DICE score, Intersection over union (IoU), Hausdorff Distance (HD), and segmentation volume (segV). Additionally, the contrast-to-noise ratio (CNR) was evaluated using a bounding box with a one-pixel offset around segmentations. Statistical analysis was performed using a one-way Repeated Measures ANOVA with scipy (version 1.9.1) considering a p-value < 0.05 as significant.

3 Results

3.1 Neural Network Performance

Generated vDCE images were evaluated on similarity and error metrics for both SCO-Net and MCO-Net on the holdout test set. Mean values across all five time points are presented in Table 1. SCO-Net reached marginally higher values for SSIM and marginally lower values for PSNR in the image volume and mean NRMSE and MEDSYMAC values were lower or similar for MCO-Net. In the segmentations, MCO-Net showed higher similarity and lower error metrics compared to SCO-Net.

Table 1. Mean (±Std) similarity and error metrics of vDCE in image volume and segmentations of SCO-Net and MCO-Net.

	Image Volume		Segmentation	
	SCO-Net	MCO-Net	SCO-Net	MCO-Net
SSIM (↑)	0.864 ± 0.025	0.863 ± 0.026	0.591 ± 0.133	0.596 ± 0.131
PSNR [dB] (↑)	24.288 ± 2.379	24.424 ± 2.416	22.065 ± 3.448	22.204 ± 3.395
NRMSE (↓)	0.089 ± 0.015	0.087 ± 0.016	0.174 ± 0.049	0.173 ± 0.049
MEDSYMAC (↓)	0.020 ± 0.011	0.022 ± 0.012	0.106 ± 0.032	0.105 ± 0.032

Furthermore, similarity metric values separated per time point for each of the above-described setups are presented in Fig. 2. It can be noted that the later time points result in significantly higher SSIM values and lower PSNR. These trends are visible both in the image volume and segmentations. Error metric values per time point are present in Supplement Fig. 2, showing also better performance for later time points.

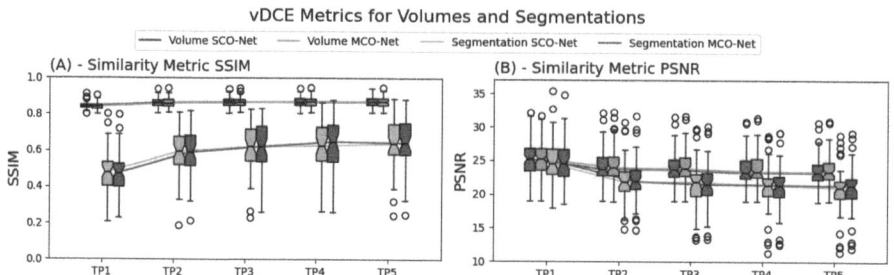

Fig. 2. Similarity metrics for vDCE SCO-Net and MCO-Net in image volume as well as segmented findings are presented. SSIM values show an increase and PSNR values a decrease for later time points both for the volume and segmentations.

The metrics in Table 1 and Fig. 2 indicate a generally worse performance inside segmentations compared to image volume. SSIM indicated no statistically significant ($p > 0.05$) differences between SCO-Net and MCO-Net in image volume. However, all other metrics showed significant effects ($p < 0.05$) between the two approaches. Significant differences ($p < 0.05$) were found for SSIM, PSNR, MEDYSMAC across different time points and approaches in image volume. NRMSE showed non-significant differences ($p > 0.05$) across different time points.

In Fig. 3 five consecutive time points of two representative cases of both vDCE approaches and of the original DCE series are shown. In both vDCE approaches the localization of the lesion is well correlating with the DCE images as well as the signal intensity uptake over time. An additional case with a false-positive prediction is presented in Supplement Fig. 3.

3.2 Evaluation of Ability to Depict Target Findings

Figure 4 displays a lesion with its corresponding segmentations performed on DCE as well as vDCE SCO-Net and MCO-Net. The lesion shapes and location appear similarly. However, this also shows how lesion depiction appears differently for the different approaches. Another segmentation case is presented in Supplement Fig. 4.

Table 2 shows the quantitative evaluation of segmentation correctness using SCO-Net and MCO-Net for vDCE generation. MCO-Net shows marginally higher mean DICE scores and IOU values and a lower HD. For the original DCE series a CNR = 2.483 ± 1.350 could be reached. This wasn't significantly different from the CNR values reached by both of the vDCE approaches. No significant changes ($p > 0.05$) were observed between SCO-Net and MCO-Net for any of the investigated segmentation metrics. Figure 5 shows the Bland-Altman plot for the segmented volume segV.

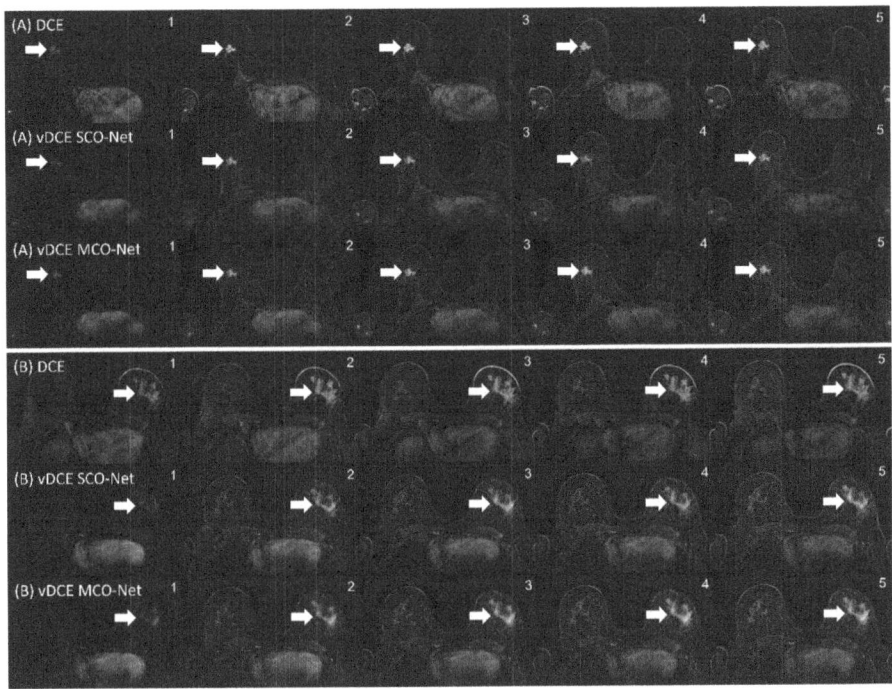

Fig. 3. (A) - Exemplary case of a 65-year-old patient with a histopathologically confirmed malignant lesion in the right breast. (B) - Exemplary case of a 60-year-old patient with a histopathologically confirmed non-mass enhancement in the left breast. For each case: Top: DCE series, Middle: vDCE SCO-Net, Bottom: vDCE MCO-Net. In each series the depiction of the lesions is visible with an increasing signal intensity over time. In (A), stronger lesion enhancement is observed in the DCE image when compared to the vDCE. The 4th time point of the vDCE SCO-Net shows weaker enhancement compared to both the vDCE MCO-Net and DCE series.

Fig. 4. Segmentation differences of a malignant lesion in DCE and the two vDCE approaches.

Table 2. Quantitative Mean (±Std) Segmentation Metrics

Metric	SCO-Net	MCO-Net
DICE Score (↑)	0.605 ± 0.210	0.610 ± 0.213
IoU (↑)	0.465 ± 0.211	0.471 ± 0.216
HD (↓)	9.454 ± 10.709	9.179 ± 10.650
CNR (↑)	2.103 ± 1.438	2.161 ± 1.525

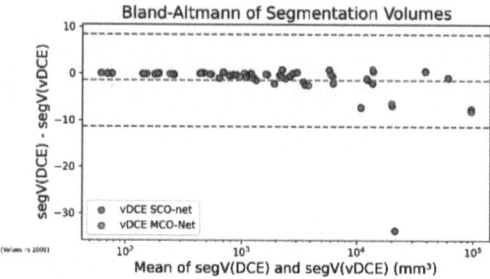

Fig. 5. Bland-Altmann plot compares findings' segV in the 2nd time point of the DCE and vDCE series. An increase in variation in larger segmentations for both vDCE approaches, not meeting the DCE segV observed similarly for SCO-Net and MCO-Net. Overall, there is a systematic bias of -1.49 for vDCE approaches indicating underestimation of finding sizes, although this bias diminishes for smaller segmentations. Outlier segmentation is shown in Supplement Fig. 4.

4 Discussion

This study evaluates the technical feasibility of generating a vDCE series for breast MRI comprising individual images for each time point post GBCA injection using two neural network approaches. One approach was trained on tissue characteristics at a specific time point, blinded to information of other time points (SCO-Net), while the other was trained to consider the entire dynamic cycle (MCO-Net), potentially benefiting from exploring cross-timepoint latency information. Both approaches depicted image characteristics similar to DCE images. MCO-Net showed a higher performance with significant differences across metrics except the SSIM compared to SCO-Net, in both image volume and segmented benign and malignant findings.

For SCO-Net, lowest SSIM scores and highest error metrics were observed for the 1st time point of the DCE series, gradually increasing towards the later time points. The SCO-Net trained for the 2nd DCE series time point, which correlates to an acquisition approx. 80 s after GBCA administration, reached a mean SSIM of 0.864 ± 0.025 aligning with prior studies by Chung et al. [9] and Kim et al. [10], both trained networks on contrast-enhanced breast MRI data acquired approx. During this timeframe. Mean SSIM scores across all time points (0.84–0.87) align with previously noted literature values of 0.76–0.91 [9, 10, 12, 13, 18], while PSNR scores 23.64–25.37 dB fall to lower end of previously noted literature ranges of 23.18–54.8 dB [10, 12, 13, 18]).

Despite minimal metric differences, a more homogenous tissue appearance over time points was observed when using MCO-Net (see Fig. 3). The MCO-Net approach aimed to incorporate contextual information of time dependency of contrast-enhancement during training. It utilizes the interdependent information of various post-contrast images and their time dependency of different tissue compartments in the breast. The MCO-Net achieved higher PSNR and lower error metrics compared to SCO-Net and non-significant differences in SSIM. The improvement in SSIM and error metrics over time might correlate with higher signal in later time points. Despite this higher signal, the increased noise level in tissue, decreased PSNR due to its sensitivity to noise.

Compared to Chung et al.'s study [9], our segmentations yielded a lower DICE coefficient between DCE and vDCE approaches. This might be attributed to including more challenging cases with all findings independent of malignancy or mass/non-mass enhancement type. Incorporating segmentations into the loss function, as demonstrated by Chen et al. [16], may enhance performance on finding-delineation and signal intensity representation. However, in this study, neither network approach significantly outperformed the other in regards of comparing manual segmentations.

Utilizing 2D Networks increased dataset size and reduced resources needed for training networks with high resolution images. Still, the images showed high inter-slice homogeneity in z-direction. Exploring 3D architectures for vDCE prediction might further improve capabilities of such technique by incorporating information of adjacent slices.

Our study has limitations, including the absence of a qualitative reader study to assess clinical applicability, evaluations on enhancement kinetics over time and a potential segmentation bias. Further clinical evaluations should be pursued in future research with larger cohorts. Additionally, the study's reliance on data from a single MRI scanner model limits the generalizability of our findings, emphasizing the need for research incorporating diverse equipment. Future work should also investigate which MRI sequences are required for vDCE generation, in analogue to investigation of Liebert et al. [21] to further explore dependency on acquisition techniques and generalizability.

5 Conclusion

In conclusion, providing a neural network information on tissue enhancement kinetics during training in form of additional input channels, like in MCO-Net approach, significantly improved metrics for generating a time-dependent series of vDCE breast MRI images from unenhanced acquisitions. Further research in this area might be justified based on these findings and should incorporate individual assessment of lesion specific enhancement characteristics as clinically relevant targets.

Acknowledgments. This project is funded by the Bavarian State Ministry of Science and Arts in the framework of the bidt Graduate Center for Postdocs. The work was performed in (partial) fulfillment of the requirements for obtaining the degree „Dr. Rer. Biol. Hum." at the Friedrich-Alexander-Universität Erlangen-Nürnberg (FAU).

Disclosure of Interests. Authors H.S., A.L., S.B. have pending patent EPO No. 21197259.1 on topic of this manuscript.

References

1. Mann, R.M., Cho, N., Moy, L.: Breast MRI: state of the art. Radiology **292**(3), 520–536 (2019). https://doi.org/10.1148/radiol.2019182947
2. Tollens, F., Baltzer, P.A., Dietzel, M., Rübenthaler, J., Froelich, M.F., Kaiser, C.G.: Cost-effectiveness of digital breast tomosynthesis vs. abbreviated breast MRI for screening women with intermediate risk of breast cancer—how low-cost must MRI be? Cancers **13**(6), 1241 (2021)

3. Kočo, L., Balkenende, L., Appelman, L., Moman, M.R., Sponsel, A., Schimanski, M., et al.: Optimized, person-centered workflow design for a high-throughput breast mri screening facility—a simulation study. Invest. Radiol. **10**, 1097 (2023)
4. Borthakur, A., Weinstein, S.P., Schnall, M.D., Conant, E.F.: Comparison of study activity times for "Full" versus "Fast MRI" for breast cancer screening. J. Am. Coll. Radiol. **16**(8), 1046–1051 (2019). https://doi.org/10.1016/j.jacr.2019.01.004
5. McDonald, R.J., Weinreb, J.C., Davenport, M.S.: Symptoms associated with gadolinium exposure (SAGE): a suggested term. Radiology **302**(2), 270–273 (2022). https://doi.org/10.1148/radiol.2021211349
6. Brünjes, R., Hofmann, T.: Anthropogenic gadolinium in freshwater and drinking water systems. Water Res. **182**, 115966 (2020). https://doi.org/10.1016/j.watres.2020.115966
7. Le Goff, S., Barrat, J.-A., Chauvaud, L., Paulet, Y.-M., Gueguen, B., Ben Salem, D.: Compound-specific recording of gadolinium pollution in coastal waters by great scallops. Sci. Rep. **9**(1), 8015 (2019)
8. Rogowska, J., Olkowska, E., Ratajczyk, W., Wolska, L.: Gadolinium as a new emerging contaminant of aquatic environments. Environ. Toxicol. Chem. **37**(6), 1523–1534 (2018). https://doi.org/10.1002/etc.4116
9. Chung, M., et al.: Deep learning to simulate contrast-enhanced breast MRI of invasive breast cancer. Radiology **306**(3), e213199 (2022). https://doi.org/10.1148/radiol.213199
10. Kim, E., Cho, H.-H., Kwon, J., Oh, Y.-T., Ko, E.S., Park, H.: Tumor-attentive segmentation-guided GAN for synthesizing breast contrast-enhanced MRI without contrast agents. IEEE J. Transl. Eng. Health Med. **11**, 32–43 (2022)
11. Müller-Franzes, G., et al.: Using machine learning to reduce the need for contrast agents in breast MRI through synthetic images. Radiology **307**(3), e222211 (2023). https://doi.org/10.1148/radiol.222211
12. Zhang, T., et al.: Synthesis of contrast-enhanced breast MRI using T1- and multi-b-value DWI-based hierarchical fusion network with attention mechanism. In: Greenspan, H., et al. (eds.) Medical Image Computing and Computer Assisted Intervention – MICCAI 2023, pp. 79–88. Springer, Cham (2023)
13. Zhang, T.Y., Tan, T., Han, L.Y., Wang, X., Gao, Y., van Dijk, J., et al.: IMPORTANT-Net: integrated MRI multi-parametric increment fusion generator with attention network for synthesizing absent data. Inf. Fusion **108**, 102381 (2024). https://doi.org/10.1016/j.inffus.2024.102381
14. Li, X., Morgan, P.S., Ashburner, J., Smith, J., Rorden, C.: The first step for neuroimaging data analysis: DICOM to NIfTI conversion. J. Neurosci. Methods **264**, 47–56 (2016). https://doi.org/10.1016/j.jneumeth.2016.03.001
15. Liebert, A., et al.: Feasibility to virtually generate T2 fat-saturated breast MRI by convolutional neural networks (2024)
16. Chen, C., Raymond, C., Speier, W., Jin, X., Cloughesy, T.F., Enzmann, D., et al.: Synthesizing MR image contrast enhancement using 3D high-resolution ConvNets. IEEE Trans. Biomed. Eng. (2022)
17. Wang, Z., Bovik, A.C., Sheikh, H.R., Simoncelli, E.P.: Image quality assessment: from error visibility to structural similarity. IEEE Trans. Image Process. **13**(4), 600–612 (2004)
18. Wang, P., Nie, P., Dang, Y., Wang, L., Zhu, K., Wang, H., et al.: Synthesizing the first phase of dynamic sequences of breast MRI for enhanced lesion identification. Front. Oncol. **11**, 792516 (2021). https://doi.org/10.3389/fonc.2021.792516
19. Morley, S.K., Brito, T.V., Welling, D.T.: Measures of model performance based on the log accuracy ratio. Space Weather- Int. J. Res. Appl. **16**(1), 69–88 (2018). https://doi.org/10.1002/2017sw001669

20. Fedorov, A., Beichel, R., Kalpathy-Cramer, J., Finet, J., Fillion-Robin, J.C., Pujol, S., et al.: 3D Slicer as an image computing platform for the Quantitative Imaging Network. Magn. Reson. Imaging **30**(9), 1323–1341 (2012). https://doi.org/10.1016/j.mri.2012.05.001
21. Liebert, A., et al.: Impact of non-contrast enhanced imaging input sequences on the generation of virtual contrast-enhanced breast MRI scans using neural networks. medRxiv 2024.2005.2003.24306067 (2024). https://doi.org/10.1101/2024.05.03.24306067

Optimizing BI-RADS 4 Lesion Assessment Using Lightweight Convolutional Neural Network with CBAM in Contrast Enhanced Mammography

Oladosu Oladimeji[1,2,3](✉)[iD], Hamail Ayaz[1,2,3][iD], Ian McLoughlin[4][iD], and Saritha Unnikrishnan[1,2,3][iD]

[1] Mathematical Modelling and Intelligent Systems for Health and Environment (MISHE), Faculty of Engineering and Design, Atlantic Technological University, Sligo, Ireland
{S00243011,hamail.ayaz,saritha.unnikrishnan}@atu.ie
[2] Health and Biomedical Strategic Research Centre, Atlantic Technological University, Sligo, Ireland
[3] Center for Precision Engineering, Materials and Manufacturing Research (PEM), Faculty of Engineering and Design, Atlantic Technological university, F91 YW50 Sligo, Ireland
[4] Department of Computer Science and Applied Physics, Atlantic Technological university, Galway, Ireland
ian.mcloughlin@atu.ie

Abstract. Breast cancer is the leading cause of cancer-related mortality and morbidity among women worldwide. Early detection plays a crucial role in improving survival rates and BI-RADS classification is one of the effective ways of predicting breast cancer. However, BI-RADS Category 4 encompasses a broad spectrum of malignancy probabilities, ranging from over 2% to 95%. Due to the wide malignancy likelihood range and the ambiguous qualitative attributes of BI-RADS 4, patients are subjected to overdiagnosis and unnecessary procedures, such as biopsy, which entail a certain degree of physical trauma as well as financial strain. This study proposed a lightweight CNN where MobileNet serves as the backbone architecture, augmented with the Convolutional Block Attention Module (CBAM), resulting in the MobileNet-CBAM model. The model demonstrated good performance in discriminating BI-RADS 4 category malignant and benign cases in Contrast Enhanced Spectral Mammogram (CESM) with a prediction of 82%, 82% and 0.91 for accuracy, f1-score and roc-auc respectively. Additionally, for clinical friendliness, the model explanation was given using SHAP. Hence, the model presents potential utility in predicting breast cancer for lesions categorized as BI-RADS category 4 in breast imaging.

Keywords: Breast cancer · Breast Imaging Reporting and Data System (BI-RADS) · MobileNet · CBAM (Convolution Block Attention Module) · Contrast Enhanced Spectral Mammogram · cancer screening

1 Introduction

Deep learning-based techniques have gained popularity recently and made significant advancements in tasks related to breast cancer diagnosis [2,25,26]. Hence, Deep Convolutional Neural Networks (DCNNs) have been instrumental in assisting radiologists and other practitioners with the classification of tumors as benign or malignant [19]. However, out of the seven Breast Imaging Reporting and Data System (BI-RADS) categories by the American College of Radiology (ACR) [12], the BI-RADS 4 category is often misdiagnosed. Due to the unclear qualitative attributes of the BI-RADS 4 category, the malignancy rate spans widely from 2% to 95% [17]. As a result, patients are subjected to overdiagnosis and unnecessary treatment or surgical procedures, such as biopsy to affirm the status of the malignancy in microscopic view [11], which entails a certain degree of physical trauma as well as financial strain [18,23].

Hence, few researchers have devised deep learning models utilising distinct imaging modalities and characteristics. Additionally, eXplainable AI frameworks were then used to explain the model and highlight the significant region in the medical image. Liu *et al.* [9] proposed a combined deep learning model that incorporates both full-field digital mammography and clinical variables to predict malignancy in BI-RADS 4 category lesions. The clinical variables were transformed into a 512-bit vector through a fully connected layer. This vector was then concatenated with the image (mammography) feature vectors extracted from the MobileNetV2 network for the prediction. The model had an AUC of 0.910, and a sensitivity and specificity of 0.853 and 0.919, respectively. Grad-CAM was then utilized to highlight important regions in the classification and provide explanations for the model. Mao *et al.* [13] utilized heavyweight networks including DenseNet-121, Xception, and ResNet-50 pre-trained architecture coupled with convolutional block attention module (CBAM) to classify breast lesions on Contrast Enhanced Spectral Mammography images (CESM). The CBAM-based Xception performed best among the three models for the BI-RADS 4 category with an AUC of 0.906 and an accuracy of 0.805. Thereafter, heatmaps were generated through Grad-CAM to highlight the most significant region in the image.

Despite these works, challenges still exist in classifying BI-RADS 4 category lesions as a result of the computational complexity of the heavyweight models or clinical information added to lightweight models which increases the number of parameters. Furthermore, Grad-CAM used for explainability is not effective enough to distinguish the tumor region. This is because Grad-CAM operates on a single convolutional layer at a time.

Similarly, this study focuses on BI-RADS 4 category due to its wide range of malignancy likelihood and ambiguous qualitative attributes, which typically lead to biopsy recommendation Additionally, this research uses CESM which is a novel breast imaging that integrates conventional mammography with the administration of contrast medium to offer enhanced information [10]. Summarily, the major contributions of this work are highlighted as follows:

- Unlike most of the existing works that combined clinical information with imaging features or used heavy-weight models, which increases the model complexity and can cause model instability, this study uses pre trained lightweight MobileNet to extract features.
- Attention Mechanisms were used to focus on tumor relevant features thereby reducing the irrelevant features, number of training parameters, and consuming less computational time.
- Extensive empirical experimentation was conducted to elucidate model predictions, utilizing the absolute SHAP difference between image and SHAP values. Hence, providing clinical friendliness and applicability.

2 Methodology

2.1 Dataset Description and Augmentation

The Categorized Digital Database for Low Energy and Subtracted Contrast Enhanced Spectral Mammography images (CDD-CESM) by [8] sourced from the Cancer Imaging Archive [5] was used for this study. The dataset entails six BI-RADS categories with 801, 331, 189, 319, 358 and 8 for categories one to six respectively. The BI-RADS category 4 of the dataset which entails 126 (92 malignant and 34 benign) subtracted images and 193 (153 malignant, 39 benign and a normal) low-energy images was utilized. This study uses both the subtracted and low-energy images and the normal case was used as benign summing up to 319 images that entail both the Mediolateral Oblique (MLO) and Craniocaudal (CC) views. CESM was chosen because it can serve as a sensitive diagnostic tool for detecting and staging breast cancer, offering higher specificity but lower sensitivity compared to contrast-enhanced breast MRI [21]. The images were resized to 224×224 and normalized with division by 255. Basic augmentation techniques were used to address the limited dataset challenge and address overfitting concerns during the training of the model. To increase the dataset, the benign instances were rotated at 180°, flipped horizontally and vertically, translated and a combination of rotation and translation. To balance the classes, the malignant instances were rotated at 180°. Rotation, flipping and translation commonly used in medical imaging were applied [4]. Figure 1 showcases instances of these augmentation techniques in the dataset. After applying these augmentation techniques, the malignant class was increased to 490 cases and the benign class to 444 cases, respectively.

2.2 MobileNet-CBAM

In this study, the MobileNet-CBAM entails MobileNet and CBAM as shown in Fig. 2., the MobileNet architecture [14] with pre-trained weights from ImageNet, was used to extract features from the CESM. To maintain the integrity of the weights in the convolutional and max-pooling layers and prevent their alteration, the decision was made to freeze them during the training process. The

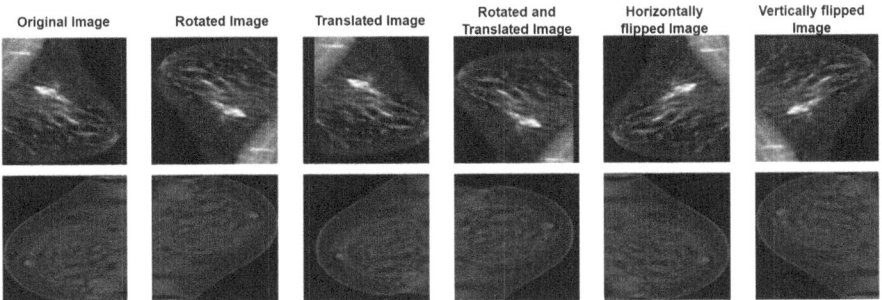

Fig. 1. The data augmentation technique visualization used in the dataset (where the first row is low-energy samples and the second row is the subtracted energy samples)

reason for the choice of MobileNet is that it is a lightweight model. Hence, it effectively addresses the challenges of training small datasets and mitigates the risk of overfitting. Its efficient design optimizes memory consumption and faster processing speed compared to other convolutional neural networks (CNNs), facilitating experimentation and parameter optimization [7] (Fig. 2).

The MobileNet layers including the Convolutional and global pooling layers were used to extract the features which was passed to the CBAM block. The attention mechanism focuses on discerning the crucial features within the input image [3]. By directing the convolutional neural network (CNN) to prioritize these vital features during training, computational resources are efficiently allocated, leading to enhanced model efficiency and accuracy. The CBAM (the dashed box in Fig. 2) which is a lightweight attention module developed by [20] was used in this study, it comprises two sub-modules: the Channel Attention Module (blue box in Fig. 3) and the Spatial Attention Module (green box in Fig. 3). These components compute attention weights for both channel and spatial dimensions, respectively [15]. As shown in Fig. 2, the channel attention module, the feature $\mathbf{F} \epsilon \mathbb{R}^{H \times W \times C}$, (Where C is the Channel, H is the height and W is the Width, F is the feature) obtained from the MobileNet is fed into both an average pooling layer and a maximum pooling layer. Subsequently, two shared dense layers are employed to process the input features unlike the conventional CBAM, ReLU activations were used to capture more complex channel relationships specifically non-linear interactions within the feature maps resulting in two processed channel features.

$$\mathbf{M}_{lp} = \sigma(\mathbf{W}_2 \cdot ReLU(\mathbf{W}_1 \cdot \mathbf{F}_{avg})) + \sigma(\mathbf{W}_2 \cdot ReLU(\mathbf{W}_1 \cdot \mathbf{F}_{max}))$$

where $\mathbf{W}$ is the weights of the dense layers. Following the element-wise addition of the average and maxpooled features, the Sigmoid activation function [22] is applied to acquire the weight $\mathbf{M}_c = \sigma(\mathbf{F}_{avg} + \mathbf{F}_{max})$, and the channel attention feature is derived by multiplying the weight with the initial input feature $\mathbf{F}_c = \mathbf{M}c \odot \mathbf{F}$. The channel feature ($\mathbf{F}_c$) is fed into the spatial attention module. The module operates on the feature using average pooling

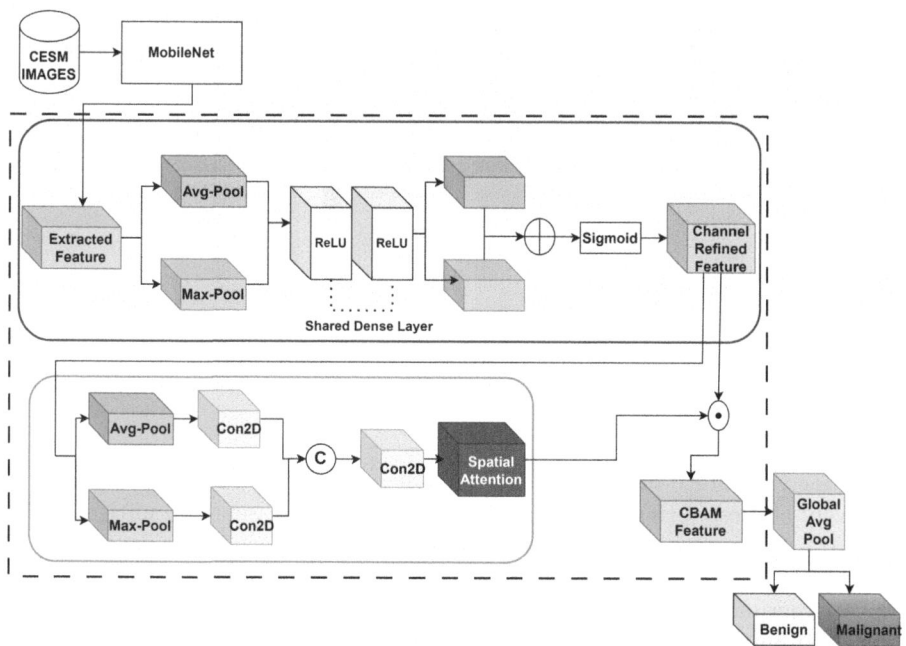

Fig. 2. The MobileNet-CBAM Architecture illustrating MobileNet for feature extraction, the integration of the Channel (in the blue box) and Spatial (in the green box) Attention Mechanisms.

$\mathbf{F}_{avg}^{spatial} = AvgPool(\mathbf{F}_c)$ and max pooling layers $\mathbf{F}_{max}^{spatial} = MaxPool(\mathbf{F}_c)$. In this study, a 1 × 1 convolutional layer with a ReLU activation was used for each pooling to produce single-channel feature maps

$$\mathbf{M}_{avg}^{spatial} = ReLU(\mathbf{W}_3 \cdot \mathbf{F}_{avg}^{spatial}), \mathbf{M}_{max}^{spatial} = ReLU(\mathbf{W}_3 \cdot \mathbf{F}_{max}^{spatial})$$

where $\mathbf{W}$ is the weights of the convolutional layer. These feature maps are then concatenated along the channel axis and activated using a ReLU function $\mathbf{F}_{concat} = ReLU(Concat[\mathbf{M}_{avg}^{spatial}, \mathbf{M}_{max}^{spatial}]$ unlike the originally proposed CBAM without ReLU, here ReLU is utilized in capturing non-linear relationships between the concatenated features, potentially improving the model's ability to distinguish between relevant and irrelevant spatial regions. A 1 × 1 convolutional layer with a sigmoid activation function is applied to the fused feature map to generate the spatial attention map $\mathbf{M}_s = \sigma(\mathbf{W} \cdot \mathbf{F}_{concat})$. The output of the CBAM module $\mathbf{F}_{out} = \mathbf{M}_s \odot \mathbf{F}_c$ is then subjected to global average pooling, which is then fed into a fully connected layer with Sigmoid activation, yielding the final output of the CBAM module.

2.3 Model Explainability

For the model explainability and clinical friendliness, SHapley Additive exPlanations (SHAP) were used to provide explainability for the model. A SHAP

Gradient Explainer was instantiated using the model and the background data. Hence, computing the SHAP values, to provide insight into the contribution and importance of each feature to the model's predictions. Thereafter, for comparison and visualization, the SHAP values were scaled to a range between 0 and 1. To highlight discrepancies between the model's interpretation and the actual image features, the absolute difference between the scaled SHAP values and the actual image values is computed. The absolute differences were visualized using a heatmap to highlight regions of high discrepancy between the SHAP values and the actual image. For comparison purpose, Gradient-weighted Class Activation Mapping (Grad-CAM) which was used in the existing state-of-the-art studies was also utilized for explainability. Hence, saliency maps were generated by applying Grad-CAM to the last convolutional layer of the network.

3 Experimental Results and Discussion

The algorithms utilized in this research were built upon Tensorflow 2.10.0 [16] and Keras 2.10.0, Python 3.9.16, and OpenCV, an open-source computer vision library. The computing environment is based on Windows 11 (64-bits) with Intel (R) Core(TM) I7-12850HX @ 2.10 GHz. The dataset was split into 80% training and 20% testing. The training and test set entails 747 and 187 images respectively. The model was trained using five-fold cross-validation on the training set and the remaining 20% was used for independent tests. For the experiment, an Adam optimizer with a batch size of 16 and binary cross-entropy loss function was used for the parameter. The model was made to train for 40 epochs for each fold.

This section gives the results of MobileNet-CBAM performance. The evaluation of the model was based on metrics such as accuracy, precision, recall, and Area under the ROC Curve (AUC). Figure 3 showcases the Receiver Operating Characteristic (ROC) curve, AUC of the training folds and the mean and standard deviation performance of the model.

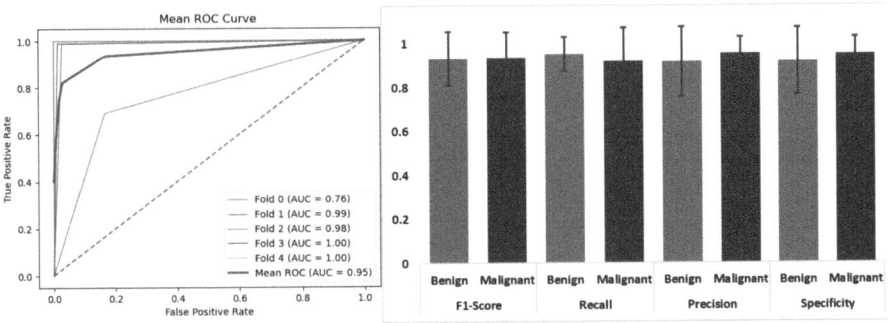

Fig. 3. The five folds training ROC Curve and Results of the MobileNet-CBAM Mean Performance.

The average performance of the model is promising and the error bars (standard deviation) are below 0.15 indicating the stability and reliability of the model. Based on the ROC curve, the true positive rate is zero when the false positive rate is zero. When the true positive rate exceeds 0.9 for the last four folds, the false positive rate reaches one. All the folds are above the diagonal line, indicating better-than-random performance.

3.1 Compared with Existing State-of-the-Art Methods

This section compares the efficacy of MobileNet-CBAM against other existing methods in terms of accuracy, AUC, F1-score, precision, recall and training time in minutes. The existing methods were developed, trained and tested on the same dataset. The results of the comparison based on the testset are showcased in Table 1.

Table 1. Comparison of classification results for lightweight models.

Architecture	Accuracy	Recall	Precision	F1-score	AUC	Time (Minutes)
DenseNet-201 [1]	0.5187	0.5187	0.7597	0.3907	0.7597	241.038
EfficientNetB7 [6]	0.7326	0.7326	0.8018	0.71966	0.9059	488.927
MobileNetV2 [9]	0.5187	0.5187	0.7597	0.3907	0.7597	106.727
Xception+CBAM [13]	0.7326	0.7326	0.7378	0.7322	0.8048	197.551
Proposed	**0.8235**	**0.8235**	**0.8248**	**0.8235**	**0.9149**	**72.347**

From Table 1 one can observe that results obtained from MobileNet-CBAM achieved superior performance compared to the existing state-of-the-art approaches including EfficientNetB7, MobileNetV2, DenseNet201 and Xception with the conventional CBAM in terms of the accuracy, precision, F1-score as well as the prediction time. MobileNet incorporates depth-wise separable convolutions to improve accuracy while maintaining efficiency by reducing the number of parameters and computational costs based on the depthwise convolutions. MobileNet-CBAM had a mean accuracy of 0.9439 and AUC of 0.9457 in the five-fold cross-validation. The experimental analysis on a separate test-set validates the performance of the MobileNet-CBAM. Figure showcases the ROC-AUC of the five-fold cross-validation of CBAM as well as the confusion matrix for the independent testset. Additionally, the training time for Mobile-CBAM is lower compared to the existing state-of-the-art approaches as they require more time for training due to their larger size and complexity, while they all have comparable testing times.

3.2 Model Interpretability

To highlight discrepancies between the model's interpretation and the actual image features, the absolute difference between the SHAP values and the actual image is computed. Fig 4 shows the input image with the given annotations (A), Grad-CAM (B), SHAP value visualization (C) and the absolute difference between SHAP XAI and input image (D). However, as shown in B and C, it is challenging to explain the model. Hence, the absolute difference was calculated. Based on the results of the absolute difference, the relevant tumor regions are highlighted in blue and pink while the background is in orange and other breast regions are green and yellow. For the Grad-CAM, red and yellow regions indicate areas with higher predictive significance compared to the green and blue regions. The absolute difference visualization was consistent with the lesion regions based on the annotations provided as it is able to identify the tumor homogeneity and heterogeneity. The visualizations indicate that SHAP absolute difference provided better visualization compared to Grad-CAM used in the previous works as Grad-CAM relies on the last convolutional layer while SHAP rely on the entire model layers. Therefore, providing better explainability.

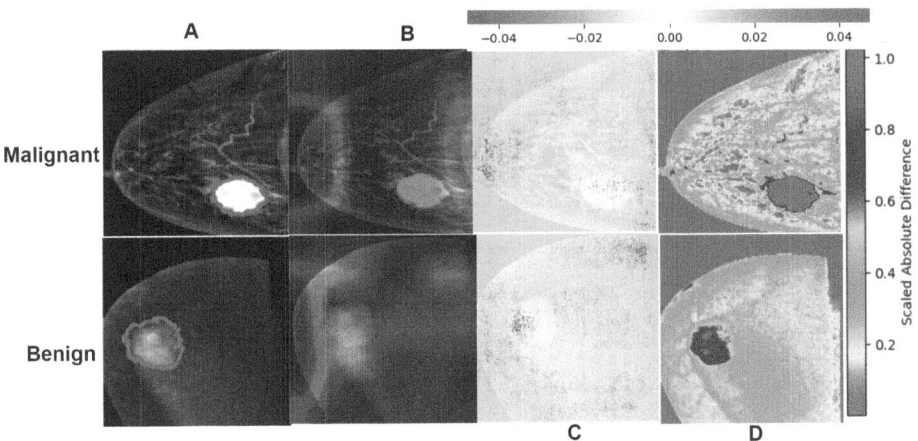

Fig. 4. The result of the Model Explainability including the annotation provided for the dataset (A), Grad-CAM (B), SHAP Value (C) and Absolute Difference (D). (Color figure online)

This study focuses on malignancy classification in BI-RADS 4 CESM using MobileNet-CBAM. In clinical practice, patients with BI-RADS 4 category still require a biopsy to determine the malignancy which comes with several risks [24]. This study aims to reduce unnecessary biopsies without compromising diagnostic accuracy. In the clinical context, the results suggest that integrating the MobileNet-CBAM model into real-world settings could result in more accurate and timely diagnoses of BI-RADS 4 breast cancer. The experimental results indicate that the approach outperforms the existing state-of-the-art approaches including large-scale CNN DenseNet-201 [1], lightweight CNNs including EfficientNetB7 [6] and MobileNetV2 [9] and attention-based CNN Xception+CBAM [13] this further proves the superiority of the model. Despite the substantial number of parameters of backbone models, it is overfitting due to the size of the dataset. The dataset is not large enough to justify its complexity. Additionally, the model is more generalizable as it has been trained on both CC and MLO views. This study demonstrated that the attention mechanisms of the model enable the model to selectively emphasize pertinent features while suppressing noise, thus contributing to its exceptional performance as well as reducing the training time. It would be interesting in future research to explore the combination of radiomic features with the imaging features to have a more robust model; as radiologists often utilize morphological characteristics like size, volume, and contour to evaluate breast lesions and make diagnoses [24]. One of the limitations of this study is the limited dataset, as CESM is a relatively new technology [13]; future research would evaluate the model on large data size.

4 Conclusions

Despite advancements in experience and technology, the subjective nature of BI-RADS category 4 remains a concern. Hence, this study proposed and developed a model for automatic BI-RADS category 4 malignancy prediction in CESM images. The MobileNet-CBAM model demonstrated an accuracy and AUC of 82% and 91% respectively. For clinical friendliness, the model explanation was given using SHAP. The model has the potential to assist, improve the efficiency and reduce the workloads of radiologists in diagnosing breast cancer. In future work, the model would be evaluated on a larger dataset to enhance the generalizability.

Acknowledgments. This research is funded by the Modelling & Computation for Health And Society (MOCHAS) Postgraduate Research Training Programme (PRTP) Scholarship, Atlantic Technological University, Ireland .

Disclosure of Interests. The authors have no competing interests to declare that are relevant to the content of this article.

References

1. Achak, A., Hedyehzadeh, M.: Determining the differentiation of benign and malignant nme lesions in contrast-enhanced spectral mammography images based on convolutional neural networks. J. Med. Biol. Eng. **43**(5), 585–595 (2023)
2. Boumaraf, S., Liu, X., Ferkous, C., Ma, X.: A new computer-aided diagnosis system with modified genetic feature selection for bi-rads classification of breast masses in mammograms. Biomed. Res. Int. **2020**(1), 7695207 (2020)
3. Chen, L., Yao, H., Fu, J., Ng, C.T.: The classification and localization of crack using lightweight convolutional neural network with cbam. Eng. Struct. **275**, 115291 (2023)
4. Chlap, P., Min, H., Vandenberg, N., Dowling, J., Holloway, L., Haworth, A.: A review of medical image data augmentation techniques for deep learning applications. J. Med. Imaging Radiat. Oncol. **65**(5), 545–563 (2021)

5. Clark, K., et al.: The cancer imaging archive (tcia): maintaining and operating a public information repository. J. Digit. Imaging **26**, 1045–1057 (2013)
6. Helal, M., et al.: Validation of artificial intelligence contrast mammography in diagnosis of breast cancer: Relationship to histopathological results. Eur. J. Radiol. 111392 (2024)
7. Kaya, Y., Gürsoy, E.: A mobilenet-based cnn model with a novel fine-tuning mechanism for covid-19 infection detection. Soft. Comput. **27**(9), 5521–5535 (2023)
8. Khaled, R., et al.: Categorized contrast enhanced mammography dataset for diagnostic and artificial intelligence research. Sci. Data **9**(1), 122 (2022)
9. Liu, H., et al.: A deep learning model integrating mammography and clinical factors facilitates the malignancy prediction of bi-rads 4 microcalcifications in breast cancer screening. Eur. Radiol. **31**, 5902–5912 (2021)
10. Long, R., et al.: Improving the diagnostic accuracy of breast bi-rads 4 microcalcification-only lesions using contrast-enhanced mammography. Clin. Breast Cancer **21**(3), 256–262 (2021)
11. Luo, L., et al.: Deep learning in breast cancer imaging: a decade of progress and future directions. IEEE Rev. Biomed. Eng. (2024)
12. Magny, S.J., Shikhman, R., Keppke, A.L.: Breast Imaging Reporting and Data System. In: StatPearls [Internet]. StatPearls publishing (2022)
13. Mao, N., et al.: Attention-based deep learning for breast lesions classification on contrast enhanced spectral mammography: a multicentre study. Br. J. Cancer **128**(5), 793–804 (2023)
14. Nan, Y., Ju, J., Hua, Q., Zhang, H., Wang, B.: A-mobilenet: an approach of facial expression recognition. Alex. Eng. J. **61**(6), 4435–4444 (2022)
15. Oladimeji, O.O., Ibitoye, A.O.J.: Brain tumor classification using resnet50-convolutional block attention module. Appl. Comput. Inf. (ahead-of-print) (2023)
16. Pang, B., Nijkamp, E., Wu, Y.N.: Deep learning with tensorflow: a review. J. Educ. Behav. Stat. **45**(2), 227–248 (2020)
17. Spak, D.A., Plaxco, J., Santiago, L., Dryden, M., Dogan, B.: Bi-rads® fifth edition: a summary of changes. Diagn. Interv. Imaging **98**(3), 179–190 (2017)
18. Tang, Y., Liang, M., Tao, L., Deng, M., Li, T.: Machine learning-based diagnostic evaluation of shear-wave elastography in bi-rads category 4 breast cancer screening: a multicenter, retrospective study. Quant. Imaging Med. Surg. **12**(2), 1223 (2022)
19. Wang, J., et al.: Information bottleneck-based interpretable multitask network for breast cancer classification and segmentation. Med. Image Anal. **83**, 102687 (2023)
20. Woo, S., Park, J., Lee, J.Y., Kweon, I.S.: Cbam: convolutional block attention module. In: Proceedings of the European Conference on Computer Vision (ECCV), pp. 3–19 (2018)
21. Yasin, R., El Ghany, E.A.: Birads 4 breast lesions: comparison of contrast-enhanced spectral mammography and contrast-enhanced mri. Egypt. J. Radiol. Nucl. Med. **50**, 1–10 (2019)
22. Yin, X., Goudriaan, J., Lantinga, E.A., Vos, J., Spiertz, H.J.: A flexible sigmoid function of determinate growth. Ann. Bot. **91**(3), 361–371 (2003)
23. Zhang, R., et al.: An MRI-based radiomics model for predicting the benignity and malignancy of bi-rads 4 breast lesions. Front. Oncol. **11**, 733260 (2022)
24. Zhang, S., et al.: Intra-and peritumoral radiomics for predicting malignant birads category 4 breast lesions on contrast-enhanced spectral mammography: a multi-center study. Eur. Radiol. **33**(8), 5411–5422 (2023)
25. Zhang, T., Mann, R.M.: Contrast-enhanced mammography: better with AI? Eur. Radiol. **34**(2), 914–916 (2024)

26. Zhang, T., et al.: Radiomics and artificial intelligence in breast imaging: a survey. Artif. Intell. Rev. **56**(Suppl 1), 857–892 (2023)

Mammographic Breast Positioning Assessment via Deep Learning

Toygar Tanyel[1]($\boxtimes$), Nurper Denizoglu[2], Mustafa Ege Seker[3], Deniz Alis[4], Esma Cerekci[5], Ercan Karaarslan[4], Erkin Aribal[4], and Ilkay Oksuz[6]

[1] Biomedical Engineering Graduate Program, Istanbul Technical University, Istanbul, Turkey
tanyel23@itu.edu.tr
[2] Department of Radiology, Acibadem Healthcare Group, Istanbul, Turkey
[3] Department of Radiology, University of Wisconsin-Madison, Madison, WI, USA
[4] Department of Radiology, School of Medicine, Acibadem University, Istanbul, Turkey
[5] Sisli Hamidiye Etfal Training and Research Hospital, Istanbul, Turkey
[6] Department of Computer Engineering, Istanbul Technical University, Istanbul, Turkey

Abstract. Breast cancer remains a leading cause of cancer-related deaths among women worldwide, with mammography screening as the most effective method for the early detection. Ensuring proper positioning in mammography is critical, as poor positioning can lead to diagnostic errors, increased patient stress, and higher costs due to recalls. Despite advancements in deep learning (DL) for breast cancer diagnostics, limited focus has been given to evaluating mammography positioning. This paper introduces a novel DL methodology to quantitatively assess mammogram positioning quality, specifically in mediolateral oblique (MLO) views using attention and coordinate convolution modules. Our method identifies key anatomical landmarks, such as the nipple and pectoralis muscle, and automatically draws a posterior nipple line (PNL), offering robust and inherently explainable alternative to well-known classification and regression-based approaches. We compare the performance of proposed methodology with various regression and classification-based models. The CoordAtt UNet model achieved the highest accuracy of 88.63% ± 2.84 and specificity of 90.25% ± 4.04, along with a noteworthy sensitivity of 86.04% ± 3.41. In landmark detection, the same model also recorded the lowest mean errors in key anatomical points and the smallest angular error of 2.42°. Our results indicate that models incorporating attention mechanisms and CoordConv module increase the accuracy in classifying breast positioning quality and detecting anatomical landmarks. Furthermore, we make the labels and source codes available to the community to initiate an open research area for mammography, accessible at https://github.com/tanyelai/deep-breast-positioning.

Keywords: Breast cancer · Mammography · Deep learning · Positioning assessment

1 Introduction

Breast cancer remains the most common cancer and leading cause of cancer-related deaths among women globally [3]. Mammography screening is the most effective method for early detection, significantly reducing mortality rates [12]. Thus, many countries have adopted national screening programs [4].

A standard mammogram includes craniocaudal (CC) and mediolateral oblique (MLO) views, with the MLO view being crucial as it captures nearly the entire breast tissue, especially the upper quadrant where cancer frequently occurs. Proper positioning in mammography is vital, as poor positioning can lead to diagnostic errors and necessitate repeat exams, increasing costs and causing stress for patients [5,9,11,17]. There is a pressing need for automated systems that can instantly evaluate the quality of mammogram positioning, allowing technologists to take immediate corrective action if necessary.

Recent advancements in deep learning (DL) have shown promising results in breast cancer diagnostics, often matching or surpassing radiologists in accuracy [7,14]. However, less focus has been given to using DL for assessing mammography positioning. This gap presents an opportunity to improve the evaluation process right after image acquisition. Traditionally, studies have relied on classification-based DL approaches involving qualitative expert assessments [2,18] or by dividing related tasks into separate regression processes [8], which can introduce additional complexity and affect the explainability and objectivity of the results.

Our work introduces a novel deep learning methodology that quantitatively evaluates image positioning quality in MLO views. By identifying key anatomical features such as the nipple and pectoralis muscle, and automatically drawing a perpendicular posterior nipple line (PNL) to the pectoralis muscle or film edge, our methodology provides a robust and superior alternative to traditional classification-based approaches. We demonstrate the effectiveness of our method on existing models, showcasing its potential to enhance mammography positioning assessments.

2 Materials

In this section we provide information on the dataset and the ground truth criteria for correct MLO positioning.

2.1 Study Sample

We used the VinDr Mammography dataset [13], an open-access collection of 5000 exams from two hospitals in Vietnam (2018–2020). From this, we selected 1000 exams, each with two MLO view mammograms from both breasts, totaling 2000 images. Exams were split into training, validation, and testing sets with an 80%/10%/10% split, ensuring a balanced representation of clinical outcomes. According to the PNL criteria, MLO-view positioning in the datasets was classified as 967 good and 633 poor for training, 108 good and 92 poor for validation, and 123 good and 77 poor for testing.

2.2 Image Positioning Quality Criterion

Several international systems assess the quality of mammography images in MLO views based on criteria like the angle, width, and length of the pectoral muscle, its border angulation, and the distance between the pectoral muscle and the nipple. The primary goal is to ensure maximum breast tissue coverage. Some criteria, such as the distance from the pectoral muscle to the nipple, are subjective and impractical [16]. The angle and dimensions of the pectoral muscle lack universal standards. A consistent criterion is that the PNL, drawn from the nipple to the pectoralis muscle at a right angle, intersects the pectoralis muscle. This method is endorsed by the American College of Radiology and the Royal Australian and New Zealand College of Radiologists [1,10,15,16,19] and is adopted as our study's reference standard.

2.3 Ground Truthing Process

Ground truth annotations were performed by a board-certified breast radiologist (N.D.) with over five years of experience in breast imaging. The radiologist used a specialized workstation, featuring a browser-based annotation tool (https://matrix.md.ai) and a 6-megapixel diagnostic monitor (Radiforce RX 660, EIZO), to annotate mammograms. All mammograms were examined in the Digital Imaging and Communications in Medicine (DICOM) format. The radiologist marked the nipple and pectoralis muscle line on MLO views.

3 Methods

In this section we provide details of our pre-processing operation, loss function, model architecture and experimental setup.

3.1 Pre-processing Steps

The pre-processing steps for mammography images are designed to prepare the data for analysis while preserving anatomical features and spatial relationships. Initially, the midpoint of the nipple bounding boxes and the endpoints of the pectoralis muscle are extracted, yielding three critical landmarks for orientation and scale adjustments. Next, the endpoints of the pectoralis muscle are standardized by extending each line to the image boundary with a 10-pixel margin to minimize variability from radiologists' arbitrary line terminations. Significant breast regions are then isolated by removing extensive black pixel areas around the periphery and below the breast. This involves thresholding the image to create a binary version, applying morphological opening, labeling connected regions, and cropping the image to the bounding box of the largest region. Zero-padding is applied to make the images square, preventing distortion during resizing and maintaining uniformity across the dataset. Subsequently, all images are resized to 512×512 pixels to facilitate computational efficiency and model training while preserving necessary detail.

3.2 Landmark-Aware Wing Loss

Landmark-Aware Wing Loss is tailored to improve the model's accuracy in predicting landmark coordinates. It employs a piecewise function that combines the Wing Loss's sensitivity to small errors with a linear part to moderate the response to larger errors. The Wing Loss [6] formula is given by:

$$\mathcal{L}_{Wing}(y) = \begin{cases} w \cdot \log(1 + \frac{|y|}{\epsilon}), & \text{if } |y| < w \\ |y| - C, & \text{otherwise} \end{cases} \quad (1)$$

where y represents the absolute error between the predicted and target coordinates, w is the parameter that defines the width of the non-linear region, ϵ controls the curvature within this region, and C is a continuity constant, defined as $C = w - w \cdot \log(1 + \frac{w}{\epsilon})$.

Practically, the $\mathcal{L}_{LAW}(y)$ is calculated for each coordinate of the landmarks, leading to a comprehensive loss for each landmark by summing up the mean losses of the coordinates, i.e., mean of x and y, expressed as:

$$\mathcal{L}_{LAW} = \alpha \cdot \mathcal{L}_{Wing(L1)} + \beta \cdot \mathcal{L}_{Wing(L2)} + \gamma \cdot \mathcal{L}_{Wing(L3)} \quad (2)$$

where α, β, and γ are the weights for the landmarks.

3.3 Model Architectures and Techniques for Landmark Detection

We used U-Net as the backbone with coordinate convolution module (CoordConv) and attention mechanisms for landmark detection (Fig. 1). CoordConv and attention refine feature maps, improving spatial information. We also used ResNeXt50 as the backbone for landmark regression, adjusting it for single-channel input and comparing its classification and regression results. This section details these components and the landmark regression process.

CoordConv Integration. To improve spatial awareness, we replaced the initial convolutional layer with a CoordConv layer, integrating spatial coordinates into the convolution operation. CoordConv augments the input by adding normalized spatial coordinates across height (H) and width (W), improving the model's ability to learn spatial hierarchies:

$$\mathcal{CC}(I) = \mathcal{R}\left(\mathcal{B}\left(\mathcal{C}\left(\mathcal{A}(I, \{x, y\})\right)\right)\right),$$

where $\mathcal{A}(I, \{x, y\})$ adds coordinate channels to input tensor I. The x-coordinates $\{x\}$ and y-coordinates $\{y\}$ are normalized in the range $[0, 1]$, calculated as:

$$x_j = \frac{j}{W-1}, \quad y_i = \frac{i}{H-1},$$

for each pixel (i, j) in the feature map. These coordinates are repeated across the batch size and stacked to form two new channels appended to I.

$\mathcal{C}$ performs convolution with these channels, and $\mathcal{B}$ and $\mathcal{R}$ represent batch normalization and ReLU activation.

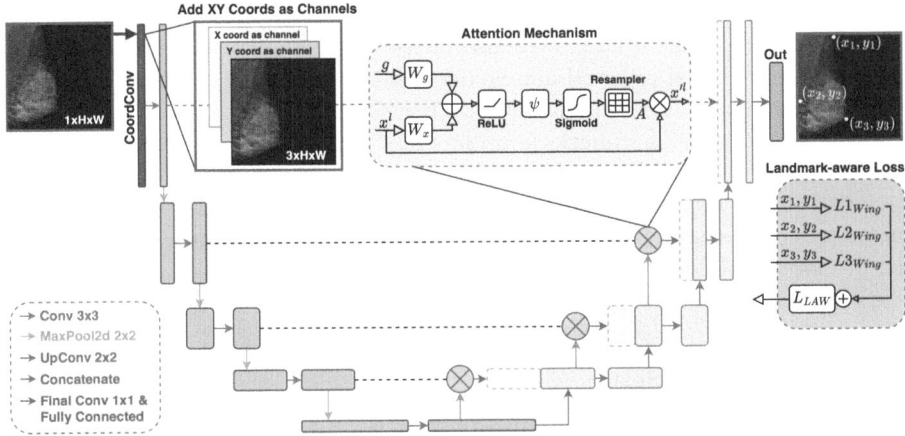

Fig. 1. Illustration of concepts utilized in this study as part of an ablation study. At the input layer, a single-channel grayscale mammogram is augmented to a three-channel image by introducing two additional channels that encode the X and Y spatial coordinates of each pixel. The attention mechanism refines features, and skip connections preserve spatial information. The final layer outputs landmark coordinates, optimized using landmark-aware wing loss.

Attention Mechanism. Attention mechanisms in the U-Net model selectively focus on important features. The attention block integrates features from both encoder and decoder paths by computing attention coefficients (ψ) using the following formulations: $g = W_{\text{gate}} * G$ and $x = W_x * X$. Here, W_{gate} and W_x are convolutional filters, with G representing the gating signal from the decoder and X the feature map from the encoder. The attention coefficients ψ are computed as $\psi = \sigma(\text{ReLU}(g + x))$, where σ denotes the sigmoid activation. The attended output A is then calculated as $A = X \cdot \psi$. This mechanism ensures that only the most relevant features are propagated through the network to improve the precision of the output.

ResNeXt50. We used ResNeXt50, a 50-layer deep residual network with a cardinality of 32, featuring grouped convolutions for enhanced feature learning. For landmark regression, we modified ResNeXt50 to accept single-channel input and output the required landmark coordinates. Additionally, we used the raw classification model to compare image-level classification with regression results, evaluating differences in accuracy and robustness, and demonstrating the model's versatility and effectiveness.

3.4 Evaluation

The evaluation checks our model's accuracy in predicting the nipple and endpoints of the pectoral muscle line. We verify if the perpendicular intersection from the nipple to the pectoral muscle (i.e., PNL) falls within the image boundaries to indicate image quality. We also measure the angular error between the original and predicted pectoral muscle lines. Additionally, we compute accuracy, sensitivity, and specificity for the model's decisions. Euclidean distance between predicted and original landmarks in millimeters is calculated, ensuring real-world measurement accuracy. The angle error is normalized to 0-180° to represent the deviation from vertical. Performance metrics are based on image quality classification, with accuracy as the proportion of correct predictions, sensitivity as the proportion of correctly identified bad quality images, and specificity as the proportion of correctly identified good quality images.

3.5 Experimental Setup

Regression. We employed the R-ResNeXt50, UNet, Attention UNet, and CoordAtt UNet models, each configured with a single input channel and six output channels corresponding to the x, y coordinates of three landmarks. Training was conducted on an NVIDIA L4 GPU for 300 epochs. The Adam optimizer was used with an initial learning rate of 1×10^{-4}, dynamically adjusted by a CyclicLR scheduler oscillating between 1×10^{-5} and 5×10^{-4} using a triangular policy without cycle momentum. The loss function integrated Wing Loss ($w = 3$, $\epsilon = 1.5$) and additional parameters ($\alpha = 1.0$, $\beta = 1.0$, $\gamma = 1.0$) to capture both precision and geometric intricacies in landmark detection. The model with the lowest validation loss was preserved for subsequent evaluation. As an exception, the R-ResNeXt50 model was initially fine-tuned with pretrained ImageNet weights using a batch size of 8 for 150 epochs.

Classification. For classification, we utilized a ResNeXt50 model to classify images into two positioning quality classes. Training was conducted on an NVIDIA L4 GPU with a batch size of 8 for 30 epochs, fine-tuning the model with pretrained ImageNet weights. The same optimizer and learning rate progression as in the regression setup were applied. Categorical Cross-Entropy Loss was used for loss calculations. The best-performing model, determined by a range of metrics, was preserved for subsequent evaluation.

4 Results

In this section, we provide results on landmark detection and binary image quality assessment.

Models' Performance on Landmark Detection
Table 1 details models' performance on landmark detection, focusing on distance errors. Direct landmark regression with ResNeXt50 (R-ResNeXt50) and vanilla UNet regression (UNet) showed higher errors for pectoral and nipple landmark detection. Attention UNet considerably improved performance both in terms of median errors, and an angular errors. CoordAtt UNet outperformed others

Table 1. Distance errors in millimeters (mm), presented as mean (μ), standard deviation (σ) and median ($x \sim$) to mitigate the influence of challenging cases (primarily due to subjectivity of the task). Perp: Perpendicular intersection error for the line drawn from the nipple to the pectoral line. Pec1: Lower endpoint of the pectoral muscle line error. Pec2: Upper endpoint of the pectoral muscle line error. Nipple: Nipple location error. Angular: Angular difference between the predicted and original pectoral muscle line.

Models	Perp			Pec1			Pec2			Nipple			Angular		
	μ	σ	$x \sim$	μ	σ	$x \sim$	μ	σ	$x \sim$	μ	σ	$x \sim$	μ	σ	$x \sim$
R-ResNeXt50	7.13	4.23	6.49	7.33	6.01	5.24	7.93	7	6.2	4.63	1.99	4.45	2.71	2.44	1.96
UNet	9.62	7.86	8.03	8.19	6.89	6.01	14.01	14.01	10.9	6.8	5.25	5.72	3.52	3.15	2.66
Attention UNet	5.12	5.04	**3.56**	6.01	5.87	**4.03**	6.94	8.25	**3.95**	2.98	2.4	2.52	2.58	2.73	1.81
CoordAtt UNet	**4.99**	4.88	3.82	**5.62**	5.29	4.14	**6.49**	7.37	4.26	**2.97**	2.46	**2.45**	**2.42**	2.56	**1.75**

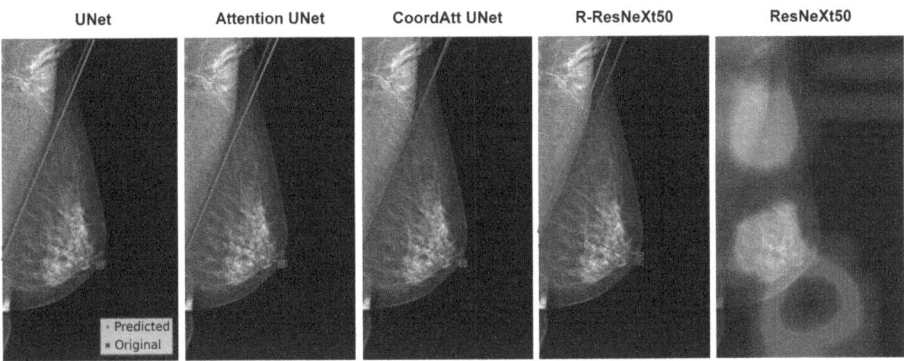

Fig. 2. Comparison of predicted (red) versus original (blue) landmarks in mammograms using different models: UNet, Attention UNet, CoordAtt UNet, R-ResNeXt50, and ResNeXt50. The rightmost column shows heatmaps for ResNeXt50. (Color figure online)

with mean errors of 4.99 mm (Perp), 5.62 mm (Pec1), 6.49 mm (Pec2), 2.97 mm (nipple), and the smallest angular error of 2.42°.

Models' Performance on Breast Positioning Labels

The models' performance on breast positioning labels is summarized in Table 2. The raw ResNeXt50 model used for binary classification without landmark regression achieved the lowest performance measures. Addition of landmark regression and rule-based binary classification (R-ResNeXt50), improved the performance dramatically. Vanilla UNet regression of the landmark points showed poor performance, where Attention block addition (Attention UNet) outperformed previous models. Addition of coordinate points (CoordAtt UNet) achieved comparable performance to Attention UNet showcasing superior performance in accuracy and specificity.

Table 2. Test results on automatically generated quality labels extracted from radiologists' label drawings. The raw ResNeXt50 model was trained for binary classification based on image-level labels. The R-ResNeXt50 model had its last layer modified to function as a landmark regressor, predicting coordinates and overall positioning quality, similar to our proposed pipeline. Results are presented as the mean ± standard deviation of 5 different training runs.

Model	Accuracy	Specificity	Sensitivity
ResNeXt50	73.7 ± 3.35	76.91 ± 6.26	68.57 ± 11.41
R-ResNeXt50	82.3 ± 5.03	81.42 ± 12.34	83.38 ± 10.49
UNet	70.63 ± 1.49	78.46 ± 1.56	58.12 ± 2.68
Attention UNet	88.2 ± 2.51	88.62 ± 4.11	**87.53 ± 3.51**
CoordAtt UNet	**88.63 ± 2.84**	**90.25 ± 4.04**	86.04 ± 3.41

5 Discussion

In this study, we presented a novel deep learning methodology for assessing the quality of mammogram positioning, focusing on the MLO views. Our method quantitatively evaluates image positioning by identifying key anatomical features and drawing a perpendicular PNL, providing a robust alternative to traditional classification-based approaches. The evaluation of various deep learning models, including ResNeXt50, UNet, Attention UNet, and CoordAtt UNet, demonstrated considerable improvements in accuracy, specificity, and sensitivity. Notably, the CoordAtt UNet model achieved the highest performance, highlighting the effectiveness of incorporating attention mechanisms and CoordConv module (Fig. 2). This study addresses a critical unmet need in mammography screening, offering an automated, objective, and explainable solution for assessing breast positioning quality, which is crucial for accurate breast cancer diagnosis.

Despite the promising results, several limitations must be acknowledged. Our study focused exclusively on MLO views, which, while comprehensive, do not cover all diagnostic perspectives. Future work will extend the model to include CC views to provide a more holistic evaluation of mammogram positioning. Additionally, our primary criterion for evaluating positioning quality was the PNL. While robust for MLO views, the models' effectiveness might be limited when considering other criteria, such as the angle and shape of the pectoral muscle. Future studies will aim to incorporate these additional criteria to improve the models' versatility. The clinical impact of this research is significant, as it paves the way for more reliable and efficient mammography screening, ultimately improving early breast cancer detection and patient outcomes.

Acknowledgments. This study has been supported by the TUBITAK 1501 Industrial R&D Projects Support Program (Project No: 3230942). Additionally, partial support was provided by the Health Institutes of Turkiye (TUSEB) under the 2022-EKG-01 Program (Project No: 20101).

Disclosure of Interests. Deniz Alis is the CEO and co-founder of Hevi AI Health Tech, and Toygar Tanyel is employed as a medical AI engineer at the same company. The other authors have declared no conflicts of interest.

References

1. Australian Screening Advisory Committee: National Accreditation Standards BreastScreen Australia Quality Improvement Program (Revised) (2001)
2. Brahim, M., Westerkamp, K., Hempel, L., Lehmann, R., Hempel, D., Philipp, P.: Automated assessment of breast positioning quality in screening mammography. Cancers **14**(19), 4704 (2022)
3. Cancer (IARC), T. I. A. for R. on Global Cancer Observatory: Global Cancer Observatory. https://gco.iarc.fr/. Accessed 14 May 2024
4. Duffy, S.W., et al.: The impact of organized mammography service screening on breast carcinoma mortality in seven Swedish counties: a collaborative evaluation. Cancer: Interdisc. Int. J. Am. Cancer Soc. **95**(3), 458–469 (2002)
5. Feig, S.A.: Image quality of screening mammography: effect on clinical outcome. AJR Am. J. Roentgenol. **178**, 805–807 (2002)
6. Feng, Z.H., Kittler, J., Awais, M., Huber, P., Wu, X.J.: Wing loss for robust facial landmark localisation with convolutional neural networks. In: Proceedings of the IEEE Conference on Computer Vision and Pattern Recognition, pp. 2235–2245 (2018)
7. Geras, K.J., Mann, R.M., Moy, L.: Artificial intelligence for mammography and digital breast tomosynthesis: current concepts and future perspectives. Radiology **293**(2), 246–259 (2019)
8. Gupta, V., et al.: Deep learning-based automatic detection of poorly positioned mammograms to minimize patient return visits for repeat imaging: a real-world application. arXiv preprint arXiv:2009.13580 (2020)
9. Gürdemir, B., Arıbal, E.: Assessment of mammography quality in Istanbul. Diagn. Interv. Radiol. **18**, 468–472 (2012)
10. Hendrick, R.E., Bassett, L., Botsco, M.A., et al.: Mammography quality control manual. Roy. Am. Coll. Radiol. (1999)
11. Mackenzie, A., et al.: The relationship between cancer detection in mammography and image quality measurements. Physica Med. **32**(4), 568–574 (2016)
12. Magnus, M.C., Ping, M., Shen, M.M., Bourgeois, J., Magnus, J.H.: Effectiveness of mammography screening in reducing breast cancer mortality in women aged 39–49 years: a meta-analysis. J. Womens Health **20**(6), 845–852 (2011)
13. Nguyen, H.T., et al.: Vindr-mammo: a large-scale benchmark dataset for computer-aided diagnosis in full-field digital mammography. Sci. Data **10**(1), 277 (2023)
14. Rodriguez-Ruiz, A., et al.: Stand-alone artificial intelligence for breast cancer detection in mammography: comparison with 101 radiologists. JNCI: J. Natl. Cancer Inst. **111**(9), 916–922 (2019)
15. Royal Australian and New Zealand College of Radiologists: Mammography quality assurance program (2002)
16. Spuur, K., Hung, W.T., Poulos, A., Rickard, M.: Mammography image quality: model for predicting compliance with posterior nipple line criterion. Eur. J. Radiol. **80**(3), 713–718 (2011)

17. U.S. Food and Drug Administration: Positioning Responsible For Most Clinical Image Deficiencies, Failures (2016). https://www.fda.gov/Radiation-EmittingProducts/MammographyQualityStandardsActandProgram/FacilityScorecard/ucm495378.html. Accessed 14 May 2024
18. Watanabe, H., et al.: Quality control system for mammographic breast positioning using deep learning. Sci. Rep. **13**(1), 7066 (2023)
19. Wilson, R., Liston, J.: Quality Assurance Guidelines for Radiographers, 2nd edn. NHSBSP Publication (2011)

Endpoint Detection in Breast Images for Automatic Classification of Breast Cancer Aesthetic Results

Nuno Freitas[1,2](✉), Carlos Veloso[1,2], Carlos Mavioso[3], Maria J. Cardoso[3], Hélder P. Oliveira[1,2], and Jaime S. Cardoso[1,2]

[1] Faculdade de Engenharia, Universidade do Porto, Porto, Portugal
[2] Institute for Systems and Computer Engineering, Technology and Science, Porto, Portugal
{nuno.p.silva,jaime.s.cardoso}@inesctec.pt
[3] Breast Unit, Champalimaud Foundation, Lisbon, Portugal

Abstract. Breast cancer is the most common type of cancer in women worldwide. Because of high survival rates, there has been an increased interest in patient Quality of Life after treatment. Aesthetic results play an important role in this aspect, as these treatments can leave a mark on a patient's self-image. Despite that, there are no standard ways of assessing aesthetic outcomes. Commonly used software such as BCCT.core or BAT require the manual annotation of keypoints, which makes them time-consuming for clinical use and can lead to result variability depending on the user.

Recently, there have been attempts to leverage both traditional and Deep Learning algorithms to detect keypoints automatically. In this paper, we compare several methods for the detection of Breast Endpoints across two datasets. Furthermore, we present an extended evaluation of using these models as input for full contour prediction and aesthetic evaluation using the BCCT.core software. Overall, the YOLOv9 model, fine-tuned for this task, presents the best results considering both accuracy and usability, making this architecture the best choice for this application. The main contribution of this paper is the development of a pipeline for full breast contour prediction, which reduces clinician workload and user variability for automatic aesthetic assessment.

Keywords: Breast Cancer · Deep Learning · Aesthetic Assessment · Keypoint Detection

1 Introduction

Breast cancer is one of the most common types of cancer in the world. In recent years, the incidence of this type of cancer has been rising. Despite that, mortality rates have been decreasing in high-income countries due to early-stage diagnosis and high-quality treatment [1]. This increase in survival rates has led to a bigger concern about a patient's Quality of Life (QoL) after treatment [3]. Locoregional treatments (surgery and radiation therapy) are a standard option for breast cancer patients. This sort of treatment can negatively affect body image and, consequently, negatively impact psychosocial recovery and QoL. Thus, several attempts have been made to create automatic Breast Cancer aesthetic assessment methods. Despite more recent works, BCCT.core [2] and BAT [8] remain the most relevant works done in this area. Both of these systems require manual annotation of key points, which makes these types of software more time-consuming and the results vary depending on user input. We propose an effective pipeline for Breast Endpoint and Keypoint automatic detection that has shown to be robust in out of distribution evaluation.

In 2008, Cardoso developed a method for breast contour detection that consists of computing the image gradient with the Sobel Filter and calculating the shortest path between breast endpoints [4]. This algorithm presented impressive results and is still used in the BCCT.core and Cinderella trial [13]. However, this algorithm requires manual annotation of Endpoints. In this paper, we compare several models for breast endpoint detection and test them on two different datasets. Furthermore, we present the impact these models have on the prediction of the remaining keypoints when using them as inputs for the shortest path algorithm and the subsequent result of Aesthetic Assessment using the BCCT.core with the images annotated with the predicted keypoints.

The rest of this paper is structured as follows. Section 2 introduces important concepts in Object Detection and previous approaches in the Literature for this application. Section 3 details the models compared in this paper for endpoint detection and the pipeline presented for full contour detection and aesthetic classification. Section 4 presents the results of the experiments conducted. Finally, Sect. 5 concludes the paper by giving an overall assessment of the results and the future work still to be done.

2 Background

This section overviews common methods for automatic Object Detection in images, as well as the previous work developed for this specific task in photographs of breast cancer patients.

2.1 Object Detection in Images

Object Detection is one of the most common tasks in Computer Vision. In recent years, Deep Learning models have shown impressive results in automatic Object Detection and Recognition and images. In order to limit the scope of our literature review, we focus on object and keypoint detection in human faces. There are obvious similarities between this application and ours, as both focus on the detection of human skin and the detection of specific parts of the human anatomy. Colaco & Han [6] showed impressive results in this task by training Convolutional Neural Networks (CNNs) to predict the coordinates of 15 Keypoints. Another successful approach in the literature is using Segmentation models in order to Segment Regions of Interest (ROIs) in the face [15].

You Only Look Once (YOLO) is a state-of-the-art, real-time object detection algorithm introduced in 2015 [17]. Because of its success, it has also been widely adapted for this task, with several examples of adapting different versions of YOLO for Face Detection and Recognition [5,10,21]. In 2024, a new generation of YOLO architectures was introduced (YOLOv9) which outperformed existing versions and other object detectors [20].

2.2 ElastiX: Medical Image Alignment

Medical image registration is an important task in medical image processing. It allows clinicians to align different data based on common points in images [14,16]. Elastix introduced an Image Registration algorithm that can apply different Elastic and Rigid transformations to images to maximize similarity between two images: a moving image (image we want to register) and a fixed image (image already present in the dataset). This methodology is simple to use and specifically designed for medical images for diagnosis [19]. In Sect. 3 we propose a method that does keypoint prediction using Image Alignment between a new image and an image already annotated and in the dataset (working as a template).

2.3 Previous Work

In 2007, Cardoso et al. proposed a Computer Vision algorithm for breast contour detection [4]. This algorithm initially detected breast endpoints using the image gradient and the strong paths present in the image. Then, with the endpoints as input, it defines the breast contour as the shortest path between endpoints using the Dijkstra algorithm [7]. This is done by modeling the Sobel result of the image as a graph (every pixel is a node n and connected to a 3×3 neighborhood by a weight set of weights w). Having w as the weight between adjacent nodes n_i and n_{i+1}, the value of w is small if both nodes are edge pixels and high if at least one of the nodes is not. This notation forces the shortest path algorithm to choose edge pixels as they have a lower weight. More recently, this model was integrated with a Deep Edge Detector [9], although this model presented poor performance in out-of-distribution images.

Two similar Deep Learning models with complex architectures were developed on an in-house dataset of 221 images [11,18]. They consisted of refining Breast Heatmaps using U-Nets and finally using a CNN for Keypoint Prediction. Despite that, these models showed poor generalization capabilities on new datasets, which suggests that the models were overfitting to the statistics of the training set [9]. In 2020, in a paper that presented the development of an aesthetic assessment software, the authors used a YOLOv3 for the automatic detection of breast keypoints, which presented positive results, and so our paper presents a YOLOv9 model integrated into our pipeline for contour detection [12].

3 Methodology

This section details the different models proposed for Breast contour endpoint detection and the pipeline for full contour prediction and aesthetic classification.

3.1 Breast Endpoint Prediction

We compare six different models for Endpoint Prediction: two using standard Deep Learning models, one using the *state-of-the-art* YOLOv9 model, one using an Image Alignment algorithm and two established models in the literature.

A. Traditional Contour Detection (Baseline): In 2008, Cardoso et al. [4] proposed not only an algorithm for breast contour detection but also a model that can predict Breast endpoints based on the Sobel of the Image. It computes the strongest paths between bottom and middle rows of the image, discards unwanted paths and selects the endpoints in the paths closer to the center. This model was tested on new datasets to compare with our proposed models.

B. Elastix: The Elastix software was developed in 2009 in order to provide tools for medical image elastic alignment [14]. It applies rigid and elastic transformation to images in order to maximize similarities between two images: the fixed image and the moving image (the moving image is the one that suffers the transformation). Let n be e a new image for which we need to predict endpoints and D be our dataset of fully annotated images. In our method, we select ten random images from the dataset D and the image i that is most similar to our current image using the Structural Symmetry Index Measure (SSIM). Image i is selected as the Moving Image and Morphed to match image n using the Elastix Software. It is easy to calculate the New Endpoints of image i after the transformation by applying the same transformation. The new location of the keypoints is finally used as a prediction for keypoints in the Fixed Image n. Figure 1 shows an example of this algorithm.

Fig. 1. Example of the Elastix Algorithm in our application. From Left to right: Fixed Image with Keypoints; Moving Image after transformation; Moving Image with predicted Keypoints.

C. Regression: It is straightforward to model this task as a regression problem, where the model must predict the x and y coordinates of the endpoints. For this task, we used the VGG16 as the backbone, a common choice among CNNs, pre-trained on the ImageNet Dataset. The regression model is useful as a baseline against other Deep Learning models in order to understand if a simple Pre-Trained CNN can be easily Fine-Tuned for this task. In our application, we replaced the fully-connected layers and added three smaller layers. The last output was obtained by a 4-output layer and a sigmoid activation function.

D. Heatmap: Wilson et al. proposed a sequential model of Deep Neural Networks (DNN) [18]. The first part of the algorithm used two sequential U-Nets to predict and refine heatmaps based on the Annotated Keypoints. The second part uses a VGG16 to predict Keypoints from the generated heatmaps. For this paper, we simply retrained the model on the new dataset.

E. Segmentation: U-Nets are commonly used models for image segmentation tasks. They have the convolutional part of a common CNN, but instead of fully connected layers, we add deconvolutional layers that will have an output of the same shape as the input image. In this task, we want the U-Net to output a binary mask of the breast. This approach can increase a model's ability to learn from data as it segments the whole Region of Interest. The Endpoints were then automatically detected from the binary segmented masks, as they are the points belonging to the mask that are closest to the top corners of the Image.

F. YOLOv9: The YOLO architecture has been very successful in object detection. Our proposed model used the recent YOLOv9 and adapted it to detect Breast Endpoints that are defined with a square bounding box centered in the endpoints with a side that was defined as the width of the breast divided by 10. Similarly to the segmentation approach, this allows us to detect the Endpoint as a region rather than a specific point in the image. This is positive when there is a lot of variance in the annotation of Endpoint Location. Furthermore, we present an algorithm that combines a model of YOLOv9 with image post-processing (**F2. YOLOv9-pp**) for the shortest path. This model is trained to detect both the endpoints and a bounding box surrounding the breast area. This bounding box is then used to crop the image for the shortest path algorithm to the breast area (see Fig. 2).

3.2 Contour Prediction and Aesthetic Assessment

In order to evaluate the utility of these models in a clinical context, a more comprehensive analysis is necessary. In that sense, we devised a pipeline for complete automatic contour detection using the models detailed in Sect. 3.1 for endpoint detection and the shortest path algorithm for contour detection with the endpoints as inputs [4]. After that, the predicted fully annotated contour was

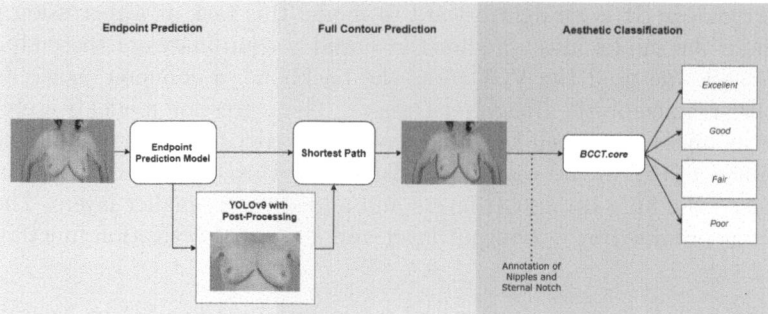

Fig. 2. Full Pipeline of Using the models for Keypoint Prediction and Aesthetic Classification.

used as input for the BCCT.core aesthetic classifier. For this, it was necessary to use the ground truth values for nipple and sternal notch coordinates. Figure 2 shows a diagram of this pipeline for automatic contour detection and breast aesthetic assessment. For evaluation, we also compute the shortest path using the ground truth endpoints as input and subsequent aesthetic classification (**G. ShortPath(GT)**). This allows us to understand which errors are caused by our models and which are caused by the shortest path algorithm.

4 Results and Discussion

Breast Endpoint Prediction: For the first set of experiments we evaluated breast endpoint prediction (see Sect. 3.1). The Cinderella project has an in-house dataset of over 2000 photographs of pre- and post-surgery patients with annotated keypoints. Furthermore, a dataset of over 3000 images of patients post-surgery with annotated keypoints has been made available [12]. This dataset presents some differences from the Cinderella dataset in illumination and distance to the camera (see Fig. 3). In our experiments, the Cinderella dataset was used for preliminary training and testing. Additionally, the models were tested on the out-of-distribution (OOD) dataset made available [12].

The error of endpoint prediction was defined as the average Euclidean Distance between the ground-truth endpoints e_{gt} and the predicted endpoints e_p, normalized by the width of the breasts w_{gt} (this can be defined as the difference in the x coordinates of the two endpoints: $w_{gt} = k_{gt}^x[2] - k_{gt}^x[1]$).

Table 1 compares all the models implemented (see Sect. 3) for endpoint prediction. It presents the mean and median error for both test sets and the average computation time for all models. Overall, the YOLOv9-based models have the best performance across both datasets. The segmentation and regression models also perform well. The traditional model performs well in the ID dataset but fails when confronted with new data. The Elastix and Heatmap models fail to perform adequately on both datasets. Overall, Deep Learning models present a lower computation time than other models.

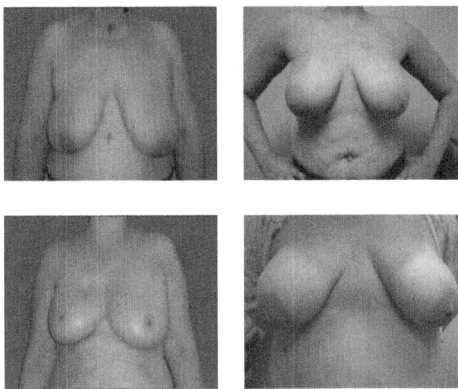

Fig. 3. Example of images from the Cinderella dataset (left) and the out-of-distribution dataset made available by [12] (right).

Table 1. Results for the endpoint detection task in the Cinderella Test Set (In Distribution - ID) and the AmericaN dataset (OOD). All models were trained in the Cinderella training set. The best results are in **bold**.

Model	Test Set (ID)		Test Set (OOD)		Time(s)
	Mean Err	Median Err	Mean Err	Median Err	
A. Traditional	0.0625	0.0384	0.1914	0.1577	2.352
B. Elastix	0.1770	0.1090	0.3666	0.2380	14.594
C. Regression	0.0431	0.0381	0.0774	0.0800	**0.071**
D. Heatmap	0.1347	0.1066	0.1269	0.1269	0.158
E. Segmentation	0.0323	0.0238	0.1016	0.0744	0.257
F. YOLOv9	0.0282	**0.0204**	0.0858	**0.0294**	0.102
F2. YOLOv9-pp	**0.0268**	0.0220	**0.0700**	0.0373	0.090

Contour Prediction and Aesthetic Assessment: The second set of experiments evaluated the impact of using these models as input on contour prediction and subsequent aesthetic classification (see Sect. 3.2). The best-performing models of the previous experiments were tested on the Cinderella Test Set for full contour prediction and aesthetic classification (see Fig. 2). Keypoint prediction is evaluated as before (but for full contour prediction). For aesthetic classification, we present the accuracy for 4-class classification, binary classification, and the Mean Squared Error. The ground truth values for classification are defined as the results output of BCCT.core when using the keypoints annotated by clinicians. These experiments introduce the ShortPath(GT) model as a baseline for keypoint prediction (see Sect. 3.2).

Looking at Table 2, we can see that the ShortPath(GT) achieves impressive results on full contour prediction. Despite that, it fails to perform as well for

Table 2. Results for the full breast contour detection and aesthetic classification tasks in the Cinderella Test Set. Acc. indicates the Accuracy of Aesthetic prediction while 4c and 2c indicate 4 and 2 classes respectively and MSE is the Mean Squared Error.

Model	Keypoint Pred		Aesthetic Classification		
	Mean Err	Median Err	Acc. (4c)	Acc. (2c)	MSE
C. Regression	0.0343	0.0234	79.74%	90.01%	0.2658
E. Segmentation	0.0336	0.0207	78.98%	90.63%	0.2658
F. YOLOv9	0.0312	0.0199	77.97%	91.13%	0.2632
F2. YOLOv9-pp	0.0263	0.0203	**81.77%**	**94.43%**	**0.2075**
G. ShortPath(GT)	**0.0126**	**0.0047**	80.75%	90.17%	0.2607

aesthetic classification. This difference in performance indicates that a part of the aesthetic classification error can be attributed to the Shortest Path algorithm. Furthermore, YOLOv9-pp outperforms the ShortPath(GT) model on aesthetic classification, which indicates that post-processing improves the effectiveness of contour detection.

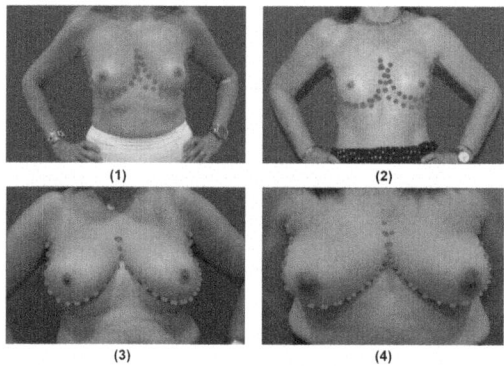

Fig. 4. Examples of predicted Keypoints with YOLOv9-pp that cause an error in aesthetic prediction. Red dots are the predicted keypoints and green dots are the ground truth. (Color figure online)

Figure 4 shows the first four images where the YOLOv9-pp model produced an incorrect prediction. It is visible that in images **1** and **2** the problem is that the breast contour is not accentuated in the image and, thus, the shortest path algorithm has some deviation from the ground truth. On the other hand, for images **3** and **4** the problem is endpoint location. Despite that, the predicted keypoints are still acceptable for a subjective evaluation, which suggests that the BCCT.core classifier should be more robust to variation of endpoint annotation.

5 Conclusion

This paper offers a detailed comparison of several approaches for breast endpoint detection and the effect this has on full keypoint prediction using the shortest path. Out of all the models compared, YOLOv9-based models present the best results for predicting endpoints and contour estimation using the shortest path. They also present a positive effect on aesthetic classification. Furthermore, it is fast and easy to train on new data. Additionally, we present a complete pipeline for automatic breast contour keypoint annotation and aesthetic assessment. With minimal clinical effort on keypoint annotation, this can be an effective tool to improve automatic aesthetic assessment, reducing workload and variability between users. Future work should focus on the detection of the nipples and sternal notch for fully automatic breast cancer aesthetic assessment. Furthermore, it is important to develop robust methods of aesthetic classification using standardized keypoint annotation with methods such as this one.

Acknowledgments. This work has received funding from the European Union's Horizon Europe research and innovation programme under the Grant Agreement 101057389-CINDERELLA project.

Disclosure of Interests. The authors have no competing interests to declare that are relevant to the content of this article.

References

1. Arnold, M., et al.: Current and future burden of breast cancer: global statistics for 2020 and 2040. Breast **66**, 15–23 (2022). https://doi.org/10.1016/j.breast.2022.08.010. https://www.sciencedirect.com/science/article/pii/S0960977622001448
2. Cardoso, J.S., Cardoso, M.J.: Towards an intelligent medical system for the aesthetic evaluation of breast cancer conservative treatment. Artif. Intell. Med. **40**(2), 115–126 (2007)
3. Cardoso, J.S., Silva, W., Cardoso, M.J.: Evolution, current challenges, and future possibilities in the objective assessment of aesthetic outcome of breast cancer locoregional treatment. Breast **49**, 123–130 (2020)
4. Cardoso, J., Luís, T., Cardoso, M.: Automatic breast contour detection in digital photographs, vol. 2, pp. 91–98 (2008)
5. Chen, W., Huang, H., Peng, S., Zhou, C., Zhang, C.: Yolo-face: a real-time face detector (2021). https://doi.org/10.1007/s00371-020-01831-7
6. Colaco, S., Han, D.S.: Facial keypoint detection with convolutional neural networks. In: 2020 International Conference on Artificial Intelligence in Information and Communication (ICAIIC), pp. 671–674 (2020). https://doi.org/10.1109/ICAIIC48513.2020.9065279
7. Dijkstra, E.W.: A note on two problems in connexion with graphs. Numer. Math. **1**(1), 269–271 (1959). https://doi.org/10.1007/bf01386390
8. Fitzal, F., et al.: The use of a breast symmetry index for objective evaluation of breast cosmesis. The Breast **16**(4), 429–435 (2007). https://doi.org/10.1016/j.breast.2007.01.013. https://www.sciencedirect.com/science/article/pii/S0960977607000422

9. Freitas, N., Silva, D., Mavioso, C., Cardoso, M.J., Cardoso, J.S.: Deep edge detection methods for the automatic calculation of the breast contour. Bioengineering **10**(4) (2023). https://doi.org/10.3390/bioengineering10040401. https://www.mdpi.com/2306-5354/10/4/401
10. Garg, D., Goel, P., Pandya, S., Ganatra, A., Kotecha, K.: A deep learning approach for face detection using yolo. In: 2018 IEEE Punecon, pp. 1–4 (2018). https://doi.org/10.1109/PUNECON.2018.8745376
11. Gonçalves, T., Silva, W., Cardoso, M.J., Cardoso, J.S.: Deep image segmentation for breast keypoint detection. Proceedings **54**(1) (2020). https://doi.org/10.3390/proceedings2020054035. https://www.mdpi.com/2504-3900/54/1/35
12. Guo, C., et al.: A fully automatic framework for evaluating cosmetic results of breast conserving therapy. Mach. Learn. Appl. **10**, 100430 (2022). https://doi.org/10.1016/j.mlwa.2022.100430. https://www.sciencedirect.com/science/article/pii/S2666827022001050
13. Kaidar-Person, O., Antunes, M., Cardoso, J.S., Ciani, O., et al.: Evaluating the ability of an artificial-intelligence cloud-based platform designed to provide information prior to locoregional therapy for breast cancer in improving patient's satisfaction with therapy: the cinderella trial. PLOS ONE **18**(8) (2023)
14. Klein, S., Staring, M., Murphy, K., Viergever, M.A., Pluim, J.P.W.: elastix: a toolbox for intensity-based medical image registration. IEEE Trans. Med. Imaging **29**(1), 196–205 (2010). https://doi.org/10.1109/TMI.2009.2035616
15. Lin, K., et al.: Face detection and segmentation with generalized intersection over union based on mask R-CNN. In: Ren, J., et al. (eds.) BICS 2019. LNCS (LNAI), vol. 11691, pp. 106–116. Springer, Cham (2020). https://doi.org/10.1007/978-3-030-39431-8_11
16. Marstal, K., Berendsen, F., Staring, M., Klein, S.: Simpleelastix: a user-friendly, multi-lingual library for medical image registration. In: Proceedings of the IEEE Conference on Computer Vision and Pattern Recognition (CVPR) Workshops (2016)
17. Redmon, J., Divvala, S., Girshick, R., Farhadi, A.: You only look once: unified, real-time object detection (2016)
18. Silva, W., Castro, E., Cardoso, M.J., Fitzal, F., Cardoso, J.S.: Deep keypoint detection for the aesthetic evaluation of breast cancer surgery outcomes. In: 2019 IEEE 16th International Symposium on Biomedical Imaging (ISBI 2019), pp. 1082–1086 (2019). https://doi.org/10.1109/ISBI.2019.8759331
19. Staring, M., Klein, S., Reiber, J., Niessen, W., Stoel, B.: Pulmonary image registration with elastix using a standard intensity-based algorithm. In: Book Pulmonary Image Registration with Elastix Using a Standard Intensity-Based Algorithm (2010)
20. Wang, C.Y., Yeh, I.H., Liao, H.Y.M.: Yolov9: learning what you want to learn using programmable gradient information (2024). https://arxiv.org/abs/2402.13616
21. Yang, W., Jiachun, Z.: Real-time face detection based on yolo. In: 2018 1st IEEE International Conference on Knowledge Innovation and Invention (ICKII), pp. 221–224 (2018). https://doi.org/10.1109/ICKII.2018.8569109

Thick Slices for Optimal Digital Breast Tomosynthesis Classification With Deep-Learning

Paul Terrassin[1,2]([✉]), Mickael Tardy[1,2], Hassan Alhajj[1], Nathan Lauzeral[1], and Nicolas Normand[2]

[1] Hera-MI, SAS, Saint-Herblain, France
paul.terrassin@hera-mi.com
[2] Nantes Université, École Centrale Nantes, CNRS, LS2N, UMR 6004, 44000 Nantes, France

Abstract. Digital breast tomosynthesis (DBT) is a recent medical imaging tool that increases accuracy and interpretability compared to traditional full-field digital mammogram (FFDM). However, DBT interpretation time is estimated to be twice longer than for FFDM, explainable by its 3D nature. Computer-aided diagnosis (CAD) systems can help radiologists in their diagnostic tasks and workload reduction. However, computation times and costs are important for CADs, thus facing the same challenge as health practitioners. This study addresses the problem concerning the processing of DBTs with high cancer detection rates while meeting the constraints of the clinical world. To this end, we propose a method relying on the slabbing approach which generates a set of 2D thick slices "slabs" that summarize a whole DBT volume. We propose a comprehensive benchmark on slabbing exploring several parameters such as slab thickness and overlap between slabs. Our method uses a fully 2D convolutional neural network (CNN) as a binary classifier, trained solely on FFDMs, exploiting the similarity between FFDMs and slabs. We report metrics on the two publicly available datasets containing DBTs: Breast Cancer Screening-DBT (BCS-DBT) and EA1141. This is the first study to explore DBTs of the EA1141 dataset, so we provide data strategy details and make it publicly available on GitHub (https://github.com/racoon-z/dbt-slabbing). We report breast-wise AUC$_{ROC}$ of **0.90** on both BCS-DBT validation and test subsets and **0.97** on EA1141. We achieve competitive specificities at 90% of sensitivity breast-wise with **0.84** and **0.79** on BCS validation and test respectively, while not training on DBTs.

Keywords: Breast Cancer · Digital Breast Tomosynthesis · Slab · Thick slices · Deep Learning · Classification · CNN

1 Introduction

Breast cancer is the most diagnosed type of cancer among women and the second leading cause of death worldwide [19]. Digital breast tomosynthesis (DBT)

is a recent 3D medical imaging tool that can be used in breast cancer screening programs. Compared to the traditional full-field digital mammography (FFDM), DBT can lead to better accuracy in the diagnosis of breast cancer [11,12]. Its 3D nature offers better context and interpretability for complex lesions such as micro-calcifications [9]. While overdiagnosis can lead to invasive surgical procedures for patients and increased workload for radiologists, early detection of breast disease remains crucial to patient care [19].

Despite its advantages, DBT analysis results in a significant increase in reading time, with the estimated interpretation time for radiologists using DBT being twice as long as for radiologists using FFDM [15]. Computer-aided diagnosis (CAD) systems aim to help health practitioners increase their cancer detection rates and reduce their workload [18]. The main current and future challenges for DBT concern the reduction of CAD computation time while maintaining high performance. Indeed, end-to-end DBT processing is resource-hungry for deep-learning-based methods, especially for convolutional neural network (CNN) due to the high resolution of the modality[1].

The current literature can be divided into three DBT processing strategies: 1) a single synthesized 2D view (S2D) summarizing a DBT entirely, 2) focusing on 3D patches of the region of interest (ROI), and 3) using the entire DBT in slices or generating thick slices, called "slabs".

The first approach is based on methods that process S2Ds generated by DBT manufacturers, comparable to the processing of FFDMs using a single 2D projection of the breast [6,20]. It cancels out the advantages of DBT which offers 3D visualization of the lesion, and therefore reverts to FFDM usage. In addition, these views are not systematically provided by manufacturers and S2Ds can generate high-intensity artifacts that could be mistaken for lesions.

The second strategy relies on global model which identifies 3D ROI patches and then exploit neighborhood pixel information, fusing inter-slices features along the z axis of the DBT [21,26]. These methods take greater account of the DBT nature by extracting multi-dimensional features from patches using both 2D and 3D grouped convolutions. While this approach remains interesting, it does not answer the stated clinical constraints above, as a global model is required to analyze all slices to extract ROIs.

The last identified strategy consists in DBT slices [5,13,14,24] or thick slices processing [4,22]. El-Shazli et al. [5] and Mota et al. [13] propose a per-slice DBT processing approach solely based on 2D convolutions, without using inter-slice information. Moreover, they both do a harsh slice resizing ($\approx$224 × 224 and 512 × 512 respectively) which induces a significant loss of information on the xy planes. Park et al. [14] and Wang et al. [24] process DBT in an end-to-end manner and use both 2D and 3D information. However, these methods require large-scale computing infrastructures and significant costs which are not meeting clinical resources limitations. Lastly, Doganay et al. [4] and Tardy et al. [22] summarize

---

[1] Standard slice thickness is approximately 1 mm, and the in-plane resolution is around 50 μm to 140 μm. For example, for a DBT with dimensions of 80 × 2500 × 2000, the total number of pixels is approximately 400 million.

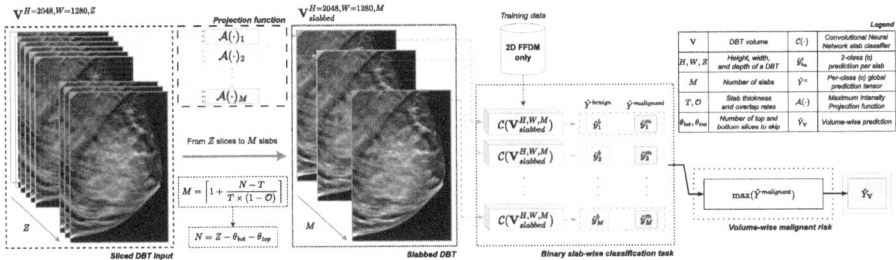

Fig. 1. Schema of the proposed method for an end-to-end classification of DBT volumes. First, we summarize a DBT volume $\mathbf{V}$ into M slabs. Then, a CNN architecture process the slabbed DBT to assess the risk of malignancy of the entire volume.

DBT pixel information along the z axis generating thick slices (slabs). However, they present relatively low performances on limited datasets (Fig. 1).

Given the above constraints and our analysis of the state of the art, we propose a method leveraging the anisotropic property of DBT. While in-plane pixel information is crucial to detect small lesions such as micro-calcifications, we believe dimensionality reduction can be done along the z axis. A CNN-based classifier aims to assess the risk of malignancy for a slabbed DBT, summarizing all slices into a subset of slabs. In addition, our CNN is trained only on FFDMs to solve the problem of the lack of well-annotated DBT datasets. Finally, our contributions can be summarized as follows:

1. A comprehensive benchmark on the impact of slabbing for a CNN-based method to classify DBT volumes according to their risk of malignancy;
2. Large-scale metrics on all state-of-the-art clinically relevant DBT public datasets: Breast Cancer Screening DBT (BCS-DBT) validation and test sets [1], and EA1141 [2];
3. To the best of our knowledge, we are the first study to specifically use DBTs from EA1141, paving the way for the community to use a new dataset by providing details on data management and free access to our code.

2 Method

The specific details of our approach are: 1) the generation of slabs to summarize DBT volumes (slabbing) in Sect. 2.1 and 2) the use of a 2D CNN-based classifier trained solely on FFDMs in Sect. 2.2.

2.1 Slabbing

Slabbing is an effective approach for radiologists to reduce the interpretation time while having similar diagnostic accuracy [16,17]. Indeed, DBT pixel information is not equally distributed along the volume as the in-plane (xy) resolution is higher than in the z axis, proving the anisotropic nature of DBT. Our method relies on this property to generate a sequence of slabs from the input volume. This reduces the dimensionality, and therefore the computation time and cost, required to perform the whole volume classification task.

Let a DBT volume $\mathbf{V}^{H,W,Z}$ where H, W, and Z denote slice height, width, and depth respectively. The main aim of slabbing is to divide the volume $\mathbf{V}$ into a set of M slabs, along the z axis. Each slab is a 2D projection of a subset of slices from a DBT. The number of generated slabs is computed according to several parameters: the slab thickness $T \in [1, N]$, the overlapping ratio between slabs $\mathcal{O} \in [0, 1)^2$, and the number of slices $N = Z - \theta_{top} - \theta_{bot}$. $\theta \in \mathbb{N}$ represents the number of skipped slices at the boundaries usually suffering from substantial noise due to the nature of reconstruction. The number of slabs M is defined as in Eq. (1).

$$M = \left\lceil 1 + \frac{N - T}{T \times (1 - \mathcal{O})} \right\rceil \tag{1}$$

Once the new slabbed DBT thickness is defined, we use an aggregation function $\mathcal{A}$ to generate the 2D slabs. The new volume $\mathbf{V}^{H,W,M}_{slabbed} = \mathcal{A}(\mathbf{V}^{H,W,Z})$ is dimensionally reduced along the z axis. In our method, we use the maximum intensity projection (MIP) as $\mathcal{A}$, computing the maximum value of a voxel stack along the z axis [3]. This strategy has the advantage of enhancing the microcalcifications contrasts, however, it may generate high-intensity artifacts [3].

2.2 CNN

The classification is performed using a deep convolutional neural network (CNN) relying on UNet3+ [7] and with architecture modifications as described in [23]. These modifications include the multi-task and multi-scale output strategies designed to improve classification performance. Despite the use of a U-shape architecture recognized for segmentation tasks, this modified version of the UNet3+ improves classification performance compared to other state-of-the-art CNN classification methods [23]. Moreover, architectural changes such as the use of depth-wise separable 2D convolutions, and the reduction of convolution filters by a factor 2 aim to decrease model complexity. This is crucial for processing FFDM or DBT slabs which are high-resolution 2D images.

We introduce further adaptations to fit the needs of the study. We trained our CNN for the binary classification task of full FFDM images assessing the risk of malignancy. Our CNN classifier has been trained solely on 2D mammography images and without using a single DBT exam due to the lack of well annotated datasets. Moreover, our method takes advantage of the similarity between FFDM and DBT slabs allowing us to minimize training resources.

In our method, we propose to use this CNN architecture as a classifier for our slabbed volume $\mathbf{V}_{slabbed}$ as follows. Classification function $\mathcal{C}$ generates a set

---

[2] $\mathcal{O} = 1$ is excluded as it indicates that each slab fully overlaps the previous one, resulting in a stride of 0, which causes the algorithm to get stuck in an infinite loop.

of M predictions ($\hat{y}$) according to binary classification problem as in Eq. (2). The two classes c predicted are benign ($c = b$) and malignant ($c = m$).

$$\mathcal{C}(\mathbf{V}_{slabbed}^{H,W,M}) = [\{\hat{y}_1^b, \hat{y}_2^b, \cdots, \hat{y}_M^b\}, \{\hat{y}_1^m, \hat{y}_2^m, \cdots, \hat{y}_M^m\}] \quad (2)$$

where $\hat{y}_i^c$ is the generated prediction for the i_{th} slab of the c class. Global tensors are: $\hat{Y}^{benign} = \{\hat{y}_1^b, \cdots, \hat{y}_M^b\}$ and $\hat{Y}^{malignant} = \{\hat{y}_1^m, \cdots, \hat{y}_M^m\}$.

Finally, we aim to obtain a single score for the entire volume $\hat{Y}_V$ to assess the risk of malignancy from the above set of predictions. To that end, we compute the maximum from the malignant class predictions, i.e., $\hat{Y}_\mathbf{V} = \max(\hat{Y}^{malignant})$, meaning capturing a malignancy on one slab at least.

Table 1. IW and BW data distribution between benign and malignant classes for each dataset. BCS$_{test}$ and BCS$_{val}$ denote BCS-DBT Validation and Test subsets while EA$_{DBT}$ and EA$_{MRI}$ refer to the two sets, excluding or including MRI biopsy outcomes.

		BCS$_{val}$	BCS$_{test}$	EA$_{DBT}$	EA$_{MRI}$
Image-wise	Benign	1126	1661	1425	1803
	Malignant	37	60	4	17
Breast-wise	Benign	565	830	679	861
	Malignant	20	30	2	8

3 Experiments

3.1 Datasets

The two public datasets containing DBT exams from clinical practice have been used: Breast Cancer Screening-Digital Breast Tomosynthesis (BCS-DBT) [1], and EA1141 [2]. BCS-DBT is a large-scale and well-annotated public DBT dataset that has become state-of-the-art since its release in 2021 in the context of a DBTex Lesion Detection Challenge [8]. To allow the comparison to the results of the challenge we used the validation and test subsets. These subsets are referred to as BCS$_{val}$ and BCS$_{test}$ respectively. EA1141 is a dataset composed of multi-modal exams, including FFDMs, DBTs, and magnetic resonance images (MRIs). All required information to understand the specific processing applied to sort images according to modalities and identify DBT exams is available on the GitHub mentioned on the first page.

We evaluate the method in two scopes: image-wise (IW) and breast-wise (BW). Our goal is to distinguish benign and normal DBTs from malignant ones focusing on biopsy-proven malignant lesions. For the two BCS-DBT subsets, it means that "Cancer" labels only were considered as malignant and "Benign", "Actionable", and "Normal" ground truths were assigned to the benign class (we refer the reader to the original manuscript for the details). The sorting strategy for EA1141 was different as the dataset contains both an MRI and a DBT clinical outcome. Therefore, we propose the two following strategies: 1) samples with malignant biopsy outcome from DBT vs. the rest, excluding malignant exams detected from MRIs (this subset is referred to as EA_{DBT}), and 2) malignant biopsy outcome from DBT and MRI vs. the rest (referred to as EA_{MRI}). The malignancy class was assigned when "DCIS" or "Invasive" words were present in the biopsy outcomes of DBTs and MRIs. Table 1 summarizes the distribution between benign and malignant sets.

3.2 Implementation Details

The CNN architecture exploited in the study follows the training procedure similar to Terrassin et al. [23] except that we use full FFDMs instead of patches and train on the image-wise binary classification task. The neural network was optimized to be trained on the NVIDIA GeForce RTX 2080 Ti GPU, fitting 11 GB RAM, and is capable of inferring on CPU.

We standardized DBT slices before the inference as follows. First, erasing noisy background pixels, using the triangle threshold method [27]. Then, we removed skin borders [1] and cropped slices aiming to suppress irrelevant pixels [25]. DBT slices were resized to 2048 × 1280 pixels to align with the input expected by the CNN used, and at last, we truncated the histogram from extreme values and normalized pixel intensity in the range [0, 1] as in [23].

We aimed to evaluate several parameters of our method by creating an experimental plan with different slab thicknesses $T = [1, 6, 8, 10, 12, 15, 20, N]$. When $T = 1$, it consists of processing all DBT slices and $T = N$ a single in-plane, similar to S2D. We evaluated $\mathcal{O} = 0.5$ and $\mathcal{O} = 0$ corresponding to 50% and no overlap between slabs, respectively. We also evaluated $\theta = 0$ and $\theta = T \times 0.5$, i.e., keeping noisy slices or removing them.

4 Results

We computed the following classification metrics: Area Under the ROC Curve (AUC_{ROC}), the Area under Precision-Recall curve (AUC_{PR}), and Spec@90%. AUCs allow us to measure the classifier's ability to distinguish between the benign and malignant classes, while sensitivities and specificities assess the true positive and true negative rates. Aiming to improve the detection rate in clinical practice, we also evaluated the specificity (Spec@90%) of the method when setting the sensitivity to above 90% (i.e., higher than an average of human reading of 87.4% [10]). We report IW and BW metrics with 95% confidence intervals (CIs), using the bootstrap approach presented by Buda et al. [1].

Based on our experiments, we found that $T = N$ was the worst slab thickness, with drastically lower AUCs and Spec@90%. It can be explained by the maximum intensity projection method used for slabbing, which generates important noisy artifacts on thick slabs and prevents them from benefitting from the

3D nature of DBT. No clear trend is observed in performances with and without overlap between slabs ($\mathcal{O} = 0$ and $\mathcal{O} = 0.5$) as very comparable AUC$_{PR}$, AUC$_{PR}$ and Spec@90% are achieved. However, excluding overlapping allows to reduce the inference time as fewer slabs are processed. We observed identical metrics varying θ values, meaning the CNN is not influenced by the noise in the volume boundaries. The slab thicknesses ablation is reported in Table 2.

Clinically meaningful BW AUC$_{ROC}$ scores are obtained on the BCS$_{val}$ and BCS$_{test}$ sets reaching **0.90** in both cases. Those performances are remarkable as they are achieved using a classifier trained only on FFDMs. Interestingly, it mimics the radiologists' performances on slabbed volumes observed in [16]. The highest IW and BW AUC$_{ROC}$ are generally obtained with 8 and 10-mm slabs on the three datasets. Best AUC$_{PR}$ scores are also achieved with these thicknesses on the BCS$_{val}$ subset, with only the 20-mm slab outperforming on BCS$_{test}$.

Table 2. Metrics table with the ROC AUC (AUC$_{ROC}$), Precision-Recall AUC (AUC$_{PR}$), and Spec@90%. IW and BW metrics are reported on the three datasets BCS$_{val}$, BCS$_{test}$, and EA$_{DBT}$ following the ablation on several slab thicknesses: $T \in [6, 8, 10, 15, 20]$ mm.

Dataset	T	Image-Wise (IW)			Breast-Wise (BW)		
		AUC$_{ROC}$	AUC$_{PR}$	Spec@90%	AUC$_{ROC}$	AUC$_{PR}$	Spec@90%
BCS$_{val}$	6	0.86 (0.78–0.93)	0.25 (0.14–0.39)	0.55 (0.52–0.58)	**0.90** (0.79–0.97)	0.28 (0.14–0.51)	**0.87** (0.84–0.90)
	8	0.87 (0.79–0.94)	0.26 (0.15–0.42)	**0.66** (0.64–0.69)	**0.90** (0.79–0.97)	0.31 (0.16–0.54)	0.84 (0.81–0.87)
	10	**0.88** (0.81–0.93)	**0.29** (0.16–0.44)	0.65 (0.63–0.68)	**0.90** (0.80–0.97)	**0.36** (0.17–0.59)	0.80 (0.77–0.83)
	15	0.86 (0.78–0.92)	0.25 (0.13–0.39)	0.50 (0.48–0.53)	0.88 (0.78–0.95)	0.29 (0.12–0.50)	0.79 (0.76–0.83)
	20	0.86 (0.78–0.92)	0.23 (0.13–0.38)	0.61 (0.58–0.64)	0.89 (0.78–0.96)	0.25 (0.12–0.48)	0.81 (0.77–0.84)
BCS$_{test}$	6	**0.86** (0.81–0.91)	0.25 (0.16–0.37)	**0.58** (0.56–0.60)	0.88 (0.82–0.94)	0.25 (0.14–0.42)	0.73 (0.69–0.76)
	8	**0.86** (0.81–0.91)	0.29 (0.18–0.42)	0.49 (0.46–0.51)	**0.90** (0.84–0.95)	0.32 (0.17–0.51)	**0.79** (0.76–0.81)
	10	**0.86** (0.82–0.91)	0.27 (0.17–0.40)	0.54 (0.52–0.57)	0.89 (0.82–0.94)	0.28 (0.16–0.45)	0.74 (0.71–0.76)
	15	0.85 (0.80–0.90)	0.25 (0.16–0.38)	0.53 (0.51–0.56)	0.85 (0.76–0.92)	0.25 (0.13–0.43)	0.46 (0.43–0.50)
	20	0.82 (0.77–0.88)	**0.32** (0.20–0.45)	0.51 (0.48–0.53)	0.85 (0.77–0.91)	**0.33** (0.16–0.51)	0.49 (0.46–0.53)
EA$_{DBT}$	6	0.84 (0.48–0.98)	0.02 (0.00–0.07)	0.47 (0.45–0.50)	**0.97** (0.95–0.98)	**0.04** (0.02–0.12)	**0.97** (0.95–0.98)
	8	0.85 (0.48–0.99)	**0.03** (0.00–0.08)	0.48 (0.45–0.50)	**0.97** (0.95–0.98)	**0.04** (0.02–0.12)	0.96 (0.95–0.98)
	10	**0.86** (0.54–0.98)	0.02 (0.00–0.07)	0.53 (0.51–0.56)	0.96 (0.94–0.97)	0.03 (0.01–0.09)	0.96 (0.94–0.97)
	15	0.80 (0.34–0.98)	0.02 (0.00–0.06)	0.33 (0.31–0.36)	0.92 (0.84–0.98)	0.02 (0.00–0.08)	0.86 (0.83–0.88)
	20	0.84 (0.58–0.99)	0.02 (0.00–0.08)	**0.57** (0.55–0.60)	0.86 (0.72–0.99)	0.02 (0.00–0.09)	0.74 (0.71–0.77)

Table 3. State-of-the-art comparison table between our method using a 8-mm slab and methods proposed from the DBTex phase 2 challenge [8]. We report binary classification metrics using the same methodology as mentioned above.

Methods	BCS$_{val}$			BCS$_{test}$		
	AUC$_{ROC}$	AUC$_{PR}$	Spec@90%	AUC$_{ROC}$	AUC$_{PR}$	Spec@90%
NYU BTeam	0.95 (0.93–0.97)	**0.39** (0.20–0.64)	0.89 (0.86–0.93)	**0.93** (0.91–0.95)	0.27 (0.15–0.41)	**0.86** (0.78–0.90)
Vicorob	0.93 (0.89–0.96)	0.33 (0.15–0.55)	0.85 (0.74–0.90)	**0.93** (0.90–0.96)	**0.33** (0.19–0.52)	0.78 (0.68–0.95)
Zedus	**0.96** (0.93–0.98)	0.35 (0.19–0.58)	**0.90** (0.85–0.94)	0.92 (0.88–0.95)	0.25 (0.14–0.40)	**0.86** (0.59–0.90)
Ours (8 mm slab)	0.90 (0.79–0.97)	0.31 (0.16–0.54)	0.84 (0.81–0.87)	0.90 (0.84–0.95)	0.32 (0.17–0.51)	0.79 (0.76–0.81)

Regarding EA_{DBT}, we achieved an AUC_{ROC} of **0.97** and a Spec@90% of **0.97**, yet noting a very small malignant population (4 malignant DBTs, 2 breasts) as shown by the low AUC_{PR} average to ≈0.03. When we consider EA_{MRI}, *i.e.*, including clinical outcomes from MRI, we observe a remarkable drop in performance with the best AUC_{ROC} scores of 0.67 and 0.76 IW, BW respectively. Still, we note the sensitivity of the method to be higher than that of the radiologists when compared to DBT BI-RADS assessments.

We explored the ways to maximize predictions from different thicknesses by aggregating predictions from slabs of different thicknesses, but no improvements have been observed with similar averaged BW AUC_{ROC} of 0.90, 0.88, and 0.97 for BCS_{val}, BCS_{test}, and EA_{DBT} respectively.

To compare with other state-of-the-art methods, we computed the same metrics using the predictions published from the DBTex phase 2 challenge [8] as shown in Table 3. We can see that NYU BTeam [8] and Zedus [8] teams outperformed our method on all but AUC_{PR} metrics. Nevertheless, the performances remain comparable, given the reported CIs. Noteworthy, we achieved these results by learning from FFDMs only, while all top-performing challenges included DBT data in training.

The processing time decreases when reducing the number of slabs M. We timed the inferences of 2787 volumes (BCS_{val} and BCS_{test}) on 2 CPUs (AMD EPYC9474@3.6 GHz 48 cores). The obtained average times per volume are: 74 s ($T = 6$), 55 s ($T = 8$), 45 s ($T = 10$), and 37 s ($T = 12$), resulting in an average ≈3.72 s per image. Hence, processing slices separately gives a volume-wise inference time of ≈372 s for DBT with 100 slices, which may not be acceptable in practice. Moreover, no performance gain was observed in none of the dataset when processing slices independently compared to 6–10 mm thicknesses.

5 Conclusion

In this study, we evaluate a DBT classification method in the context of breast cancer screening. To align with the lack and heterogeneity of DBT training data, we used a 2D CNN architecture trained solely on FFDMs. To preserve the resolution and reduce computation times and costs, we propose to use a slabbing approach to summarize an entire DBT volume into several 2D slabs. This strategy leverages the anisotropic property of DBT, copes with the scarcity of isolated slices, and mimics the running clinical practices.

We propose a comprehensive benchmark evaluating different sets of parameters to generate slabs. We place the proposed method in the realistic screening scenario (*i.e.*, strongly imbalanced towards benign and normal cases), evaluating on two public screening datasets: BCS-DBT and EA1141. We share the splits used for EA1141 in a GitHub repository to facilitate future works.

Our method achieves high performances with breast-wise AUC_{ROC} of **0.90** on BCS-DBT validation and test subsets and **0.97** on EA_{DBT}. To evaluate the clinical viability, we show specificity at 90% of sensitivity on the three datasets obtaining **0.87**, **0.79**, and **0.97** for BCS_{val}, BCS_{test}, and EA_{DBT} respectively.

Future works will focus on the integration of DBTs in training data, and the design of a method that fuses both 2D and 3D features to exploit inter-slices information to improve both classification and detection performance.

Acknowledgements. This research is supported by the CIFRE program granted by the French ANRT organism under contract no. 2022/155. Computational resources were provided by the CPER Pays de la Loire Datacenter et Calcul Scientifique (DaCaS) project and GLiCID cluster.

References

1. Buda, M., et al.: A data set and deep learning algorithm for the detection of masses and architectural distortions in digital breast tomosynthesis images. JAMA Netw. Open **4**(8), e2119100–e2119100 (2021)
2. Comstock, C.E., et al.: Abbreviated breast MRI and digital tomosynthesis mammography in screening women with dense breasts (EA1141). The Cancer Imaging Archive (2023)
3. Diekmann, F., et al.: Thick slices from tomosynthesis data sets: phantom study for the evaluation of different algorithms. J. Digit. Imaging **22**, 519–526 (2009)
4. Doganay, E., Li, P., Luo, Y., Chai, R., Guo, Y., Wu, S.: Breast cancer classification from digital breast tomosynthesis using 3D multi-subvolume approach. In: Medical Imaging 2020: Imaging Informatics for Healthcare, Research, and Applications, vol. 11318, pp. 103–109. SPIE (2020)
5. El-Shazli, A.M.A., Youssef, S.M., Soliman, A.H.: Intelligent computer-aided model for efficient diagnosis of digital breast tomosynthesis 3D imaging using deep learning. Appl. Sci. **12**(11), 5736 (2022)
6. Hassan, L., Saleh, A., Singh, V.K., Puig, D., Abdel-Nasser, M.: Detecting breast tumors in tomosynthesis images utilizing deep learning-based dynamic ensemble approach. Computers **12**(11), 220 (2023)
7. Huang, H., et al.: UNet 3+: a full-scale connected UNet for medical image segmentation. In: ICASSP 2020-2020 IEEE International Conference on Acoustics, Speech and Signal Processing (ICASSP), pp. 1055–1059. IEEE (2020)
8. Konz, N., et al.: A competition, benchmark, code, and data for using artificial intelligence to detect lesions in digital breast tomosynthesis. JAMA Netw. Open **6**(2), e230524–e230524 (2023)
9. Kopans, D., Gavenonis, S., Halpern, E., Moore, R.: Calcifications in the breast and digital breast tomosynthesis. Breast J. **17**(6), 638–644 (2011)
10. Lee, C.I., et al.: National performance benchmarks for screening digital breast tomosynthesis: update from the breast cancer surveillance consortium. Radiology **307**(4), e222499 (2023)
11. McDonald, E.S., McCarthy, A.M., Akhtar, A.L., Synnestvedt, M.B., Schnall, M., Conant, E.F.: Baseline screening mammography: performance of full-field digital mammography versus digital breast tomosynthesis. Am. J. Roentgenol. **205**(5), 1143–1148 (2015)
12. Michell, M., et al.: A comparison of the accuracy of film-screen mammography, full-field digital mammography, and digital breast tomosynthesis. Clin. Radiol. **67**(10), 976–981 (2012)

13. Mota, A.M., Clarkson, M.J., Almeida, P., Matela, N.: Automatic classification of simulated breast tomosynthesis whole images for the presence of microcalcification clusters using deep cnns. J. Imaging **8**(9), 231 (2022)
14. Park, J., et al.: An efficient deep neural network to classify large 3D images with small objects. IEEE Trans. Med. Imaging (2023)
15. Partridge, G.J.W., et al.: How long does it take to read a mammogram? Investigating the reading time of digital breast tomosynthesis and digital mammography. Eur. J. Radiol. 111535 (2024)
16. Pujara, A.C., et al.: Digital breast tomosynthesis slab thickness: impact on reader performance and interpretation time. Radiology **297**(3), 534–542 (2020)
17. Sauer, S.T., et al.: Artificial-intelligence-enhanced synthetic thick slabs versus standard slices in digital breast tomosynthesis. Br. J. Radiol. **96**(1145), 20220967 (2023)
18. Shoshan, Y., et al.: Artificial intelligence for reducing workload in breast cancer screening with digital breast tomosynthesis. Radiology **303**(1), 69–77 (2022)
19. Siegel, R.L., Miller, K.D., et al.: Cancer statistics, 2023. CA: Cancer J. Clini. **73**(1), 17–48 (2023). https://doi.org/10.3322/caac.21763
20. Singh, S., et al.: Adaptation of a deep learning malignancy model from full-field digital mammography to digital breast tomosynthesis. In: Medical Imaging: Computer-Aided Diagnosis, vol. 11314, pp. 25–32. SPIE (2020)
21. Sun, H., et al.: SAH-NET: structure-aware hierarchical network for clustered microcalcification classification in digital breast tomosynthesis. IEEE Trans. Cybern. (2022)
22. Tardy, M., Mateus, D.: Trainable summarization to improve breast tomosynthesis classification. In: International Conference on Medical Image Computing and Computer-Assisted Intervention, pp. 140–149. Springer (2021)
23. Terrassin, P., Tardy, M., Lauzeral, N., Normand, N.: Annotation-free deep-learning framework for microcalcifications detection on mammograms. In: Medical Imaging 2024: Computer-Aided Diagnosis, vol. 12927, pp. 208–217. SPIE (2024)
24. Wang, J., et al.: CAPNet: context attention pyramid network for computer-aided detection of microcalcification clusters in digital breast tomosynthesis. Comput. Methods Programs Biomed. **242**, 107831 (2023)
25. Wu, N., et al.: Deep neural networks improve radiologists' performance in breast cancer screening. IEEE Trans. Med. Imaging **39**(4), 1184–1194 (2019)
26. Xiao, B., et al.: Classification of microcalcification clusters in digital breast tomosynthesis using ensemble convolutional neural network. Biomed. Eng. Online **20**, 1–20 (2021)
27. Zack, G.W., Rogers, W.E., Latt, S.A.: Automatic measurement of sister chromatid exchange frequency. J. Histochem. Cytochem. **25**(7), 741–753 (1977)

Predicting Aesthetic Outcomes in Breast Cancer Surgery: A Multimodal Retrieval Approach

Mohammad Hossein Zolfagharnasab[1,2](✉), Nuno Freitas[1,2], Tiago Gonçalves[1,2], Eduardo Bonci[3], Carlos Mavioso[3], Maria J. Cardoso[3], Hélder P. Oliveira[1,2], and Jaime S. Cardoso[1,2]

[1] University of Porto, Porto, Portugal
[2] Institute for Systems and Computer Engineering, Technology and Science, Porto, Portugal
{mohammad.h.zolfagharnasab,nuno.p.silva}@inesctec.pt
[3] Breast Unit, Champalimaud Foundation, Lisbon, Portugal

Abstract. Breast cancer treatments often affect patients' body image, making aesthetic outcome predictions vital. This study introduces a Deep Learning (DL) multimodal retrieval pipeline using a dataset of 2,193 instances combining clinical attributes and RGB images of patients' upper torsos. We evaluate four retrieval techniques: Weighted Euclidean Distance (WED) with various configurations and shallow Artificial Neural Network (ANN) for tabular data, pre-trained and fine-tuned Convolutional Neural Networks (CNNs) and Vision Transformers (ViTs), and a multimodal approach combining both data types. The dataset, categorised into Excellent/Good and Fair/Poor outcomes, is organised into over 20K triplets for training and testing. Results show fine-tuned multimodal ViTs notably enhance performance, achieving up to 73.85% accuracy and 80.62% Adjusted Discounted Cumulative Gain (ADCG). This framework not only aids in managing patient expectations by retrieving the most relevant post-surgical images but also promises broad applications in medical image analysis and retrieval. The main contributions of this paper are the development of a multimodal retrieval system for breast cancer patients based on post-surgery aesthetic outcome and the evaluation of different models on a new dataset annotated by clinicians for image retrieval.

Keywords: Aesthetic Evaluation · Breast Cancer · Decision Support Systems · Medical Image Retrieval Systems · Vision Transformers

1 Introduction

Breast cancer (BrCa) remains a prevalent global health concern, though advancements in screening and treatment have significantly improved survival rates,

---

M. H. Zolfagharnasab and N. Freitas—These authors contributed equally.

exceeding 90% at 5 years in many high-income countries [1]. Consequently, attention within the clinical community has shifted towards enhancing post-surgery patient quality of life (QoL) [2]. Locoregional (LoRe) treatments, such as radiation therapy and surgery, commonly employed in patients, often impact aesthetic outcomes, influencing body image significantly. Ongoing research aims to establish a standard for evaluating these outcomes [3]. Recent studies on QoL of breast cancer patients after treatment, show that a patient's body image has a high correlation to QoL [4]. Despite that, the current methods for objective assessment using panel scores or software do not adequately correlate with the patient's self-image [5]. Currently, clinicians use visual examples of similar cases to discuss potential outcomes of breast cancer surgery with patients [3]. However, as databases grow, selecting cases becomes time-consuming and subjective, highlighting the need for objective methods to efficiently retrieve clinically and visually relevant examples that meet both criteria. Artificial intelligence (AI) algorithms, have emerged as crucial tools in this context, enabling accurate analysis of complex medical images [6,7]. Thus, a retrieval system can be effective by allowing clinicians to show patients previous cases and allow them to fully understand the possible outcomes of treatment. These systems enhance efficiency and objectivity in retrieving relevant samples, thereby improving diagnostic accuracy and patient outcomes. Despite these advancements, challenges such as the *semantic gap* between system analysis and user expectations, variability in image quality, and limited data availability persist, needing ongoing attention and innovation [8,9].

Considering these challenges, this paper introduces a DL-based multimodal retrieval pipeline for predicting aesthetic outcomes in BrCa patients post-LoRe treatments. Given a query image from the upper torso, our proposed algorithm retrieves the top 10 most analogous patient cases from the image database. While our focus is on pre-surgery and post-surgery comparisons in BrCa, this pipeline is adaptable to various domains. Key contributions include:

1. A novel multimodal retrieval framework for the prediction of aesthetic outcomes of LoRe treatments of BrCa patients that combines tabular clinical data and image features trained and evaluated on an annotated dataset.
2. A comparative study with ViTs and CNNs regarding the impacts of feature extraction on retrieval quality.

The code for the implementation of this paper is publicly available on GitHub.

2 Background

2.1 Image Retrieval

Image retrieval systems are designed to efficiently retrieve samples from extensive databases [10]. They fall into two main categories of content-based image

https://github.com/MsainZn/bcs-aesth-mmodal-retrieval.

retrieval (CBIR), which analyses the visual content of a query image to find similar images, and collaborative filtering image retrieval (CFIR), which employs scoring mechanisms to identify similarities among available entities.

In medical applications, CBIR systems are quite common due to operating without requiring detailed clinician annotation [11]. Examples include chest X-rays [12,13] and brain MRIs [14]. While CFIR systems are less explored, some studies with CFIR systems [15,16] report improved performances, likely because they incorporate more clinician input, which translates to learning more from the data. In this regard, the model proposed in this paper can be categorised as a weak CFIR since it is trained to imitate the clinicians' rankings as well taking advantage of visual features.

2.2 Mathematical Modelling: Triplet Loss

The triplet loss is a robust technique used in tasks like face recognition, image retrieval, and metric learning to learn embeddings that capture semantic similarity among data points [17]. It involves three entities: a query, a positive sample (similar to the query), and a negative sample (dissimilar to the query). Equation 1 shows the triplet loss formulation:

$$L(A, P, N) = \max(0, dist(A, P) - dist(A, N) + \alpha), \tag{1}$$

where A, P, and N are embedding of the query, positive, and negative samples, respectively, $dist(A, P)$ and $dist(A, N)$ represent distances (e.g., Euclidean or cosine) between these samples, and α is a margin hyper-parameter enforcing a minimum difference between distances for the loss to be zero. This ensures that semantically similar samples are closer to each other while dissimilar samples are farther apart in the embedding space. This approach effectively mimics the exact ranking determined by clinicians during training, and optimises the weights to enhance the clustering of similar samples.

2.3 Evaluation Techniques

In this study, we utilised the Adjusted Discounted Cumulative Gain (ADCG), given in Eq. 2, and Contrastive Accuracy (CAcc), presented in Eq. 3, to ensure a more accurate assessment of our models' performance.

$$DCG_p = \sum_{i=1}^{p} \frac{2^{\text{rel}_i} - 1}{\log_2(i + 1)}, \quad ADCG_p = Norm_{MinMax}(DCG_p) \tag{2}$$

$$\text{CAcc} = \sum_{cat=1}^{m} \frac{\text{Number of correct predictions per triplet}}{\text{Total number of triplets}}. \tag{3}$$

The presented metrics offer several benefits for evaluating the performance retrieval systems. For instance, ADCG accounts for prioritising the relevant instances with respect to the query, which makes it particularly interesting for our application where results ordering is crucial. In the meantime, CAcc offers insights into the model's ability to distinguish between similar and dissimilar items in relation to a query image. This metric is particularly crucial for our dataset as it ensures a detailed comparison of all catalogue elements against the query, enabling a comprehensive assessment of all samples.

3 Related Work

Recent literature on image retrieval systems focuses extensively on enhancing feature extraction algorithms [18]. This includes CNN and ViT architectures, which follow a process of feature extraction to encode image features, pattern recognition for high-level representations, and embedding these features into a space where similar images are positioned close together for efficient retrieval by comparing feature vector distances [19].

With that in mind, we point the reader to the works of Wang et al. [20], Bhandi et al. [21], and Maji et al. [22], who evaluated the performance of CNN-based image retrieval architectures against traditional computer vison methods, and concluded that the first performed better than the latter. Naturally, with the recent advancement in transformers, similar investigations are carried out using ViTs [23]. For instance, Song et al. [24] and Dubey et al. [25] published pioneer studies on the comparison between CNN-based retrieval and ViT-based retrieval, showcasing the superior performance of ViTs across multiple datasets. Using same pre-trained models, studies such as Zhou et al. [26] where viable accuracy improvement is reported using semi-supervised training in chest X-ray application. For medical applications, variations of CLIP model, especially Med-CLIP has also shown promising results in both zero-shot use-cases and image-retrieval systems [27]. Using MedCLIP and contrastive learning strategy with expert annotation, Kumar et al. [28] were able to improve the retrieval accuracy by almost 5% in all of their test-cases. Similar improvements were reported from researchers working with CLIP in X-ray [29], and MRI images [30]. Studies such as [31] has also reported on multi-view mammograms.

4 Dataset

The dataset for this study comprises 2,193 instances encompassing clinical attributes (i.e., height, weight, age, bra size, bra-cup size) organised as tabular data, along with their corresponding JPEG images depicting the upper torsos of patients (some depicted in (see Fig. 1). The images vary in size ranging from 1869 × 1117 to 6000 × 4000, with an average size of 4810 × 2903. To create the ground-truth annotations, the clinicians were asked to rank the 10–15 most similar images to a given query image such that the sample ranked i is more similar to the query image compared to the one appearing later in the list with rank $i + k$, where $k > 0$. For each query patient, there are two catalogues annotated according to the aesthetic classification of the retrieved patients. This classification is done by clinicians according to the Harris scale [32]: one group presented patients with *Excellent/Good* aesthetic outcomes and the other with *Fair/Poor* aesthetic result. Using this strategy, we constructed 160 catalogues of query-retrieved images, while ensuring no overlap between instances. These catalogues were split into training (80%) and testing (20%) sets.

For training with triplet-loss, the catalogues were organised into triplets, considering all possible combinations of query and annotated sample. Each triplet includes a query, a positive sample, and a negative sample, where the negative sample is the one ranked further from the query compared with the positive one. There are several preprocessing steps worth discussing. Concerning the tabular data, each element in the tabular feature vector is normalised according to the training set. For instance, the patient height is normalised using min-max normalisation with train set elements. For the images, we first transformed all them into 224 × 224 with zero padding. Afterwards for each model (either ViT or CNN), we used its own ImageProcessor module (available on Hugging Face) to transform the images based on the model requirement. By doing so, we were able to assess various models using the same framework. More implementation details can be found in the publicly available GitHub repository (see Sect. 1).

5 Proposed Method

This study presents four sets of techniques for patient retrieval. The first set of experiments focuses on clinical data. The second experiment used pre-trained DL image models to extract features from the images. The third experiment is similar but performs fine-tuning of the models on our training set. The fourth experiment combines both the image and clinical data. Except for the third approach, all models were trained on the data. Using clinicians' ranking, we organise the data into triplets and utilise the triplet loss to update model weights.

The first experiments used the clinical (tabular) data. We employed Weighted Euclidean Distance (WED) to optimise the retrieval process. The reason we used this model was the simplicity of the tabular data (i.e., a vector with five features); however, same triplet-loss formulation was employed to update the weights according to the clinicians' rankings. The WED is defined in Eq. 4:

$$WED(u, v, W) = |u-v|_{1\times N} W_{N \times N} |u-v|_{N \times 1}^T, \tag{4}$$

where u is the feature vector for sample A, v for B, and W is the weight matrix. By setting the weight matrix as identity ($W = I$), we recover the standard (baseline) Euclidean distance. Unlike WED, baseline euclidean contains no learnable parameter; thus, it requires no training. Besides WED, we also employed a more flexible approach using a shallow 4-layer ANN for tabular data as well. Each layer consists of 16 neurons with a tangent-hyperbolic activation function. Same as WED, the model's weights are also updated using triplet loss; however, the ANN provides a greater number of learnable parameters, which promotes capturing complex interactions between features.

---

https://huggingface.co/.

For the second experiment, we shift our attention to the images, and we leveraged competitive DL models to perform feature extraction. It is important to note that this experiment did not include any additional fine-tuning with respect to clinicians' ranking. Essentially, we did not update the models weight based on triplet-loss in this experiment and we essentially captured a zero-shot feature extraction from the image models. For this purpose, we utilised a selection of pre-trained DL models, including well-known CNNs such as ResNet50 and VGG16, as well as advanced ViTs like BEIT, DINOv2, DEIT, and Google-ViT.

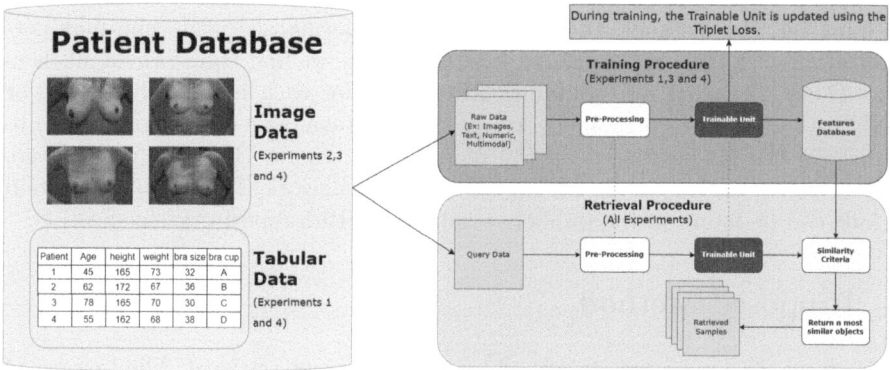

Fig. 1. Illustration of the training and retrieval procedure. During training, the trainable unit is optimised using the triplet loss to promote retrieval according to clinicians' ranking. It is worth noting that for images, the trainable unit must incorporate feature extraction, while for tabular data, it can be as simple as WED. During retrieval, the features corresponding to a given query are extracted using the trainable unit and the Euclidean distance (similarity criterion) is used to calculate the distance between the query-samples to retrieve the n most similar samples. To improve the performance, the extracted feature vector of a particular image can also be stored in a feature database.

The third experiment mirrors the second; however, we utilised triplet-loss to fine-tune the extracted feature vectors from the images to align with clinicians' ranking criteria. This approach serves dual purposes: ensuring semantic alignment with clinicians' objectives and emphasising features that aid in replicating clinicians rankings. As a result, this approach falls under weakly CFIRs, where clinicians' predefined scores enhances sample retrieval for new cases.

The fourth experiment enhances the trainable DL model by incorporating multimodal inputs. In this method, feature vectors from fine-tuned image models are concatenated with tabular feature vector. This combined vector is later used as the input of another shallow MLP with same properties of the first experiment, and the model weights are updated according to the triplet-loss formulation. Additional implementation details are available in the official GitHub repository (see Sect. 1). Figure 1 briefly summarises the retrieval pipeline described in the experiments.

6 Results and Discussion

The study's goal was to develop and evaluate a DL-based multimodal retrieval system to predict aesthetic outcomes in BrCa patients after LoRe treatments. This system combined tabular clinical data and image features to provide a robust retrieval framework. By comparing different methods and models, given in Table 1, this study offers valuable insights into the performance and practical implications of each approach. Furthermore, we developed distinct retrieval models based on varying aesthetic assessments (i.e., *Excellent/Good* and *Fair/Poor*). Clinicians typically require retrieval of both positive and negative treatment outcomes to illustrate diverse scenarios to patients. This separation enables our algorithm to specifically address these preferences, thereby improving its ability to accurately reflect the needs of clinicians. This approach highly improves the relevance and precision of the retrieval process by ensuring each scenario is appropriately represented.

Tabular Data-Based Retrieval: The first method utilised clinical (tabular) data to perform the retrieval using WED and an MLP. The WED method provided a baseline for comparison, revealing moderate performance on both datasets. The MLP approach outperformed the WED, achieving higher CAcc and ADCG values. However, no model achieves performance superior to 66% on ADCG and 65% on CAcc, both in training and testing. This suggests that the clinical data alone may not provide sufficient information to achieve high retrieval accuracy, indicating its limitations in capturing the full complexity required for precise aesthetic outcome prediction.

Image-Based Retrieval: Table 1 shows both pre-trained models and fine-tuned models for image retrieval. Overall, pre-Trained models generally exhibit lower performance compared to most tabular models across both datasets, potentially due to their limited alignment with specific aesthetic criteria used by clinicians. Nevertheless, it is still worth noting that ViTs in general, especially BEIT, emerge as the standout performers. The third scenario involved fine-tuning pre-trained DL models to better align their feature vectors with the clinicians' ranking criteria. By doing so, it can be observed that the performance of all image models were notably improved. For instance, the fine-tuned VGG16 model showed a dramatic improvement, with CAcc scores jumping from 52.10% to 69.26% and ADCG reaching from 46.71% to 76.87% in the test set. These improvements underscore the importance of tailoring pre-trained models for retrieval tasks, as it allowed the models to better capture the semantic and aesthetic considerations critical to clinicians. When comparing CNNs to ViTs, ViTs generally demonstrated greater success, showcasing the potential of ViTs for medical image retrieval. Among them, GoogleViT stood out as the top performer, achieving superior results in 5 out of 8 performance metrics evaluated.

Multimodal Retrieval: The final method integrated both tabular and image features, resulting in a more comprehensive input for the retrieval system. As expected, the multimodal approach achieved the highest performance, with an average 1–2% improvement in the retrieval accuracy metrics across all evaluation criteria. Besides improving accuracy, utilising multimodal data is valuable as it promotes robustness of the overall prediction in case the DL models underperform or encounter out-of-distribution samples. For such scenarios, the clinical data is capable of providing structured, interpretable insights that help maintain consistency and reliability in the predictions, ensuring more informed decision-making in clinical settings.

Table 1. Retrieval performance metrics for various models categorized by aesthetic quality. Each entry is of the form (**Excellent/Good, Fair/Poor**).

Type	Model	Train		Test	
		CAcc (%)	ADCG (%)	CAcc (%)	ADCG (%)
Tabular	Baseline	(61.37, 61.77)	(65.21, 63.52)	(55.68, 61.87)	(57.75, 62.05)
	Matrix	(60.41, 60.40)	(65.29, 62.02)	(**57.58**, 61.58)	(58.54, 65.31)
	MLP	(**62.65, 64.89**)	(**66.64, 64.89**)	(57.09, **64.90**)	(57.70, 66.56)
Pre-trained	VGG16	(52.02, 46.68)	(54.55, 46.42)	(52.10, 44.72)	(56.69, 46.71)
	ResNet	(54.96, 47.81)	(58.75, 50.56)	(53.38, 50.56)	(55.20, 53.74)
	DEIT	(52.08, 45.85)	(52.87, 46.24)	(53.25, 44.47)	(54.87, 53.13)
	GoogleViT	(53.24, 47.29)	(56.21, **49.99**)	(52.10, 49.09)	(54.87, 53.13)
	DINOv2	(56.00, 46.31)	(58.88, 47.82)	(**54.88**, 46.15)	(**60.231**, 44.95)
	BEIT	(**56.03**, 49.25)	(**61.06**, 49.39)	(54.79, **50.98**)	(57.58, **54.35**)
Fine-tuned	VGG16	(90.51, 90.55)	(95.18, 95.42)	(69.26, 71.16)	(71.96, 76.87)
	ResNet	(89.47, 87.11)	(94.22, 93.52)	(68.33, 72.17)	(70.30, 78.29)
	DEIT	(76.40, 73.58)	(62.75, 79.02)	(60.06, 63.09)	(64.61, 64.58)
	GoogleViT	(**92.65**, 91.95)	(**96.45, 96.28**)	(69.30, **73.18**)	(73.87, **79.86**)
	DINOv2	(89.39, 87.77)	(94.38, 93.82)	(69.92, 70.78)	(**77.89**, 76.97)
	BEIT	(89.78, **95.33**)	(93.95, 81.88)	(**71.95**, 72.76)	(73.85, 77.92)
Multimodal	GoogleViT	(98.69, **98.91**)	(99.39, 99.56)	(68.55, **73.85**)	(71.14, **80.62**)
	DINOv2	(97.89, 98.25)	(99.10, 99.33)	(70.14, 73.56)	(**77.40**, 78.96)
	BEIT	(**99.10**, 98.87)	(**99.65, 99.65**)	(**72.06**, 73.05)	(73.63, 78.45)

7 Conclusions and Future Work

Using triplet-loss optimisation, this study evaluated various configurations of clinical and image-based retrieval systems for predicting aesthetic outcomes in BrCa patients following LoRe treatments. The key findings are:

1. Clinical (tabular) data alone showed moderate performance, indicating limitations in capturing complexities for precise aesthetic outcome prediction;
2. ViTs, especially BEIT, showed superior performance compared to traditional CNNs like VGG16 and ResNet;
3. Fine-tuning enhanced retrieval across all models, especially GoogleViT and BEIT, to better align with semantic and aesthetic considerations;
4. Integrating tabular clinical data with image features resulted in the highest overall performance, due to combining structured clinical insights with nuanced image features.

Future work could explore the potential of image-segmentation models instead of image-classifiers to achieve higher performance and evaluating out-of-distribution instances as the current dataset has limited variability.

Acknowledgments. This work has received funding from the European Union's Horizon Europe research and innovation programme under the Grant Agreement 101057389-CINDERELLA project, and by the Portuguese Foundation for Science and Technology (FCT) through the Ph.D. Grant "2020.06434.BD".

Disclosure of Interests. The authors have no competing interests to declare that are relevant to the content of this article.

Data Policy. The dataset used for this study is private, but it can be accessed upon request.

References

1. Arnold, M., et al.: Current and future burden of breast cancer: global statistics for 2020 and 2040. Breast **66**, 15–23 (2022)
2. Cardoso, J.S., Silva, W., Cardoso, M.J.: Evolution, current challenges, and future possibilities in the objective assessment of aesthetic outcome of breast cancer locoregional treatment. Breast **49**, 123–130 (2020)
3. Silva, W., Carvalho, M., Mavioso, C., Cardoso, M.J., Cardoso, J.S.: Deep aesthetic assessment and retrieval of breast cancer treatment outcomes. In: Pinho, A.J., Georgieva, P., Teixeira, L.F., Sánchez, J.A. (eds.) Pattern Recognition and Image Analysis, pp. 108–118. Springer, Cham (2022)
4. Zwakman, M., et al.: Long-term quality of life and aesthetic outcomes after breast conserving surgery in patients with breast cancer. Eur. J. Surg. Oncol. **48**(8), 1692–1698 (2022)
5. Kim, M.K., et al.: Effect of cosmetic outcome on quality of life after breast cancer surgery. Eur. J. Surg. Oncol. (EJSO) **41**(3), 426–432 (2015)
6. Huan, J.: Research on the application of artificial intelligence in image and text database retrieval. Front. Comput. Intell. Syst. **2** (2022)
7. Naqvi, W.M., Sundus, H., Mishra, G., Muthukrishnan, R., Kandakurti, P.K.: AI in medical education curriculum: the future of healthcare learning. Eur. J. Therap. (2024)
8. Shirkhani, S., Mokayed, H., Saini, R., Chai, H.Y.: Study of AI-driven fashion recommender systems. SN Comput. Sci. **4** (2023)

9. Al-Jubouri, H.A.: Content-based image retrieval: survey (2019)
10. Chen, W., et al.: Deep image retrieval: a survey. arXiv preprint arXiv:2101.11282, vol. 1, no. 3, p. 6 (2021)
11. Li, X., Yang, J., Ma, J.: Recent developments of content-based image retrieval (CBIR). Neurocomputing **452**, 675–689 (2021)
12. Agrawal, S., Chowdhary, A., Agarwala, S., Mayya, V., Kamath, S.S.: Content-based medical image retrieval system for lung diseases using deep CNNs. Int. J. Inf. Technol. **14**(7), 3619–3627 (2022)
13. Boroujeni, F.Z., Afshari, D.H., Mahmoodi, F.: COVID-19 image retrieval using siamese deep neural network and hashing technique. In: 2023 14th International Conference on Information and Knowledge Technology (IKT), pp. 186–193. IEEE (2023)
14. Sampathila, N, Pavithra, Martis, R.J.: Computational approach for content-based image retrieval of k-similar images from brain MR image database. Expert Syst. **39**(7), e12652 (2022)
15. Si, L., Jin, R., Hoi, S.C.H., Lyu, M.R.: Collaborative image retrieval via regularized metric learning. Multimed. Syst. **12**, 34–44 (2006)
16. Lo, W.F., Mital, N., Wu, H., Gündüz, D.: Collaborative semantic communication for edge inference. IEEE Wirel. Commun. Lett. (2023)
17. Wang, G., Guo, Y., Xu, Z., Wong, Y., Kankanhalli, M.S.: Semantic-aware triplet loss for image classification. IEEE Trans. Multimed. **25** (2023)
18. Dubey, S.R.: A decade survey of content based image retrieval using deep learning. IEEE Trans. Circ. Syst. Video Technol. **32** (2022)
19. Yan, K., Wang, Y., Liang, D., Huang, T., Tian, Y.: CNN vs. SIFT for image retrieval: alternative or complementary? (2016)
20. Wang, H., Cai, Y., Zhang, Y., Pan, H., Lv, W., Han, H.: Deep learning for image retrieval: what works and what doesn't. In: 2015 IEEE International Conference on Data Mining Workshop (ICDMW), pp. 1576–1583 (2015)
21. Bhandi, V., Sumithra Devi, K.A.: Image retrieval by fusion of features from pre-trained deep convolution neural networks. In: 2019 1st International Conference on Advanced Technologies in Intelligent Control, Environment, Computing & Communication Engineering (ICATIECE), pp. 35–40 (2019)
22. Maji, S., Bose, S.: CBIR using features derived by deep learning. CoRR, abs/2002.07877 (2020)
23. Denner, S., et al.: Leveraging foundation models for content-based medical image retrieval in radiology (2024)
24. Song, C.H., Yoon, J., Choi, S., Avrithis, Y.: Boosting vision transformers for image retrieval (2022)
25. Dubey, S.R., Singh, S.K., Chu, W.-T.: Vision transformer hashing for image retrieval. In: 2022 IEEE International Conference on Multimedia and Expo (ICME), pp. 1–6 (2022)
26. Zhou, H.-Y., Chen, X., Zhang, Y., Luo, R., Wang, L., Yu, Y.: Generalized radiograph representation learning via cross-supervision between images and free-text radiology reports. Nat. Mach. Intell. **4**(1) (2022)
27. Sain, A., Bhunia, A.K., Chowdhury, P.N., Koley, S., Xiang, T., Song, Y.-Z.: Clip for all things zero-shot sketch-based image retrieval, fine-grained or not (2023)
28. Kumar, Y., Marttinen, P.: Improving medical multi-modal contrastive learning with expert annotations (2024)
29. You, K., et al.: CXR-CLIP: toward large scale chest x-ray language-image pre-training. In: International Conference on Medical Image Computing and Computer-Assisted Intervention, pp. 101–111. Springer (2023)

30. Aono, M., Shinoda, H., Asakawa, T., Shimizu, K., Togawa, T., Komoda, T.: Multi-stage medical image captioning using classification and clip. In: CLEF (Working Notes), pp. 1387–1395 (2023)
31. Gao, Y., et al.: Visualize what you learn: a well-explainable joint-learning framework based on multi-view mammograms and associated reports (2023)
32. Rose, M.A., et al.: Conservative surgery and radiation therapy for early breast cancer: long-term cosmetic results. Arch. Surg. **124**(2), 153–157 (1989)

Vision Mamba for Classification of Breast Ultrasound Images

Ali Nasiri-Sarvi[1(✉)], Mahdi S. Hosseini[1], and Hassan Rivaz[2]

[1] Department of Computer Science and Software Engineering (CSSE), Concordia University, Montreal, Canada
ali.nasiri.sarvi7@gmail.com
[2] Department of Electrical and Computer Engineering (ECE), Concordia University, Montreal, Canada

Abstract. Mamba-based models, VMamba and Vim, are a recent family of vision encoders that offer promising performance improvements in many computer vision tasks. This paper compares Mamba-based models with traditional Convolutional Neural Networks (CNNs) and Vision Transformers (ViTs) using the breast ultrasound BUSI dataset and Breast Ultrasound B dataset. Our evaluation, which includes multiple runs of experiments and statistical significance analysis, demonstrates that some of the Mamba-based architectures often outperform CNN and ViT models with statistically significant results. For example, in the B dataset, the best Mamba-based models have a 1.98% average AUC and a 5.0% average Accuracy improvement compared to the best non-Mamba-based model in this study. These Mamba-based models effectively capture long-range dependencies while maintaining some inductive biases, making them suitable for applications with limited data. The code is available at https://github.com/anasiri/BU-Mamba.

Keywords: Vision Mamba · State Space Models · Breast Ultrasound · Breast Cancer

1 Introduction

Processing breast ultrasound images using deep learning can benefit from pre-trained weights and a transfer learning paradigm, especially when dealing with smaller datasets [1]. Several factors influence the effectiveness of transfer learning. One crucial factor is the choice of the pretrained dataset [2], and another critical factor is the selection of the encoder architecture [2].

Convolutional Neural Networks (CNNs) [3] and Vision Transformers (ViTs) [4,5] have been studied for breast ultrasound applications in works such as [6–8]. Recently, a new family of encoders, Vim [9] and VMamba [10], based on State Space Models (SSMs), has emerged in computer vision, leveraging the Mamba architecture [11]. Although studies like UMamba [12] have recently investigated the Mamba architecture for medical imaging dataset segmentation, its performance in breast ultrasound classification has yet to be explored.

In this work, we adopt these architectures from natural image processing, utilizing pretrained weights trained on ImageNet [13], and compare them with common CNN and ViT architectures on two breast ultrasound datasets, BUSI [14] and B dataset [15]. We also conduct a statistical analysis to ensure that the performance improvements are significant. Our results show that Mamba-based architectures frequently outperform other encoder types with significant results. They are also never outperformed by the other encoders in terms of statistical significance.

2 Related Work

CNNs [3] have shown tremendous capability in computer vision tasks, with AlexNet [16] achieving breakthrough performance in the ImageNet Challenge [13], leading to widespread adoption of deep learning models in the field with models such as ResNet [17] and VGG [18]. While CNNs excel at capturing local patterns, they are limited in capturing long-range dependencies due to their limited receptive field.

ViTs [4,5] have been proposed as an alternative to CNN models. They generally outperform these CNN models due to a lack of inductive bias present in CNNs, allowing ViT models to freely learn from the dataset using the attention mechanism [19,20] and effectively capture long-range dependencies. However, this lack of inductive bias also means these models require more data and training to achieve similar performance to CNNs or outperform them.

Recently, a new family of architectures based on the Mamba model [11] has emerged, leveraging State Space Models (SSMs) in deep learning [21]. These architectures, including VMamba [10] and Vision Mamba (Vim) [9], show potential in various applications like video understanding [22], remote sensing [23], pathology datasets [24], and point clouds [25]. In medical imaging, Mamba-based models have demonstrated significant potential, particularly for segmentation tasks, as explored in [12,26–29].

We aim to do a comparative analysis between the Mamba-based models compared to CNN and ViT architectures on two widely adopted breast ultrasound datasets BUSI [14] and B dataset [15]. Since these datasets are small, our analysis uses transfer learning for the comparison. Similar work on comparative analysis for CNN and ViT has been explored for breast ultrasound datasets. For example, the impact of transfer learning on CNNs for breast ultrasound images is explored in [6,7,30]. In [8], ViTs are compared to CNNs through transfer learning. Our goal is to extend these studies to Mamba-based models.

3 Preliminaries

In this section, we provide an overview of the state space models. These preliminaries would help with understanding the Mamba model.

3.1 State Space Models

State space models are mathematical frameworks that describe continuous linear systems. The state equation defines how the state $h(t)$ evolves as a function of the input $x(t)$, as shown in Eq. 1.

$$h_t = Ah_{t-1} + Bx_t \tag{1}$$

The output equation links the connection between the output, the hidden state, and the input based on Eq. 2.

$$y_t = Ch_t + Dx_t \tag{2}$$

The parameters $A, B,$ and C are time-invariant and remain unchanged across the sequence in the S4 model [21]. This time-invariance allows using a global convolution to represent the sequential data, thereby avoiding the slowdown typically seen in recurrent modeling. The global convolution for a sequence of length L is defined based on the Eq. 3 ($\overline{CAB}$ is used to showcase discretized parameters):

$$\begin{aligned} y &= \bar{K} * x \\ \bar{K} \in \mathbb{R} &:= \mathcal{K}_L(A, B, C) = (\overline{CB}, \overline{CAB}, ..., \overline{CA}^{L-1}\overline{B}) \end{aligned} \tag{3}$$

Although this time-invariance accelerates processing speed, it restricts the model's ability to behave dynamically based on each input token, thus constraining its overall performance.

3.2 Mamba

In Mamba [11], selective state spaces are used where the state space parameters B, C, and Δ (a discretization parameter) are computed dynamically based on each input sequence, with A as the only time-invariant parameter. This dependence on the input improves the model's ability to capture temporal variations and complex dependencies in the data. However, this dependence on the input prevents the option of using a global convolution, limiting the ability to utilize the parallel processing capabilities of GPUs due to the recurrent processing.

Mamba uses a hardware-aware algorithm to increase the processing speed, considering that modern GPUs have two types of memory, SRAM and HBM, with the first being faster but having less capacity. Since the parameter A is still time-invariant, they move it to the fast SRAM for the sequential processing. At each time step, they compute $B, C,$ and Δ in HBM and move B and Δ to SRAM to compute the state space recurrence. The state vectors are then moved to HBM to compute the output based on Eq. 2 using the previously computed C. This hardware-aware algorithm makes Mamba's throughput a sequential model comparable to parallel transformers.

4 Methods

In this section, we explain two vision models based on Mamba Architecture.

4.1 Vim

In Vim, images are divided into smaller patches, each projected into a patch embedding. A bidirectional Mamba processes these patches by considering both previous and next tokens. Additionally, positional encoding is added to each token to retain spatial information about neighboring patches. The architecture is illustrated in Fig. 1. Vim has similar processing to ViT models but uses Mamba-based blocks instead of attention-based Transformer blocks.

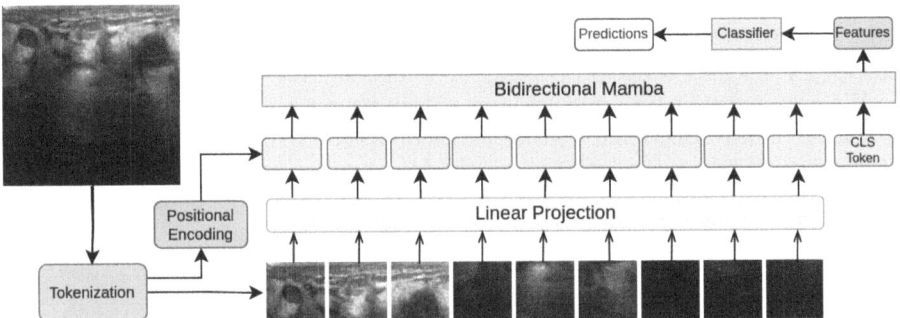

Fig. 1. An over view of the Vim model

4.2 VMamba

VMamba introduces "2D Selective Scan" to the Mamba's original scan. Furthermore, instead of breaking the image into tokens and processing each token similarly to ViT and Vim, the image patches are treated as feature maps and are processed using VSS blocks similar to CNN models, where the feature maps are down-sampled at each layer. The overall pipeline is demonstrated in Fig. 2.

4.3 Model Comparison

Figure 3 shows how different encoders process images. In CNNs, if patches P1 and P2 do not fall in the same receptive field, the model will struggle to capture long-range dependencies. In the ViT model, the attention mechanism would allow the model to process the relationship between P1 and P9. However, distinguishing between pairs like P1-P2 and P1-P9 relies primarily on positional encoding. As a result, the model needs more data and training to differentiate these pairs accurately and focus on close-range dependencies. This increased demand for

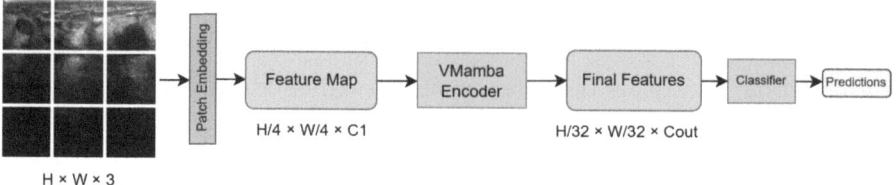

Fig. 2. An over view of the VMamba model

training arises from the absence of the inductive bias, where neighboring patches are assumed to have similar content.

In Mamba-based models, the inductive bias is reintroduced through Mamba's sequential processing, similar to models like PixelRNN [31]. However, unlike PixelRNN, Mamba allows for long-range information processing and more efficiently utilizes GPUs. Consequently, Mamba-based models combine CNNs' inductive bias with ViT's long-range processing capability, offering the best of both worlds.

When comparing Vim and VMamba, Vim uses a bidirectional Mamba scan to achieve multi-directional feature extraction across the patches. In contrast, VMamba's 2D selective Scan employs the Mamba scan in four directions to capture more comprehensive and complex relationships between the image patches, enhancing the feature representation and in-context learning.

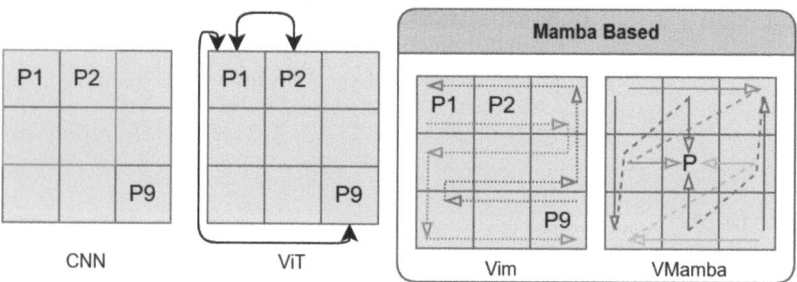

Fig. 3. An abstract comparison between different architecture types.

5 Experiments

This section summarizes the performance of various encoder types on different datasets. For our classification task, we use the BUSI [14] dataset (three classes of benign, malignant, and normal), the Dataset B of [15] (two classes of benign and malignant), and a combined BUSI+B dataset (three classes of normal, benign, and malignant). Each table reports the Area Under the Curve (AUC), Accuracy (ACC) metrics, and the number of parameters for each encoder. Since the experiment datasets are imbalanced, AUC is required as a more valuable metric. For

BUSI and BUSI+B, which have three classes, the AUC is calculated individually for each class by comparing it against the other two classes. The final AUC for an experiment is then determined by averaging these individual AUC scores.

We use ResNet50 [17] and VGG16 [18] as the CNN-based models. For ViT models, we use ViT-ti16, ViT-s16, ViT-s32, ViT-b16, and ViT-b32 [4], where the prefixes 'ti', 's', and 'b' denote tiny, small, and base model sizes, respectively, and the numbers indicate the patch size used (16 × 16 or 32 × 32 pixels). For Mamba-based models, we use Vim-s16 [9], VMamba-ti, VMamba-s, and VMamba-b [10]. These Mamba-based models have the default parameters and definition as provided in the papers. We use pretrained weights of each of these encoders from ImageNet for transfer learning.

We conduct each experiment across five training runs, using different seeds to minimize randomness in experiments. The data is split into training, validation, and test sets with respective splits of 0.7, 0.15, and 0.15. The validation set is used for early stopping; we select the checkpoint that shows the best performance on the validation set to prevent overfitting to the test set. Results are reported based on the test set's performance for each fold.

We assess statistical significance between two encoders using a paired t-test on their prediction. This analysis is conducted across all five folds, using the checkpoints from each model trained on the training set of a fold and subsequently tested on the test set.

5.1 Results on the BUSI+B Dataset

The classification performance of Mamba-based and ViT/CNN models is provided in Table 1. We ran our experiments five times and averaged the results to obtain mean and standard deviation measurements. Mamba-based models achieve higher or comparable results to ViT and CNN models. However, the high variance in the results and the small dataset size necessitate statistical significance analysis to compare the results.

Statistical Significance Analysis: To further evaluate the differences in performance between Mamba-based models and ViT/CNN models on the BUSI + B dataset, statistical tests are conducted using t-tests, and the threshold for the p-value is set to 0.05. The p-values were computed by comparing the accuracy of predictions between two models and testing for a zero mean difference.

This analysis reveals that VMamba-ti outperforms VGG16 (p-value: 0.004), ViT-ti16 (p-value: 0.003), ViT-s32 (p-value: 0.014), and ViT-b32 (p-value: 0.022), and the difference is significant. VMamba-b outperforms VGG16 (p-value: 0.037) and ViT-ti16 (p-value: 0.015). Additionally, ViT-b16 performs better than VGG16 (p-value: 0.044) and ViT-ti16 (p-value: 0.013). There are no other significant differences between pairs of models (the p-value is bigger than 0.05). This showcases that Mamba-based models perform similarly or outperform other encoders on the BUSI+B dataset with respect to statistical significance.

Table 1. Transfer Learning Results for BUSI+B datasets. The values of AUC and ACC are scaled between 0 to 100. The results are averaged over five runs.

Encoder Type	Encoder	# Params (Millions)	BUSI+B AUC	ACC
CNN	ResNet50	23.5	95.74 ± 1.42	87.66 ± 2.04
	VGG16	134.3	94.25 ± 1.28	85.82 ± 1.49
ViT	ti-16	5.5	94.19 ± 1.74	85.39 ± 1.93
	s-16	21.7	95.39 ± 0.54	87.23 ± 2.33
	s-32	22.5	93.85 ± 0.72	86.24 ± 1.65
	b-16	85.8	95.76 ± 0.77	88.51 ± 2.67
	b-32	87.5	95.51 ± 1.53	86.52 ± 3.23
Vim	s-16	25.4	95.84 ± 0.96	87.38 ± 3.22
VSSM	VMamba-ti	29.9	95.71 ± 1.01	89.36 ± 2.33
	VMamba-s	49.4	96.12 ± 0.75	87.80 ± 2.78
	VMamba-b	87.5	95.60 ± 0.79	88.51 ± 2.22

It is important to note that while ResNet50, as shown in Table 1, achieves a higher mean AUC of 95.74 compared to some of the other models, the statistical significance analysis indicates that this improvement is not significant. For example, when testing for ResNet50 against ViT-s32, the p-value is 0.27, even though the mean AUC and ACC for ResNet50 are better. Due to the experiments' small dataset size and inherent randomness, we report both mean and standard deviation for each metric, which makes direct comparisons between models more complex. Therefore, statistical analysis is necessary to reduce this randomness and better identify instances where the differences between pairs of models are statistically significant and not due to randomness in the experiments.

5.2 Results on the BUSI Dataset

The classification results for the BUSI dataset are provided in Table 2. We ran our experiments five times and averaged the results to obtain the mean and standard deviation measurements. The results suggest that the Mamba-based models outperform the other encoders on the B dataset.

Statistical Significance: We performed p-value tests on the BUSI dataset. The analysis demonstrates that ViT-b16, VMamba-s, and Vim-s outperform ViT-s32 (with a p-value of 0.036, 0.027, and 0.011, respectively). VMamba-ti model outperforms ResNet50 (p-value: 0.032), VGG16 (p-value: 0.024), and ViT-s32 (p-value: 0.002). The VMamba-b model notably surpasses ResNet50 (p-value: 0.015), VGG16 (p-value: 0.006), ViT-ti16 (p-value: 0.018), ViT-s16 (p-value: 0.022), ViT-s32 (p-value: 0.0001), and ViT-b32 (p-value: 0.029). There are no other pairs with p-values smaller than 0.05. These results indicate that the Mamba-based models frequently performed at or above the level of other models with respect to statistical significance.

Table 2. Transfer Learning Results for BUSI dataset. The values of AUC and ACC are scaled between 0 to 100. The results are averaged over five runs.

Encoder Type	Encoder	# Params (Millions)	BUSI	
			AUC	ACC
CNN	ResNet50	23.5	93.23 ± 1.93	85.64 ± 2.72
	VGG16	134.3	93.69 ± 2.18	85.47 ± 4.59
ViT	ti-16	5.5	93.52 ± 3.07	85.98 ± 4.48
	s-16	21.7	93.60 ± 4.04	86.50 ± 4.44
	s-32	22.5	93.59 ± 2.59	84.10 ± 3.81
	b-16	85.8	94.11 ± 2.12	87.18 ± 2.70
	b-32	87.5	94.10 ± 1.23	85.98 ± 1.39
Vim	s-16	25.4	95.63 ± 1.66	87.86 ± 2.72
VSSM	VMamba-ti	29.9	95.28 ± 1.89	88.55 ± 1.67
	VMamba-s	49.4	94.48 ± 3.48	87.18 ± 4.15
	VMamba-b	87.5	94.67 ± 2.53	89.06 ± 3.72

5.3 Results on the B Dataset

The classification results for the B dataset are provided in Table 3. We conducted our experiments five times and calculated the average and standard deviation of the results. VMamba-ti is the best model, outperforming all other encoders on average AUC and having a large margin on average ACC. Other Mamba encoders also perform competitively and often surpass other models.

Table 3. Transfer Learning Results for B dataset. The values of AUC and ACC are scaled between 0 to 100. The results are averaged over five runs.

Encoder Type	Encoder	# Params (Millions)	B	
			AUC	ACC
CNN	ResNet50	23.5	90.05 ± 4.19	78.33 ± 5.53
	VGG16	134.3	88.24 ± 7.10	80.00 ± 6.67
ViT	ti-16	5.5	80.90 ± 9.98	77.50 ± 7.26
	s-16	21.7	90.68 ± 7.89	82.50 ± 6.67
	s-32	22.5	87.55 ± 8.89	79.17 ± 9.50
	b-16	85.8	88.32 ± 6.24	76.67 ± 7.26
	b-32	87.5	83.14 ± 12.82	77.50 ± 12.25
Vim	s-16	25.4	87.42 ± 9.83	84.17 ± 8.50
VSSM	VMamba-ti	29.9	92.66 ± 9.07	87.50 ± 12.08
	VMamba-s	49.4	88.70 ± 9.30	83.33 ± 10.54
	VMamba-b	87.5	92.19 ± 5.43	81.67 ± 6.24

Statistical Significance: Our statistical significance analysis for the B dataset reveals that ViT-s16 outperforms ViT-b16 (p-value: 0.034). Vim-s performs better than both ViT-ti16 (p-value: 0.032) and ViT-b16 (p-value: 0.019). VMamba-ti model shows remarkable performance by outperforming ResNet50 (p-value: 0.011), VGG16 (p-value: 0.028), ViT-ti16 (p-value: 0.004), ViT-s32 (p-value: 0.012), ViT-b16 (p-value: 0.003), ViT-b32 (p-value: 0.007), and even VMamba-b (p-value: 0.034). There are no other pairs of models with p-values smaller than 0.05. These results underscore VMamba-ti as the top performer among the models evaluated. Furthermore, there are no instances with statistical significance where non-Mamba-based models outperformed Mamba-based models.

6 Discussion

The overall performance on the three datasets demonstrates the advantages of using Mamba-based models for breast cancer ultrasound datasets. Additionally, Mamba-based models' ability to capture long-range dependencies while retaining some inductive bias makes them a suitable alternative to CNN and ViT models, especially in scenarios with limited data and resources. Furthermore, VMamba showed better performance overall compared to Vim. This could be due to 2D selective scan of VMamba, which allows better representation learning.

One limitation of this study is that the statistical significance analysis is not considering the imbalance in the dataset due the multi-class analysis and complexity of comparing AUC for pairs of models. Despite this, some Mamba-based models frequently have higher average AUC as provided in the experiments section. A more comprehensive statistical analysis, including the multi-class AUC, would provide stronger support for our results.

7 Conclusion

In this work, we conducted a comprehensive comparison of three families of vision encoders—ViT, CNN, and Mamba-based models—using the BUSI and B datasets and a combined BUSI+B dataset. Our evaluation included multiple runs, averages, and standard deviations, and we performed a statistical significance analysis for each experiment. Overall, Mamba-based models frequently demonstrated competitive performance compared to the other models, with statistically significant results. Additionally, they were never outperformed by any other encoder type regarding statistical significance.

Acknowledgments. This project was funded by the Natural Sciences and Engineering Research Council of Canada (NSERC) and Fonds de recherche du Québec – Nature et technologies (FRQNT). We also extend our gratitude to Behnaz Gheflati for their valuable time.

Disclosure of Interests. The authors have no competing interests to declare that are relevant to the content of this article.

References

1. Yasaka, K., Akai, H., Kunimatsu, A., Kiryu, S., Abe, O.: Deep learning with convolutional neural network in radiology. Jpn. J. Radiol. **36**, 257–272 (2018)
2. Zhuang, F., et al.: A comprehensive survey on transfer learning. Proc. IEEE **109**(1), 43–76 (2020)
3. Lecun, Y., Bengio, Y.: Convolutional networks for images, speech, and time-series (1995)
4. Dosovitskiy, A., et al.: An image is worth 16×16 words: transformers for image recognition at scale. *arXiv preprint* arXiv:2010.11929 (2020)
5. Touvron, H., Cord, M., Douze, M., Massa, F., Sablayrolles, A., Jégou, H.: Training data-efficient image transformers & distillation through attention. In: International Conference on Machine Learning, pp. 10347–10357. PMLR (2021)
6. Lazo, J.F., Moccia, S., Frontoni, E., De Momi, E.: Comparison of different CNNs for breast tumor classification from ultrasound images. arXiv preprint arXiv:2012.14517 (2020)
7. Al-Dhabyani, W., Gomaa, M., Khaled, H., Aly, F.: Deep learning approaches for data augmentation and classification of breast masses using ultrasound images. Int. J. Adv. Comput. Sci. Appl. **10**(5), 1–11 (2019)
8. Gheflati, B., Rivaz, H.: Vision transformers for classification of breast ultrasound images. In: 2022 44th Annual International Conference of the IEEE Engineering in Medicine & Biology Society (EMBC), pp. 480–483. IEEE (2022)
9. Zhu, L., Liao, B., Zhang, Q., Wang, X., Liu, W., Wang, X.: Vision mamba: efficient visual representation learning with bidirectional state space model. arXiv preprint arXiv:2401.09417 (2024)
10. Liu, Y., et al.: VMamba: visual state space model. arXiv preprint arXiv:2401.10166 (2024)
11. Gu, A., Dao, T.: Mamba: linear-time sequence modeling with selective state spaces. arXiv preprint arXiv:2312.00752 (2023)
12. Ma, J., Li, F., Wang, B.: U-mamba: enhancing long-range dependency for biomedical image segmentation. arXiv preprint arXiv:2401.04722 (2024)
13. Deng, J., Dong, W., Socher, R., Li, L.-J., Li, K., Fei-Fei, L.: ImageNet: a large-scale hierarchical image database. In: 2009 IEEE Conference on Computer Vision and Pattern Recognition, pp. 248–255. IEEE (2009)
14. Al-Dhabyani, W., Gomaa, M., Khaled, H., Fahmy, A.: Dataset of breast ultrasound images. Data Brief **28**, 104863 (2020)
15. Yap, M.H., et al.: Automated breast ultrasound lesions detection using convolutional neural networks. IEEE J. Biomed. Health Inform. **22**(4), 1218–1226 (2017)
16. Krizhevsky, A., Sutskever, I., Hinton, G.E.: ImageNet classification with deep convolutional neural networks. In: Advances in Neural Information Processing Systems, vol. 25 (2012)
17. He, K., Zhang, X., Ren, S., Sun, J.: Deep residual learning for image recognition. In: Proceedings of the IEEE Conference on Computer Vision and Pattern Recognition, pp. 770–778 (2016)
18. Simonyan, K., Zisserman, A.: Very deep convolutional networks for large-scale image recognition. arXiv preprint arXiv:1409.1556 (2014)
19. Bahdanau, D., Cho, K., Bengio, Y.: Neural machine translation by jointly learning to align and translate. arXiv preprint arXiv:1409.0473 (2014)
20. Vaswani, A., et al.: Attention is all you need. In: Advances in Neural Information Processing Systems, vol. 30 (2017)

21. Gu, A., Goel, K., Ré, C.: Efficiently modeling long sequences with structured state spaces. arXiv preprint arXiv:2111.00396 (2021)
22. Li, K., et al.: VideoMamba: state space model for efficient video understanding. arXiv preprint arXiv:2403.06977 (2024)
23. Chen, K., Chen, B., Liu, C., Li, W., Zou, Z., Shi, Z.: RSMamba: remote sensing image classification with state space model. IEEE Geosci. Remote Sens. Lett. (2024)
24. Nasiri-Sarvi, A., Trinh, V.Q.-H., Rivaz, H., Hosseini, M.S.: Vim4Path: self-supervised vision mamba for histopathology images. In: Proceedings of the IEEE/CVF Conference on Computer Vision and Pattern Recognition (CVPR) Workshops, pp. 6894–6903 (2024)
25. Liu, J., et al.: Point mamba: a novel point cloud backbone based on state space model with octree-based ordering strategy. arXiv preprint arXiv:2403.06467 (2024)
26. Liao, W., Zhu, Y., Wang, X., Pan, C., Wang, Y., Ma, L.: LightM-UNet: mamba assists in lightweight UNet for medical image segmentation. arXiv preprint arXiv:2403.05246 (2024)
27. Ruan, J., Xiang, S.: VM-UNet: vision mamba UNet for medical image segmentation. arXiv preprint arXiv:2402.02491 (2024)
28. Wang, Z., Zheng, J.-Q., Zhang, Y., Cui, G., Li, L.: Mamba-UNet: UNet-like pure visual mamba for medical image segmentation. arXiv preprint arXiv:2402.05079 (2024)
29. Xing, Z., Ye, T., Yang, Y., Liu, G., Zhu, L.: SegMamba: long-range sequential modeling mamba for 3D medical image segmentation. arXiv preprint arXiv:2401.13560 (2024)
30. Amiri, M., Brooks, R., Rivaz, H.: Fine-tuning u-net for ultrasound image segmentation: different layers, different outcomes. IEEE Trans. Ultrason. Ferroelectr. Freq. Control **67**(12), 2510–2518 (2020)
31. Van Den Oord, A., Kalchbrenner, N., Kavukcuoglu, K.: Pixel recurrent neural networks. In: International Conference on Machine Learning, pp. 1747–1756. PMLR (2016)

Breast Cancer Molecular Subtyping from H&E Whole Slide Images Using Foundation Models and Transformers

Lauren Jimenez-Martin, Carlos Hernández-Pérez, and Veronica Vilaplana(✉)

Image Processing Group - Universitat Politècnica de Catalunya (UPC),
Carrer de Jordi Girona 31, 08034 Barcelona, Spain
{lauren.jimenez,carlos.hernandez.p,veronica.vilaplana}@upc.edu

Abstract. This study tackles the challenge of classifying breast cancer molecular subtypes using H&E-stained Whole Slide Images (WSI), avoiding the cost and labor limitations of the commonly used immunohistochemistry. We leverage the Attention-Challenging Multiple Instance Learning framework and introduce a variant, ACTrans, which utilizes a transformer aggregator for a more flexible feature aggregation. We also compare two publicly available foundation feature extractors pre-trained on large pathology datasets. A comparison of the impact of two different patch sizes at two different resolutions is made. The results obtained in our in-house dataset demonstrate that ACTrans yields superior results than existing methods, particularly with the UNI model at lower resolutions and larger patch sizes. In this setting, ACTrans achieves an average F1 score of 0.687, a precision of 0.755, a recall of 0.667, and an AUC of 0.812. Furthermore, these approaches enhance interpretability when displaying the attention weights. This method can potentially advance breast cancer diagnostics by leveraging the rich information within H&E-stained WSIs.

Keywords: Molecular Subtype · H&E Slides · Breast Cancer · Multiple Instance Learning

1 Introduction

Accurately classifying breast cancer molecular subtypes is crucial for tailoring treatment strategies and improving patient outcomes. While some studies have explored this task through radiology imaging [9,12,28], Immunohistochemistry (IHC) staining on Whole Slide Images (WSI) is a widely used technique to identify these subtypes based on specific molecular markers present in a biopsy sample displayed on a selected paraffin block. These markers, linked to cellular processes like growth or death, help diagnose and classify tumors [26]. However, IHC can be costly and suffers from limitations. Hematoxylin and Eosin (H&E) staining, which highlights tissue morphology and architecture, shows promise as a complementary approach by providing a broad view of tumor heterogeneity [8,13] across multiple tissue blocks. Computational analysis of H&E staining can offer insights into this heterogeneity, potentially predicting the molecular subtype. This information can guide the selection of the most appropriate paraffin block for confirmatory IHC analysis. Despite its clinical significance, classifying molecular subtypes through H&E staining presents challenges due to limited samples, weak annotations, and the aforementioned tumor heterogeneity.

While research on this area has been limited, recent years have witnessed a surge of interest. For instance, [18] proposed deep tissue fingerprints to predict the expression status of ER, PR, and HER2 molecular markers by learning distinctive features from H&E images. In [8] a molecular subtype classifier was introduced based on H&E slides and analyzed tumor heterogeneity within slides. Furthermore, to solve this task, other studies have investigated domain adaptation or Multiple Instance Learning (MIL) methods for selecting discriminative image patches and filtering noise in private datasets [13,20].

Self-supervised learning (SSL) has emerged as a powerful tool for developing robust feature extractors by exploiting the inherent patterns and structures in unlabeled data to learn meaningful representations, even in the presence of heterogeneous data [3,10]. Researchers have employed self-supervised contrastive learning [3] to enhance the quality of extracted representations [5,17]. However, the DINO framework [1,16] and Vision Transformers (ViT) [6] have gained popularity as the field is increasingly shifting towards transformer-based architectures [19,24,25]. These ViT systems not only produce superior results but also offer an additional layer of explainability.

Due to computational limitations, analyzing WSIs in digital pathology often requires dividing them into smaller patches. A significant challenge arises when these patches must be analyzed under a single slide-level label. Multiple Instance Learning, a variant of weakly-supervised learning, addresses this challenge by treating a WSI as a "bag" with its patches as "instances" [11,21,27,29]. This paradigm allows for slide-wide classification based on the collective feature representation of all patches, eliminating the need for individual annotations. Recent advancements in MIL leverage attention mechanisms [7] to improve feature extraction and offer interpretability by highlighting the contributory weight of each patch [4,15,22].

This work proposes an approach based on Attention-Challenging Multiple Instance Learning (ACMIL) [29] to select discriminative image patches, address overfitting, and improve generalizability on small datasets. We leverage two different foundation self-supervised feature extractors pre-trained on large histopathology datasets, specifically TCGA and Mass-100K, which is the largest histology slide collection used in self-supervised learning to date. Additionally, we propose an ACMIL extension, named ACTrans, incorporating a transformer for robust instance aggregation. Our study also compares the influence of different resolutions and patch sizes on this task. We demonstrate the effectiveness of our proposed framework on an in-house dataset.

2 Methodology

In this study, we present a computational framework for breast cancer molecular subtype classification from H&E stained WSIs. Our work leverages two pre-trained ViTs for feature extraction and weakly-supervised classification strategies, shown in Fig. 1. In this section, we describe the data used and the steps involved in image preprocessing. We also discuss two state-of-the-art histopathological pre-trained feature extractors and present our ACTrans method, a variation of ACMIL for a deeper contextual analysis of the patch-level features.

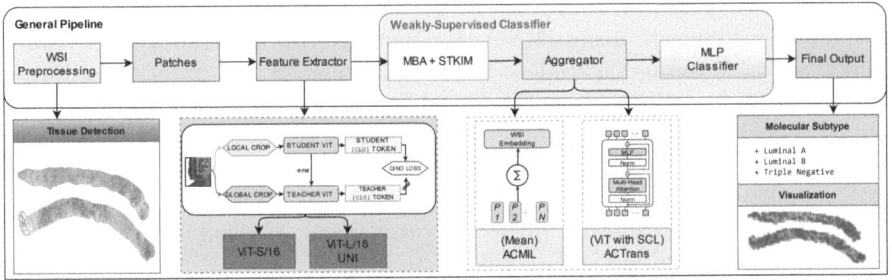

Fig. 1. Pipeline of WSIs analysis for breast cancer molecular subtyping. Steps include tissue detection, patch extraction, feature extraction using pre-trained models, ViT-S/16 or UNI, input into a weakly-supervised classifier with ACMIL or ACTrans, and final output with predictions and patch importance heatmap.

2.1 Data

We use an in-house dataset of WSIs with H&E staining collected from five local hospitals managed by the Catalan Health Institute (ICS). As Table 1 shows, the dataset contains 170 core needle biopsy WSIs distributed in 63 Luminal A, 83 Luminal B, and 24 Triple Negative.

Table 1. Distribution of molecular subtyping in the dataset.

Set	Luminal A	Luminal B	Triple Negative	Total
Train-Val	56	75	22	153
Test	7	8	2	17
Total	63	83	24	170

2.2 Preprocessing

Our data pre-processing follows the method detailed in CLAM [15] to separate tissue from background in WSIs. The images are first downsampled and converted from RGB to HSV color space to facilitate processing. Median blurring is then applied to smoothen edges, followed by binarization using a threshold on the saturation channel (often more informative for tissue segmentation). Morphological closing fills small holes within the foreground regions. Finally, foreground objects are filtered based on their area to remove noise artifacts. Patches are extracted from the identified tissue areas.

2.3 Backbone Models

Building on the recent success of self-supervised learning for feature extraction in histopathology [17,19,23,25], this work leverages two publicly available pre-trained Vision Transformer models. These ViTs were trained on large histopathology datasets using DINO [1]/DINOv2 [16], a self-supervised learning method that leverages a student-teacher paradigm. This approach facilitates knowledge transfer between a smaller, local-feature-focused student network and a larger, global-information-learning teacher network. The teacher's parameters are dynamically adjusted based on an exponential moving average of the student's parameters. This strategy empowers the ViTs to extract robust features from histopathological images for downstream tasks. The foundational models are a ViT-S/16 [1] and a ViT-L/16 called UNI [2].

Vit/S-16: For pre-training, the model leverages a collection of Hematoxylin & Eosin stained Whole Slide Images from The Cancer Genome Atlas (TCGA), a publicly available resource widely used for deep learning model training. A total of 19 million patches of size 512×512 pixels were extracted from 20,994 TCGA WSIs to ensure a balance between dataset diversity and computational efficiency. The pre-training data encompasses WSIs captured at two distinct magnifications (resolutions): $20\times$ (0.5 µm/px) and $40\times$ (0.25 µm/px) objective field of view (FoV).

UNI: A general-purpose self-supervised model for pathology, pre-trained using Mass-100K dataset, more than 100,000 diagnostic H&E-stained whole slide images across 20 major tissue types, including breast tissue. Unlike other pre-trained encoders, UNI is developed on mostly non-public histology collections. The pretraining stage directly applied DINOv2 using tissue patches at 256×256 pixels at $20\times$. As part of their training, for high-resolution finetuning in DINOv2, the authors used additional images at 512×512 pixels at $20\times$.

2.4 Multiple Instance Learning Models

This study builds upon a weakly-supervised learning approach called Attention Challenging MIL (**ACMIL**) designed to address overfitting particularly relevant when analyzing whole slide images in pathology. ACMIL integrates two techniques: 1) Multiple Branch Attention (MBA): This approach identifies M distinctive patterns within the data. Each pattern is identified through a gated attention branch [7]. To ensure these patterns capture diverse and informative aspects, the method incorporates two regularization techniques penalizing similar patterns and encouraging semantic variety. 2) Stochastic Top-K Instance

Masking (STKIM): This technique incorporates a masking operation into the attention mechanism, positioned before feature aggregation and following attention value generation. It stochastically masks out a portion of instances with the highest attention values (top-K) with a probability p and redistributes their attention values among the remaining instances.

Building upon the strengths of the aforementioned techniques, we propose **ACTrans**, an extension of ACMIL that leverages a transformer aggregator for improved feature fusion. Unlike ACMIL's reliance on a mean-based approach, ACTrans incorporates an additional Transformer encoder. This mechanism treats patch embeddings as a sequence, allowing each element to be compared and related to every other element. Similar to vision transformers [6], a class token (CLS) is included to capture the overall information within all patch embeddings. This approach enables a more profound contextual analysis of the aggregated patch-level features outputted by the MBA module, by considering their relationships with each other. By allowing a more flexible feature aggregation, ACTrans holds the potential to enhance the model's classification capabilities.

3 Experiments and Results

This section delves into the performance of the proposed weakly-supervised classifiers for predicting breast cancer molecular subtype, ACMIL and ACTrans, while assessing the impact of two different feature extractors, ViT-S/16 and UNI on the classification task. As shown in Fig. 1, the experiments followed a three-step process: first, WSIs were preprocessed and divided into smaller image patches. Second, these patches were fed through the chosen feature extractor to generate feature vectors. Finally, the extracted features were fed into the weakly-supervised classifiers to predict the molecular subtype for each WSI. To evaluate the effectiveness of the methods, we compare their capability against two established state-of-the-art MIL approaches.

3.1 Implementation Details

To ensure robust evaluation, we employed stratified 10-fold cross-validation on the WSI dataset. Stratification ensures that the class distribution is maintained within each fold, leading to a more reliable assessment of model performance across various classes. Resolutions of 0.50 μm/px and 0.24 μm/px were used. At both resolutions, patches were cropped at sizes 256 × 256 and 512 × 512.

Five evaluation metrics were employed to assess model performance: F1-score, precision, recall, Area Under the ROC Curve (AUC), and accuracy. The first four metrics are macro-averaged. These metrics were chosen because they are standard in evaluating classification performance in medical imaging tasks, providing a comprehensive assessment of performance. The reported results represent the mean performance across all ten test sets obtained through 10-fold cross-validation. We use ABMIL [7] and CLAM [15] as baseline models.

For all experiments, a fixed learning rate of 0.001 and weight decay of 0.0001 were used with the AdamW optimizer [14]. We evaluated various model configurations by testing different combinations of the number of branches (NB) {3, 5, 7} and mask probability (MProb) {0.4, 0.6, 0.8}. The number of top-K values was set to 10 as proposed in the ACMIL paper.

We extract and save features for UNI (1024 dimensions) and for ViT_S/16 (384 dimensions). The learnable components of the ACMIL/ACTRANS model include one fully-connected layer to reduce feature dimensions (to 256 for UNI and 128 dimensions for ViT-S/16), a gated attention network, and a fully-connected layer for making predictions.

3.2 Results

Our experiments evaluated the performance of various MIL models using different patch sizes, resolutions, and feature extractor backbones. Table 2 summarizes the performance metrics for each model and patch size configuration. The highest values in each category for each patch size-resolution combination are highlighted in bold. The best-performing configuration is highlighted in a light grey background for better distinction.

Patch Size and Resolution: On each resolution, models using larger patch sizes (512 × 512) generally show improved performance metrics compared to those using smaller patches (256 × 256). The improvement with larger patch sizes is consistent across all metrics. ACMIL and ACTrans perform better with lower resolution (0.5 μm/px) compared to higher resolution (0.24 μm/px), evidenced mainly by higher F1 scores.

Backbone: UNI backbone consistently outperformed the ViT-S/16 backbone across most settings. At higher resolution (0.24 μm/px), the choice of backbone has a less pronounced effect on the F1-score according to patch size. While not showing an improvement for all models, the UNI backbone still achieves the best scores for both patch sizes. At a lower resolution (0.5 μm/px), all models show a significant improvement in F1-score when using UNI backbone compared to ViT-S/16 for both patch sizes. The improvement with UNI was most prominent for the ACTrans model at 512 × 512 patch size, achieving an F1-score of 0.687 ± 0.08 (highlighted in bold) compared to 0.561 ± 0.12 with ViT-S/16. This translates to an absolute improvement of 0.126. Precision improved by 0.152, recall by 0.093, accuracy increased by 10% points, and AUC by 0.053. This suggests UNI architecture is more effective at utilizing information from lower-resolution images in this pathology task. UNI's performance on this dataset underscores its potential applicability to this specific task.

Model Performance Variations: While the leading model varied based on patch size and resolution, the backbone-model combinations UNI+ACMIL and UNI+ACTrans consistently achieved top scores. Notably, at the lower resolution (0.5 μm/px) and 512 × 512 patch size, UNI+ACTrans achieved the highest F1 score (0.687 ± 0.08), surpassing the previous best score (0.643 ± 0.10 for

Table 2. Performance metrics of various MIL models using different patch sizes and resolutions, evaluated with different feature extractor backbones.

Backbone	Model	NB	MProb	F1-score	Precision	Recall	Acc	AUC
256×256-0.24μm/px								
UNI	ACMIL	5	0.6	**0.59 ± 0.13**	**0.626 ± 0.16**	0.59 ± 0.12	**62.941 ± 9.63**	**0.767 ± 0.09**
UNI	ACTrans	7	0.6	0.541 ± 0.10	0.615 ± 0.18	0.536 ± 0.08	60.588 ± 7.36	0.752 ± 0.05
UNI	ABMIL	1	0	0.535 ± 0.12	0.584 ± 0.18	0.530 ± 0.09	60.0 ± 8.23	0.741 ± 0.07
UNI	CLAM_SB	-	-	0.364 ± 0.08	0.3768 ± 0.11	0.3897 ± 0.08	40.0 ± 7.74	0.5759 ± 0.09
ViT-S/16	ACMIL	5	0.6	0.559 ± 0.11	0.602 ± 0.13	0.566 ± 0.11	60.0 ± 6.68	0.751 ± 0.07
ViT-S/16	ACTrans	3	0.8	0.528 ± 0.11	0.563 ± 0.14	0.535 ± 0.09	56.471 ± 7.44	0.748 ± 0.07
ViT-S/16	ABMIL	1	0	0.555 ± 0.17	0.592 ± 0.2	0.568 ± 0.15	57.059 ± 13.88	0.752 ± 0.10
ViT-S/16	CLAM_SB	-	-	0.365 ± 0.07	0.344 ± 0.08	0.405 ± 0.08	47.647 ± 8.52	0.552 ± 0.08
512×512-0.24μm/px								
UNI	ACMIL	7	0.8	**0.612 ± 0.10**	**0.661 ± 0.14**	**0.616 ± 0.10**	**65.882 ± 6.08**	0.805 ± 0.08
UNI	ACTrans	5	0.6	0.57 ± 0.10	0.644 ± 0.14	0.582 ± 0.08	62.353 ± 7.44	**0.815 ± 0.05**
UNI	ABMIL	1	0	0.575 ± 0.14	0.615 ± 0.18	0.579 ± 0.12	61.765 ± 11.85	0.769 ± 0.09
UNI	CLAM_SB	-	-	0.406 ± 0.08	0.407 ± 0.09	0.453 ± 0.09	45.882 ± 11.02	0.650 ± 0.07
ViT-S/16	ACMIL	3	0.4	0.591 ± 0.13	0.646 ± 0.15	0.598 ± 0.12	61.176 ± 10.45	0.782 ± 0.09
ViT-S/16	ACTrans	3	0.6	0.601 ± 0.11	0.653 ± 0.11	0.609 ± 0.12	62.941 ± 7.87	0.8 ± 0.05
ViT-S/16	ABMIL	1	0	0.556 ± 0.13	0.592 ± 0.17	0.565 ± 0.11	58.235 ± 10.54	0.794 ± 0.07
ViT-S/16	CLAM_SB	-	-	0.360 ± 0.07	0.367 ± 0.10	0.396 ± 0.06	45.294 ± 9.22	0.635 ± 0.08
256×256-0.5μm/px								
UNI	ACMIL	7	0.8	0.618 ± 0.13	0.678 ± 0.16	0.615 ± 0.11	**66.471 ± 9.22**	**0.8 ± 0.07**
UNI	ACTrans	7	0.4	0.618 ± 0.15	**0.723 ± 0.16**	**0.625 ± 0.13**	64.118 ± 12.54	0.785 ± 0.08
UNI	ABMIL	1	0	0.566 ± 0.13	0.583 ± 0.14	0.575 ± 0.13	61.765 ± 7.47	0.772 ± 0.06
UNI	CLAM_SB	-	-	0.452 ± 0.13	0.480 ± 0.15	0.490 ± 0.11	51.176 ± 9.63	0.672 ± 0.07
ViT-S/16	ACMIL	5	0.4	0.517 ± 0.18	0.558 ± 0.19	0.528 ± 0.16	58.235 ± 15.05	0.769 ± 0.08
ViT-S/16	ACTrans	3	0.4	0.539 ± 0.13	0.556 ± 0.16	0.548 ± 0.12	60.0 ± 7.74	0.759 ± 0.05
ViT-S/16	ABMIL	1	0	0.533 ± 0.14	0.567 ± 0.18	0.546 ± 0.13	59.412 ± 10.54	0.795 ± 0.08
ViT-S/16	CLAM_SB	-	-	0.368 ± 0.11	0.368 ± 0.10	0.405 ± 0.12	45.294 ± 12.42	0.632 ± 0.11
512×512-0.5μm/px								
UNI	ACMIL	7	0.6	0.643 ± 0.10	0.698 ± 0.13	0.633 ± 0.10	68.235 ± 5.68	**0.822 ± 0.05**
UNI	ACTrans	5	0.4	**0.687 ± 0.08**	**0.755 ± 0.08**	**0.667 ± 0.08**	**68.235 ± 9.69**	0.812 ± 0.05
UNI	ABMIL	1	0	0.581 ± 0.12	0.605 ± 0.16	0.596 ± 0.11	61.177 ± 8.41	0.812 ± 0.03
UNI	CLAM_SB	-	-	0.472 ± 0.12	0.501 ± 0.16	0.531 ± 0.10	51.176 ± 10.76	0.718 ± 0.08
ViT-S/16	ACMIL	5	0.6	0.573 ± 0.12	0.653 ± 0.16	0.566 ± 0.10	58.824 ± 11.43	0.781 ± 0.07
ViT-S/16	ACTrans	5	0.6	0.561 ± 0.12	0.603 ± 0.18	0.574 ± 0.08	58.235 ± 9.69	0.759 ± 0.06
ViT-S/16	ABMIL	1	0	0.550 ± 0.12	0.595 ± 0.15	0.563 ± 0.10	57.647 ± 9.15	0.802 ± 0.04
ViT-S/16	CLAM_SB	-	-	0.359 ± 0.11	0.361 ± 0.11	0.414 ± 0.11	45.294 ± 14.15	0.662 ± 0.11

UNI+ACMIL at 0.5 μm/px) by more than 4% margin. UNI+ACTrans also achieved the highest precision (0.755 ± 0.08) and recall (0.667 ± 0.08) in this setting.

Figure 2 shows how the ACTrans model with UNI backbone assigns importance scores to image patches from a test WSI using 512 × 512 patch size at 0.5 μm/px. The left image highlights areas marked by a pathologist as invasive tumors (shown in red), which would later be analyzed with IHC stains. The right image shows a heatmap where red hues indicate high importance (highly attended regions) and blue indicates low importance (less attended regions). The heatmap shows that the model focuses more on pathologist-identified invasive

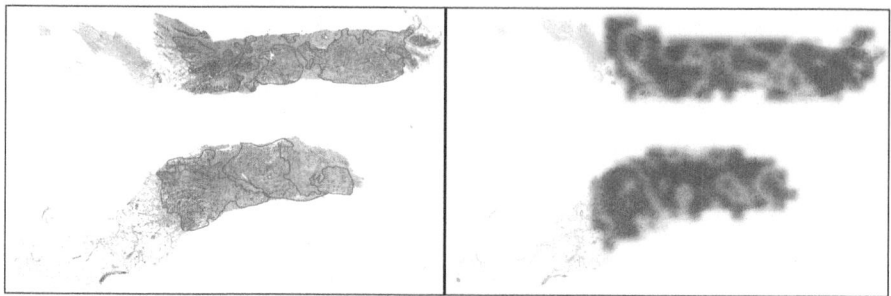

Fig. 2. ACTrans assigns importance scores to WSI patches with UNI backbone (512 × 512–0.5μm/px). Left: Pathologist-marked invasive tumor areas (red). Right: Heatmap (red: high importance, blue: low). The model focuses on invasive tumor regions and potentially areas with high nuclei density, suggesting interest in factors like nuclei interaction or growth. (Color figure online)

tumor regions. The main focus areas suggest regions with high nuclei concentration, which might be informative for factors like nuclei interaction, growth, or division.

4 Conclusion

This study demonstrates the utility of weakly-supervised learning for classifying breast cancer molecular subtypes directly from H&E-stained WSIs. We introduce ACTrans, a variation of the ACMIL that leverages a transformer aggregator for a more flexible feature aggregation. ACMIL and ACTrans reach superior results than existing methods on our in-house dataset, showcasing their ability to extract information and learn better with a small dataset compared to previous models. ACMIL and ACTrans models with UNI backbone consistently achieve better results across various metrics and resolutions. The combination of lower resolution (0.5 μm/px) and larger patch size (512 × 512) provides the best performance, especially for the ACTrans model. This suggests the model benefits from observing a larger area and consequently capturing correlations between features of distant cells.

This framework is readily applicable to other pathology image classification tasks. Our findings highlight its capability for classifying molecular subtypes from H&E WSIs, especially with limited data. By overcoming the limitations of traditional IHC and leveraging the rich information within WSIs, this approach has the potential to improve diagnostic accuracy and guide personalized treatment decisions. For future work, two promising avenues are identified. First, the automatic segmentation of tumoral tissue for independent processing from healthy tissue could be explored. Second, techniques to dynamically filter out low-importance patches during training may also be investigated. Both approaches can reduce overfitting and eliminate noise patches, likely leading to enhanced model performance.

Acknowledgments. This research was supported by the Spanish Research Agency (AEI) under projects PID2020-116907RB-I00 and PID2023-148614OB-I00 of the calls MCIN/ AEI /10.13039/501100011033, (Challenges of Society 2020 and Knowledge Generation 2023) and the FI-AGAUR (2022 FI_B 00634) grant funded by Direcció General de Recerca (DGR), Departament de Recerca i Universitats (REU) of the Generalitat de Catalunya and the European Social Fund.

Disclosure of Interests. The authors have no competing interests to declare that are relevant to the content of this article.

References

1. Caron, M., et al.: Emerging properties in self-supervised vision transformers. In: Proceedings of the IEEE/CVF International Conference on Computer Vision, pp. 9650–9660 (2021)
2. Chen, R.J., et al.: Towards a general-purpose foundation model for computational pathology. Nat. Med. (2024)
3. Chen, T., Kornblith, S., Norouzi, M., Hinton, G.: A simple framework for contrastive learning of visual representations. In: International Conference on Machine Learning, pp. 1597–1607. PMLR (2020)
4. Chikontwe, P., Kim, M., Nam, S.J., Go, H., Park, S.H.: Multiple instance learning with center embeddings for histopathology classification. In: Martel, A.L., et al. (eds.) MICCAI 2020. LNCS, vol. 12265, pp. 519–528. Springer, Cham (2020). https://doi.org/10.1007/978-3-030-59722-1_50
5. Ciga, O., Xu, T., Martel, A.L.: Self supervised contrastive learning for digital histopathology. Mach. Learn. Appl. **7**, 100198 (2022)
6. Dosovitskiy, A., et al.: An image is worth 16x16 words: transformers for image recognition at scale. arXiv preprint arXiv:2010.11929 (2020)
7. Ilse, M., Tomczak, J., Welling, M.: Attention-based deep multiple instance learning. In: International Conference on Machine Learning, pp. 2127–2136. PMLR (2018)
8. Jaber, M.I., et al.: A deep learning image-based intrinsic molecular subtype classifier of breast tumors reveals tumor heterogeneity that may affect survival. Breast Cancer Res. **22**, 1–10 (2020)
9. Jiang, M., et al.: Deep learning with convolutional neural network in the assessment of breast cancer molecular subtypes based on us images: a multicenter retrospective study. Eur. Radiol. **31**, 3673–3682 (2021)
10. Kang, M., Song, H., Park, S., Yoo, D., Pereira, S.: Benchmarking self-supervised learning on diverse pathology datasets. In: Proceedings of the IEEE/CVF Conference on Computer Vision and Pattern Recognition, pp. 3344–3354 (2023)
11. Laleh, N.G., et al.: Benchmarking weakly-supervised deep learning pipelines for whole slide classification in computational pathology. Med. Image Anal. **79**, 102474 (2022)
12. Leithner, D., et al.: Radiomic signatures with contrast-enhanced magnetic resonance imaging for the assessment of breast cancer receptor status and molecular subtypes: initial results. Breast Cancer Res. **21**, 1–11 (2019)
13. Liu, H., et al.: Breast cancer molecular subtype prediction on pathological images with discriminative patch selection and multi-instance learning. Front. Oncol. **12**, 858453 (2022)

14. Loshchilov, I., Hutter, F.: Decoupled weight decay regularization. arXiv preprint arXiv:1711.05101 (2017)
15. Lu, M.Y., Williamson, D.F., Chen, T.Y., Chen, R.J., Barbieri, M., Mahmood, F.: Data-efficient and weakly supervised computational pathology on whole-slide images. Nat. Biomed. Eng. **5**(6), 555–570 (2021)
16. Oquab, M., et al.: Dinov2: learning robust visual features without supervision. arXiv preprint arXiv:2304.07193 (2023)
17. Perez, C.H., Escudero, M.C., Puig, S., Malvehy, J., Besler, V.V.: Contrastive and attention-based multiple instance learning for the prediction of sentinel lymph node status from histopathologies of primary melanoma tumours. In: Ali, S., van der Sommen, F., Papież, B.W., van Eijnatten, M., Jin, Y., Kolenbrander, I. (eds.) CaPTion 2022. LNCS, vol. 13581, pp. 57–66. Springer, Cham (2022). https://doi.org/10.1007/978-3-031-17979-2_6
18. Rawat, R.R., et al.: Deep learned tissue "fingerprints" classify breast cancers by ER/PR/HER2 status from h&e images. Sci. Rep. **10**(1), 7275 (2020)
19. Roth, B., Koch, V., Wagner, S.J., Schnabel, J.A., Marr, C., Peng, T.: Low-resource finetuning of foundation models beats state-of-the-art in histopathology. arXiv preprint arXiv:2401.04720 (2024)
20. Shang, Z., Liu, H., Wang, K., Wang, X.: BM-SMIL: a breast cancer molecular subtype prediction framework from h&e slides with self-supervised pretraining and multi-instance learning. In: Qin, W., Zaki, N., Zhang, F., Wu, J., Yang, F., Li, C. (eds.) CMMCA 2023. LNCS, vol. 14243, pp. 81–90. Springer, Cham (2023). https://doi.org/10.1007/978-3-031-45087-7_9
21. Shao, Z., Bian, H., Chen, Y., Wang, Y., Zhang, J., Ji, X., et al.: Transmil: transformer based correlated multiple instance learning for whole slide image classification. Adv. Neural. Inf. Process. Syst. **34**, 2136–2147 (2021)
22. Tourniaire, P., Ilie, M., Hofman, P., Ayache, N., Delingette, H.: Attention-based multiple instance learning with mixed supervision on the camelyon16 dataset. In: MICCAI Workshop on Computational Pathology, pp. 216–226. PMLR (2021)
23. Wagner, S.J.: Transformer-based biomarker prediction from colorectal cancer histology: a large-scale multicentric study. Cancer Cell **41**(9), 1650–1661 (2023)
24. Wang, X., et al.: Transformer-based unsupervised contrastive learning for histopathological image classification. Med. Image Anal. **81**, 102559 (2022)
25. Wessels, F., et al.: A self-supervised vision transformer to predict survival from histopathology in renal cell carcinoma. World J. Urol. **41**(8), 2233–2241 (2023)
26. Whiteside, G., Munglani, R.: TUNEL, hoechst and immunohistochemistry triple-labelling: an improved method for detection of apoptosis in tissue sections–an update. Brain Res. Protoc. **3**(1), 52–53 (1998)
27. Yao, J., Zhu, X., Jonnagaddala, J., Hawkins, N., Huang, J.: Whole slide images based cancer survival prediction using attention guided deep multiple instance learning networks. Med. Image Anal. **65**, 101789 (2020)
28. Zhang, T., et al.: Predicting breast cancer types on and beyond molecular level in a multi-modal fashion. NPJ Breast Cancer **9**(1), 16 (2023)
29. Zhang, Y., Li, H., Sun, Y., Zheng, S., Zhu, C., Yang, L.: Attention-challenging multiple instance learning for whole slide image classification. arXiv preprint arXiv:2311.07125 (2023)

Graph Neural Networks for Modelling Breast Biomechanical Compression

Hadeel Awwad(✉), Eloy García, and Robert Martí

Computer Vision and Robotics Institute, University of Girona, Girona, Spain
hadeel.awwad@udg.edu, robert.marti@udg.edu

Abstract. Breast compression simulation is essential for accurate image registration from 3D modalities to X-ray procedures like mammography. It accounts for tissue shape and position changes due to compression, ensuring precise alignment and improved analysis. Although Finite Element Analysis (FEA) is reliable for approximating soft tissue deformation, it struggles with balancing accuracy and computational efficiency. Recent studies have used data-driven models trained on FEA results to speed up tissue deformation predictions. We propose to explore Physics-based Graph Neural Networks (PhysGNN) for breast compression simulation. PhysGNN has been used for data-driven modelling in other domains, and this work presents the first investigation of their potential in predicting breast deformation during mammographic compression. Unlike conventional data-driven models, PhysGNN, which incorporates mesh structural information and enables inductive learning on unstructured grids, is well-suited for capturing complex breast tissue geometries. Trained on deformations from incremental FEA simulations, PhysGNN's performance is evaluated by comparing predicted nodal displacements with those from finite element (FE) simulations. This deep learning (DL) framework shows promise for accurate, rapid breast deformation approximations, offering enhanced computational efficiency for real-world scenarios.

Keywords: Breast computed tomography · Digital breast phantom · Multimodal imaging fusion · 2D-3D image registration · Mammography · Finite element models

1 Introduction

Breast cancer is one of the most prevalent and, life-threatening cancers affecting women worldwide. The high incidence rate underscores the critical need for early and accurate diagnosis to improve patient outcomes [19,25]. Common diagnostic modalities include mammography, magnetic resonance imaging (MRI), ultrasound, and dedicated breast computed tomography (BCT), each offering unique benefits in detecting and characterizing breast lesions [2,20,23,24]. Integrating and correlating information from these diverse imaging techniques can significantly enhance diagnostic accuracy. By synthesizing and simulating data from 3D modalities like MRI and BCT into 2D representations as seen in mammography, clinicians can leverage the comprehensive structural details of MRI or BCT with the practical format of mammography. This multi-modal strategy provides a more comprehensive perspective of breast tissue, enhancing lesion detection and assessment, and ultimately improving diagnostic outcomes and patient care.

Achieving realistic breast compression simulation is crucial for multi-modal breast imaging correspondence, commonly approached using Finite Element Analysis (FEA) methods. However, the limited computational efficiency of FEA poses a significant challenge in medical image registration, as it requires substantial time and resources to solve biomechanical models accurately. This limitation affects the performance of existing multimodal registration techniques. To address this issue, researchers have proposed data-driven models that train different machine learning algorithms with FEA results to speed up tissue deformation approximations by prediction [9,10,12–14]. However, these methods overlook valuable information contained within the FE mesh structure, such as node connections and distances, and their number of parameters depends on the mesh resolution.

To the best of our knowledge, this study is the first to adapt the PhysGNN model proposed by Salehi [15] for simulating breast compression. It provides a comparative analysis of the results using both quantitative and qualitative metrics against existing FEA methods and discusses its benefits and limitations.

2 Materials

BCT is an advanced imaging modality that provides high-resolution, three-dimensional breast images, offering superior tissue contrast compared to digital mammography, see Fig. 1(a). This enhanced imaging capability facilitates better detection and characterization of breast lesions. This work used a publicly available dataset of computational digital phantoms generated from clinical BCT images previously obtained at UC Davis (California, USA) [1,7,16], utilizing a semi-automatic tissue classification algorithm [11]. Each voxel of the breast phantom was segmented into various classes: air, fatty tissue, glandular tissue, and skin tissue. In this work, we have used a single phantom (Uncompressed-Breast3) for generating the geometry of the biomechanical model. We chose to use a single phantom because generating incremental FEA solutions is computationally expensive. Future research can explore additional breast phantoms to test PhysGNN's capability in predicting the deformation of various geometries.

3 Methods

Figure 1(b) outlines the workflow of the proposed method to approximate mammographic compression using a biomechanical breast model to train the PhysGNN model, detailed in the following sections.

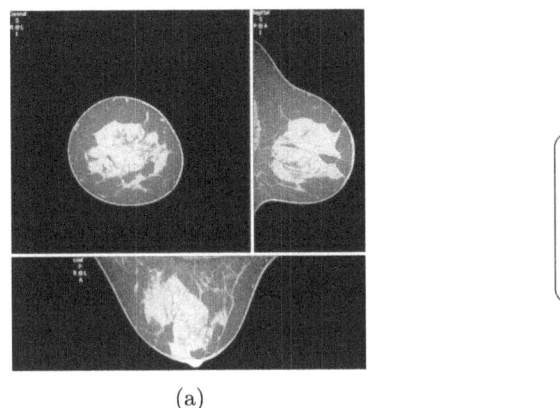 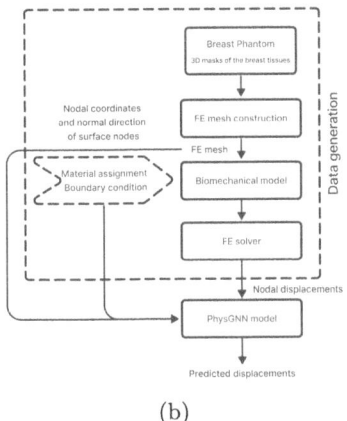

(a) (b)

Fig. 1. (a) Reconstructed dataset from breast CT [7]. (b) Flow chart of the proposed method to simulate the breast compression using PhysGNN.

3.1 Biomechanical Breast Model

The breast biomechanical model is derived from García's work [5]. An overview of generating a biomechanical breast model is shown in Fig. 2 involving breast geometry and mesh generation, material properties and boundary conditions definition, and the finite element solver.

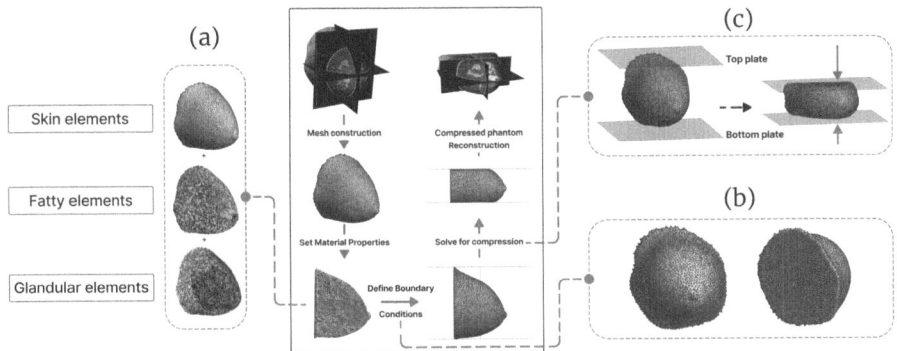

Fig. 2. Overview of steps to set up and solve compressed breast geometry using FEA, then apply deformation to reposition and compress the breast phantom. (Color figure online)

Generation of the Finite Element Mesh. To represent the breast geometry, we used a meshing technique that discretizes the breast volume into small tetrahedral elements [18]. These elements form a graph-like structure, approximating the breast's complex geometry with tetrahedrons, each having four triangular

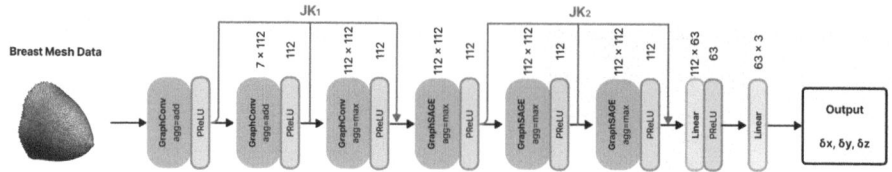

Fig. 3. Architectural diagram of PhysGNN [15]

faces and four nodes. The FE volume mesh for running FE simulations was generated by running Pygalmesh [17], a Python interface to the CGAL library [21] to generate high-quality 3D volume mesh. Figure 2 (a) illustrates the FE volume mesh of the breast phantom, which consists of 17595 nodes and 95865 tetrahedral elements. More details on the FE volume mesh may be found in Table 3, Appendix A.

Material Properties and Boundary Conditions. The material behaviour of breast tissues was characterized as nearly incompressible, with a Poisson ratio of 0.49, using homogeneous and isotropic Neo-Hookean material models as reported in the literature [22]. The stiffness measures were assigned using Young's modulus ($E_{fatty} = 4.46$ kPa, $E_{glandular} = 15.1$ kPa, $E_{skin} = 20.0$ kPa). The boundary condition was set to restrict rigid motion by constraining the posterior surface of the breast in the anterior-posterior direction. See Fig. 2(b), which is colour-coded by boundary conditions: free nodes (blue) throughout the breast and constrained nodes (red) on the posterior surface to mimic chest wall restriction.

Finite Element Simulations. While FEA is a common method for solving the compression, this work specifically focuses on simulating compression for the Cranio Caudal (CC) view during mammography. The results from FEA simulations are utilized as ground truth to train the PhysGNN model in predicting breast compression, see next section. NiftySim (v.2.3.1; University College London, UK) [8] is used to conduct incremental FE simulations on the FE mesh, modelled using two frictionless infinite linear planes [5], see Fig. 2(c).

3.2 PhysGNN

In this work, we explore PhysGNN proposed by Salehi [15], which approximates soft tissue deformation under prescribed forces by leveraging Graph Neural Networks (GNN)s. Figure 3 illustrates the architecture of PhysGNN, integrating GraphSAGE and GraphConv layers with Jumping Knowledge (JK) connections. This design facilitates inductive learning over graphs through *parameter sharing*, ensuring a constant number of parameters regardless of the mesh size. This approach enhances computational feasibility when learning from high-quality meshes with numerous nodes [15].

A training and testing dataset was generated from the incremental simulations of NiftySim by applying a force of 90 N to the breast surface nodes, incrementally over 30-time steps and in 40 directions, to capture the non-linear behaviour of soft tissue under large forces. The forces applied to each surface node are directed along its surface normal (x, y, and z) and three additional randomly sampled directions. Each additional direction is represented as a tuple (x, y, and z) randomly selected from a unit-radius hemisphere. Note that this is slightly different from the original implementation of [15] where only 10 distinct batches of random directions were included, along with the surface normal direction. Further details on the generated dataset can be found in Table 4, Appendix B.

The input features for PhysGNN include force values applied to surface nodes in Cartesian coordinates (F_x, F_y, F_z) and spherical coordinates (F_ρ, F_θ, F_ϕ). Each node is also assigned a Physical Property value: 0.1 for skin, 0.6 for glandular tissue, 1 for fatty tissue under free boundary conditions, and 0 for fixed boundary conditions. This value impacts the node's displacement, influenced by its boundary condition and Young's modulus. Fatty tissue tends to experience larger displacements due to its smaller Young's modulus compared to glandular and skin tissues. PhysGNN outputs displacement values ($\delta_x, \delta_y, \delta_z$) for the mesh nodes. Edge weights ($e_{u,v}$) in the GNN model are computed as the inverse of the Euclidean distance between adjacent nodes u and v, with $u, v \in \mathcal{N}$. Information about PhysGNN hyperparameters and infrastructure settings can be found in Appendix C.

3.3 Voxelised Compressed Phantom Reconstruction

Predicted deformations by FEA and PhysGNN are used to reconstruct the compressed voxel phantom following the method in [3,6]. The compressed FE mesh is converted into a voxelized phantom, with elements stored on a uniform grid. Each voxel's position is mapped to the uncompressed model using barycentric coordinates [3]. This transforms points along a ray in the compressed model to a curve in the segmented BCT image, with labels obtained using nearest neighbour interpolation.

3.4 PhysGNN Training Experiments

We evaluate the performance of PhysGNN model on Hold-out and Leave-one-deformation-out (LODO) strategies against the results of FEA (our baseline).

Hold-Out Experiment. The dataset from step-wise compression of a single BCT phantom obtained using FEA NiftySim was randomly split into training (70%), validation (20%), and testing (10%) sets. Despite using a single breast phantom with 30 deformation states, this experiment provides valuable groundwork for future studies involving additional breast models.

Leave-One-Deformation-Out Experiment. To evaluate the model's ability to generalize to unseen deformations, a specific testing strategy was used. From 30 NiftySim-simulated deformations, one (the final compression state) was isolated for testing. The remaining 29 were split into training (80%) and validation

(20%) sets. This approach reflects real-world scenarios where models train on known deformations and predict new ones for a complete breast geometry. Note that the training data is from a single BCT phantom.

3.5 Evaluation Metrics

Similar to previous research [9,14], the PhysGNN model predictions are evaluated against FEA results, which serve as the ground truth. We use several evaluation metrics to assess model performance and accuracy. The Dice coefficient measures the agreement between segmented images. The Mean Euclidean Error (MEE) and Mean Absolute Error (MAE) assess prediction accuracy based on node positions, with MEE measuring the average distance between predicted and ground truth positions, and MAE evaluating the average error magnitude of node displacements. Lastly, the Volume Loss metric measures the difference in breast tissue volume before and after compression, reflecting the physical realism and accuracy of the biomechanical models. These metrics collectively provide a comprehensive assessment of the model's performance.

4 Results and Discussion

4.1 Performance of PhysGNN Model

Table 1 shows PhysGNN's performance in predicting breast deformation under mammographic compression. PhysGNN effectively predicts deformations, with 99.96% of nodal position errors under 1 mm in the Hold-out experiment and 81.22% in the LODO experiment. The Hold-out evaluation offers more stable performance estimates than LODO, which is computationally expensive and limits model complexity and hyperparameter tuning. Additionally, single-deformation testing in LODO may not accurately reflect performance on diverse deformations. Table 5 in Appendix D presents the PhysGNN test set statistics.

Table 1. The performance of PhysGNN model on Hold-out and Leave-one-deformation-out on the test set. Exp. stands for Experiment

Exp.	MAE (δx) (mm)	MAE (δy) (mm)	MAE (δz) (mm)	Mean Euclidean Error (mm)	Euclidean Error $\leq$ 1 mm (%)	Mean Absolute Position Error (mm)	Absolute Position Error $\leq$ 1 mm (%)
Hold-out	0.17 ± 0.18	0.20 ± 0.20	0.13 ± 0.14	0.34 ± 0.15	97.50	0.17 ± 0.03	99.96
LODO	0.56 ± 0.44	0.52 ± 0.39	0.67 ± 0.52	1.21 ± 0.44	33.51	0.59 ± 0.07	81.22

In the Hold-out experiment, predicting tissue deformation took 0.42 ± 0.04 s on CPU and 0.01 ± 0.06 s on GPU. In the LODO experiment, it took 0.82 s on CPU and 0.47 s on GPU. Incremental NiftySim simulations, with GPU acceleration, totalled 4640.5 s (154.7 s per simulation). This indicates a speedup of 329 times with GPU and 188 times with CPU in the LODO experiment compared to a single NiftySim simulation.

4.2 Quantitative and Qualitative Analysis of Leave-One-Deformation-Out Experiment

We present here additional quantitative and qualitative results only for the LODO experiment. For the Hold-out experiment, since graphs from different deformations are mixed in the test set, a specific evaluation cannot be provided.

Figure 4 compares the reconstructed phantoms from PhysGNN-predicted deformation using the LODO strategy to the final compression state by NiftySim, which serves as the ground truth. The results show that PhysGNN closely matches FEA in breast deformation predictions, demonstrating its effectiveness and potential as a reliable alternative to traditional FEA methods. The similarity is further quantified by the Dice scores: 0.94 for fat tissue, 0.83 for glandular tissue, and 0.53 for skin tissue, indicating high values for primary tissues (excluding skin, which is very thin and thus results in a compromised Dice score).

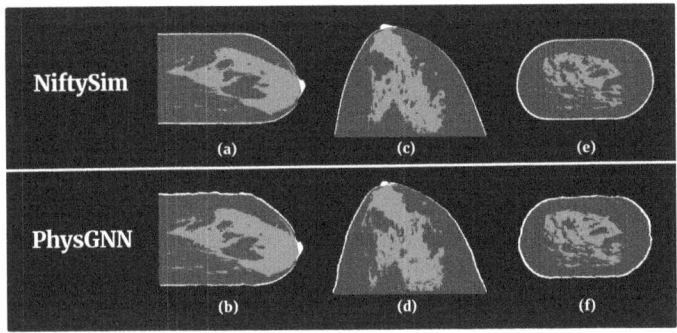

Fig. 4. Cross-sectional views of compressed digital phantoms from NiftySim and PhysGNN: (a) and (b) sagittal sections, (c) and (d) axial sections, (e) and (f) coronal sections

Finally, Table 2 summarizes the volume loss percentages for total breast, fatty, glandular, and skin tissues. PhysGNN predictions show a slightly increased overall breast tissue loss.

Table 2. Breast tissue loss during compression

FEA/DL	Total breast volume loss (%)	Fatty tissue volume loss (%)	Glandular tissue volume loss (%)	Skin tissue volume loss (%)
NiftySim	1.03	0.38	0.03	10.33
PhysGNN	1.26	0.55	0.34	10.94

We can also visually assess the displacement magnitudes on the BCT model with each method as shown in Fig. 5. Figure 5(a) shows NiftySim's displacements, Fig. 5(b) shows PhysGNN's predicted displacements, and Fig. 5(c) highlights the differences. While overall patterns are similar, noticeable dissimilarity exists on the breast surface, with a maximum displacement difference of 5.2 mm.

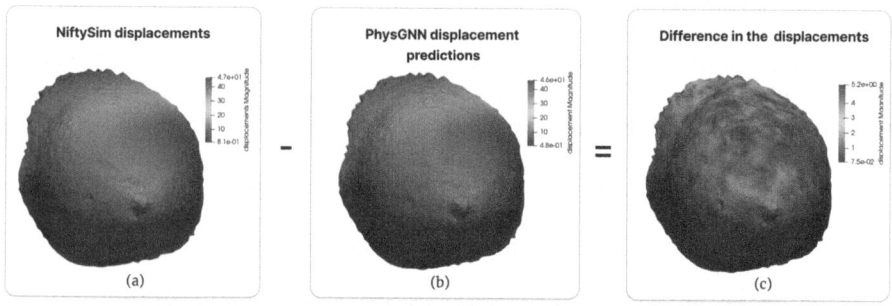

Fig. 5. Output displacements (mm) of NiftySim and PhysGNN on the FE model

The overall results show strong performance with low errors and visual similarity to the NiftySim ground truth, suggesting the model is nearing practical applicability. However, the necessity for training on incremental FEA simulations, which requires significant training time, remains a challenge. Despite this, the method holds promise for multiple compression simulations, particularly within an optimization framework for 2D/3D registration, as demonstrated by García's work [4]. Thus, PhysGNN has significant potential for specialized scenarios requiring detailed and repeated simulations.

5 Conclusion

This work is the first to apply GNNs for predicting breast deformation during mammographic compression, comparing quantitatively and qualitatively with standard FEA models. The PhysGNN model, trained on FEA displacement data, achieved a Mean Euclidean Error of 0.34 ± 0.15 mm in the Hold-out experiment. The PhysGNN model achieved accurate results comparable to the FEA, with a speedup of factor 329 and 188 using GPU and CPU, respectively in the Leave-one-deformation-out experiment, suggesting its potential to replace FEA simulations for real-time clinical applications. For future work, it is important to include simulations of compression for the Mediolateral Oblique (MLO) view during mammography. Further efforts should focus on comparing PhysGNN with other FEA methods to assess relative performance. Additionally, the study should be extended to generalize the model to multiple geometries, examining its robustness and accuracy across diverse scenarios. Finally, integrating PhysGNN into 2D/3D registration frameworks could further enhance its applicability and effectiveness in clinical settings.

Acknowledgments. This work has been partially funded by the Erasmus+: Erasmus Mundus Joint Master's Degree (EMJMD) scholarship (2022–2024), with project reference 610600-EPP-1-2019-1-ES-EPPKA1-JMD-MOB and the project VICTORIA, "PID2021-123390OB-C21" from the Ministerio de Ciencia e Innovación of Spain.

Disclosure of Interests. The authors have no competing interests to declare relevant to this article's content.

A   Appendix

Table 3 provides information on the finite element (FE) volume mesh that was used for generating the dataset.

Table 3. Finite element volume mesh statistics

Attribute	Value
Mesh points	17595
Mesh tetrahedra	95865
Mesh triangular faces	33594
Mesh faces on the exterior surface	2300

B   Appendix

Further details on the generated training and testing datasets can be found in Table 4.

Table 4. Characteristics of the Dataset. B.C. stands for Boundary Condition

No. Fixed B.C. Nodes	No. Free B.C. Surface Nodes	No. Force magnitudes	Max. Force Applied (N)	No. Directions	No. Simulations
1171	1129	30	90	40	1200

C   Appendix

PhysGNN Hyperparameters. The loss function used for learning the trainable parameters is the mean Euclidean error computed as:

$$MEE = \frac{1}{\mathcal{N}} \sum_{n \in \mathcal{N}} \sqrt{\sum_{i=1}^{3} (y_n^i - \hat{y}_n^i)^2} \qquad (1)$$

where $\mathcal{N}$ is the number of mesh nodes, $\mathbf{y} \in \mathbb{R}^{\mathcal{N} \times 3}$ represents the FEM-approximated displacement in the x, y, and z directions, and $\hat{\mathbf{y}} \in \mathbb{R}^{\mathcal{N} \times 3}$ represents the displacement predicted by PhysGNN. The AdamW optimizer, with an initial learning rate of 0.005, was used to minimize the loss value, reducing the rate by a factor of 0.1 to a minimum of 1×10^{-8} if validation loss did not improve after 5 epochs. Early stopping, halting training after 15 epochs without validation loss improvement, was employed to prevent overfitting. Additionally, a dropout rate of 0.1 was applied to the penultimate layer of PhysGNN to enhance generalization. The model was trained in 8 batches for faster convergence.

Infrastructure Settings. The FE simulations and PhysGNN model training in our study were carried out on an NVIDIA GeForce RTX 2080 Ti GPU with 46 GB.

D Appendix

Table 5 presents the PhysGNN test set statistics of Hold-out and Leave-one-deformation-out experiments.

Table 5. The test set statistics of Hold-out and Leave-one-deformation-out, where y is the displacement, and Max. Euclidean Error$_{\text{mean}}$ is computed as the average of the maximum Euclidean error observed for each data element—i.e., each simulation.

Experiment	$\delta y_{\max}$ (mm)	δy_{mean} (mm)	Max. Euclidean Error$_{\text{mean}}$ (mm)
Hold-out	46.56	24.02 ± 13.27	2.60 ± 1.40
LODO	46.56	46.56 ± 0.00	5.16 ± 0.00

References

1. Boone, J.M., Nelson, T.R., Lindfors, K.K., Seibert, J.A.: Dedicated breast CT: radiation dose and image quality evaluation. Radiology **221**(3), 657–667 (2001)
2. Caballo, M., et al.: Multi-marker quantitative radiomics for mass characterization in dedicated breast CT imaging. Med. Phys. (2021)
3. García, E., et al.: Multimodal breast parenchymal patterns correlation using a patient-specific biomechanical model. IEEE Trans. Med. Imaging **37**(3), 712–723 (2018)
4. García, E., et al.: Breast MRI and x-ray mammography registration using gradient values. Med. Image Anal. **54**, 76–87 (2019)
5. García, E., Fedon, C., Caballo, M., Martí, R., Sechopoulos, I., Diaz, O.: Realistic compressed breast phantoms for medical physics applications. In: 15th International Workshop on Breast Imaging (IWBI2020), p. 73. SPIE (2020)
6. García, E., et al.: Mapping 3d breast lesions from full-field digital mammograms using subject-specific finite element models. In: Society of Photo-Optical Instrumentation Engineers (SPIE) Conference Series, vol. 10135, p. 1013504 (2017)

7. Gazi, P.M., Yang, K., Burkett, G.W., Aminololama-Shakeri, S., Seibert, J.A., Boone, J.M.: Evolution of spatial resolution in breast CT at UC Davis. Medical physics **42**(4), 1973–1981 (2015)
8. Johnsen, S.F., Taylor, Z.A., Clarkson, M.J., et al.: NiftySim: a GPU-based nonlinear finite element package for simulation of soft tissue biomechanics. Int. J. Comput. Assist. Radiol. Surg. (Int. J. CARS) **10**(7), 1077–1095 (2015)
9. Martínez-Martínez, F., et al.: A finite element-based machine learning approach for modeling the mechanical behavior of the breast tissues under compression in real-time. Comput. Biol. Med. **90**, 116–124 (2017)
10. Mendizabal, A., Tagliabue, E., Brunet, J.-N., Dall'Alba, D., Fiorini, P., Cotin, S.: Physics-based deep neural network for real-time lesion tracking in ultrasound-guided breast biopsy. In: Miller, K., Wittek, A., Joldes, G., Nash, M.P., Nielsen, P.M.F. (eds.) MICCAI 2018-2019, pp. 33–45. Springer, Cham (2020). https://doi.org/10.1007/978-3-030-42428-2_4
11. Mettivier, G., Sarno, A., Boone, J.M., Bliznakova, K., di Franco, F., Russo, P.: Virtual clinical trials in 3D and 2D breast imaging with digital phantoms derived from clinical breast CT scans. In: Medical Imaging 2020: Physics of Medical Imaging, vol. 11312, p. 1131259 (2020)
12. Phellan, R., Hachem, B., Clin, J., Mac-Thiong, J.M., Duong, L.: Real-time biomechanics using the finite element method and machine learning: Review and perspective. Med. Phys. **48**(1), 7–18 (2021)
13. Rupérez, M.J., et al.: Modeling the mechanical behavior of the breast tissues under compression in real time. In: Tavares, J.M.R.S., Natal Jorge, R.M. (eds.) ECCOMAS 2017. LNCVB, vol. 27, pp. 583–592. Springer, Cham (2018). https://doi.org/10.1007/978-3-319-68195-5_63
14. Said, S., Yang, Z., Clauser, P., Ruiter, N., Baltzer, P., Hopp, T.: Estimation of the biomechanical mammographic deformation of the breast using machine learning models. Clin. Biomech. **110**, 106117 (2023)
15. Salehi, Y., Giannacopoulos, D.: PhysGNN: a physics-driven graph neural network based model for predicting soft tissue deformation in image-guided neurosurgery. Adv. Neural. Inf. Process. Syst. **35**, 37282–37296 (2022)
16. Sarno, A., et al.: Dataset of patient-derived 3D digital breast phantoms for research in breast computed tomography (2021)
17. Schlömer, N.: pygalmesh: Python interface for CGAL's meshing tools. Zenodo (2021)
18. Shewchuk, J.: Tetrahedral mesh generation by delaunay refinement. In: Proceedings of 14th Annual ACM Symposium Computational Geometry (1970)
19. Sung, H., et al.: Global cancer statistics 2020: globocan estimates of incidence and mortality worldwide for 36 cancers in 185 countries. a Cancer J. Clin. CA (2021)
20. Tan, T., et al.: Multi-modal artificial intelligence for the combination of automated 3D breast ultrasound and mammograms in a population of women with predominantly dense breasts. Insights into Imaging (2023)
21. The CGAL Project: CGAL User and Reference Manual. CGAL Editorial Board, 5.6.1 edn. (2024)
22. Wellman, P., Howe, R.D., Dalton, E., Kern, K.A.: Breast tissue stiffness in compression is correlated to histological diagnosis. Harvard BioRobotics Laboratory Technical Report **1** (1999)

23. Zhang, T., Han, L., Gao, Y., Wang, X., Beets-Tan, R., Mann, R.M.: Predicting molecular subtypes of breast cancer using multimodal deep learning and incorporation of the attention mechanism. In: Medical Imaging with Deep Learning (2021)
24. Zhang, T., et al.: Predicting breast cancer types on and beyond molecular level in a multi-modal fashion. NPJ Breast Cancer **9**(1), 16 (2023)
25. Zhang, T., et al.: Radiomics and artificial intelligence in breast imaging: a survey. Artif. Intell. Rev. **56**(1), 857–892 (2023)

A Generative Adversarial Approach to Remove Moiré Artifacts in Dark-Field and Phase-Contrast X-Ray Images

Eloy García[1(✉)], Diego García-Pinto[2], Victor Sánchez-Lara[2], Ricardo Montoya delÁngel[1], and Robert Martí[1]

[1] Institute of Computer Vision and Robotics (ViCOROB), University of Girona, Girona, Spain
eloy.garcia@udg.edu
[2] Laboratory of Micro-CT Universidad Complutense de Madrid, Madrid, Spain

Abstract. X-ray phase contrast is a promising breast image modality. This technique is capable of simultaneously providing three types of images: absorption, differential phase contrast (DPC) and dark-field (DF) images, allowing to obtain complementary information from each one. However, the Talbot-Lau interferometer, the device used to acquire this type of images, can yield Moiré artifacts in the corresponding images. The aim of this work is to introduce a deep learning approach, using a generative adversarial network, in particular the *pix2pix* neural network, to reduce Moiré artifacts efficiently. Our approach was tested using simulated DPC and DF images obtained from the INbreast dataset. Moiré and mammography-based images are fused using a novel approach which aims to eliminate the bias yielded by the traditional one. Results shows a significant image quality improvement for the DF dataset, reaching a structural similarity (SSIM) index of $SSIM = 0.96 \pm 0.02$, in average, after applying the neural network. However, under the same training conditions, the denoised DPC images do not show such a clear improvement, yielding checkerboard and discontinuity artifacts.

Keywords: Deep Learning · Moire Pattern · Dark-field images · differential phase-contrast images

1 Introduction

Talbot-Lau x-ray phase contrast imaging is a promising technique in biological imaging since it can provide three different type of images: the absorption, differential phase contrast (DPC), and dark-field (DF) images simultaneously [1]. These different types of images can provided complementary information of the internal distribution of the sample, for instance, the glandular and adipose tissue distributions, as well as tumour location and microcalcifications, as corresponds in breast imaging. The DPC signal corresponds to the x-ray refraction information, instead of the transmitted signals as corresponds to the absorption one [2].

Compared to the traditional absorption image, x-ray differential phase images can provide superior contrast for soft (i.e. glandular, adipose and tumour) tissues [3,4]. Furthermore, the complementary DF images are mainly generated from small-angle x-ray scattering signals, that are particularly sensitive to fine structures, below the spatial resolution of the imaging system, such as microcalcifications [5,6]. Due to these potential advantages, numerous research interests have been attracted with the hope to translate x-ray grating interferometry into practical applications [4]. However, high accuracy motorized translation stages and high stability of the imaging system are needed to avoid Moiré artifacts in the reconstructed images [1].

Moiré artifacts are the most common artifact in this type of images [7]. A group of Moiré patterns can be obtaining by moving one of the three gratings, that compose the interferometer, within one period in Talbot-Lau interferometry. As a result, each detector records a group of phase stepping data, which form the phase stepping curve and are used to extract the absorption, DPC, and DF signals [2]. In this way, the final image is composed of equispaced black-and-white regular pattern on the acquired images [7]. The constructive part of the interference is shown as a white area, while the destructive part is shown as darker lines. For a deeper explanation about the Talbout-Lau interferometer, as well as the Moiré artifact that can be yielded, we encourage the reader to review [7–9]. To reduce this type of artifacts after the image acquisition, different method have been proposed [1,10]. Lately, convolutional neural networks (CNN) have attracted research interest to reduce Moiré artifacts because they have demonstrated to obtain high image quality for noise reduction [11]. In particular, Chen et al. [2] propose to use a traditional U-net to reduce Moiré image artifacts induced by system instabilities, Ge et al. [12] introduced a phase signal extraction and noise suppression algorithm for DPC images, using their network architecture called XP-NET, and similarly Ren et al. [4] propose their own CNN architecture called DnCNN, which can significantly reduce the noise in retrieved x-ray differential phase and dark-field images.

The aim of this work is to introduce a deep learning method to remove Moiré artifacts from attenuation, DPC and DF images using generative adversarial neural networks. A set of image are acquired using a Talbot-Landau interferometer, modifying the grid positions but without any object in the device, yielding interference Moiré artifacts without attenuation of the signal (beyond to that produced by the interference). Later, an open-access mammography dataset is used to directly obtain mammography images, that are considered as the attenuation one. Phase-contrast and dark field images are simulated using morphological approaches. While the simulated images do not contain the same information than a real DPC and DF image, they are useful to test our approach, as it is performed in the work of Chen et al. [2]. Conversely to the exposed work, the artifacts are not included in the original images but directly adding the pattern. We propose a new methodology that takes into account the corresponding x-ray attenuation which is presented in the mammograms. Furthermore, we analyze the performance of a generative adversarial network, in particular the well know *pix2pix* GAN, to generate images without artifacts.

The rest of this document is organized as follows: Sect. 2 summarizes the methodology to obtain Moiré pattern images, as well as to fuse this type of artifact with simulated dark-field and differential phase-contrast images. Furthermore, the proposed generative network to denoise the images is exposed in Sect. 2.2. Experimental results, stratified considering each type of images independently is shows in Sect. 3, while Sect. 4 corresponds to the discussion and conclusion of our experiments.

2 Materials and Methods

Unfortunately, there is not an open-access dataset of DPC and DF breast images. Therefore, inspired by the work of Chen et al. [2], on the one hand, we aim at simulating dark-field and differential phase-contrast images using the open-access mammography dataset INbreast[1] [13]. These images are considered as the attenuation ones, without artifacts. To simulate DPC images, a sobel filter was used on the mammograms, while to simulate DF images, grayscale pixels intensity are directly inverted.

On the other hand, to obtain the Moiré artifacts, image acquisitions were carried out in the laboratory of micro-CT at the University Complutense of Madrid (Madrid, Spain), using a Talbot-Lau interferometer. Moiré patterns were obtained by modifying the grating position in the interferometer, without any object in the x-ray path. Eventually, 10 different temporal acquisitions, at different time points along the x-ray phase were obtained from every procedure. A total of 13 procedures were performed, modifying the grating position for each one. Attenuation, dark-field and differential phase contrasts patterns were simultaneously obtained.

Moiré temporal acquisition can be permuted in order to obtain a large number of different patterns, within the stack of images obtained in the same procedure and taking into consideration the image type. Considering the number of temporal points, the maximum number of permutations is $10! = 3,628,800$, where each one represents a different Moiré pattern. To fuse the information of both mammogram and artifact images, we propose a new approach, taking into consideration the x-ray absorption performed when an object is situated within the interferometer.

2.1 Image Composition

In the work of Chen et al. [2], artifacts are included in the original DF or DPC images, as corresponds, by a simple weighted addition, using the following equation:

$$A_{Moiré} = (1 - \alpha) \cdot I + \alpha \cdot M_A \qquad (1)$$

---

[1] https://www.kaggle.com/datasets/tommyngx/inbreast2012.

where I represent the original image, M_A correspond to the Moiré artifact image and α is an attenuation value, defined in the interval $\alpha \in [0, 0.3]$. We have to point out that using this equation, the final image $A_{Moiré}$ contains a bias in the constructive part of the interference. For instance, let suppose an image obtained by the Talbot-Landau interferometer using a completely opaque object which does not allow the x-ray transmission. The expected value in the image is $I(x, y) = 0$. However, if this pixel is situated on the constructive part of the Moiré artifact, where $M_A(x, y) = 1$, the final image obtains a value equal to the proposed attenuation coefficient α. That is $A_{Moire}(x, y) = (1 - \alpha) \cdot 0 + \alpha \cdot 1 = \alpha$.

Therefore, in order to avoid this bias, we propose to normalize the Moiré images taking into consideration the attenuation α value. Later, the normalized image $M_A norm$ is directly multiplied by the original image, in order to obtain the unbiased one, which contains the artifact. The corresponding equation can be expressed as follows:

$$A_{Moiré} = I \cdot norm(M_A)_\alpha^1 \qquad (2)$$

To illustrate the different behaviour, with respect to the previous exposed approach, similarly to the previous example, let suppose a region of interest where $I(x, y) = 1$ (i.e. maximum value in the normalized attenuation image). If this area is localized in the constructive part of the interference $M_A(x, y) = 1$, the expected value is preserved $A_{Moiré} = 1$. However, if the area is localized in the destructive part of the interference, the value in the normalized Moiré image is $M_A = \alpha$ and, therefore, the final images is an attenuated version of the original region $A_{Moiré}(x, y) = 1 \cdot \alpha = \alpha$. While, if the region of interest in the original image has value $I(x, y) = 0$ (i.e. minimum of the image), the final image, which is composed of the two real and artifact images, preserves the initial value $A_{Moiré} = 0 \cdot norm(M_A)_\alpha^1$, regardless the artifact pattern.

2.2 Moiré Pattern Removal

After including the artifacts on the corresponding images, an image-to-image generative adversarial network such as *pix2pix* [14] is proposed to remove Moiré pattern of the images. This neural network is trained using an Adam optimization algorithm [15], with learning rate equal to $lr = 0.0005$, which is constant during 150 iterations and using a linear decay for 100 more iterations. he backbone generative network corresponds to a traditional U-net [16], while the discriminator corresponds to patch-gan discriminator [14], known for its ability to enforce desirable local detail generation. We used a least-squared (ls-gan) loss to train the network, with a L1 factor of $\lambda = 10$. Two different networks were trained under the same conditions. The first was trained using DF images, while the second was focused on DPC.

To quantitative evaluate the performance of the denoising procedure, we compute the structural similarity (SSIM) index, and peak signal-to noise (psnr) ratio before and after applying the neural network.

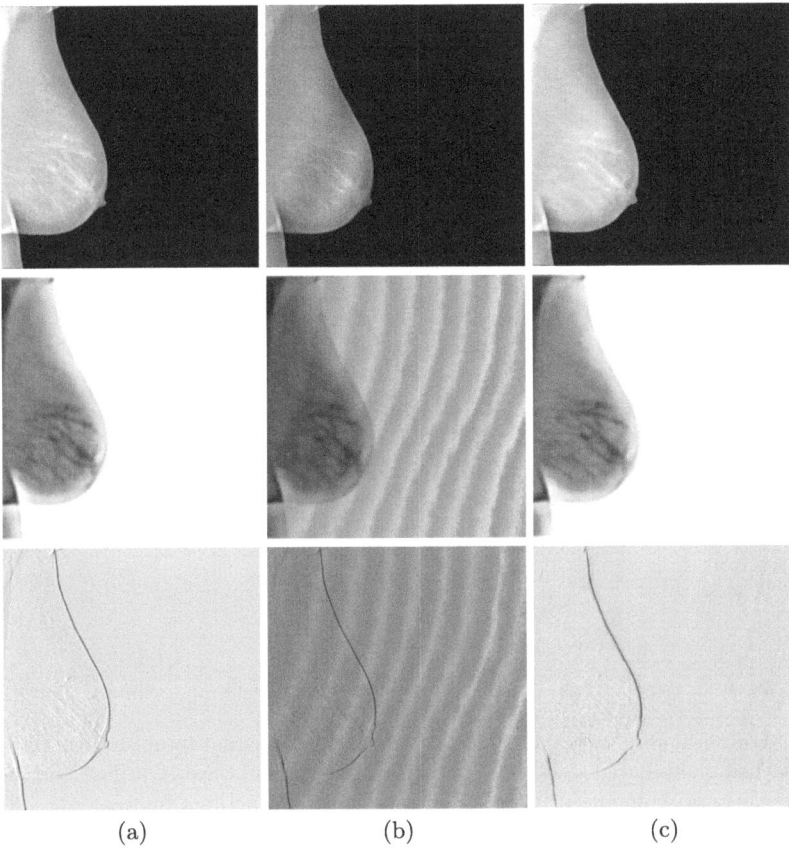

Fig. 1. Example of attenuation (upper row), dark-field (middle row) and phase-contrast (bottom row) images. Column (a) shows the original (i.e. simulated) image without artifacts, while (b) shows the image including the Moiré artifact. The attenuation value was $\alpha = \mathbf{0.49}$ in the current example for the three images. Finally, column (c) shows the results after applying the neural network

3 Experimental Results

The final dataset is composed of 400 FFDM, obtained from the open-access dataset INbreast. These images are considered as the attenuation ones, without artifacts. Furthermore, the same number of Moiré pattern was obtained, from the 13 grating positions, using different order permutation for every temporal acquisition. In this way, each FFDM is associated with one single artifact pattern to avoid repetitions. To fuse the two images, both FFDM and Moiré images are resampled to 512×512 pixels, and the pattern is superimposed in the mammograms using the Eq. 2, using a randomly selectected attenuation α value, between 0.9 and 0.1, for every pair of images.

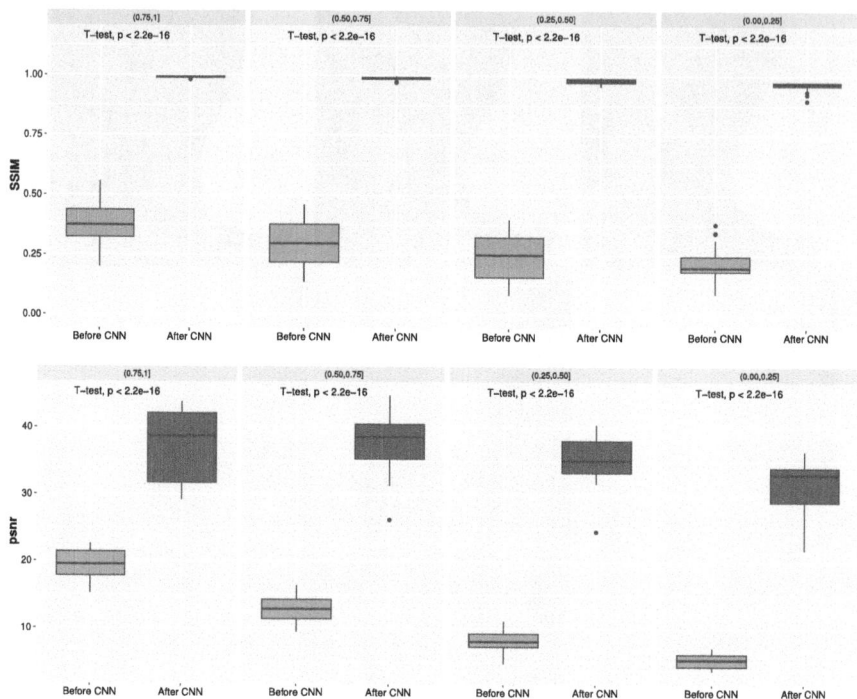

Fig. 2. Structural similarity index (top) index and peak signal-to-noise ratio (bottom) obtained using simulated dark-field mammograms. Results are stratified considering the attenuation α value used to fuse mammography and artifact images.

The dataset is divided into training a test set in a ratio of 75/25, stratified considering the Moiré acquisition. Therefore, 9 acquisitions were used in the training set, while only 4 temporal Moiré patterns were included in the test set. Patterns belonging to the training set were not included in the test set.

Simulated DPC and DF image are obtained as exposed in Sect. 2. Figure 1 shows an example of the three type of images, with and without artifacts, and before and after the denoising procedure carried out using the generative network *pix2pix*.

3.1 Dark-Field Images Dataset

Figure 2 shows the results obtained using the simulated dark-field images, stratified considering the attenuation α value used to fuse simulated dark-field mammograms and Moiré artifact images.

In all cases, before applying the neural network, the best structural similarity value, $SSIM = 0.38 \pm 0.08$ in average, is obtained for larger α values, between 0.75 and 1.00, that corresponds to low attenuation. Obviously, the worst case, with value $SSIM = 0.22 \pm 0.08$, corresponds to the smaller α values, in the

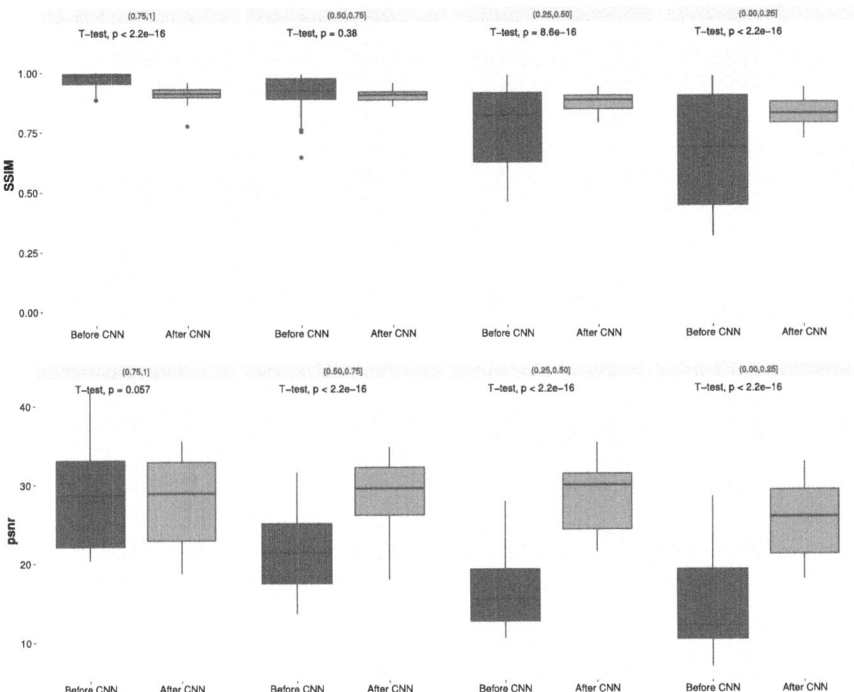

Fig. 3. Structural similarity index (top) index and peak signal-to-noise ratio (bottom) obtained using simulated dark-field mammograms. Results are stratified considering the attenuation α value used to fuse mammography and artifact images.

interval $(0.00, 0.25]$, that yield a large opacity on the mammographic images. The same behaviour is shown when evaluating the peak signal-to-noise ratio. In the first α interval, the PSNR value is $psnr = 19.30 \pm 2.16$, while for the largest attenuation the value corresponds to $psnr = 5.33 \pm 1.09$.

After applying the trained neural network, all values obtain a significant improvement. Similarly to the previous results, the best similarity is obtained for the low attenuation case, while still the worst case corresponds to the smallest α values. In this case, the smallest structural similarity value is $SSIM = 0.96 \pm 0.02$, while the peak signal-to-noise ratio increase up to $psnr = 31.40 \pm 4.11$, in average.

3.2 Differential Phase-Contrast Images Dataset

Regarding the differential phase-contrast images, Fig. 3 shows the results obtained using the simulated DPC images, stratified considering the attenuation α value used to fuse simulated dark-field mammograms and Moiré artifact images.

In this case, the structural similarity is larger than that obtained in the previous case. Largest SSIM values are obtained using larger α values, reaching

$SSIM = 0.97 \pm 0.04$ before applying the denoising procedure. Also, the worst case correspond to the largest attenuation case, where $\alpha \in (0, 0.25]$, which corresponds to $SSIM = 0.66 \pm 0.23$. The same behaviour is shown for the peak signal-to-noise ratio, where the worst value is obtained in the same α interval, with value $psnr = 14.6 \pm 6.16$.

However, results obtained after applying the neural network show a differential behaviour. While for the large attenuation cases, i.e. small α values, between 0.00 and 0.50 there is a clear improvement, when $\alpha > 0.50$ the results show poor image quality. In particular, the worst case is obtained in the interval $\alpha \in (0.75, 1.00]$ where the structural similarity index is $SSIM = 0.90 \pm 0.04$, smaller than that obtained before applying the neural network, and peak signal-to-noise ratio of $psnr = 27.70 \pm 5.26$ which does not show an actual improvement with respect to the image with artifacts dataset.

4 Discussion and Conclusion

The aim of this work is to introduce a deep-learning based framework to reduce Moiré artifacts in dark-field and differential phase-contrast images, using a generative adversarial networks. Inspired by the work of Chen et al. [2], that use a traditional U-net to eliminate this type of artifacts, we use the generative network *pix2pix*, using the U-net network as the backbone, but also include a discriminator network to improve the denoised image quality. The open-access INbreast dataset is used to simulate dark-field an differential phase-contrast images. Later, Moiré artifacts, acquired using a Talbot-Lau interferometer, are included in the breast images using our proposed methodology which aims to avoid the bias obtained by the traditional approach.

Results using DF images show a significant improvement in all the cases, using different attenuation α values to join the information of both breast and artifact images. However, surprisingly, DPC images show a differential behaviour considering the α interval. While our approach obtains a significant improvement for those cases with largest attenuation, i.e. α values between 0.0 and 0.5, in the small attenuation case, $\alpha \in (0.50, 1.00]$, there is not a clear improvement. Even, in the worst cases, with α between 0.75 and 1.00, the peak signal-to-noise value does not show a significant difference between the images before and after applying the neural network, while the structural similarity index shows a better results before the denoising procedure.

A visual assessment demonstrated that, so far, the neural network is yielding checkerboard and discontinuity artifacts on in the final DPC images, mainly localized in the contour of the breast and in those areas that corresponds to the constructive part of the Moiré interference. Considering the number of cases in the training set, just 300 images, and the number of training iterations as well as the learning rate, we theorized that this artifacts may be reduced using a larger dataset as well as modifying the training sample size and/or the learning rate.

The main idea of this work was to evaluate the denoising procedure under the same conditions, i.e. similar number of cases, training epochs as well as the same learning rate. However, dark-field and attenuation images may have low requirements to obtain high quality images, compared to the DPC images. Therefore, as future work, we aim at localizing the optimal training configuration in order not only to improve the results obtained in the DPC dataset but also to avoid overfitting in the neural network when it is trained in an attenuation or DF dataset.

Acknowledgments. This research was partially supported from the Ministry of Science, Innovation, and Universities of Spain, under the project **MODELLING** (ref. PID2020-114769RB-100), and the joint project **VICTORIA:linux** Virtual Clinical Trials and pre-clinical experiments for optimising new Imaging and AI algorithms in Breast Cancer (ref. PID2021-123390OB-C21 & PID2021-123390OB-C22, UdG and UCM respectively).

Disclosure of Interests. The authors have no competing interests to declare that are relevant to the content of this article.

References

1. Tao, S., et al.: Moiré artifacts reduction in Talbot-Lau x-ray phase contrast imaging using a three-step iterative approach. Opt. Express **30**(20), 35096–35111 (2022)
2. Chen, J., et al.: Automatic image-domain Moiré artifact reduction method in grating-based x-ray interferometry imaging. Phys. Med. Biol. **64**(19), 195013 (2019)
3. Bravin, A., Coan, P., Suortti, P.: X-ray phase-contrast imaging: from pre-clinical applications towards clinics. Phys. Med. Biol. **58**(1), R1 (2012)
4. Ren, K., et al.: Deep-learning-based denoising of x-ray differential phase and dark-field images. Eur. J. Radiol. **163**, 110835 (2023)
5. Yashiro, W., et al.: On the origin of visibility contrast in x-ray talbot interferometry. Opt. Express **18**(16), 16890–16901 (2010)
6. Scherer, K., et al.: Correspondence: quantitative evaluation of x-ray dark-field images for microcalcification analysis in mammography. Nat. Commun. **7**(1), 10863 (2016)
7. Miao, H., et al.: A universal moiré effect and application in x-ray phase-contrast imaging. Nat. Phys. **12**(9), 830–834 (2016)
8. Pfeiffer, F., et al.: Grating-based X-ray phase contrast for biomedical imaging applications. Zeitschrift für medizinische Physik **23**(3), 176–185 (2013)
9. Rawlik, M., et al.: Refraction beats attenuation in breast CT. arXiv preprint arXiv:2301.00455 (2023)
10. Seifert, M., et al.: Improved reconstruction technique for Moiré imaging using an x-ray phase-contrast Talbot-Lau interferometer. J. Imaging **4**(5), 62 (2018)
11. Zhang, K., et al.: Beyond a gaussian denoiser: residual learning of deep CNN for image denoising. IEEE Trans. Image Process. **26**(7), 3142–3155 (2017)
12. Ge, Y., et al.: Enhancing the x-ray differential phase contrast image quality with deep learning technique. IEEE Trans. Biomed. Eng. **68**(6), 1751–1758 (2020)
13. Moreira, I., et al.: Inbreast: toward a full-field digital mammographic database. Acad. Radiol. **19**(2), 236–248 (2012)

14. Isola, P., et al.: Image-to-image translation with conditional adversarial networks. In: Proceedings of the IEEE Conference on Computer Vision and Pattern Recognition (2017)
15. Kingma, D.P., Jimmy, B.: Adam: a method for stochastic optimization. arXiv preprint arXiv:1412.6980 (2014)
16. Ronneberger, O., Fischer, P., Brox, T.: U-Net: convolutional networks for biomedical image segmentation. In: Navab, N., Hornegger, J., Wells, W.M., Frangi, A.F. (eds.) MICCAI 2015. LNCS, vol. 9351, pp. 234–241. Springer, Cham (2015). https://doi.org/10.1007/978-3-319-24574-4_28
17. Endrizzi, M.: X-ray phase-contrast imaging. Nucl. Instrum. Methods Phys. Res., Sect. A **878**, 88–98 (2018)
18. Heusel, M., et al.: Gans trained by a two time-scale update rule converge to a local nash equilibrium. Adv. Neural Inf. Process. Syst. **30** (2017)

MRI Breast Tissue Segmentation Using nnU-Net for Biomechanical Modeling

Melika Pooyan(✉), Hadeel Awwad, Eloy García, and Robert Martí

Institute of Computer Vision and Robotics, University of Girona, Girona, Spain
melikapooyan.id@gmail.com, robert.marti@udg.edu

Abstract. Integrating 2D mammography with 3D magnetic resonance imaging (MRI) is crucial for improving breast cancer diagnosis and treatment planning. However, this integration is challenging due to differences in imaging modalities and the need for precise tissue segmentation and alignment. This paper addresses these challenges by enhancing biomechanical breast models in two main aspects: improving tissue identification using nnU-Net segmentation models and evaluating finite element (FE) biomechanical solvers, specifically comparing NiftySim and FEBio. We performed a detailed six-class segmentation of breast MRI data using the nnU-Net architecture, achieving Dice Coefficients of 0.94 for fat, 0.88 for glandular tissue, and 0.87 for pectoral muscle. The overall foreground segmentation reached a mean Dice Coefficient of 0.83 through an ensemble of 2D and 3D U-Net configurations, providing a solid foundation for 3D reconstruction and biomechanical modeling. The segmented data was then used to generate detailed 3D meshes and develop biomechanical models using NiftySim and FEBio, which simulate breast tissue's physical behaviors under compression. Our results include a comparison between NiftySim and FEBio, providing insights into the accuracy and reliability of these simulations in studying breast tissue responses under compression. The findings of this study have the potential to improve the integration of 2D and 3D imaging modalities, thereby enhancing diagnostic accuracy and treatment planning for breast cancer.

Keywords: Multi-class Tissue Segmentation · nnU-Net · Biomechanical Modeling

1 Introduction

Breast cancer is the most common cancer among women, with 1 in 8 women developing invasive breast cancer in their lifetime, highlighting the need for early and accurate diagnosis to improve patient outcomes [1–3]. While traditional imaging techniques provide valuable information, they have inherent limitations. Advanced methods such as multi-modality correspondence can overcome

---

Supplementary Information The online version contains supplementary material available at https://doi.org/10.1007/978-3-031-77789-9_19.

© The Author(s), under exclusive license to Springer Nature Switzerland AG 2025
R. Mann et al. (Eds.): Deep Breath 2024, LNCS 15451, pp. 191–201, 2025.
https://doi.org/10.1007/978-3-031-77789-9_19

these limitations by integrating data from different sources, resulting in a more comprehensive analysis [4,5]. Combining imaging techniques such as mammography and MRI provides a comprehensive view of the breast, improving diagnosis and treatment planning. Mammography detects microcalcifications but struggles with dense tissue, whereas MRI excels in soft tissue contrast and detecting invasive cancers. Integrating these modalities enhances lesion detection and characterization [6]. However, differences in patient positioning during imaging, such as mammographic compression and prone positioning in MRI, present challenges in integration [7–9]. Hence, advanced image registration techniques have been proposed to align these images accurately [10,11]. Finite Element Analysis (FEA) commonly plays a crucial role in these registration techniques by simulating breast tissue deformation under different conditions, aiding in accurate image registration. Patient-specific models replicating the breast's physical properties improve the precision of diagnostic and therapeutic interventions [6,12,13]. Despite advancements, the deformable nature of breast tissue complicates image correlation across modalities and clinical contexts, affecting the diagnosis, biopsy guidance, and surgical planning [6]. Biomechanical modeling offers valuable insights into breast tissue behavior, understanding disease progression, and treatment planning. However, accurately identifying different tissue types within patient-specific models derived from 3D modalities like MRI is a time-consuming and error-prone manual task [14]. Due to its high soft-tissue contrast, MRI can discriminate between different structures in the breast and enable 3D visualization [15]. However, breast MRI imaging includes other organs such as the lungs, heart, pectoral muscles, and thorax. As a result, it is crucial to segment the breast region from the other organs to ensure accurate analysis in biomechanical modeling.

Recent advancements in biomechanical modeling and image segmentation have made significant strides in improving breast cancer diagnosis and treatment planning. Traditional methods primarily relied on manual segmentation, which is time-consuming and prone to errors. The advent of deep learning, particularly convolutional neural networks (CNNs) such as U-Net and its variants, has revolutionized tissue segmentation in medical imaging. Hou [16] achieved a Dice Coefficient of 0.87 for glandular tissue using nnU-Net [17], while Zafari [18] reported a Dice Coefficient of 0.89 for pectoral muscle using U-Net. Alqaoud [19] achieved a Dice Coefficient of 0.95 for fat using a Deep Neural Network (DNN). Despite these advances, current models often segment a limited number of tissue classes and require significant manual intervention, which can reduce their clinical utility. Finite element (FE) biomechanical solvers such as NiftySim and FEBio have been used to model the mechanical properties of breast tissue, aiding in tasks such as image registration and surgical planning. However, these models often lack detailed segmentation data, which is critical for accurately simulating tissue behavior.

This paper addresses challenges in integrating 2D and 3D imaging modalities for breast cancer diagnosis and treatment planning. The main contributions of this work include:

- Utilized the advanced nnU-Net framework for comprehensive segmentation of all breast tissue types in breast MRI data [17]. This approach addresses limitations in existing literature, which often only segment a subset of classes of breast MRI and require additional automatic or manual pre-processing steps.
- Conducted the first known comparative analysis of NiftySim and FEBio for biomechanical modeling of breast tissue mechanics using breast MRI images. This study provides valuable insights into their relative strengths and limitations for accurately simulating breast tissue behavior.

2 Material and Methods

The private dataset comprised 166 T1-weighted non-fat saturated Dynamic contrast-enhanced MRI (DCE-MRI) scans, including follow-ups. Acquired with a 1.5 T Siemens Magnetom Vision system and a CP Breast Array coil, the scans had a typical volume size of 512×256×120 voxels, with pixel spacing from 0.625 to 0.722 mm and a slice thickness of 1.3 mm. Pre-contrast volumes were primarily used for tissue segmentation. An experienced observer manually segmented the MRI volumes into seven categories: background, fatty tissue, glandular tissue, heart, lung area, pectoral muscles, and thorax. This involved labeling every 5–10 slices, with linear interpolation filling the gaps, and more precise structures segmented at smaller intervals. Thresholding techniques were used for segmenting the background, fatty, and glandular tissues based on selected regions [20].

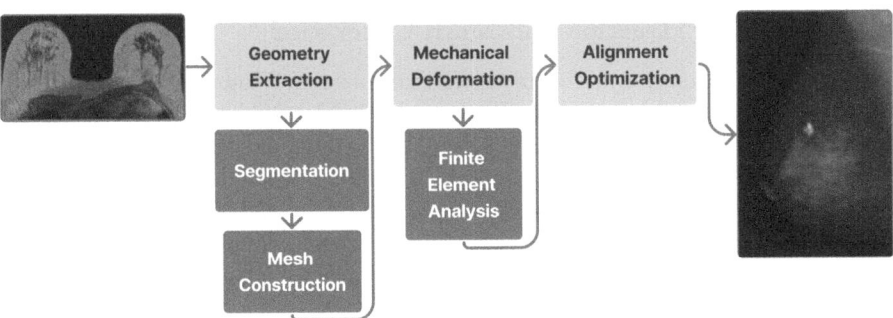

Fig. 1. Overview of the steps for integrating MRI with mammography, inspired by Garcia [14], focusing on segmentation up to finite element analysis.

2.1 Segmentation

As shown in Fig. 1, the segmentation step is a critical component of the overall process of integrating MRI with mammography. This process sets the foundation for accurate registration and biomechanical modeling. The segmentation process in this study utilized the nnU-Net framework [17], known for its high performance in medical image segmentation tasks. nnU-Net was selected due to its capability to automatically adapt its architecture to the specific dataset, thereby optimizing performance without the need for extensive manual configuration [17]. The segmentation involved several critical steps:

- Data Preprocessing: MRI volumes were normalized and resampled to an isotropic voxel size to ensure uniformity across the dataset.
- Training Configuration: The nnU-Net architecture was configured based on the dataset's characteristics, including selecting appropriate hyperparameters, loss functions (a combination of Dice and cross-entropy loss), and optimization algorithms (stochastic gradient descent with Nesterov momentum).
- Model Training: Separate models were trained using both 2D and 3D U-Net configurations. The 2D U-Net processed individual slices of MRI volumes, while the 3D U-Net handled volumetric data, providing a comprehensive analysis of the tissue structures.
- Ensembling: The final segmentation results were obtained by ensembling the outputs from the 2D and 3D models. This involved averaging the softmax probabilities from both configurations to generate the final segmentation labels.

Details on the dataset fingerprint, which includes the dataset characteristics identified by nnU-Net such as image size, voxel spacing, and intensity distributions, as well as the hyperparameters determined based on these characteristics for both 2D and 3D networks, and the architectures of the 2D and 3D networks, are provided in the supplementary material.

2.2 Geometry Extraction and Mesh Generation

Following the segmentation step in the overall process of integrating MRI with mammography, as shown in Fig. 1, the geometry extraction and mesh generation process is the next critical step. The geometry extraction and mesh generation process begins by utilizing the segmentation results obtained from the nnU-Net framework [17]. The initial step involves isolating the breast region from the MRI volumes, excluding non-breast tissues. This isolation is achieved by applying a pre-obtained breast region mask from Gubern-Mérida [20], which effectively segments the image background, leaving only the volumes of interest, such as fat and glandular tissue. The sternum serves as a reference point to ensure accurate segmentation. Following the segmentation, the isolated breast volume, including its internal fat and glandular tissues, is resampled to isotropic voxels of $1\,\text{mm}^3$. Although nnU-Net automatically resamples data based on the median image spacing of the dataset, this additional resampling after segmentation ensures consistency and better mesh quality. The volume mesh is then generated using pygalmesh [21], a Python interface for CGAL's meshing tools [22]. This tool is capable of generating both 2D and 3D meshes. The element count in these meshes varies between 50,000 and 500,000, depending on the volume of the breast, which helps minimize errors during finite element simulations [6].

2.3 Finite Element Analysis: Simulating Compression

Finite Element Analysis (FEA), which is the next step in the pipeline, is essential for simulating the mechanical behavior of breast tissue under conditions like mammography compression. FEA models were constructed using segmented MRI data, incorporating mechanical properties to simulate deformation and stress distribution accurately. NiftySim [23] and FEBio [24] are open-source software for biomechanical simulations of soft tissues. They support properties like position, and orientation of the patient, to adapt the registration process to the patient-specific conditions. Moreover, the initial parameters of the elastic materials were set based on literature values reported in the work of Garcia [23], specifically Young's modulus (4.46 kPa for fatty tissue, 15.1 kPa for glandular tissue) and Poisson's ratio (0.45 to 0.499). Both tools generate uncompressed and compressed breast models, suitable for detailed analysis under different conditions. NiftySim's efficiency in handling large-scale simulations made it ideal for this study [23]. FEBio offers advanced features for simulating complex tissues and incorporates sophisticated material models and boundary conditions. It has been used to simulate breast compression using high-resolution CT data, handling detailed anatomical models and complex tissue interactions [25]. In this study, FEBio validated and compared NiftySim's results. Using FEBio, breast tissue's response to mechanical forces were analyzed, further validating NiftySim's results. The compression process is similar for both tools, as illustrated for NiftySim in Fig. 2.

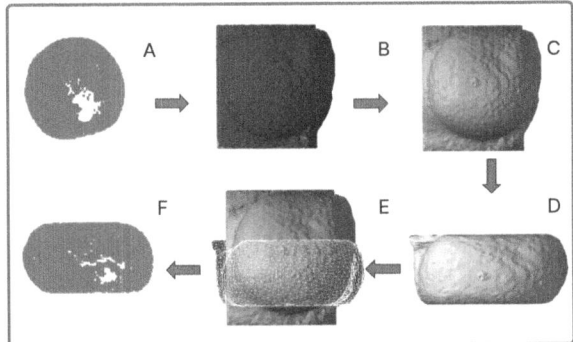

Fig. 2. Process of compression: (A) Segmentation Map, (B) Generated Mesh, (C) NiftySim Displacement, (D) Compressed Map, (E) Wireframe overlay comparing pre- and post-compression maps, (F) Final Compressed Map.

3 Experimental Results

3.1 Evaluation Metrics

The performance of the segmentation and biomechanical modeling processes was evaluated using two critical metrics: the Dice Coefficient and breast volume

(BV) measurements. These metrics are essential for assessing the accuracy of breast tissue deformation under compression in our study. Firstly, the Dice Coefficient was utilized to measure segmentation accuracy by quantifying the overlap between the predicted and ground truth labels. Additionally, it was employed to assess the accuracy of biomechanical modeling using NiftySim and FEBio by comparing compressed and uncompressed segmentation maps, focusing on the center of mass for fat and glandular tissues. A high Dice score close to 1 indicates that the tissues did not deform significantly under compression, suggesting the need for further analysis to ensure accurate simulation. To complement the Dice Coefficient, breast volume changes were analyzed to evaluate the model's ability to simulate realistic tissue behavior under compression. Ideally, the breast volume should remain constant, indicating no tissue loss. However, due to inherent imperfections in simulations, a smaller reduction in breast volume is preferable, indicating better compression with minimal tissue loss. This metric is crucial for understanding the extent of tissue deformation and loss during compression. The study by Garcia [23] supports the use of breast volume changes as an evaluation metric, highlighting its relevance in biomechanical modeling. For a comprehensive statistical analysis, the mean and standard deviation (SD) of the deviations were examined between the analyzed cases. These metrics allow for assessing the consistency and reliability of the segmentation and biomechanical modeling processes, offering insights into the overall performance and robustness of the models.

3.2 Segmentation Results

The nnU-Net framework demonstrated high performance in segmenting breast tissues and organs, including in breast MRI data. The quantitative results, summarized in Table 1, show robust segmentation accuracy across different tissue types. The Dice Coefficients indicate that the framework effectively captures the details of breast tissues, comparable to state-of-the-art methods in the literature. Additionally, the mean and standard deviation (SD) values provide an overview of the average segmentation performance and the variability across different tissues, indicating consistent performance by the nnU-Net framework. The boxplots demonstrate the Dice coefficients for six tissue types segmented using 2D U-Net, and 3D U-Net, and their ensemble. The ensemble method generally shows higher or similar median Dice Coefficients compared to the individual 2D and 3D U-Nets, especially for fat and pectoral tissues. The narrower interquartile ranges for the ensemble method in tissues like fat and pectoral suggest more consistent performance, while individual methods show more variability (Fig. 3). Detailed boxplots, particularly highlighting the high Dice coefficients for the fat class, are included in the supplementary material. Moreover, visual assessments confirmed the accuracy of the segmentation, accurately delineating tissue boundaries even in challenging regions. These segmentation results provide a strong foundation for subsequent biomechanical modeling and analysis, as illustrated in Fig. 4.

Table 1. Comparison of nnU-Net results with State-of-the-Art [16,18,19].

Methods	Fat	Glandular	Heart	Lung	Pectoral	Thorax	Mean ± SD
2D-UNet	**0.94**	**0.88**	0.77	0.72	**0.87**	0.72	0.82 ± 0.14
3D-UNet	0.93	0.86	**0.79**	0.72	0.85	0.72	0.81 ± 0.13
Ensemble	**0.94**	**0.88**	0.79	0.73	0.87	**0.74**	**0.83 ± 0.13**
State of the Art	0.95 [19]	0.87 [16]	-	-	0.89 [18]	-	-

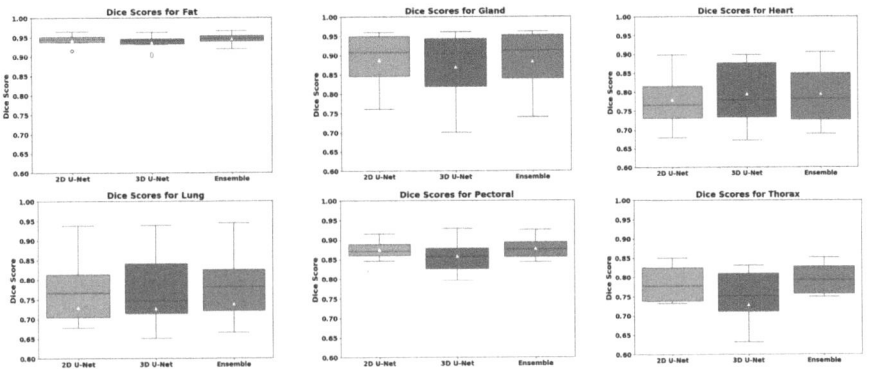

Fig. 3. Dice Coefficients for six tissue types segmented by 2D U-Net, 3D U-Net, and their ensemble, shown from a scale of 0.60 as the Dice Coefficients for all classes were above this value.

3.3 Biomechanical Modeling Results

A subset of 10 cases was chosen to obtain their biomechanical models. Out of these, 4 cases were successfully compressed, while the rest were not, potentially due to issues with the mesh or segmentation affecting the biomechanical models. The biomechanical modeling results, summarized in Table 2, show that NiftySim consistently outperformed FEBio in modeling accuracy and breast volume preservation. NiftySim achieved higher Dice Coefficients for both fat (0.78 to 0.91) and glandular tissues (0.19 to 0.31) compared to FEBio's lower values for fat (0.59 to 0.72) and glandular tissues (0.14 to 0.28). Despite concerns about higher Dice Coefficients after compression, NiftySim showed less breast volume loss (1.52% to 1.94%) compared to FEBio (3.22% to 4.30%), indicating better preservation of anatomical integrity and more accurate tissue deformation modeling. Additionally, mean and standard deviation (SD) values for these measurements are included in Table 2.

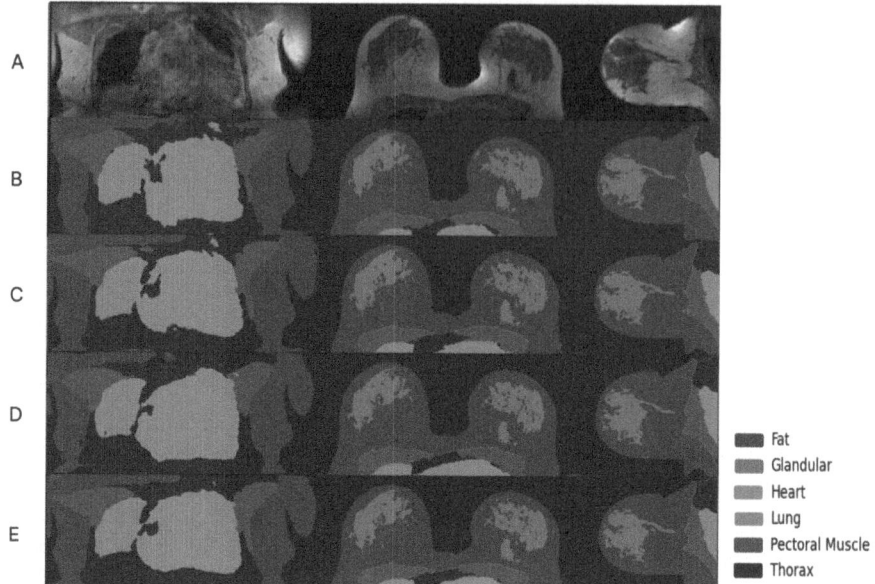

Fig. 4. Qualitative segmentation results for six tissue types (Fat, Glandular, Heart, Lung, Pectoral Muscle, and Thorax) using MRI data. A: Original MRI images. B: Ground truth segmentation. C: 2D U-Net results. D: 3D U-Net results. E: Ensemble method results. The ensemble method (E) shows the most consistent and accurate segmentation, closely matching the ground truth (B).

Table 2. Dice Coefficients, BVs of two FEA Methods for 4 Cases

Cases	FEA	Fat	Gland	BV
Case 1	NiftySim	0.91	0.22	1.52%
Case 1	FEBio	0.69	0.20	3.22%
Case 2	NiftySim	0.78	0.31	1.63%
Case 2	FEBio	0.59	0.28	4.11%
Case 3	NiftySim	0.85	0.20	1.87%
Case 3	FEBio	0.72	0.19	4.30%
Case 4	NiftySim	0.89	0.19	1.94%
Case 4	FEBio	0.65	0.14	4.18%
Mean ± SD	NiftySim	0.85 ± 0.05	0.23 ± 0.05	-
Mean ± SD	FEBio	0.66 ± 0.05	0.20 ± 0.05	-

4 Discussion and Conclusions

In this work, we presented a comprehensive approach for six-class segmentation of breast MRI data using the nnU-Net framework, followed by detailed biomechanical modeling with NiftySim and FEBio. Our study aims to compare and analyze the performance of these tools in segmenting and modeling breast tissues, thereby providing insights into their respective strengths and limitations. The nnU-Net framework demonstrated high Dice Coefficients and precise tissue boundaries, effectively segmenting all breast tissue types. In the comparative analysis, NiftySim generally outperformed FEBio in biomechanical modeling, achieving expected Dice Coefficients for fat and glandular tissues with less volume loss. This indicates that NiftySim may provide a superior simulation of tissue biomechanics under compression, maintaining anatomical integrity during simulations. Accurate biomechanical models facilitate the correlation of breast structures across imaging modalities, support CAD algorithms and needle biopsy procedures, and help radiologists evaluate suspicious areas over time. Despite these advancements, only 4 out of the 10 cases analyzed were successfully compressed. This limited success rate may be due to segmentation issues, mesh quality, or other complexities in finite element analysis, highlighting the need for further research and improvement in these areas.

In conclusion, while the nnU-Net framework effectively segments breast tissue types in MRI data and NiftySim shows promise in biomechanical modeling, the current success rate indicates significant areas for improvement. Challenges such as segmentation accuracy, mesh quality, and the complexity of finite element analysis need to be addressed to enhance the robustness and reliability of biomechanical simulations. Recognizing both the strengths and the areas needing improvement, this work lays the foundation for future advancements in breast tissue segmentation and biomechanical modeling. Future work should focus on refining these aspects to improve simulation success rates, better support personalized treatment planning, and ultimately improve outcomes for patients undergoing breast cancer diagnosis and treatment.

Acknowledgments. This work has been partially funded by the Erasmus+: Erasmus Mundus Joint Master's Degree (EMJMD) scholarship (2022–2024), with project reference 610600-EPP-1-2019-1-ES-EPPKA1-JMD-MOB and the project VICTORIA, "PID2021-123390OB-C21" from the Ministerio de Ciencia e Innovación of Spain.

Disclosure of Interests. The authors have no competing interests to declare that are relevant to the content of this article.

References

1. Smith, T.J.: Breast cancer surveillance guidelines. J. Oncol. Pract. **9**, 65 (2013)
2. Sung, H., et al.: Global cancer statistics 2020: GLOBOCAN estimates of incidence and mortality worldwide for 36 cancers in 185 countries. CA: Cancer J. Clin. **71**(3), 209–249 (2021)
3. Zhang, T., et al.: Radiomics and artificial intelligence in breast imaging: a survey. Artif. Intell. Rev. **56**(Suppl 1), 857–892 (2023)
4. Zhang, T., et al.: Predicting breast cancer types on and beyond molecular level in a multi-modal fashion. NPJ Breast Cancer **9**(1), 16 (2023)

5. Tan, T., et al.: Multi-modal artificial intelligence for the combination of automated 3D breast ultrasound and mammograms in a population of women with predominantly dense breasts. Insights Imaging **14**(1), 10 (2023)
6. Garcia, E., et al.: Multimodal breast parenchymal patterns correlation using a patient-specific biomechanical model. IEEE Trans. Med. Imaging **37**, 712–723 (2017)
7. van Engeland, S., Snoeren, P., Hendriks, J., Karssemeijer, N.: A comparison of methods for mammogram registration. IEEE Trans. Med. Imaging **22**, 1436–1444 (2003)
8. Pinto Pereira, S.M., et al.: Automated registration of diagnostic to prediagnostic x-ray mammograms: evaluation and comparison to radiologists' accuracy. Med. Phys. **37**, 4530–4539 (2010)
9. Rueckert, D., Sonoda, L.I., Hayes, C., Hill, D.L., Leach, M.O., Hawkes, D.J.: Non-rigid registration using free-form deformations: application to breast MR images. IEEE Trans. Med. Imaging **18**, 712–721 (1999)
10. Arlinghaus, L.R., et al.: Motion correction in diffusion-weighted MRI of the breast at 3T. J. Magn. Reson. Imaging **33**, 1063–1070 (2011)
11. Siegler, P., Ebrahimi, M., Holloway, C.M., Thevathasan, G., Plewes, D.B., Martel, A.: Supine breast MRI and assessment of future clinical applications. Eur. J. Radiol. **81**, S153–S155 (2012)
12. Babarenda Gamage, T.P., Rajagopal, V., Nielsen, P.M., Nash, M.P.: Patient-specific modeling of breast biomechanics with applications to breast cancer detection and treatment. Patient-Specif. Model. Tomorrow's Med. 379–412 (2012)
13. Melbourne, A., Cahill, N.D., Tanner, C., Hawkes, D.J.: Image registration using an extendable quadratic regulariser. In: 2011 IEEE International Symposium on Biomedical Imaging: From Nano to Macro, pp. 557–560. IEEE (2011)
14. García, E., et al.: A step-by-step review on patient-specific biomechanical finite element models for breast MRI to x-ray mammography registration. Med. Phys. **45**, e6–e31 (2018)
15. Giess, C.S., Yeh, E.D., Raza, S., Birdwell, R.L.: Background parenchymal enhancement at breast MR imaging: normal patterns, diagnostic challenges, and potential for false-positive and false-negative interpretation. Radiographics **34**, 234–247 (2014)
16. Huo, L., Hu, X., Xiao, Q., Gu, Y., Chu, X., Jiang, L.: Segmentation of whole breast and fibroglandular tissue using NNU-net in dynamic contrast enhanced MR images. Magn. Reson. Imaging **82**, 31–41 (2021)
17. Isensee, F., Jaeger, P.F., Kohl, S.A., Petersen, J., Maier-Hein, K.H.: NNU-net: a self-configuring method for deep learning-based biomedical image segmentation. Nat. Methods **18**, 203–211 (2021)
18. Zafari, S., et al.: Automated segmentation of the pectoral muscle in axial breast MR images. In: Bebis, G., et al. (eds.) ISVC 2019. LNCS, vol. 11844, pp. 345–356. Springer, Cham (2019). https://doi.org/10.1007/978-3-030-33720-9_26
19. Alqaoud, M., et al.: Multi-modality breast MRI segmentation using NNU-net for preoperative planning of robotic surgery navigation. In: 2022 Annual Modeling and Simulation Conference (ANNSIM), pp. 317–328. IEEE (2022)
20. Gubern-Mérida, A., Kallenberg, M., Martí, R., Karssemeijer, N.: Segmentation of the pectoral muscle in breast MRI using atlas-based approaches. In: Ayache, N., Delingette, H., Golland, P., Mori, K. (eds.) MICCAI 2012. LNCS, vol. 7511, pp. 371–378. Springer, Heidelberg (2012). https://doi.org/10.1007/978-3-642-33418-4_46

21. Schlömer, N.: pygalmesh: Python interface for CGAL's meshing tools (2021). https://doi.org/10.5281/zenodo.5628848
22. The CGAL Project: CGAL User and Reference Manual. 5.6.1 ed., CGAL Editorial Board (2024). https://doc.cgal.org/5.6.1/Manual/packages.html
23. García, E., Fedon, C., Caballo, M., Martí, R., Sechopoulos, I., Diaz, O.: Realistic compressed breast phantoms for medical physics applications. In: 15th International Workshop on Breast Imaging (IWBI2020), SPIE, pp. 30–37 (2020)
24. Maas, S.A., Ellis, B.J., Ateshian, G.A., Weiss, J.A.: FEBio: finite elements for biomechanics. J. Biomech. Eng. **134**, 011005 (2012)
25. Hsu, C.M.L., Palmeri, M.L., Segars, W.P., Veress, A.I., Dobbins, J.T., III.: An analysis of the mechanical parameters used for finite element compression of a high-resolution 3D breast phantom. Med. Phys. **38**, 5756–5770 (2011)

Fat-Suppressed Breast MRI Synthesis for Domain Adaptation in Tumour Segmentation

Lidia Garrucho[1,2(✉)], Eve Delegue[1,3], Richard Osuala[1,4,5], Dimitri Kessler[1], Kaisar Kushibar[1], Oliver Díaz[1], Karim Lekadir[1,6], and Laura Igual[1]

[1] Departament de Matemàtiques i Informàtica, Universitat de Barcelona, Barcelona, Spain
lgarrucho@ub.edu
[2] Department of Oncology-Pathology, Karolinska Institutet, Stockholm, Sweden
[3] Ecole Normale Supérieure de Paris Saclay, Gif-Sur-Yvette, France
[4] Helmholtz Center Munich, Munich, Germany
[5] Technical University of Munich, Munich, Germany
[6] Institució Catalana de Recerca i Estudis Avançats (ICREA), Barcelona, Spain

Abstract. Heterogeneity in dynamic contrast-enhanced breast MRI acquisition protocols hinders the generalization of automatic tumour segmentation tools. While fat-suppressed MRI acquisition is common, some vendors do not provide these sequences, making a segmentation model trained with fat-suppressed images unusable for non-fat-suppressed cases. In this study, we propose two strategies to alleviate this issue. The first approach involves translating non-fat-suppressed to fat-suppressed breast MRI. The second approach integrates synthetic non-fat-suppressed MRI into the training pipeline of tumour segmentation models. Our experimental results demonstrate that both approaches significantly improve segmentation performance on non-fat-suppressed MRI, suggesting that domain adaptation techniques based on image synthesis can enhance the accuracy and reliability of tumour segmentation in breast MRI. The generative models will be made publicly available at *medigan* library (*medigan* [18] GitHub repository).

Keywords: Synthetic Data · Breast Cancer · Deep Learning · Generative Models · Image-to-image Translation · Fat Suppression

1 Introduction

A frequent issue in breast MRI encompasses the high signal from fat, which can obscure cancerous lesions thereby impacting accurate diagnosis and timely treatment. To address this, fat suppression techniques such as fat-saturation and subtraction, are commonly used to reduce artifacts and enhance gadolinium

---

L. Garrucho and E. Delegue—These authors contributed equally to this work.

contrast visualization, crucial for determining malignancy [2]. The application of fat suppression techniques varies widely among hospitals, patients, and scans due to factors such as clinical context, diagnostic goals, breast fat content, magnetic field, technology, and institutional protocols [10,14]. This variability can degrade the performance of automated medical image analysis methods, particularly deep learning models, which are sensitive to domain shifts. Therefore, research into consistent automated fat-suppression methodologies for clinical application is essential as a complement or even an alternative to existing methods.

Volumetric tumour segmentation is crucial for assessing cancer volume and extension. Currently, deep learning-based segmentation methods, such as *nnU-Net* [8], have shown excellent results in various biomedical image segmentation tasks. However, these methods are data-intensive and rely on the availability of ground-truth segmentations for training. In T1-weighted breast MRI, publicly available ground-truth segmentations of breast cancer are predominantly restricted to images with fat suppression. However, as mentioned above, imaging protocols differ across hospitals, complicating the generalization of these models to non-fat-suppressed T1-weighted images, as well as across different fat-suppressed breast MRI domains.

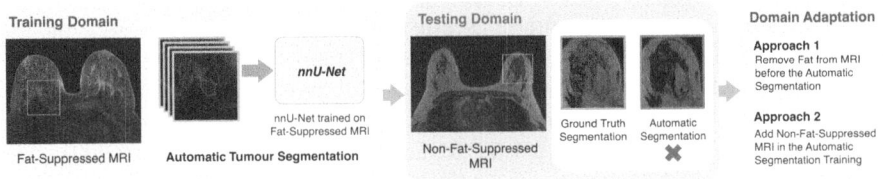

Fig. 1. Overview of our proposed domain adaptation pipeline illustrating two alternative methods validated in this study for volumetric tumour segmentation in non-fat-suppressed T1-weighted breast MRI.

As depicted in Fig. 1, given automatic tumour segmentation models trained on fat-suppressed MRI, we propose two domain adaptation (DA) techniques to improve the performance of tumour segmentation on non-fat-suppressed MRI. The first approach involves applying fat suppression to non-fat-suppressed MRI using Generative Adversarial Networks (GANs) [4,5,12,23] and subsequently performing tumour segmentation on the synthetic fat-suppressed images. This largely unexplored approach is motivated by some promising initial results [14] reported for synthetic fat-suppressed images, which, however, have not been assessed in terms of their utility for clinical applications. To this end, our goal is to evaluate the effectiveness of synthetic fat-suppressed MRI for tumour segmentation, potentially as useful replacement for real non-fat-suppressed MRI. Our second approach constitutes the first study to include and evaluate synthetic non-fat-suppressed MRI in automatic tumour segmentation model training pipelines. In this case, instead of performing fat suppression, the GAN learns to inpaint fat into the real fat-suppressed MRI. Incorporating synthetic non-fat-suppressed images into the training pipeline can eliminate the need for MRI post-processing steps (synthesizing fat-suppressed MRI from non-fat-suppressed ones), thereby reducing computational resources and time. In sum, the key contributions of our work are as follows:

- Design, implementation and multi-metric validation of a conditional Generative Adversarial Network for synthesizing fat-suppressed and non-fat-suppressed breast MRI.
- Evaluation of the effect of domain shift in fat-suppressed T1-weighted breast MRI on tumour segmentation.
- Contribute with the first in-depth comparative analysis and validation of synthetic non-fat-suppressed MRI (i) as target inference domain and (ii) as training data augmentation method, demonstrating its potential to improve tumour segmentation performance.

2 Materials and Methods

2.1 Datasets

The MAMA-MIA dataset [3], a collection of 1506 ground-truth breast MRI tumour segmentations from four public datasets [11,15,16,20], was used in this study to train the automatic tumour segmentation models. The dataset encompasses 1271 axial and 235 sagittal T1-weighted dynamic contrast-enhanced scans (DCE-MRI) with fat suppression from three different vendors. The Advanced MRI Breast Lesions (AMBL) dataset [1] was used to train the GANs. AMBL contains 632 cases acquired on a 1.5T MR system between 2018 and 2021. The patients were screened with various MRI modalities and ground-truth tumour segmentations are available for 99 cases. In this study, we use the non-fat-suppressed T1-weighted MRI and the first phase (pre-contrast) of the axial T1-weighted DCE-MRI as image pairs for image synthesis. Additionally, 47 test cases with ground-truth tumour segmentations were randomly excluded from image-to-image translation training to evaluate the tumour segmentation performance in an external test set.

2.2 Fat-Suppressed and Non-Fat-Suppressed MRI Synthesis

We adopt *pix2pix* [9], a conditional Generative Adversarial Network (cGAN) framework for paired image-to-image translation, was trained to synthesized fat-suppressed and non-fat-suppressed 2D axial MRI slices. As depicted in Fig. 2, we design a pre-processing pipeline involving several steps to assemble MRI image pairs for our training setup. First, the pre-contrast fat-suppressed T1-weighted DCE-MRI phase and the pre-contrast non-fat-suppressed T1-weighted MRI were registered using rigid-affine registration [19]. Next, the MRI were resampled to isotropic pixel spacing to ensure consistent resolution across all three axes (axial, sagittal, and coronal), utilizing B-Spline interpolation implemented using the SimpleITK library [13]. Lastly, the MRI were cropped to the breast region using Otsu's thresholding to discard the background before extracting slices and pairing corresponding axial MRI slices.

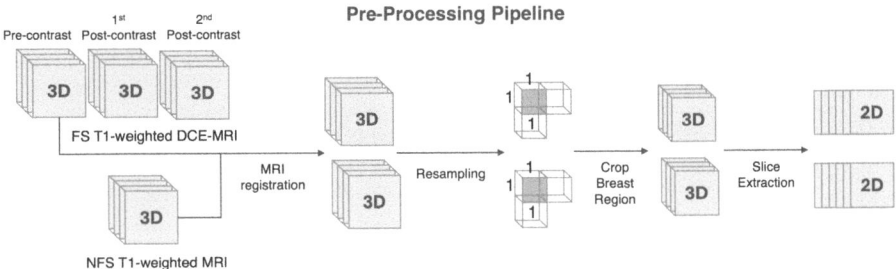

Fig. 2. Steps to extract the paired fat-suppressed (FS) and non-fat-suppressed (NFS) MRI slices to train our conditional GAN models.

After image pre-processing, the AMBL dataset was split in 471 MRI cases for training and 160 for testing. Two *pix2pix* models were trained using paired fat-suppressed and non-fat-suppressed MRI 2D slices with input size 256 × 256, as exemplified by Fig. 3. We follow the *pix2pix* hyperparameter setup [9], training during 200 epochs, using serial batches, and the Adam optimizer with $\beta_1 = 0.5$. The training schedule consisted of 100 epochs with an initial learning rate of 0.0002, followed by 100 epochs with a linearly decreasing learning rate.

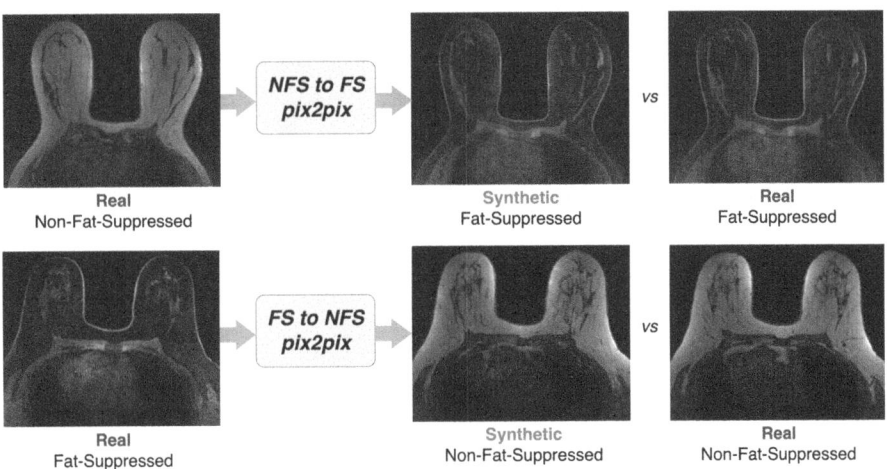

Fig. 3. Bi-directional image-to-image translation using *pix2pix* for synthesizing either FS or NFS T1-weighted MRI slices, illustrated alongside their real counterparts.

2.3 Automatic Tumour Segmentation

We integrate *nnU-Net* [8] as an automatic tumour segmentation model into our pipeline. Tumour volumes (VOI) of 1506 real fat-suppressed pre-contrast T1-weighted MRI with an additional 20% margin were used to train a 3D *nnU-Net* in a 5-fold cross-validation setting. The training parameters include using z-score normalization, isotropic pixel spacing, an initial learning rate of 1e−2, and a weight decay of 3e−5 during 1000 epochs.

As shown in Fig. 4, we design two different DA approaches to improve the automatic tumour segmentation in out-of-domain non-fat-suppressed MRI.

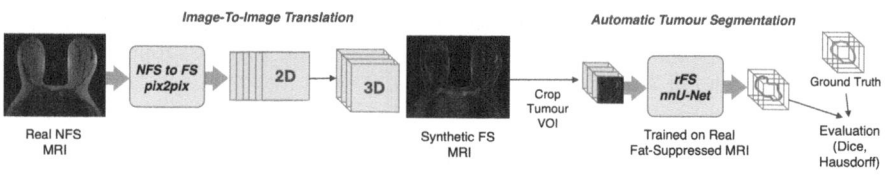

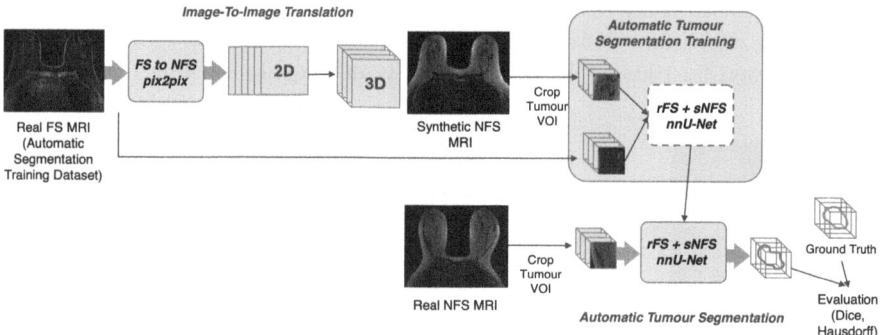

Fig. 4. Our domain adaptation approaches for tumour segmentation of non-fat-suppressed (NFS) T1-weighted breast MRI.

Approach 1: Tumour Segmentation on Synthetic Fat-Suppressed MRI
The first approach involves performing image-to-image translation prior to automatic tumour segmentation. The *pix2pix*, trained to translate non-fat-suppressed to fat-suppressed MRI (*NFS to FS pix2pix*), is applied to synthesize 2D axial slices that are stacked to respective 3D MRI volumes back to their original space. Further, these synthetic MRI volumes are then cropped to extract the volume of interest to segment using the *rFS nnU-Net*.

Approach 2: Synthetic Non-Fat-Suppressed MRI Data Augmentation
The second approach involves the addition of synthetic non-fat-suppressed MRIs in the *nnU-Net* training pipeline. Synthetic non-fat-suppressed MRI are generated using the *FS to NFS pix2pix* for each of the 1271 axial MRI cases in the MAMA-MIA dataset. The final segmentation model (*rFS+sNFS nnU-Net*) is,

thus, trained using real fat-suppressed (rFS) and synthetic non-fat-suppressed (sNFS) MRI.

2.4 Evaluation Metrics and Statistical Analysis

The performance of the *pix2pix* models is evaluated using Peak Signal-to-Noise Ratio (PSNR), Structural Similarity Index (SSIM) [21], Fréchet Inception Distance (FID) [6], and Fréchet Radiomics Distance (FRD) [17]. High PSNR values indicate close resemblance to ground-truth images, while SSIM aligns with human perception, crucial for clinical evaluation. FID assesses image realism, and FRD evaluates dataset similarity based on radiomics features, providing a more accurate complementary assessment for breast MRI. These metrics offer insights into pixel-level similarity, structural fidelity, realism, and radiomics feature alignment.

Automatic tumour segmentation performance is evaluated using the Dice Coefficient and the 95th percentile of the Hausdorff Distance (HD95). The Dice Coefficient measures the overlap between predicted and ground-truth segmentations, indicating accuracy, while HD95 assesses boundary accuracy by measuring the largest distance between predicted and ground-truth boundaries, excluding outliers [7].

Statistical differences in segmentation performances are assessed using the Wilcoxon signed-rank test with Bonferroni Correction, a non-parametric test suitable for non-normally distributed data common in biomedical research [22].

3 Experiments and Results

3.1 Fat-Suppressed and Non-Fat-Suppressed MRI Synthesis

The quantitative evaluation of both *pix2pix* models is depicted in Table 1. The *NFS to FS* model achieved a promising PSNR of 25.58 ± 3.50, an SSIM of 0.75 ± 0.11, an FID of 5.54, and an FRD of 13.24, indicating high pixel-level similarity, structural fidelity, and radiomic imaging biomarker accuracy. The *FS to NFS* model had a higher PSNR of 26.39 ± 0.46 but lower structural fidelity with an SSIM of 0.69 ± 0.26. As indicated by an FID of 34.10 and an FRD of 52.14, the model generated synthetic images of high quality, however, they resulted overall less realistic than their synthetic *NFS to FS* counterparts.

Table 1. Performance metrics for *pix2pix* models synthesizing fat-suppressed (FS) and non-fat-suppressed (NFS) MRI.

pix2pix	PSNR ↑	SSIM ↑	FID ↓	FRD ↓
NFS to FS	25.58 ± 3.50	0.75 ± 0.11	5.54	13.24
FS to NFS	26.39 ± 0.46	0.69 ± 0.26	34.10	52.14

3.2 Automatic Tumour Segmentation

The mean 5-fold cross-validation Dice coefficients for the automatic tumour segmentation models trained on MAMA-MIA were 0.76 ± 0.01 for *rFS nnU-Net* in Approach 1 (A1) and 0.76 ± 0.01 for *rFS + sNFS nnU-Net* in Approach 2 (A2), indicating that incorporating synthetic non-fat-suppressed (Synth NFS) MRI did not negatively affect overall performance. The segmentation performance on real FS tumours in the external test set (47 cases from AMBL dataset containing 79 tumours) decreased due to domain shift (Dice of 0.59 for *rFS nnU-Net* in A1 and 0.61 for *rFS + sNFS nnU-Net* in A2).

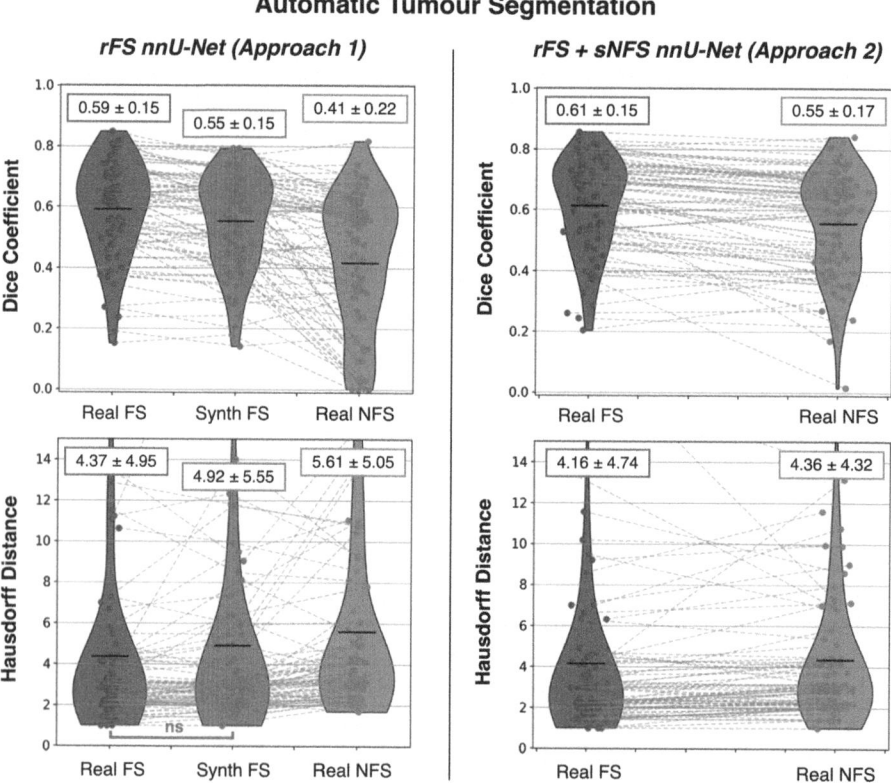

Fig. 5. Comparison of automatic tumour segmentation evaluation metrics for both DA approaches on the test set. 'FS' stands for Fat-Suppressed, 'NFS' for Non-Fat-Suppressed, and 'Synth' for Synthetic. *ns* indicates no statistical difference between metrics.

Both DA approaches, with results summarized in Fig. 5, improved segmentation metrics compared to real non-fat-suppressed (Real NFS) images segmented with *rFS nnU-Net* in A1. Metrics show similar performance between Synth FS in A1 and Real NFS in A2 (Dice: 0.55 ± 0.15 vs. 0.55 ± 0.17, HD: 4.92 ± 5.55 vs. 4.36 ± 4.32). The Dice coefficient in Real FS is slightly better in A2 (0.61 ± 0.15 vs. A1: 0.59 ± 0.15), indicating that Synth NFS data augmentation improved the segmentation model. Despite statistical differences in Dice coefficient between Real FS and Synth FS, this difference is not observed in the Hausdorff Distance metric, which evaluates boundary accuracy. Figure 6 presents qualitative results for four test cases, supporting our findings. Although the tumour segmentations are volumetric, only the middle slice of each tumour is displayed for clarity.

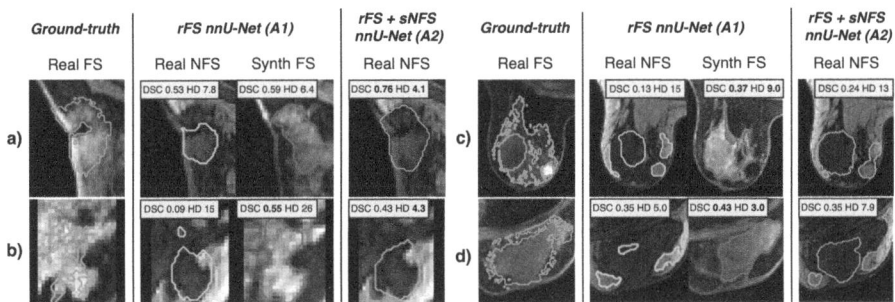

Fig. 6. Four examples (a), b), c) and d)) of tumour segmentation contours highlighting the differences between the ground-truth in real FS and the results of the DA approaches. 'A1' stands for Approach 1, 'A2' for Approach 2, 'FS' for Fat-Suppressed, 'NFS' for Non-Fat-Suppressed, 'Synth' for Synthetic, 'DSC' for Dice Coefficient, and 'HD' for Hausdorff Distance.

4 Discussion and Conclusion

Our study investigates DA techniques leveraging image synthesis to enhance tumour segmentation in non-fat-suppressed (NFS) breast MRI. We employed two distinct DA approaches: Approach 1 (A1), which runs tumour segmentation in synthetic fat-suppressed (Synth FS) MRI obtained using the *NFS to FS pix2pix* model, and Approach 2 (A2), which incorporates synthetic non-fat-suppressed (Synth NFS) MRI generated with the *FS to NFS pix2pix* model into the automatic tumour segmentation pipeline (*rFS + sNFS nnU-Net* model) to improve the tumour segmentation in real NFS MRI.

Our FS MRI synthesis with *NFS to FS pix2pix* model showed superior performance across multiple evaluation metrics. The *FS to NFS pix2pix* model, while delivering higher PSNR, faced challenges related to structural and radiomic fidelity, evident from higher FID and FRD values. Nevertheless, integrating Synth NFS MRI into the training pipeline in A2 did not compromise overall tumour segmentation performance. On the contrary, it bolstered the Dice coefficient for Real NFS, underscoring the efficacy of data augmentation with synthetic images.

Both DA approaches exhibited notable improvements in tumour segmentation metrics compared to real NFS MRI segmented with *rFS nnU-Net* in A1. Although statistical differences in Dice coefficients were observed between Real FS and Synth FS, there was no statistical difference for the Hausdorff distance, demonstrating remarkable synthetic data utility.

Our findings highlight the potential of both DA approaches for enhancing tumour segmentation on NFS MRI. Moreover, the synthetic NFS images generated by the *NFS to FS pix2pix* model offer a promising alternative to conventional fat suppression techniques. Future research aims to address current study limitations by exploring their utility in diverse clinical tasks related to breast cancer using MRI, such as comprehensive cancer detection in high-risk screening populations and prediction of treatment response. Additionally, future efforts will focus on synthesizing 3D MRI to maintain spatial continuity across 2D slices, integrating perceptual loss in the training pipeline to enhance synthetic MRI fidelity, and validating models externally with additional datasets.

Acknowledgments. This project was funded by the EU's Horizon 2020 programmes under grants No 952103 (EUCanImage) and No 101057699 (RadioVal). It was partially supported by Spain's Ministry of Science and Innovation (FUTURE-ES PID2021-126724OB-I00), MICINN Grant PID2022-136436NB-I00, and AGAUR Grant 2021-SGR-01104. Co-author K.K. holds a Juan de la Cierva fellowship (FJC2021-047659-I).

Disclosure of Interests. The authors declare no competing interests.

References

1. Daniels, D., Last, D., Cohen, K., Mardor, Y., Sklair-Levy, M.: Standard and delayed contrast-enhanced MRI of malignant and benign breast lesions with histological and clinical supporting data (advanced-MRI-breast-lesions) (version 2) [data set]. The Cancer Imaging Archive (2024). https://doi.org/10.7937/C7X1-YN57
2. Delfaut, E.M., Beltran, J., Johnson, G., Rousseau, J., Marchandise, X., Cotten, A.: Fat suppression in MR imaging: techniques and pitfalls. Radiographics **19**(2), 373–382 (1999). https://doi.org/10.1148/radiographics.19.2.g99mr03373
3. Garrucho, L., Reidel, C.A., Kushibar, K., et al.: MAMA-MIA: a large-scale multi-center breast cancer DCE-MRI benchmark dataset with expert segmentations. arXiv preprint (2024). https://doi.org/10.48550/arXiv.2406.13844. https://arxiv.org/abs/2406.13844
4. Goodfellow, I., et al.: Generative adversarial nets. In: Ghahramani, Z., Welling, M., Cortes, C., Lawrence, N., Weinberger, K.Q. (eds.) Advances in Neural Information Processing Systems, vol. 27, pp. 2672–2680. Curran Associates, Inc. (2014)
5. Han, L., et al.: Synthesis-based imaging-differentiation representation learning for multi-sequence 3D/4D MRI. Med. Image Anal. **92**, 103044 (2024)
6. Heusel, M., Ramsauer, H., Unterthiner, T., Nessler, B., Hochreiter, S.: GANs trained by a two time-scale update rule converge to a local Nash equilibrium. In: Advances in Neural Information Processing Systems 30 (2017)

7. Huttenlocher, D.P., Klanderman, G.A., Rucklidge, W.J.: Comparing images using the Hausdorff distance. IEEE Trans. Pattern Anal. Mach. Intell. **15**(9), 850–863 (1993). https://doi.org/10.1109/34.232073
8. Isensee, F., Jaeger, P.F., Kohl, S.A.A., Petersen, J., Maier-Hein, K.H.: nnU-Net: a self-configuring method for deep learning-based biomedical image segmentation. Nat. Methods **18**(2), 203–211 (2021). https://doi.org/10.1038/s41592-020-01008-z
9. Isola, P., Zhu, J.Y., Zhou, T., Efros, A.A.: Image-to-image translation with conditional adversarial networks. In: Proceedings of the IEEE Conference on Computer Vision and Pattern Recognition, pp. 1125–1134 (2017)
10. Kuhl, C.: The current status of breast MR imaging part I. Choice of technique, image interpretation, diagnostic accuracy, and transfer to clinical practice. Radiology **244**(2), 356–378 (2007). https://doi.org/10.1148/radiol.2442051620
11. Li, W.: I-SPY 2 breast dynamic contrast enhanced MRI trial (version 1) [data set]. The Cancer Imaging Archive (2022). https://doi.org/10.7937/TCIA.D8Z0-9T85
12. Li, W., Xiao, H., Li, T., et al.: Virtual contrast-enhanced magnetic resonance images synthesis for patients with nasopharyngeal carcinoma using multimodality-guided synergistic neural network. IJROBP **112**(4), 1033–1044 (2022)
13. Lowekamp, B.C., Chen, D.T., Ibáñez, L., Blezek, D.: The design of SimpleITK. Front. Neuroinform. **7**, 45 (2013)
14. Mori, M., et al.: Feasibility of new fat suppression for breast MRI using pix2pix. Jpn. J. Radiol. **38**, 1075–1081 (2020). https://doi.org/10.1007/s11604-020-01012-5
15. Newitt, D., Hylton, N.: Multi-center breast DCE-MRI data and segmentations from patients in the I-SPY 1/ACRIN 6657 trials. The Cancer Imaging Archive (2016). https://doi.org/10.7937/K9/TCIA.2016.HdHpgJLK
16. Newitt, D., Hylton, N.: Single site breast DCE-MRI data and segmentations from patients undergoing neoadjuvant chemotherapy (version 3) [data set]. The Cancer Imaging Archive (2016). https://doi.org/10.7937/K9/TCIA.2016.QHsyhJKy
17. Osuala, R., et al.: Towards learning contrast kinetics with multi-condition latent diffusion models. arXiv preprint arXiv:2403.13890 (2024)
18. Osuala, R., et al.: medigan: a Python library of pretrained generative models for medical image synthesis. J. Med. Imaging **10**(6), 061403 (2023). https://doi.org/10.1117/1.JMI.10.6.061403
19. Ourselin, S., Roche, A., Subsol, G., Pennec, X., Ayache, N.: Reconstructing a 3D structure from serial histological sections. Image Vis. Comput. **19**(1–2), 25–31 (2001)
20. Saha, A., et al.: Dynamic contrast-enhanced magnetic resonance images of breast cancer patients with tumor locations [data set]. The Cancer Imaging Archive (2021). https://doi.org/10.7937/TCIA.e3sv-re93
21. Wang, Z., Bovik, A.C., Sheikh, H.R., Simoncelli, E.P.: Image quality assessment: from error visibility to structural similarity. IEEE Trans. Image Process. **13**(4), 600–612 (2004)
22. Wilcoxon, F.: Individual comparisons by ranking methods. Springer (1992). https://doi.org/10.1007/978-1-4612-4380-9_16
23. Zhang, T., Tan, T., Han, L., et al.: IMPORTANT-Net: integrated MRI multi-parametric increment fusion generator with attention network for synthesizing absent data. Inf. Fusion **108**, 102381 (2024)

Guiding Breast Conservative Surgery by Augmented Reality from Preoperative MRI: Initial System Design and Retrospective Trials

Rasoul Sharifian[1,3](✉), Sabrina Madad-Zadeh[2,3], Nicolas Bourdel[1,3], Alexia Giro[2], Wissam Marraoui[2], Christophe Pomel[2], and Adrien Bartoli[1,3]

[1] CHU de Clermont-Ferrand, Clermont-Ferrand, France
rasoul.sharifian.cs@gmail.com
[2] Centre Jean Perrin, Clermont-Ferrand, France
[3] EnCoV/Institut Pascal, Clermont-Ferrand, France

Abstract. Breast-Conserving Surgery (BCS) often presents significant challenges in accurately localising the tumours intraoperatively, even for expert surgeons. Augmented Reality (AR) has been attempted to improve BCS accuracy. Existing systems are still research prototypes and share two main limitations caused by a) breast deformations and b) camera projection. We propose an AR system for BCS which uses preoperative MRI and an intraoperative RGB-D camera. We mitigate a), which mainly occurs because of gravity, by collecting a preoperative MRI in supine position. We mitigate b), which occurs because of variations in the relative breast to camera position, using a vertical projection method. Retrospective qualitative and quantitative evaluations for two patients are promising.

Keywords: Breast-Conserving Surgery · Augmented Reality

1 Introduction

Breast cancer is one of the world's most prevalent malignancies, with approximately 12% of women encountering breast cancer [6]. Breast-Conserving Surgery (BCS) is a common procedure to remove cancerous tumours. However, in cases where a tumour is not palpable, which represent over 50% of cases at diagnosis [3] but is detected in imaging modalities such as ultrasound, mammography or MRI, even expert surgeons have difficulties accurately localising it intraoperatively [14]. Moreover, with chemotherapy used prior to surgery, approximately 30% of the tumours will have a complete response and become extremely tiny or even vanish, making resection even more challenging [17].

Preoperative localisation of cancerous breast tumours involves different invasive modalities including Wire Guided Localisation (WGL), carbon tattooing, and, more recently, radioactive seed and magnetic seed localisation. WGL, also called needle localisation, is the most common method performed before BCS.

This procedure is done by placing a fine thread-like wire close to the cancerous region or by targeting a biopsy clip marker deployed after the percutaneous biopsy at diagnosis. This way, the surgeon can follow the thread to reach the breast abnormality whose tissue must be extracted. This process is guided by the use of a mammogram or ultrasound. Therefore, this method usually involves two departments, radiology and surgical oncology, which complicates planning. From the patient's perspective, going through different procedures in two different settings is usually unpleasant as, even if inserting the guidance objects inside the breast is performed under local anaesthesia, it can be painful and is often very traumatic [13]. In addition, there is a small chance of wire displacement during confirmatory mammography or patient transferring [14]. Accurate localisation is essential to achieve complete resection and optimal cosmetic results. However, a significant pathological margin from the cancerous tissue may be obtained after the initial surgery. Thus, between 10% to 40% of the patients require at least one additional re-excision procedure to remove the remaining abnormal lesions [6,8].

Related Work. The development of AR systems for Mini-Invasive Surgery (MIS) has received tremendous attention [1,2,9,15]. Such systems have two main steps, 1) the creation of a digital twin as a preoperative virtual 3D model from one or several of MRI, CT and US images, and 2) the registration of this 3D model in real-time with the intraoperative laparoscopic video and their fusion. Step 1) can be achieved with existing tools available on the radiology consoles or medical image segmentation software. Step 2) is responsible for merging the digital twin and the intraoperative images, solely from the image contents or from 'natural' markers. This is challenging because these images are expressed in different coordinate frames, are issued of different modalities and show the organs in different states. With the augmented views, the surgeons do not have to look away from the surgical site to see the preoperative images repeatedly. This approach to surgical guidance has so far not been attempted in BCS.

In contrast, non-invasive or limited invasiveness navigation systems using AR in BCS use additional devices. In [16], an AR visualisation system is proposed to guide surgeons in finding the breast tumour's location. A US probe combined with a 3D position sensor is used to create a preoperative tumour 3D model. This 3D model is then superimposed on a live video stream at the time of surgery to help the surgeon visually localise the tumour. In [18], a position sensor attached to a needle is implanted into the breast tumour to have a reliable ground-truth that shows where the tumour is precisely located. Two other 3D position sensors are connected to a US imaging probe and surgical cautery tool. The tumour is segmented on US slices manually by the surgeon before starting the surgery. The tumour's relative position to the cautery tool is visualised on the screens during excision. The system was tested on a phantom and six patients with palpable tumours. However, the proposed method has two main disadvantages: the tracked needle protrudes from the breast, and the intraoperative US is required to define tumour borders. In [12], MRI scans with gadolinium-based contrast injection are used to create preoperative models. MR-visible fiducial markers are applied in different positions surrounding the breast. Preoperative 3D models are created both for the breast and tumour. These models are then uploaded to an AR headset, the Hololens, for surgeon visualisation during surgery. In [7], another use of an AR system was reported in which the surgeon can see the tumour location inside the patient's breast by wearing the Hololens. For this purpose, first, the tumour 3D model is obtained from the preoperative MRI and mammography. This 3D model is then registered to the breast intraoperative 3D models to create an AR visualisation. These systems have opened a new way for non-invasive tumour localisation during breast surgery through AR. Despite the advances offered by these AR-based navigation systems, they have limitations. One significant drawback is their reliance on additional devices such as 3D position sensors and US probes, which complicates the surgical setup and workflow. The registration of the 3D models to the surgical site is complex and often lacks accuracy, which affects the overall efficiency and effectiveness of navigation.

Contributions. We propose an AR system for BCS which follows the same strategy as in MIS. The proposed system starts by reconstructing a digital twin as a preoperative 3D model for the breast and tumours. However, there is a strong difference: whilst MIS, whether traditional or robot-assisted, uses a camera and a screen, BCS is an open surgery, and uses neither of these. Therefore, we introduce both a camera and a screen in the OR, in order to capture the intraoperative surgical images and to display the augmented images for guidance. We have chosen an RGB-D camera, which provides both a regular colour image and a depth image in real time, as the technology is mature and low-cost. We exploit the depth image for 3D model registration. We have chosen a simple regular screen as display. In contrast to existing AR systems for BCS, we propose the reconstruction of digital twins based on MRI acquired with patients in supine position. This approach mitigates the intense breast deformations caused by gravity. Further, unlike existing AR systems which render the tumours by direct virtual camera projection, we propose a vertical projection technique. Direct projection causes misguidance, as the resulting AR visualisation is then dependent on camera positioning. Lastly, we present a retrospective expert evaluation of the proposed system on two patients.

2 Materials and Methods

The proposed AR system for BCS has four steps, as illustrated in Fig. 1.

Step 1). We begin with MRI data acquisition with the patient in supine position. This is in contrast with conventional MRI data acquisition for breast imaging, which is typically performed with the patient in prone position. The prone positioning is used because it allows the breast to hang away from the body, which helps in separating the breast tissue from the chest wall and provides a clearer image. This is particularly useful for detecting and characterising breast lesions and for surgical planning. However, as a result, the breast deforms intensely because of gravity. This huge deformation makes the registration phase of AR

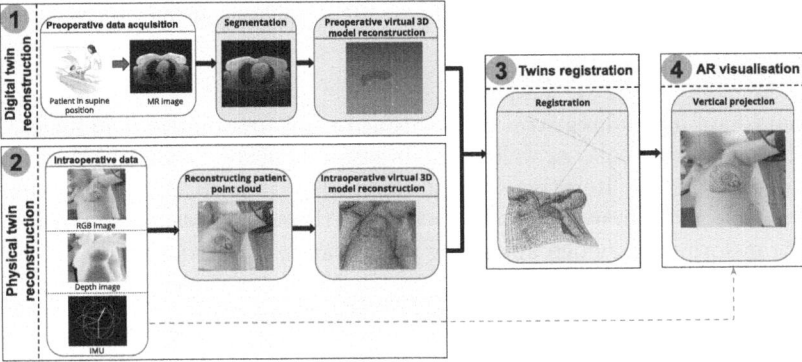

Fig. 1. Schematics of the proposed BCS guidance AR system. The inputs are in orange boxes, actions in gray boxes, and the main steps in green boxes. In step 1), the preoperative MRI is acquired with the patient in supine position. The breast and tumours are then manually segmented, and their preoperative 3D models are reconstructed. In step 2), the intraoperative data, including RGB and depth images along with IMU information, are acquired via an RGB-D camera. This is followed by the reconstruction of the patient's body surface point cloud and the intraoperative 3D model. In step 3), the preoperative 3D model is registered to the intraoperative 3D model. In step 4), the AR image is generated, using the proposed vertical projection system. The IMU data provides the gravity vector. In the absence of IMU, this vector is estimated by taking the normal of the ground floor plane. (Color figure online)

highly difficult. Recent studies [5] assess the feasibility and image quality of breast MRI imaging performed in supine position compared to prone position. The study concludes that there is no difference between supine and prone positioning in terms of image quality and number of lesions. However, a significant difference in the lesion extension and the breast shape can be observed comparing the two positions. Therefore, we use the preoperative MRI in supine position in order to mitigate intense breast deformations caused by gravity. The selected patients have a classical MRI acquisition in prone position and are then asked to lie down in supine position, with their arms alongside the body. An initial acquisition is performed without injection and then with injection of gadolinium, a commonly used contrast agent. With these MRI data, we reconstruct the preoperative 3D models of the desired structures. Concretely, we use MITK [11], to manually segment the breast and tumour on the MRI images, followed by reconstruction of their 3D models.

Step 2). We capture RGB-D images using an Intel RealSense camera at the beginning of surgery. We have used both the D415 and D435i models without noticing a difference in performance. This type of cameras provide conventional RGB images but also an image giving the depth of each pixel. Technically, using the camera parameters, we generate a point cloud of the scene, which is subsequently used to reconstruct the intraoperative model through Meshlab [10]. More precisely, we first segment the region of interest from the obtained point cloud and reconstruct its surface using the screened Poisson surface reconstruction algorithm.

Step 3). We register the 3D models obtained in steps 1) and 2). First, we perform an initial rough manual registration, focusing on key anatomical landmarks such as the nipple and aureola, as well as the breast silhouette. Second, we refine this registration using the Iterative Closest Point algorithm (ICP). Technically, we use Meshlab for the first stage and Matlab for the second stage. This results in a rigid transformation which aligns the preoperative 3D model to the intraoperative model.

Step 4). We use the rigid transformation from step 3) to transfer the preoperative tumours 3D models to the surgical camera coordinates. With the tumours positioned correctly in their intraoperative location, we have two options for their visualisation in the AR system. The first option is direct projection, in which one projects the tumours towards the camera centre. This is the conventional practice in AR systems. However, a simple geometric reasoning as illustrated in Fig. 2a, shows that this strategy can lead to inconsistent renderings, due to variations in the relative positioning of the breast and camera. To address this, we examine a second approach for which we first project the tumour to a specific location on the breast surface and subsequently project to the camera, as illustrated in Fig. 2b. We perform the first projection following the gravity vector, for two main reasons. First, the surgeons commonly use a similar vertical projection, known as orthogonal localisation [4]. This method involves measuring the distances between the tumour and the nipple along the mediolateral and craniocaudal axes on both frontal and strict profile mammograms, and then transferring these measurements to the patient's breast. Following the same clinical strategy, we hypothesise that, given that the patient is positioned horizontally, the gravity vector is orthogonal to the breast, and thus leads to the same clinical orthogonal registration technique. Second, the gravity vector is typically readily available from the camera's IMU sensor. In scenarios where the IMU data is unavailable, we fit a plane to the ground floor point cloud and use its normal as gravity vector. Finally, we project this region obtained on the breast surface to the camera to realise the AR overlay on the images captured by the RGB-D camera. Using this vertical projection, the virtually augmented tumour remains consistent.

3 Experimental Evaluation

Data. We evaluate the proposed method retrospectively in two BCS cases. All data were collected from hospital Centre Jean Perrin, Clermont-Ferrand, France, following the IRB approved protocol 00013468. The inclusion of only two patients was due to the rare availability of MRI in both the supine and prone positions. These specific patients were chosen by a radiologist who determined that a supine MRI sequence was necessary to assess the feasibility of breast-conserving surgery versus mastectomy. During intraoperative data collection, we ensured that the

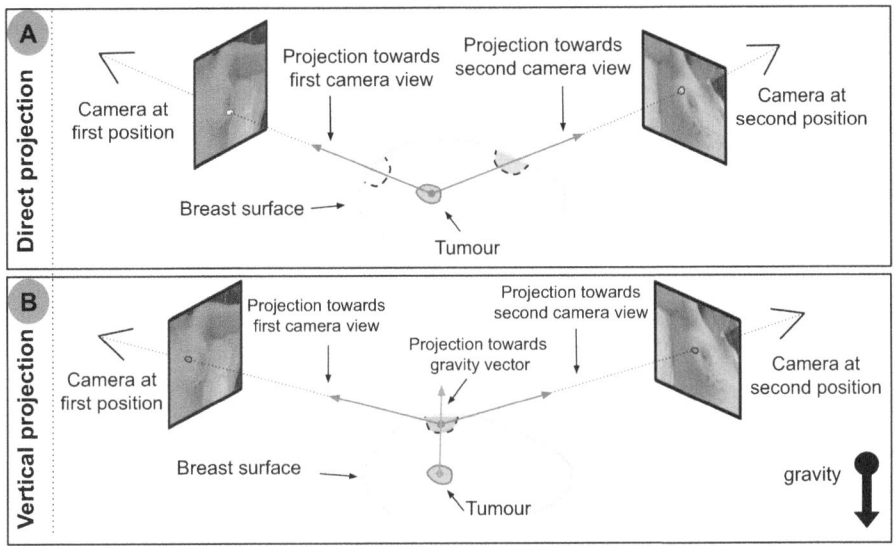

Fig. 2. Schematic representation of the projection systems. A) Direct projection: the tumour is projected directly to the camera. B) Vertical projection: the tumour is first vertically projected to the breast surface via the gravity vector, followed by projection to the camera. In B), the AR output remains consistent regardless of camera positioning, whereas in A), it varies significantly with changes in camera position.

patient bed was positioned roughly parallel to the ground floor, which is standard for BCS. We rotated the camera around the patient to examine the proposed system for different viewpoints. We selected three frames from the sequence representing extreme, middle and top views. We rendered AR visualisation using both direct projection and vertical projection methods, resulting in a total of 12 augmented images. For patient #1, the data was collected using a D415 camera, which lacks IMU data. Therefore, for this patient the gravity vector was estimated by computing the normal of the ground floor. For patient #2, the data was collected using a D435i camera which provides IMU information.

Table 1. Residual registration error for the supine and prone position MRI.

	Patient #1		Patient #2	
	Supine position	Prone position	Supine position	Prone position
RMSE (mm)	**6.21**	34.71	**5.31**	28.14

MRI Acquisition. The impact of the MRI acquisition position on registration is illustrated by Fig. 3. In prone positioning, deformable registration is required for accurate registration, whereas in supine positioning, a rigid transformation suffices for a fair alignment. We quantitatively evaluated the effectiveness of MRI acquisition in supine position by measuring the residual error obtained at the registration step. Specifically, we use the Root Mean Square Error (RMSE) of ICP for both positioning. Concretely, we identified the closest point in the transformed point cloud for each point in the intraoperative model after registration. We then calculated the Euclidean distance between these points and computed the RMSE. Finally, we averaged the RMSE values obtained from three views. The results reported in Table 1 show significantly better alignment for supine position MRI.

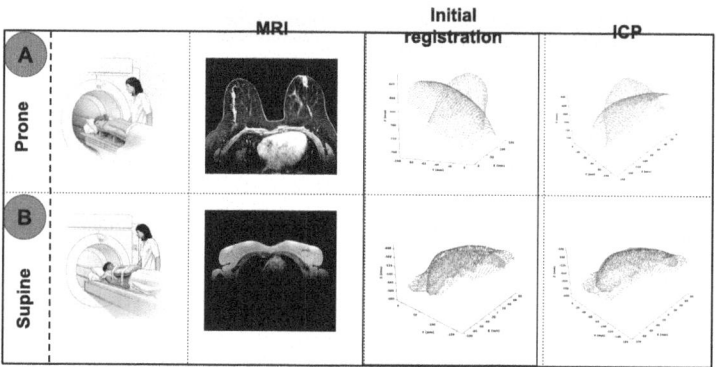

Fig. 3. Qualitative comparison of data acquisition and 3D model registration between different patient positioning. In A), the breast is intensely deformed due to gravity. Purple and green 3D points represent intraoperative and preoperative point clouds, respectively. The final rigid registration is significantly improved in supine position. The illustrated data pertain to patient #2. (Color figure online)

Projection Method. We performed quantitative evaluation of the proposed projection method by measuring the consistency of Euclidean distances between the tumours and anatomical landmarks in 3D. It is important to note that establishing a reliable ground truth for evaluating AR outputs in breast surgery has significant challenges. Although surgeons typically use the orthogonal localisation technique, as discussed in Sect. 2, this method has limitations. The transfer of coordinates from imagery is imprecise. Consequently, orthogonal registration lacks the sufficient reliability to serve as ground truth. Instead, we measured the 3D Euclidean distances between the centre of gravity of the nipple and the centre of gravity of the projected tumour on the breast surface, which should be constant. We report the standard deviation of these measurements as a metric representing the consistency of the projection methods in Table 2. The proposed vertical projection largely outperforms classical direct projection.

Expert Evaluation. A surgeon evaluated the AR outputs as Very likely, Likely or Failure, based on the expected location of the rendered tumour. All the cases are shown in Fig. 4. The results demonstrate an improvement in surgeon's overall

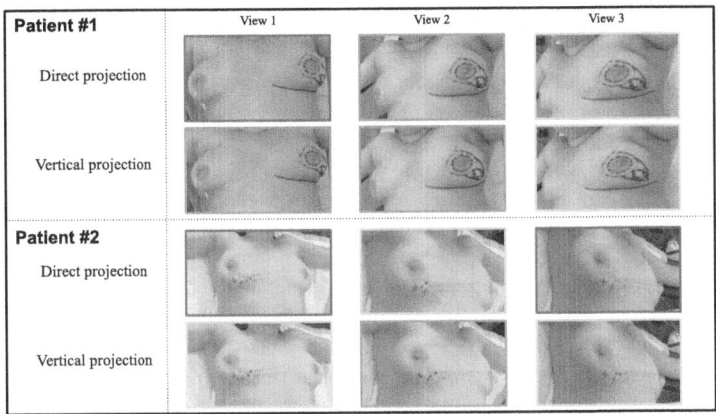

Fig. 4. Qualitative results of the proposed AR method. The augmented tumour is rendered in red. The image boundary colour shows the expert evaluation, with green for Very likely, yellow for Likely and red for Failure. The images were cropped to improve breast visualisation. (Color figure online)

Table 2. Standard deviation of measured 3D distances for both projection methods. Lower values indicate greater consistency in AR visualisation.

	Patient #1		Patient #2	
	Direct projection	Vertical projection	Direct projection	Vertical projection
Dist. std (mm)	23.15	**13.15**	31.43	**11.45**

satisfaction with the AR output when comparing the vertical to direct projection. For instance, for Patient #1 and View #1 the evaluation upgrades from Failure to Likely. Following the position of the rendered tumour in the sequence, we observe a more consistent AR output with the vertical projection for both patients.

4 Conclusion

We have proposed to use the principles of AR systems from MIS in open breast surgery. Implementing such a guidance system has many challenges, for which we have proposed solutions. Our system has shown promising results on two patients. The results reveal the importance of using a supine MRI and a vertical projection system. We now plan to 1) extend the validation of our system to a broader range of clinical cases, 2) incorporating deformable registration to account for remaining breast deformations, and 3) test our system intraoperatively.

References

1. Bernhardt, S., Nicolau, S.A., Soler, L., Doignon, C.: The status of augmented reality in laparoscopic surgery as of 2016. Med. Image Anal. **37**, 66–90 (2017)
2. Collins, T., et al.: Augmented reality guided laparoscopic surgery of the uterus. IEEE Trans. Med. Imaging **40**, 371–380 (2021)
3. Dua, S.M., Gray, R.J., Keshtgar, M.: Strategies for localisation of impalpable breast lesions. The Breast **20**, 246–253 (2011)
4. Heitz, D., Salmon, R.J., Clough, K.B.: Chirurgie locorégionale des cancers du sein. Chirurgie locorégionale des cancers du sein. Encycl Méd Chir (Elsevier SAS, Paris, tous droits réservés), Techniques chirurgicales - Gynécologie, pp. 15–31 (2003)
5. Fausto, A., et al.: Feasibility, image quality and clinical evaluation of contrast-enhanced breast MRI performed in a supine position compared to the standard prone position. Cancers **12**, 2364 (2020)
6. Fraser, V.J., Nickel, K.B., Fox, I.K., Margenthaler, J.A., Olsen, M.A.: The epidemiology and outcomes of breast cancer surgery. Trans. Am. Clin. Climatol. Assoc. **127**, 46–58 (2016)
7. Gouveia, P.F., et al.: Breast cancer surgery with augmented reality. The Breast **56**, 14–17 (2021)
8. Jung, W., et al.: Factors associated with re-excision after breast-conserving surgery for early-stage breast cancer. J. Breast Cancer **15**, 412 (2012)
9. Mirota, D.J., Ishii, M., Hager, G.D.: Vision-based navigation in image-guided interventions. Ann. Rev. Biomed. Eng. **13**, 297–319 (2011)
10. Visual Computing Lab of ISTI CNR: Meshlab: open source system for processing and editing 3D triangular meshes (2024). Accessed 20 June 2024
11. German Cancer Research Center (DKFZ) Division of Medical Image Computing: The medical imaging interaction toolkit (MITK) (2024). Accessed 20 June 2024
12. Perkins, S.L., Lin, M.A., Srinivasan, S., Wheeler, A.J., Hargreaves, B.A., Daniel, B.L.: A mixed-reality system for breast surgical planning, pp. 269–274. IEEE (2017)
13. Postma, E.L., et al.: Efficacy of 'radioguided occult lesion localisation' (ROLL) versus 'wire-guided localisation' (WGL) in breast conserving surgery for non-palpable breast cancer: a randomised controlled multicentre trial. Breast Cancer Res. Treat. **136**, 469–478 (2012)
14. Postma, E.L., Witkamp, A.J., van den Bosch, M.A.A.J., Verkooijen, H.M., van Hillegersberg, R.: Localization of nonpalpable breast lesions. Expert Rev. Anticancer Ther. **11**, 1295–1302 (2011)
15. Puerto-Souza, G.A., Cadeddu, J.A., Mariottini, G.-L.: Toward long-term and accurate augmented-reality for monocular endoscopic videos. IEEE Trans. Biomed. Eng. **61**, 2609–2620 (2014)
16. Sato, Y., et al.: Image guidance of breast cancer surgery using 3-D ultrasound images and augmented reality visualization. IEEE Trans. Med. Imaging **17**, 681–693 (1998)
17. Spring, L.M., et al.: Pathologic complete response after neoadjuvant chemotherapy and impact on breast cancer recurrence and survival: a comprehensive meta-analysis. Clin. Cancer Res. **26**, 2838–2848 (2020)
18. Ungi, T., et al.: Navigated breast tumor excision using electromagnetically tracked ultrasound and surgical instruments. IEEE Trans. Biomed. Eng. **63**, 600–606 (2016)

ELK: Enhanced Learning Through Cross-Modal Knowledge Transfer for Lesion Detection in Limited-Sample Contrast-Enhanced Mammography Datasets

Ricardo Montoya-del-Angel[1(✉)], Marawan Elbatel[2],
Jorge Patricio Castillo-Lopez[3], Yolanda Villaseñor-Navarro[3],
Maria-Ester Brandan[4], and Robert Marti[1]

[1] Computer Vision and Robotics Institute, University of Girona, Girona, Spain
ricardo.montoya@udg.edu
[2] The Hong Kong University of Science and Technology,
Hong Kong, China
[3] Instituto Nacional de Cancerología, Mexico City, Mexico
[4] Instituto de Física, Universidad Nacional Autónoma de México, Mexico City, Mexico

Abstract. Contrast-enhanced mammography (CEM) offers improved breast cancer diagnosis by enhancing vascular contrast uptake. However, the development of reliable deep learning-based computer-aided detection (CAD) systems for CEM is hindered by limited data availability. This paper introduces ELK (Enhanced Learning through cross-modal Knowledge transfer), a deep learning pipeline designed to adapt large pre-trained models into a target limited data-volume population by leveraging synthetic data augmentation. Specifically, we adapt a detection model pretrained on digital breast tomosynthesis (DBT) and digital mammography data into a target CEM population using diffusion models to generate high-resolution, realistic synthetic lesions, preserving the visual integrity of CEM images. To assess the efficacy of our synthetic lesions, we compare the detection performance of a pretrained Faster R-CNN detector fine-tuned using only real images, synthetic images, and a combination of both. Our approach improves mean sensitivity by 4% on a test sample from the same population and by 7% on a newly collected out-of-domain CEM dataset. Our code and synthetic datasets are available at https://github.com/Likalto4/CEM-Detect.

Keywords: detection · mammography · lesion inpainting · diffusion models

1 Introduction

Contrast-enhanced mammography (CEM) is a type of breast imaging modality that highlights vascular contrast uptake, improving visibility while reducing the prominence of breast tissue and enhancing the accuracy of breast cancer diagnosis [16]. CEM can be approached in two ways: Dual-energy (DE), the commonly used and commercially accessible method, and single-energy temporal (SET), which permits only one mammographic projection, thus restricting its use to controlled research settings. Traditional methods for detecting and diagnosing breast cancer rely on the expertise of radiologists and pathologists. Computer-aided detection and diagnosis (CADe and CADx) systems have emerged as primary artificial intelligence techniques to support clinical decision making, with deep learning leading the way for developing such tools [29]. Effective implementation of deep learning methods, however, requires extensive data, posing a challenge for small datasets. While large datasets of common breast imaging modalities such as digital mammography (DM) and Digital Breast Tomosynthesis (DBT) are available for CAD development [3,7], public CEM studies are rare and usually composed of few samples. Therefore methods to deal with data scarcity, such as advanced data augmentation, few-shot learning, and knowledge transfer techniques are crucial.

Some researches have proposed CAD pipelines for lesion detection and breast classification on CEM-DE images [11,12]. While the feasibility of deep learning for lesion detection was attested, these pipelines were developed using private CEM datasets, restricting the reproducibility of the results. Moreover, the studies were conducted using a large sample of Dual Energy CEM dataset, which further impedes application of such algorithms to other CEM datasets (e.g. SET), which are usually composed of less than 130 patients [11]. Cross-modal knowledge transfer or learning (CMKT) could potentially tackle this issue, by using a model pretrained on large datasets from other breast image modalities followed by domain-adaptation and fine-tuning towards the target CEM modality. CMKT has been used for natural and medical images modalities in cases when the target data has low data-volume and other more common modalities have larger datasets available [1,2,6]. Nevertheless, this alternative must deal with challenges such as catastrophic forgetting, changes in the structure of the organs when represented in different modalities, as well as differences in the spatial and intensity pixel information inherent to each modality.

Several works have explored the use of generative models for image generation and data augmentation in medical imaging [4,5,10,20] and specifically in breast imaging [8,13,15,18,19,30]. In the case of lesion inpainting, there exist diffusion-based methods to enhance lesion detection for brain imaging [22,26]. For conventional digital mammography, some authors have shown an improvement in lesion detection thanks to the inpainting of synthetic lesions on healthy patients [25,27,28]. These works, however, have not explored the implementation of such synthetic data augmentation techniques for CEM. Moreover, the proposed algorithms do not explore the use of diffusion-based models, which are known for training stability [9], few-shot-learning [23], and in the case of stable diffusion, flexible text-driven conditioning [21].

To this end, we propose ELK (Enhanced Learning through cross-modal Knowledge transfer), a deep learning pipeline tailored for knowledge transfer across modalities leveraging synthetic data augmentation. Specifically, we propose ELK for improving breast lesion detection in contrast-enhanced digital mammography (CEM). ELK employs 1) diffusion models for synthesizing high-resolution realistic mass-like lesions to enrich the datasets and enhance the model's performance and 2) a Faster-RCNN detector, pretrained on both OPTIMAM and Breast-Cancer-Screening-DBT datasets, as a base model for the knowledge transfer. Our stable diffusion inpainting pipeline allows the generation of synthetic lesions on the CEM's original spatial resolution, preserving the breast structure and visual resemblance of CEM images. To evaluate the added value of our synthetic lesions, we compared the detection performance when fine-tuning in a traditional way with real images, synthetic images, and a combination of both. The CEM dataset used for the experiments is a dual-energy CEM dataset [14]. To further revise the generalisability of our method, we perform a second testing using a private single-energy CEM dataset.

The key contributions of our work are the following: 1) we propose a novel lesion inpainting approach to enable lesion generation at the CEM image original high resolution; 2) we introduce a cross-modal knowledge transfer method to enhance the performance of lesion detection on CEM datasets; 3) we provide an advanced and accessible data augmentation technique which allows the maximum exploitation of the training dataset through the lesion inpainting of healthy cases.

2 Methodology

Our method is composed of two parts: a) a diffusion-based generative pipeline as a novel data augmentation technique to generate new synthetic lesions over real healthy CEM images in their original image size; and b) a Cross-modal knowledge transfer pipeline to exploit the prior knowledge learned by a lesion detection model trained on digital mammography (DM) and digital breast tomosynthesis (DBT), and use it to detect mass-type lesions in Contrast-enhanced mammography (CEM) using a small sample set for training. Figure 1 shows an overview of our proposed method.

2.1 Diffusion Models for Image Synthesis

Diffusion models aim at estimating the probability distribution of a target population $p(x)$ by converting a known distribution (e.g. Gaussian) into the target distribution using a Markov chain [24]. In [9], Denoising Diffusion Probabilistic Models (DDPM) was proposed for image generation, consisting on a two-step process. First, a forward diffusion process is employed to add noise to an image x_0 in an iterative manner $q(x_t|x_{t-1}) = N(x_t; \sqrt{1-\beta_t}x_{t-1}, \beta_t I)$, where the variance β_t is fixed and $t \in (1, ..., T)$. Then, an inverse diffusion process is used to remove the noise using a similar Markov chain of Gaussian sampling $p_\theta(x_{t-1}|x_t) = N(x_{t-1}; \mu_\theta(x_t, t), \beta I)$, where only the distribution mean μ_θ is learnable. According to Ho et al. [9] the problem is equivalent to predicting

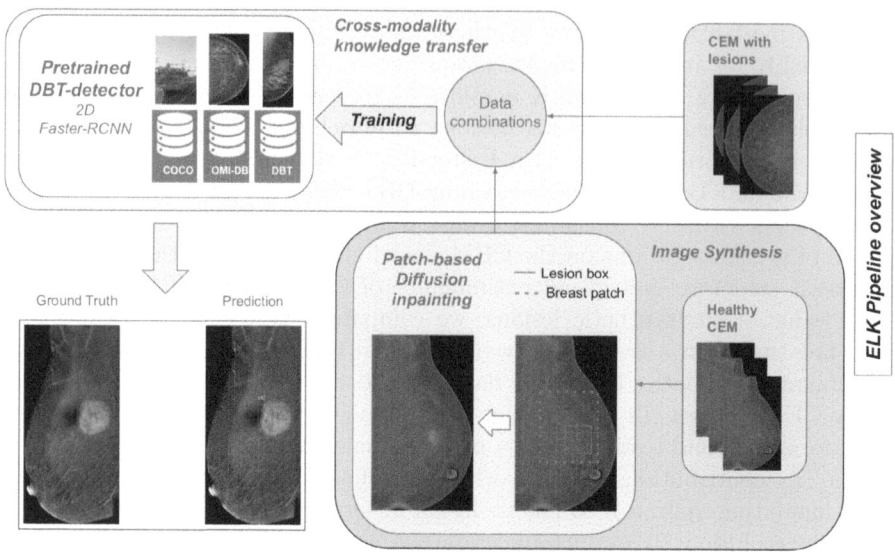

Fig. 1. ELK pipeline overview.

the Gaussian noise ϵ added during the diffusion process, which leads to a simple lost function $L = \|\epsilon - \epsilon_\theta\|^2$. A UNet can be used to predict the noise ϵ_θ from an image given its timestep t and iteratively remove it to generate new samples coming from pure Gaussian noise. Further improvements, such as the use of image encoder-decoder architectures for image compression (Latent diffusion) and text-encoders for prompt-conditioning (Stable diffusion) [21], have been proposed for a more stable, faithful and cost-effective image generation technique.

Our proposed lesion generator uses a stable diffusion (SD) architecture, modified to handle the inpainting task. As shown in Fig. 2, the training of the inpainting SD model requires an image, the lesion bounding box and a text prompt. After sampling noise, and adding it to the image according to DDPM, the image and a masked-out version of the image are encoded into a latent space using a Variational Autoencoder (VAE). The diffusion process is carried out in this space using the encoded text prompt as conditioning.

This inpainting proposal considers three main issues surrounding our objective task: large image size, inpainting conditioning and limited data availability. First, regarding the **image size problem**, we propose using a patch of 512×512 containing the lesion for inpainting. To avoid the model from memorizing the position of the lesion inside the patch, the lesion position must be random. Second, to limit the inpainting process to a specific region, a lesion bounding box is used as **conditioning** during training. Instead of feeding the conditioning lesion bounding box directly to the network, like the timestep and the text prompt, the mask conditioning is reshaped and stacked with the patch and the masked patch, which are then fed to the UNet. Finally, due to the **limited training**

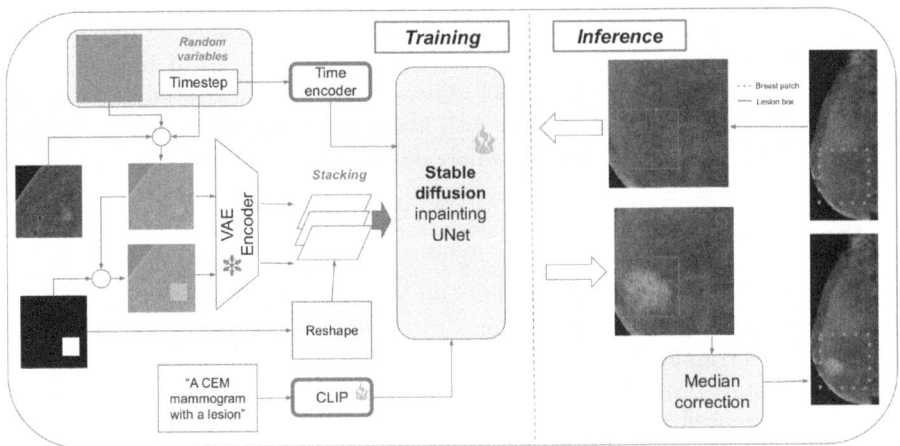

Fig. 2. Inpainting model diagram for both training and inference time.

data, we use the Dreambooth fine-tuning technique [23] which allows for few-shot learning.

During lesion generation, healthy CEM are used as base images for the inpainting. Despite the mask conditioning, some pixel intensities outside the lesion mask may be modified. To ensure the integration of the patch back into the full-field CEM, a statistical correction in the patch intensity range is performed. We call this postprocessing step **median correction** and it consists in computing the median of the pixel intensity shift between the original patch and the diffused-inpainted patch, in pixels outside of the lesion mask. The median is then used to shift the whole patch pixel intensities before reintegration.

2.2 Cross-Modal Knowledge Transfer in Medical Imaging

Cross-modal knowledge transfer (CMKT), also known as cross-modal learning, is a learning technique that addresses the problem of domain adaptation across different imaging modalities [6]. This differs from traditional intra-modality domain-adaptation where transfer is performed between images of the same modality but with different populations. We apply CMKT by fine-tuning a pre-trained out-of-modality large model using the target modality samples. To ensure reproducibility and good prior-task performance, we propose the use of a DBT lesion detection challenge top-3 winner model made available by its authors [17]. The goal is to exploit the prior lesion detection capabilities learned for DBT and DM and transfer them to the CEM space.

2.3 ELK: Enhanced Learning Through Knowledge Transfer

Our proposed pipeline, **E**nhancing **L**earning through **K**nowledge transfer (ELK), leverages the inpainting abilities of diffusion models to enhance the cross-modal knowledge transfer of a large pretrained models towards a specific population. Specifically, we apply ELK for the detection of lesions in CEM images using a pretrained lesion detector for DBT. Given that a clinical study is usually composed of normal cases and cases with lesions, we decided to inpaint lesions on the healthy cases, exploiting the whole dataset for the training process.

3 Experiments

Datasets and Pretrained Models. Our experiments were conducted using the *Categorized Digital Database* for Low energy and Subtracted Contrast Enhanced Spectral Mammography images (CDD-CESM) dataset [14]. This dataset is composed of 1003 CESM images, each with its respective low-energy mammogram as well as segmentation annotations, medical reports and pathological diagnosis. The second dataset is significantly smaller, containing 33 subtracted images from Mexican women with suspected multicentric breast cancer. These images were acquired using the single-energy temporal technique (SET), which achieves higher lesion conspicuity than the dual-energy technique, at the expense of more frequent motion artifacts. All lesions are segmented by an expert radiologist using pathology results. We used a pretrained DBT-detector used in the DBTex challenge as base detection model. The weights and model details were made available by its authors [17]. The model consists of a 2D Faster R-CNN architecture with a ResNet 101 backbone applied at a slice by slice basis, pretrained on the OPTIMAM [7] and the Breast-Cancer-Screening-DBT dataset [3]. All datasets, except from the mexican one, are publicly available, although the OPTIMAM dataset requires an application process. For the SD-inpainting model we used the pretrained weights of RunwatML for inpainting on natural images, trained with the LAION-aesthetics v2 dataset [21].

Data Preparation and Preprocessing. The CDD-CESM dataset was already preprocessed with intensities in the 0–255 range and the images cropped in the breast region, removing unnecessary background. The mexican SET dataset, originally in tiff format with intensities ranging from -200 to 250, was saved in png format, with 8 bits per pixel, to match the CESM dataset. Also, the image was cropped into the breast region. From the 1003 CEM images only 243 images contained mass-like lesions. Stratified by number of lesions and grouped by patients, the dataset was split into training, validation and testing sets at 60%, 15% and 25%, respectively, representing a patient/image distribution of 80/150, 19/37 and 32/56 per set.

Training Details. The SD-inpainting model was trained using a combination of both training and validation patches with lesion bounding box smaller than 512×512, with a total of 187 images, corresponding to 254 individual lesion samples. The model was trained for 2400 training steps with batch size of 8 and learning rate (lr) of 10^{-6}. The best model was selected by visually evaluating generated samples every 235 steps (around one epoch). The training was performed on a NVIDIA A40 GPU using 15GB of VRAM and around 1 h of training time. The inpainting inference process was performed on random regions of the breast region. The area and height/width ratio of the lesion box was selected inside ranges defined using the statistics of the training set, so the synthetic lesions have real lesions dimensions. The detector was trained for 3K steps, with a batch size of 2 and lr of 2.5×10^{-4}. Different combinations of training samples were used such as: normal fine-tuning with real images, only synthetic images, and the combination of both. Additionally, different area ranges for the lesions were tried, as well as different number of synthetic images. The metrics used for detection evaluation were the Average sensitivity at 0.5, 1, 2 and 3 FPpI as primary metric and the area under the FROC TPR vs FPRpI at 3FPpI as secondary.

3.1 Results

Our results show that using ELK to enhance the training process through synthetic lesions surpasses the performance of traditional fine-tuning when combining real and synthetic data, as shown in Table 1. The table shows two main groups of results. On the left are the metrics obtained for the best model selected using the Mean sensitivity, and the group on the right the best models selected using the AUFROC. In both cases, a model trained with real and synthetic images combined was the top performer for both metrics.

Table 1. Results of the detection pipeline for the **CESM dataset**. The percentage represents the amount of extra synthetic data used in relation to the real samples.

Method	Best model wrt Mean sensitivity		Best model wrt Mean AUFROC	
	Mean Sensitivity	AUFROC	Mean Sensitivity	AUFROC
Fine-tuning	0.72	0.71	0.68	0.67
Real-synthetic 100%	**0.76**	**0.73**	0.70	0.67
Real-synthetic 200%	0.73	0.72	**0.73**	**0.72**
Synth medium-area	0.66	0.65	0.66	0.65

Table 1 also shows the best model trained exclusively with synthetic data. We generated lesions with diverse sizes and found that the best performance was achieved when the synthetic lesions were restricted to a medium size, with respect to the overall training sample. We see that such model underperforms, concluding that for this setting the combination of real and synthetic data is necessary for a proper generalization. Further analysis must be conducted to determine the optimal type of synthetic lesion based on an analysis of the cases where the detector fails.

Testing our selected best models in the slightly out-of-domain mexican SET dataset showed that the real and synthetic combination prevails as the top performer. When selecting the best model based on the mean sensitivity, the synthetic dataset trained with 200% extra synthetic lesion samples outperforms the standard fine-tuning technique by 0.07 Mean sensitivity and 0.11 AUFROC, with a FROC curve as seen in Fig. 3a). Nevertheless, when selecting the best model based on the AUFROC during validation, there is similar performance between the real-synthetic and normal fine-tuning methods. Using the secondary metric, the real-synthetic method obtains better performance but the performance is relatively similar.

Although the quality of the generated lesions is not the primary indicator of improvement for the proposed method, we explored the realism of the final CEM image. Figure 3b) shows the effect of applying the median correction before patch reintegration into the original full-field image (Table 2).

Table 2. Results of the detection pipeline for the **SET dataset**, the second test set. The underscore highlights cases were similar result were obtained and the second metric is needed for tie-break.

Method	Best model wrt Mean sensitivity		Best model wrt Mean AUFROC	
	Mean Sensitivity	AUFROC	Mean Sensitivity	AUFROC
Fine-tuning	0.58	0.52	0.65	0.61
Real-synthetic 100%	0.53	0.53	0.64	0.63
Real-synthetic 200%	**0.65**	**0.63**	**0.65**	**0.63**
Synth medium-area	0.56	0.53	0.56	0.54

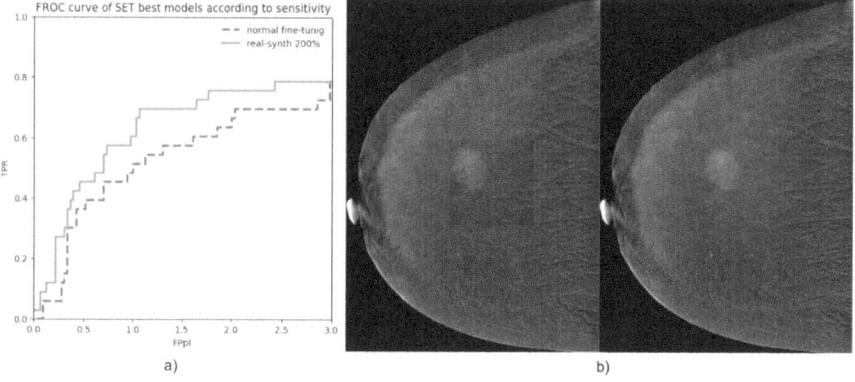

Fig. 3. a) FROC curves of best SET models according to mean sensitivity for normal and ELK fine-tuning. b) Example of an image with a generation error before and after the median correction.

4 Conclusion

This paper introduced ELK, a cross-modal knowledge transfer method to enhance the performance of lesion detection in limited-sampled datasets, such as clinical studies of contrast enhanced mammography, leveraging large cross-domain pretrained models. Our method allows boosting the performance of small datasets in a fast and relatively limited-resourced setting. Future work includes exploring the effect of adding more than one synthetic lesion per healthy image in the generation process, as well as controlling the type of lesion generated by adding text conditioning.

Acknowledgments. This research was possible thanks to funding from the VICTORIA project (PID2021-123390OB-C21) from the Ministerio de Ciencia, Innovación y Universidades of Spain, and the Joan Oró grant for the hiring of pre-doctoral research staff in training (ref. BDNS 657443) from the Government of Catalonia. Additionally, this work was partially supported by Conahcyt-Mexico CF-1311307 "Imágenes radiológicas cuantitativas para la caracterización no invasiva del cáncer de mama" and by UNAM-PAPIIT Grant IN105622.

Disclosure of Interests. The authors have no competing interests to declare that are relevant to the content of this article.

References

1. Aderghal, K., Khvostikov, A., Krylov, A., Benois-Pineau, J., Afdel, K., Catheline, G.: Classification of Alzheimer disease on imaging modalities with deep CNNs using cross-modal transfer learning. In: 2018 IEEE 31st International Symposium on Computer-Based Medical Systems (CBMS), pp. 345–350 (2018)
2. Ahmed, S.M., Lohit, S., Peng, K.C., Jones, M.J., Roy-Chowdhury, A.K.: Cross-modal knowledge transfer without task-relevant source data. In: Avidan, S., Brostow, G., Cissé, M., Farinella, G.M., Hassner, T. (eds.) Computer Vision - ECCV 2022, vol. 13694, pp. 111–127. Springer, Cham (2022)
3. Buda, M., et al.: A data set and deep learning algorithm for the detection of masses and architectural distortions in digital breast tomosynthesis images. JAMA Netw. Open **4**(8), e2119100 (2021)
4. Chambon, P., et al.: RoentGen: vision-language foundation model for chest X-ray generation (2022)
5. Dorjsembe, Z., Odonchimed, S., Xiao, F.: Three-dimensional medical image synthesis with denoising diffusion probabilistic models (2022)
6. Gupta, S., Hoffman, J., Malik, J.: Cross modal distillation for supervision transfer. In: 2016 IEEE Conference on Computer Vision and Pattern Recognition (CVPR), Las Vegas, NV, USA, pp. 2827–2836. IEEE (2016)
7. Halling-Brown, M.D., et al.: OPTIMAM mammography image database: a large-scale resource of mammography images and clinical data. Radiol. Artif. Intell. **3**(1) (2021)
8. Han, L., et al.: Synthesis-based imaging-differentiation representation learning for multi-sequence 3D/4D MRI. Med. Image Anal. **92**, 103044 (2024)

9. Ho, J., Jain, A., Abbeel, P.: Denoising diffusion probabilistic models. In: Advances in Neural Information Processing Systems, vol. 33, pp. 6840–6851. Curran Associates, Inc. (2020)
10. Hung, A.L.Y., et al.: Med-cDiff: conditional medical image generation with diffusion models. Bioengineering **10**(11), 1258 (2023)
11. Jailin, C., Milioni, P., Li, Z., Iordache, R., Muller, S.: Lesion detection in contrast enhanced spectral mammography. In: 16th International Workshop on Breast Imaging (IWBI2022), p. 24 (2022). https://doi.org/10.1117/12.2624577
12. Jailin, C., et al.: AI-based cancer detection model for contrast-enhanced mammography. Bioengineering **10**(8), 974 (2023)
13. Khader, F., et al.: Denoising diffusion probabilistic models for 3D medical image generation. Sci. Rep. **13**(1), 7303 (2023)
14. Khaled, R., et al.: Categorized contrast enhanced mammography dataset for diagnostic and artificial intelligence research. Sci. Data **9**(1), 122 (2022)
15. Kidder, B.L.: Advanced image generation for cancer using diffusion models. Preprint, Cancer Biology (2023)
16. Lobbes, M., Jochelson, M.: Contrast-Enhanced Mammography, 1st edn. Springer, Cham (2019)
17. Martí, R., et al.: Lesion detection in digital breast tomosynthesis: method, experiences and results of participating to the DBTex challenge. In: Bosmans, H., Marshall, N., Van Ongeval, C. (eds.) 16th International Workshop on Breast Imaging (IWBI2022), p. 33. SPIE, Leuven (2022)
18. Montoya-del-Angel, R., Sam-Millan, K., Vilanova, J.C., Martí, R.: MAM-E: mammographic synthetic image generation with diffusion models. Sensors **24**(7), 2076 (2024)
19. Pinaya, W.H.L., et al.: Generative AI for medical imaging: extending the MONAI framework (2023)
20. Pinaya, W.H.L., et al.: Brain imaging generation with latent diffusion models. In: Deep Generative Models: Second MICCAI Workshop, DGM4MICCAI 2022, Held in Conjunction with MICCAI 2022, Singapore, 22 September 2022, Proceedings. Springer (2022)
21. Rombach, R., Blattmann, A., Lorenz, D., Esser, P., Ommer, B.: High-resolution image synthesis with latent diffusion models. In: 2022 IEEE/CVF Conference on Computer Vision and Pattern Recognition (CVPR), New Orleans, LA, USA, pp. 10674–10685. IEEE (2022)
22. Rouzrokh, P., Khosravi, B., Faghani, S., Moassefi, M., Vahdati, S., Erickson, B.J.: Multitask brain tumor inpainting with diffusion models: a methodological report (2022)
23. Ruiz, N., Li, Y., Jampani, V., Pritch, Y., Rubinstein, M., Aberman, K.: DreamBooth: fine tuning text-to-image diffusion models for subject-driven generation. In: Proceedings of the IEEE/CVF Conference on Computer Vision and Pattern Recognition (2023)
24. Sohl-Dickstein, J., Weiss, E.A., Maheswaranathan, N., Ganguli, S.: Deep unsupervised learning using nonequilibrium thermodynamics (2015)
25. Walsh, R., Tardy, M.: A comparison of techniques for class imbalance in deep learning classification of breast cancer. Diagnostics **13**(1), 67 (2022)
26. Wolleb, J., Bieder, F., Sandkühler, R., Cattin, P.C.: Diffusion models for medical anomaly detection. In: Wang, L., Dou, Q., Fletcher, P.T., Speidel, S., Li, S. (eds.) Medical Image Computing and Computer Assisted Intervention - MICCAI 2022, vol. 13438, pp. 35–45. Springer, Cham (2022)

27. Wu, E., Wu, K., Cox, D., Lotter, W.: Conditional infilling GANs for data augmentation in mammogram classification. In: Stoyanov, D., Taylor, Z., Kainz, E.A. (eds.) Image Analysis for Moving Organ, Breast, and Thoracic Images, vol. 11040, pp. 98–106. Springer, Cham (2018)
28. Kim, Y., Jeon, K., Kim, S., Park, C.M.: Lesion in-and-out painting for medical image augmentation. In: Deep Generative Models for Health Workshop, NeurIPS 2023 (2023)
29. Zhang, T., Mann, R.M.: Contrast-enhanced mammography: better with AI? Eur. Radiol. (2023)
30. Zhang, T., et al.: Important-Net: integrated MRI multi-parametric increment fusion generator with attention network for synthesizing absent data. Inf. Fusion **108**, 102381 (2024)

Safe Breast Cancer Diagnosis Resilient to Mammographic Adversarial Samples

Degan Hao[1], Dooman Arefan[2], Margarita L. Zuley[2], Wendie A. Berg[2], and Shandong Wu[1,2,3,4(✉)]

[1] Intelligent Systems Program, University of Pittsburgh, Pittsburgh, PA, USA
[2] Department of Radiology, University of Pittsburgh, Pittsburgh, PA, USA
[3] Department of Bioengineering, University of Pittsburgh, Pittsburgh, PA, USA
[4] Department of Biomedical Informatics, University of Pittsburgh, Pittsburgh, PA, USA
wus3@upmc.edu

Abstract. Adversarial data can lead to malfunction of deep learning applications. It is essential to develop deep learning models that are resilient to adversarial data while accurate on standard, clean data. In this study, we focus on building safe breast cancer diagnosis models against mammographic adversarial samples. We proposed a novel adversarially robust feature learning (ARFL) method to facilitate adversarial training using both standard data and adversarial data, where a feature correlation measure is incorporated as an objective function to encourage learning of robust features and restrain spurious features. To show the efficacy of ARFL for robust breast cancer diagnosis, we built and evaluated deep learning diagnosis models using two independent clinically collected breast imaging datasets, comprising a total of 9,548 mammogram images. We performed extensive experiments showing that the ARFL method outperformed several state-of-the-art methods. ARFL can serve as an effective method to enhance adversarial training, towards building safe breast cancer diagnosis against adversarial attacks in clinical settings. The code repository of this study is publicly available at GitHub: https://github.com/usernamesafeai/ARFL.

Keywords: Breast cancer diagnosis · Adversarial defense · Mammogram · Safe AI

1 Introduction

Adversarial samples can fool a deep learning classification model, where small and intentional perturbations may lead to unexpected results [24]. Adversarial attacking methods, such as projected gradient descent (PGD) [14], have shown success on attacking classification of natural view images. Adversarial attacks also pose threats to deep learning-based medical applications, such as inducing unsafe diagnosis, fraudulent insurance claims, biased clinical trial outcomes, etc. [6]. In the medical imaging domain, previous studies showed adversarial samples may downgrade a model's performance, as observed in image classification, detection, and segmentation [16,18]. It is critical to develop deep learning models that are resistant to adversarial samples/attacks in order to deliver safe artificial intelligence (AI)-enabled medical applications.

Adversarial training, which trains a model by using a set of adversarially generated samples, is one of the few approaches to defend adversarial attacks [20]. Studies showed that by using the minimax optimization, adversarial training can improve a model's adversarial robustness [14]. Adversarial samples may also serve as a special type of data augmentation to increase a model's performance on the standard data (i.e., original clean data without adversarial perturbations) [26]. In the medical imaging domain, adversarial training-based methods have shown improved image diagnosis performance on either standard data [8] or adversarial data [10]. However, it remains challenging for a model to maintain stable performance simultaneously on both the standard data and adversarial data [9,17,19,25,28]. A previous study [12] indicated that the lack of exploiting the underlying manifold of data may be a key reason for this challenge.

While adversarial training has the benefits of resisting adversarial attacks, previous theoretical studies [19,25] showed that adversarial training at the same time may lower a model's performance on standard data, which is undesirable, as it is equally important to maintain the model performance on both standard data and adversarial data [17,28]. A recent study showed that adversarial training could result in even worse results when training with limited data [3]. To ensure stable model performance on both standard and adversarial data, a common approach is to merge the datasets for training [24], though this may fail when their distributions significantly differ. Researchers have considered standard data and adversarial data as two different domains to learn domain-invariant representations [22]. Another approach, as proposed in a recent work [1], is to perform training with separated batch normalization layers for standard data and adversarial data. Since the testing data's distribution is usually unknown in priori, it is difficult for this approach to choose which batch normalization layer to use. Another method, TRADES [28], demonstrates there may be a theoretical trade-off of the performance between standard and adversarial data. Overall, it remains an open research question in developing effective training methods to reconcile model performance on standard data and adversarial data.

In this study, we proposed a novel regularization method to build a breast cancer diagnosis model that is adversarially robust on both standard data and adversarial data. Our approach incorporates a feature correlation measure as an objective function, promoting robust features and reducing spurious ones when training on a mix of standard and adversarial mammogram images. We name our method ARFL (Adversarially Robust Feature Learning). Implemented on two real-world mammogram datasets (9,548 images total), ARFL's performance was compared with and without its integration, as well as against domain-specifi batch normalization (DSBN) method [1], TRADES [28], and multi-instance robust self-training (MIRST) [23]. Extensive experiment results on the two datasets showed the clear benefits of ARFL in maintaining the model's performance on both the standard data and adversarial data, and that our method outperformed the compared methods.

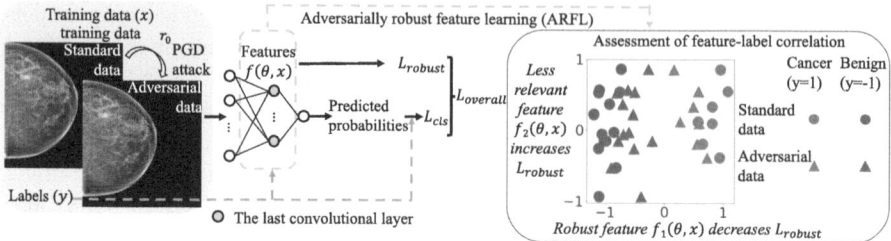

Fig. 1. Overview of the Adversarially Robust Feature Learning (ARFL) framework for breast cancer diagnosis. This figure shows the ARFL architecture using both standard and adversarial mammographic data as inputs. The adversarial training with ARFL focuses on extracting robust features $\mathbf{f}(\theta, \mathbf{x})$ for computing the robust loss $\mathbf{L_{robust}}$.

2 Related Work

AI has shown promise and early success in enhancing various tasks for medical image analysis, including detection, classification, segmentation, reconstruction, registration, etc. [2]. AI-based breast cancer diagnosis models are under active development and clinical translation [13]. It is imperative to ensure the deployment of such AI models are safe to patients, secure to clinical environments, and resilient to adversarial samples/attacks.

Adversarial security of AI models has attracted attention in the medical domain [8,15,27]. Such studies on breast cancer/imaging is scarce, but more challenging, as malignancy information in breast imaging may be more subtle and heterogeneous [11]. Researchers showed that adversarial mammogram images produced by generative adversarial networks can fool both breast cancer diagnosis models and experienced radiologists [29]. MIRST was introduced to defend adversarial attacks on breast ultrasound images [23].

3 Methods

3.1 Adversarially Robust Feature Learning (ARFL)

When training a classification model with both standard and adversarial data, the model simultaneously fits two potentially different distributions. As shown in Fig. 1, to encourage the learning of useful features from the mixed input and to reduce the chances the model learns from spurious correlations between the training data and truth labels, we introduced a regularization term, called adversarially robust feature learning (thus the name ARFL). As pointed by a previous work [9], a feature's usefulness can be measured by the expectation of feature-label multiplication, i.e., $\mathbb{E}_{(x,y)\sim\mathcal{D}}(f_{i,j}(\theta, x) \cdot y))$, and the feature is called ρ-useful if the expectation is greater than ρ. Inspired by such a correlation measurement, we designed a new loss function, named robust loss (denoted by L_{robust}), to characterize the feature-label correlation. L_{robust} is calculated by summing up the absolute values of the product of each feature and label over the feature map, as shown in Eq. 1.

$$L_{\text{robust}}(\theta, x, y) = -\frac{1}{HW} \sum_{i=1}^{H} \sum_{j=1}^{W} \sigma(\text{abs}(f_{i,j}(\theta, x) \cdot y)) \quad (1)$$

where input x can be either a standard input with an underlying distribution of $\mathbb{D}$; or an adversarial input from distribution $\mathbb{D}'$; H and W respectively denote the width and height of a feature map of input x; abs($\cdot$) denotes the absolute value function; $\sigma(\cdot)$ denotes the sigmoid function that scales the feature-label correlation; y denotes a positive or negative label $\{\pm 1\}$; θ denotes the model parameters; $f_{i,j}(\theta, x)$ denotes the value of the feature map at position (i, j). Considering that features near the output of a classification model contain more high-level information, we obtain the feature map from the last convolutional layer. L_{robust} encourages the model to learn features that are highly correlated with the labels. Different from the original method in [9], we revised the method to measure useful features by adding an absolute-value operation to consider both positive and negative correlations, and we also incorporated a sigmoid function to squash extreme loss values. Our method is appropriate as features showing either low positive correlations (yielding $\rho > f_{i,j}(\theta, x) \cdot y > 0$) or low negative correlations (yielding $-\rho < f_{i,j}(\theta, x) \cdot y < 0$) tend to be potentially less robust, leading to higher L_{robust} values. Then we integrate the adversarial loss and the robust loss as an overall loss for standard data as expressed in Eq. 2.

$$L_{\text{overall}}(\theta, x, y) = L_{\text{cls}}(\theta, x, y) + \lambda \cdot L_{\text{robust}}(\theta, x, y) \quad (2)$$

where L_{cls} denotes the binary cross entropy loss for binary classification tasks and λ is a weighting factor controlling the two objectives, i.e., the cross-entropy loss L_{cls} and the robust loss L_{robust}.

3.2 Integrating ARFL Into Minimax Optimization

To construct adversarial data, we introduced some degree of adversarial perturbation generated by PGD [14] to standard data (x). PGD generates adversarial perturbations by iteratively maximizing the perturbation towards the direction of changing the predicted output. To defend the adversarial attacks, adversarial training minimizes the loss of fitting the adversarial data while maximizing the same loss for the generated adversarial samples, as shown in Eq. 3.

$$\min_{\theta} \mathbb{E}_{(x,y) \sim \mathcal{D}} \left[\max_{\delta \in \Delta(X)} L_{\text{cls}}(\theta, x + \delta, y) \right] \quad (3)$$

where δ denotes the perturbation imposed to x within the specified set of valid perturbations Δ, and y denotes the truth label.

With both standard data and adversarial data in each training batch, we minimize the empirical loss by fitting both the standard data and adversarial data. We introduce Eq. 4 to implement the minimax optimization process.

$$\min_\theta \mathbb{E}_{(x,y)\sim\mathcal{D}}\Big[(1-r)\cdot \max_{\delta\in\Delta(X)} L_{\text{cls}}(\theta, x+\delta, y) \\ + r\cdot L_{\text{cls}}(\theta, x, y)\Big] \quad (4)$$

where r denotes the ratio of the amount of standard data relative to the total amount of the data (standard data plus adversarial data) in each training batch. After integrating ARFL into adversarial training, we propose Eq. 5 for the minimax optimization on both standard and adversarial data.

$$\min_\theta \mathbb{E}_{(x,y)\sim\mathcal{D}}\Big[(1-r)\big(\max_{\delta\in\Delta(X)} L_{\text{cls}}(\theta, x+\delta, y) \\ + \lambda \cdot L_{\text{robust}}(\theta, x+\delta, y)\big) \\ + r\cdot L_{\text{overall}}(\theta, x, y)\Big] \quad (5)$$

where r can take various values in the range $[0,1]$ to define different training schemes. The term L_{overall} is defined in Eq. 2.

4 Experiments and Results

4.1 Datasets

Our study was approved by the Institutional Review Board. We examined the effects of our method on two real-world mammogram imaging datasets for breast cancer diagnosis. The first dataset is from University of Pittsburgh Medical Center (UPMC) and the second is the publicly available Chinese Mammography Database (CMMD) [4]. The UPMC dataset was collected from a cohort of 1,284 women who underwent full field digital mammography screening. Each patient had one digital mammogram exam with up to four images of the two breasts (left craniocaudal [CC] view, left mediolateral oblique [MLO] view, right CC view, and right MLO view). Based on biopsy results, there are 366 patients diagnosed with breast cancer and 918 benign/negative cases. There are a total of 4,346 images. The images were acquired by a Hologic Lorad Selenia mammography system. The UPMC dataset is an internal private dataset and may be available to interested users upon request, after an approval from the institution along with a signed data use agreement and/or a material transfer agreement. The CMMD dataset was collected from a cohort of 1,775 patients who underwent mammography examination with both CC and MLO views. Based on biopsy, 1,310 patients are diagnosed with breast cancer and 465 patients are benign/negative, and there are a total of 5,202 images. The images were acquired by a GE Senographe DS mammography system. Using the two independent datasets, our target task is to perform computer-aided diagnosis of classifying breast cancer (i.e., malignancy) vs. benign/negative findings at patient level. The CMMD dataset is publicly available and can be downloaded from https://www.cancerimagingarchive.net/collection/cmmd/.

4.2 Experiment Settings

Model Structure and Training Settings: We used the VGG16 model [21] pre-trained on ImageNet [5] as the backbone. We fine-tuned the fully connected and last convolutional layers for binary classification of breast cancer. We implemented three training settings with parameter r: 1) standard training ($r = 1$), 2) adversarial training ($r = 0$) [14], and 3) dual adversarial training ($r = 0.5$) [10]. We trained with and without ARFL, setting L_{robust}'s weight λ to 10.0. Each model was trained for 100 epochs on both datasets.

Adversarial Sample Generation: We used PGD for adversarial attacks, with 7 iterative steps and an adversarial perturbation budget ε_1 of 0.01. The attacking perturbation budget ε_2 was set to 1e−4 to be visually imperceptible.

Comparison with Related Methods: We compared our method to three related methods, including DSBN [1], TRADES [28], and MIRST [23]. DSBN is a domain adaptation technique that allocates domain-specific affine parameters for data from different domains. DSBN was tested for adversarial training with standard data and adversarial data perturbed by the FGSM algorithm [8]. We replaced FGSM [7] with PGD [14], aiming to measure our method's resilience against this more threatening challenge. TRADES is an adversarial defense method that balances model performance on adversarial data and standard data using KL-divergence for regularization. MIRST uses different levels of perturbations to generate adversarial examples as additional data for self-training.

Performance Metric and Statistical Significance: We evaluated performance using the Area Under the Curve (AUC) and the standard deviation under five-fold cross-validation, where at each fold, 70% of the data for training, 10% for validation, and 20% for testing. Statistical significance was determined using the Mann-Whitney U test.

Visual Assessment: To visually assess feature learning effects using ARFL, we plotted feature saliency maps of mammogram images, calculated as gradients of loss with respect to the input.

4.3 Robustness Analyses of Hyperparameters

We analyzed the effects of the standard data mixing ratio (r), the weighting factor (λ), and the adversarial perturbation budget (ε_1) on model performance.

Effects of Mixing Ratio (r). We examined the effects of mixing standard data with adversarial data at varying ratios (i.e., robustness analysis of parameter r in Eq. 5). While in dual adversarial training where r is set to 0.5, it is interesting to examine whether other values of this ratio may lead to different performance. In this experiment, we measured the diagnosis model's performance additionally at $r = 0.25$ and $r = 0.75$ and compared to the effects when $r = 0.5$.

Effects of Weighting Factor (λ). The weighting factor λ, which controls the influence of L_{cls} and L_{robust} in the model, was varied from 0.1 to 100.0.

We applied ARFL in the context of dual adversarial training to determine the optimal balance point, where the model efficiently learns robust features without compromising classification performance.

Effects of Adversarial Perturbation Budget (ε_1). We investigated the impact of varying the adversarial perturbation budget ε_1 within the range of 0.005 to 0.1. We used 0.1 as the upper bound considering literatures and characteristics of mammogram images. Using the PGD method, we generated adversarial data constrained by this budget and incorporated the data into the adversarial training process. The aim was to observe how different levels of adversarial perturbation during adversarial training influence the model's defense against adversarial attacks.

5 Results

Table 1 and Table 2 show the mean AUC values and standard deviations on the test set of standard data and the test set of adversarial data, when using the UPMC dataset and CMMD dataset, respectively. As can be seen in Table 1, adversarial test had a substantially dropped performance under standard training (row A), which is the expected behavior for a standard model when facing adversarial attacks. When the model is trained by adversarial training (row C), adversarial test performance increased but at the same time the model downgraded in standard test - this sacrifice is undesirable for the slight benefit of adversarial robustness. When using dual adversarial training (row F), model performance largely increased in both standard test and adversarial test, showing the efficacy of this training method.

Table 1. Model performance comparisons on the UPMC dataset.

Training Method	Standard AUC	Adversarial AUC
A. Standard training	69.2 (1.1)	58.8 (1.4)
B. Standard training + ARFL	70.0 (1.9)	58.3 (3.5)
C. Adversarial training	61.7 (4.0)	56.9 (5.3)
D. Adversarial training + ARFL	62.5 (4.3)	59.2 (4.0)
E. Dual adversarial training	65.7 (5.9)	59.6 (9.4)
F. Dual adversarial training + ARFL	69.3 (2.3)	67.8 (2.4)
G. DSBN [1]	54.1 (8.5)	54.7 (9.0)
H. TRADES [28]	63.7 (3.5)	63.2 (3.5)
I. MIRST [23]	63.0 (1.9)	63.6 (1.7)

In terms of the benefits of ARFL, as shown in rows B, D, and F, while ARFL did not make a change in standard training (this is expected as ARFL is designed to mainly account for the mix of standard and adversarial data), it largely improved the performance for adversarial training (row D) and dual adversarial training (row F; here the benefits are the highest), showing the usefulness of our proposed method, in not only resisting adversarial attacks but also maintaining the performance in the original standard data. In the comparison, DSBN (row G), TRADES (row H), and MIRST (row I) exhibited lower performance compared to dual adversarial training with ARFL (row F). The underperformance of DSBN can be attributed to its limitation in selecting specific batch normalizations for test sets. Furthermore, this comparison highlights that ARFL's approach of regularizing through feature-label correlation is more robust than TRADES, which regularizes with prediction-label correlation. It also demonstrates ARFL can learn robust features without using multiple instances as MIRST does.

Table 2. Model performance comparisons on the CMMD dataset.

Training Method	Standard AUC	Adversarial AUC
A. Standard training	64.9 (4.2)	41.5 (3.7)
B. Standard training + ARFL	64.9 (4.4)	41.5 (4.2)
C. Adversarial training	45.5 (4.6)	43.7 (4.7)
D. Adversarial training + ARFL	48.6 (4.5)	45.7 (4.7)
E. Dual adversarial training	67.8 (3.3)	66.3 (3.3)
F. Dual adversarial training + ARFL	68.8 (3.3)	67.3 (3.4)
G. DSBN [1]	54.7 (6.9)	55.5 (2.7)
H. TRADES [28]	64.8 (5.0)	61.9 (5.1)
I. MIRST [23]	64.4 (2.6)	64.8 (2.8)

When examining the results of CMMD shown in Table 2, a very similar overall performance pattern is observed as seen in Table 2, which further verifies the efficacy and generalizability of our proposed method on an independent dataset. The dual adversarial training with ARFL also outperformed DSBN, TRADES, and MIRST. In addition, on both datasets, the AUCs of the dual adversarial training with ARFL are significantly higher (all $p < 0.05$) than the AUCs of the adversarial training with ARFL.

It is worth mentioning that in Table 2 we noticed the adversarial training (row C) did not improve adversarial AUC compared to standard training (row A), though the standard deviation of the AUCs is also larger in row C compared to row A, showing the data heterogeneity may be higher in the CMMD dataset and that may lead to what we observed. Also note that the improvement resulted from adversarial training is also modest under adversarial test on the UPMC dataset (Table 1, row C vs. row A). Previous studies showed that adversarial training may only improve adversarial AUCs under the use of a very large dataset [3]. This may partly explain the slight improvement observed in our study as our data scale is relatively small compared to large datasets.

Figure 2 illustrates on example mammogram images and the feature saliency maps for models trained with dual adversarial training with and without ARFL. In these maps, regions with sharp intensity contrast indicate important features, where higher gradients suggest stronger influence on the classification performance [25]. The comparison shows that incorporating ARFL results in a greater number of sharply contrasted regions, suggesting that ARFL enhances the learning of discriminative imaging features for the diagnosis purposes. Note that we demonstrate the saliency maps mainly on standard data as these clean data are better cases to illustrate and perceive the effects.

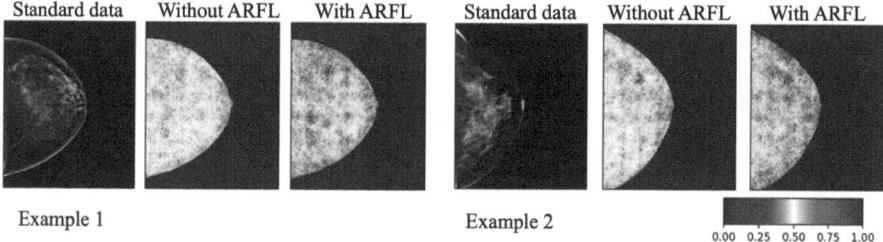

Fig. 2. Feature saliency maps of mammogram images from models trained using dual adversarial training with and without the integration of ARFL. The color bar represents the scaled gradients between zero and one. More regions with sharp contrast indicate more important features. (Color figure online)

Figures 3 shows the robustness analysis results. The sub figures in the left column shows model performance for varying r. In the UPMC dataset, $r = 0.5$ achieved the highest performance, while in the CMMD dataset, $r = 0.75$ was optimal. For consistency, results with $r = 0.5$ were reported to fairly compare with previous studies [10,24]. The sub figures in the middle column shows the effects of adjusting λ. The highest test AUC was achieved at $\lambda = 10.0$. The right sub figure shows the model's test AUCs for varying ε_1. As ε_1 increased, AUC initially increased, then stabilized at 0.01 and beyond. This suggests an optimal range for ε_1 in adversarial training for our study/data. These experiments supported the use of optimal parameter values in our main experiments. Note that optimal values may differ for other datasets or tasks.

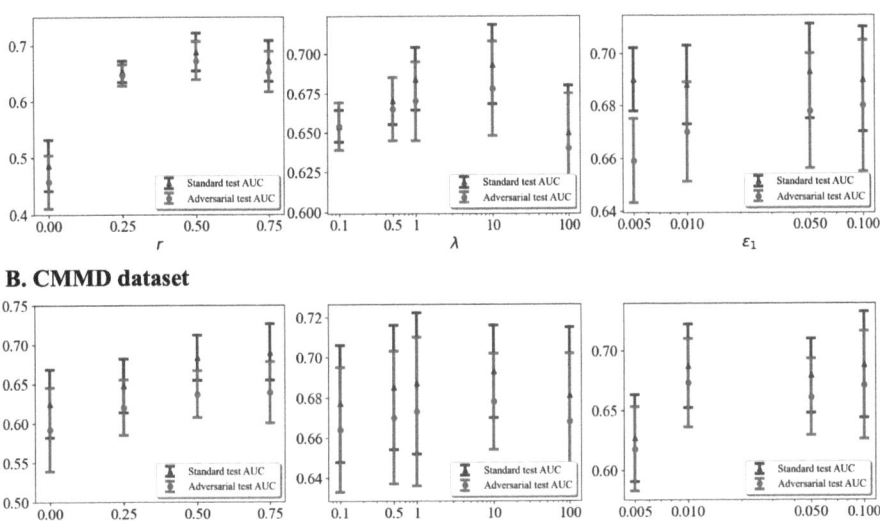

Fig. 3. Robustness analysis of hyperparameters: standard data mixing ratio (r), weighting factor (λ), and adversarial perturbation budget (ε_1). Shown are AUC values with varying values of hyperparameters. Error bars represent standard deviations.

6 Conclusion

In this work, we designed a novel method, ARFL, to facilitate adversarially robust adversarial training for safe breast cancer diagnosis. ARFL facilitates the learning process towards identifying features that are strongly correlated with true labels. On the two breast mammogram datasets, ARFL showed benefits in resisting adversarial samples and maintaining stable diagnosis performance on standard data. Our extensive experiments on the two datasets from different sources showed similar efficacy and the generalizability of our method. ARFL also outperformed the compared methods. For future work, we will extend the evaluation of our method on other imaging data and other types of adversarial attacks.

Acknowledgement. This work was supported by the 1R01EB032896 grant (and a Supplement grant 3R01EB032896-03S1) as part of the NSF/NIH Smart Health and Biomedical Research in the Era of Artificial Intelligence and Advanced Data Science Program, a NSF grant (CICI: SIVD: #2115082), the Jewish Healthcare Foundation RAPS Seed Grant Program, and the University of Pittsburgh Momentum Funds for the Pittsburgh Center for AI Innovation in Medical Imaging. This work used Bridges-2 at Pittsburgh Supercomputing Center through allocation [MED200006] from the Advanced Cyberinfrastructure Coordination Ecosystem: Services & Support (ACCESS) program, which is supported by NSF grants #2138259, #2138286, #2138307, #2137603, and #2138296.

References

1. Chang, W.G., You, T., Seo, S., Kwak, S., Han, B.: Domain-specific batch normalization for unsupervised domain adaptation. In: Proceedings of the IEEE/CVF Conference on Computer Vision and Pattern Recognition, pp. 7354–7362 (2019)
2. Chen, X., et al.: Recent advances and clinical applications of deep learning in medical image analysis. Med. Image Anal. **79**, 102444 (2022)
3. Clarysse, J., Hörmann, J., Yang, F.: Why adversarial training can hurt robust accuracy. arXiv preprint arXiv:2203.02006 (2022)
4. Cui, C., et al.: The Chinese Mammography Database (CMMD): an online mammography database with biopsy confirmed types for machine diagnosis of breast. The Cancer Imaging Archive (2021)
5. Deng, J., Dong, W., Socher, R., Li, L.J., Li, K., Fei-Fei, L.: ImageNet: a large-scale hierarchical image database. In: 2009 IEEE Conference on Computer Vision and Pattern Recognition, pp. 248–255. IEEE (2009)
6. Finlayson, S.G., Bowers, J.D., Ito, J., Zittrain, J.L., Beam, A.L., Kohane, I.S.: Adversarial attacks on medical machine learning. Science **363**(6433), 1287–1289 (2019)
7. Goodfellow, I.J., Shlens, J., Szegedy, C.: Explaining and harnessing adversarial examples. arXiv preprint arXiv:1412.6572 (2014)
8. Han, T., et al.: Advancing diagnostic performance and clinical usability of neural networks via adversarial training and dual batch normalization. Nat. Commun. **12**(1), 1–11 (2021)
9. Ilyas, A., Santurkar, S., Tsipras, D., Engstrom, L., Tran, B., Madry, A.: Adversarial examples are not bugs, they are features. In: Advances in Neural Information Processing Systems, vol. 32 (2019)
10. Joel, M.Z., et al.: Using adversarial images to assess the robustness of deep learning models trained on diagnostic images in oncology. JCO Clin. Cancer Inform. **6**(2), e2100170 (2022)
11. Kim, J.H., et al.: Breast cancer heterogeneity: MR imaging texture analysis and survival outcomes. Radiology **282**(3), 665–675 (2017)
12. Lin, W.A., Lau, C.P., Levine, A., Chellappa, R., Feizi, S.: Dual manifold adversarial robustness: defense against LP and non-LP adversarial attacks. In: Advances in Neural Information Processing Systems, vol. 33, pp. 3487–3498 (2020)
13. Lotter, W., et al.: Robust breast cancer detection in mammography and digital breast tomosynthesis using an annotation-efficient deep learning approach. Nat. Med. **27**(2), 244–249 (2021)
14. Madry, A., Makelov, A., Schmidt, L., Tsipras, D., Vladu, A.: Towards deep learning models resistant to adversarial attacks. arXiv preprint arXiv:1706.06083 (2017)
15. Mirsky, Y., Mahler, T., Shelef, I., Elovici, Y.: CT-GAN: malicious tampering of 3D medical imagery using deep learning. In: 28th USENIX Security Symposium (USENIX Security 19), pp. 461–478 (2019)
16. Paschali, M., Conjeti, S., Navarro, F., Navab, N.: Generalizability vs. robustness: exploring adversarial examples in medical imaging. In: Medical Image Computing and Computer-Assisted Intervention - MICCAI 2018. Springer (2018)
17. Picot, M., Messina, F., Boudiaf, M., Labeau, F., Ayed, I.B., Piantanida, P.: Adversarial robustness via fisher-rao regularization. IEEE Trans. Pattern Anal. Mach. Intell. (2022)
18. Qi, G., Gong, L., Song, Y., Ma, K., Zheng, Y.: Stabilized medical image attacks. arXiv preprint arXiv:2103.05232 (2021)

19. Raghunathan, A., Xie, S.M., Yang, F., Duchi, J.C., Liang, P.: Adversarial training can hurt generalization. arXiv preprint arXiv:1906.06032 (2019)
20. Shafahi, A., et al.: Adversarial training for free! In: Advances in Neural Information Processing Systems, vol. 32 (2019)
21. Simonyan, K., Zisserman, A.: Very deep convolutional networks for large-scale image recognition. arXiv preprint arXiv:1409.1556 (2014)
22. Song, C., He, K., Wang, L., Hopcroft, J.E.: Improving the generalization of adversarial training with domain adaptation. In: International Conference on Machine Learning, pp. 4934–4943. PMLR (2018)
23. Sun, S., Xian, M., Vakanski, A., Ghanem, N.: MIRST-DM: multi-instance RST with drop-max layer for robust classification of breast cancer. In: International Conference on Medical Image Computing and Computer-Assisted Intervention, pp. 401–410. Springer (2022)
24. Szegedy, C., et al.: Intriguing properties of neural networks. arXiv preprint arXiv:1312.6199 (2013)
25. Tsipras, D., Santurkar, S., Engstrom, L., Turner, A., Madry, A.: Robustness may be at odds with accuracy. arXiv preprint arXiv:1805.12152 (2018)
26. Xie, C., Tan, M., Gong, B., Wang, J., Yuille, A.L., Le, Q.V.: Adversarial examples improve image recognition. In: Proceedings of the IEEE/CVF Conference on Computer Vision and Pattern Recognition, pp. 819–828 (2020)
27. Yao, Q., He, Z., Han, H., Zhou, S.K.: Miss the point: targeted adversarial attack on multiple landmark detection. In: Martel, A.L., et al. (eds.) MICCAI 2020. LNCS, vol. 12264, pp. 692–702. Springer, Cham (2020). https://doi.org/10.1007/978-3-030-59719-1_67
28. Zhang, H., Yu, Y., Jiao, J., Xing, E., El Ghaoui, L., Jordan, M.I.: Theoretically principled trade-off between robustness and accuracy. In: International Conference on Machine Learning, pp. 7472–7482. PMLR (2019)
29. Zhou, Q., et al.: A machine and human reader study on AI diagnosis model safety under attacks of adversarial images. Nat. Commun. **12**(1) (2021)

Author Index

A
Alhajj, Hassan   127
Alis, Deniz   107
Arefan, Dooman   232
Aribal, Erkin   107
Ashraf, Tajamul   13
Astaraki, Mehdi   65
Awwad, Hadeel   169, 191
Ayaz, Hamail   96

B
Balkenende, Luuk   32
Bartoli, Adrien   212
Berg, Wendie A.   232
Bickelhaupt, Sebastian   85
Bonci, Eduard   137
Bourdel, Nicolas   212
Brandan, Maria-Ester   221

C
Cardoso, Jaime S.   117, 137
Cardoso, Maria J.   117, 137
Castillo-Lopez, Jorge Patricio   221
Cerekci, Esma   107
Chairi, Ikram   1

D
De Neve, Wesley   75
delÁngel, Ricardo Montoya   181
Delegue, Eve   202
Denizoglu, Nurper   107
Díaz, Oliver   202
Diaz, Oliver   54

E
Eberle, Jessica   85
Elbatel, Marawan   221
Emons, Julius   85
Erber, Ramona   85

F
Freitas, Nuno   117, 137

G
Gao, Yuan   42
García, Eloy   169, 181, 191
García-Pinto, Diego   181
Garrucho, Lidia   202
Giro, Alexia   212
Gonçalves, Tiago   137

H
Hadler, Dominique   85
Han, Luyi   32
Hao, Degan   232
Hernández-Pérez, Carlos   159
Hosseini, Mahdi S.   148
Huang, Jiaju   23

I
Idri, Ali   1
Igual, Laura   202

J
Jimenez-Martin, Lauren   159
Jimoh, Abdulganiyu   1

K
Kaissis, Georgios   54
Kang, Solha   75
Kapsner, Lorenz A.   85
Karaarslan, Ercan   107
Kessler, Dimitri   202
Kushibar, Kaisar   202

L
Lang, Daniel M.   54
Laun, Frederik B.   85
Lauzeral, Nathan   127
Lekadir, Karim   54, 202

Liang, Xinglong 23
Liebert, Andrzej 85
Luo, Wuman 23

M

Ma, Junqiang 23
Madad-Zadeh, Sabrina 212
Madame, Tisha 13
Mann, Ritse M. 32, 42
Marraoui, Wissam 212
Martí, Robert 169, 181, 191
Marti, Robert 221
Mavioso, Carlos 117, 137
McLoughlin, Ian 96
Mok, SengPeng 23
Montoya-del-Angel, Ricardo 221
Morche, Karine R. 32
Moreno, Rodrigo 65

N

Nakach, Fatima-Zahrae 1
Nasiri-Sarvi, Ali 148
Normand, Nicolas 127

O

Ohlmeyer, Sabine 85
Oksuz, Ilkay 107
Oladimeji, Oladosu 96
Oliveira, Hélder P. 117, 137
Osuala, Richard 54, 202
Ozbulak, Utku 75

P

Pomel, Christophe 212
Pooyan, Melika 191

R

Rameau, Francois 75
Rasoolzadeh, Nika 32, 42
Riess, Anneliese 54
Rivaz, Hassan 148

S

Sánchez-Lara, Victor 181
Schnabel, Julia A. 54
Schreiter, Hannes 85
Seker, Mustafa Ege 107
Sharifian, Rasoul 212
Skorupko, Grzegorz 54
Smedby, Örjan 65
Song, Jinhong 23
Sun, Yue 23
Szafranowska, Zuzanna 54

T

Tan, Tao 23, 42
Tanyel, Toygar 107
Tardy, Mickael 127
Terrassin, Paul 127

U

Uder, Michael 85
Unnikrishnan, Saritha 96

V

van Dijk, Jarek M. 32, 42
Veloso, Carlos 117
Vilaplana, Veronica 159
Villaseñor-Navarro, Yolanda 221

W

Wang, Ying 23
Wenkel, Evelyn 85
Wu, Shandong 232

Y

Yang, Qiuhui 42
Yang, Xiao 23
Yang, Zhikai 65

Z

Zhang, Tianyu 32, 42
Zolfagharnasab, Mohammad Hossein 137
Zuley, Margarita L. 232

The manufacturer's authorised representative in the EU is Springer Nature Customer Service Centre GmbH, Europaplatz 3, 69115 Heidelberg, Germany. If you have any concerns regarding our products, please contact ProductSafety@springernature.com

Printed and bound by CPI Group (UK) Ltd, Croydon, CR0 4YY

26/03/2026

02078935-0007